Communicating Science

Communicating Science

The Scientific Article from the 17th Century to the Present

Alan G. Gross
Joseph E. Harmon
Michael Reidy

UNIVERSITY PRESS
2002

Oxford New York
Auckland Bangkok Buenos Aires Cape Town Chennai
Dar es Salaam Delhi Hong Kong Istanbul Karachi Kolkata
Kuala Lumpur Madrid Melbourne Mexico City Mumbai Nairobi
São Paulo Shanghai Singapore Taipei Tokyo Toronto

and an associated company in Berlin

Published by Oxford University Press, Inc.
198 Madison Avenue, New York, New York 10016

www.oup.com

Oxford is a registered trademark of Oxford University Press

Library of Congress Cataloging-in-Publication Data
Gross, Alan G.
Communicating science : the scientific article from the 17th century to the present/
Alan G. Gross, Joseph E. Harmon, Michael Reidy.
p. cm.
Includes bibliographical references.
ISBN 0-19-513454-0 (cloth)
1. Scientific literature—History. 2. Science—Language—History. 3. Technical writing—History.
I. Gross, Alan G. II. Harmon, Joseph (Joseph E.) III. Reidy, Michael (Michael S.) IV. Title
Q225.5 .G79 2001
808′.0665—dc21 2001039089

9 8 7 6 5 4 3 2 1

Printed in the United States of America
on acid-free paper

To Rona E. Harmon (1955–2001)

PREFACE

In January 1665, Denis de Sallo published the first issue of the French *Journal des Sçavans* (Journal of the Learned), one of whose stated purposes was "to make known experiments that might serve to explain natural phenomena." Two months later in England, Henry Oldenburg decided to expand his role as unofficial letter box for scientific correspondence in England and Europe and inaugurated the monthly publication of technical letters in *Philosophical Transactions*—"Giving some accompt of the . . . ingenious in many considerable parts of the world." Thus the scientific journal article was born. This birth was key in the then-fledgling enterprise of science. It permitted the relatively rapid and accurate transmittal of new discoveries and ideas from one researcher to a community of researchers—who could then propagate, refute, accept, ignore, or extend the original claims. Emerging from letters and essays and competing with books, this new medium developed a style and format that, eventually, would make it the preferred mode of presentation and debate for new claims of scientific knowledge.

Despite the obvious importance of the scientific article, there exists as yet no comprehensive survey of its development as a representation of science and as a medium for its communication. There are many studies of rhetorical and linguistic elements of the scientific article based on small samples selected from a single journal covering a limited historical period, as well as samples selected for the reputation of their authors as scientists rather than their typicality as examples of scientific prose. In addition, while numerous European countries actively participated in the origin and development of modern science, most studies are of English science exclusively or of existing translations. Few trustworthy generalizations can be drawn from these limited studies. And to neglect telling the rhetorical history of the scientific article is to leave an important gap in our understanding of the history of science. This book is meant to fill that gap.

By examining the scientific article from its debut in the 17th century to the present, we will track the progress of an evolving genre of discourse continuously engaged in three acts: the creation of arguments for and against knowledge claims about the natural world, the artful deployment of these arguments in a text, and their representation in the syntax and semantics of natural languages. Not coincidentally, these three acts parallel the central categories of classical rhetoric: the invention of arguments, their presentation, and the style in which they are embodied. (We have changed Aristotle's "arrangement" to "presentation" to include tables, graphics, and features of format.)

Our goal is not to reduce science to mere rhetoric, only to acknowledge that communicative and argumentative theory forms a legitimate intellectual basis for viewing the practice of science. It is, after all, only through publication that new knowledge claims become fully engaged in a struggle for existence. And only in this public context do scientists take full responsibility for the veracity of their claims, or lack thereof.

Any contemporary reader of the scientific literature knows intuitively that 20th-century scientific prose is a very specialized use of language distant from the general register of contemporary intellectual prose and from its 17th-century counterpart. What is not known, however, is when or how this change came about. This book seeks to explore and map this change as it occurred in English, French, and German—three very different languages, all of which were adapted to the same intellectual purpose. In particular, we address the following questions: (1) In the scientific article viewed over time, what are the trends in style, presentation, and argument—the traditional components of rhetoric? (2) Can the trends, or patterns of development, that our analysis uncovers be explained? In answering these questions, we tried to take into consideration both national differences, such as those between France and England in the 17th century, and disciplinary differences, such as those between a well-established discipline (e.g., astronomy in the 18th century) and an emerging discipline (e.g., geology in the 18th century).

The introduction will set forth our method for gathering a representative sample of scientific texts spanning four centuries and three languages and for analyzing the selected texts. It reports not only how we performed these tasks, but also why. Then chapter 1 presents an example of our method by applying it to two articles in the life sciences, one from the 17th century, the other from the 20th. Our purpose here is twofold: to serve as a trial run for our analysis method and to dramatize the many changes in style, presentation, and argument that have occurred by comparing two articles published nearly 300 years apart. Next come four pairs of chapters devoted to the implementation of our method on a century-by-century basis: each pair consists of one chapter on style and presentation and one on argument. Within these eight chapters, we discuss our results from an analysis of 1,804 short passages for style and 430 whole articles for presentation and argument. By analyzing this large sample in a systematic manner, we hoped to arrive at plausible generalizations about communicative and argumentative practices as they changed over time.

In each pair of century chapters, we deliberately omitted any overarching theoretical explanation for the trends and patterns detected. Although we left this task, on purpose, to the final chapter, we need to establish up front that any explanation of the developing patterns of communicative and argumentative behavior must avoid intentional language.

In "Three Ways of Spilling Ink" (1966), John L. Austin differentiates carefully among three expressions: "on purpose," "intentionally," and "deliberately." While in many contexts these words can be used interchangeably without confusion, Austin insists that they have meanings that are importantly different from each other. If I shoplift a candy bar, I certainly acted intentionally. But did I steal the candy bar on purpose? Deliberately?

Our interest is not in how these words differ, but in the fact that all of them, and all of their siblings—"he meant it," "it's his doing," "he's to blame," and so forth—assign some degree of responsibility to the actors involved. But of the changes we have chronicled—changes in titles and sentence length, in headings and the use of verbs—we cannot say that they were done on purpose, or intentionally, or deliberately.

Of course, in the latter part of the 20th century especially, some of these have been codified in style manuals, in the stylistic requirements of specific journals, and in academic textbooks on technical writing. At least as far as these codified factors are concerned, scientists do now act intentionally, deliberately, and on purpose. But we must not confuse this codification with the fact of the changes as they originally appeared. And we must also acknowledge that there are simply too many changes ever to codify them all. What individual or institution could possibly document, much less intentionally orchestrate, the large suite of changes we are chronicling? "No one" is the obvious answer.

Any explanation of these changes must be causal in some sense of that difficult word. Our last chapter, therefore, explains the trends and patterns of development described in the preceding chapters as an instance of evolutionary change. To make this claim, we adapted a version of selection theory, an offshoot of the evolutionary epistemology championed by philosophers Stephen Toulmin, David Hull, and James Griesemer and William Wimsatt. In our evolutionary model, the population of scientific articles constitutes the species; each individual article, an organism, the locus for change. Over time, the style, presentation, and argument in scientific articles continually vary, and these variants selectively reproduce as a consequence of the changing needs of the diverse scientific disciplines. This process of selection creates the communicative and argumentative lineage whose origin and progress our model is meant to explain.

We divided the time span covered in this book into centuries for convenience only: this approach greatly facilitates our comparisons among style, presentation, and argument over time. It might be argued that nothing has been more productive of historical bias than the tendency to regard calendar demarcations as freighted with significance. Despite the recent ballyhoo, for example, the "21st century" and the "new millennium" mean only another year. But in the end, we decided this arbitrary division of time worked best for expository purposes.

Our primary audience for the book is students and scholars interested in scientific communication from a combined historical, rhetorical, social, and linguistic perspective. This is now a robust and eclectic group housed in many disciplines—in sharp contrast to the anemic condition a mere 15 years ago. We also hope that at least some working scientists will be interested in our book since our arguments and conclusions have some bearing on the soundness of their process of writing, an act that occupies much of their workday.

Against widespread opinion to the contrary, we contend that the current scientific article is, on the whole, an accurate reflection of the world as science conceives it, an effective means of securing the claims of science, and an efficient medium for communicating the knowledge it creates. Our conclusions thus challenge the critiques of stylistic "purists" who insist that modern scientific prose is a communicative scandal.

Acknowledgments

It is important to acknowledge that this book would not have been completed without the assistance of Suzanne Gross. It was she who insisted at its inception that we use electronic spreadsheets to record and analyze the data rather than the paper-and-pencil methods we were initially considering. Moreover, several years ago, when we discovered some serious flaws in the grammatical analysis, she graciously offered to reanalyze the English passages. None of this material assistance is meant to slight her constant encouragement and support throughout a "five-year" project that, in fact, has lasted for closer to 10 years. She is not an author; none of the ideas is hers, and none of the prose. But she made us realize that the ideas and the prose in which they are expressed are merely necessary conditions for scholarship. It is not by these alone that the relevant past, always concealed in the deepest shadow, reveals its shape to interested readers, however imperfectly.

At various stages in this project, we also greatly benefited from the help of Kirk Allison, a graduate student with expertise in technical German; Betsy Foster and Joe Little, undergraduate seniors in Scientific and Technical Communication; and Audrey Styer, a computer consultant and Excel wizard. This team was assembled with the aid of a generous grant from the Society of Technical Communication and support from the Agricultural Experiment Station of the University of Minnesota. In the early years of the project, we received constructive criticism from Jane Andrew, John Angus Campbell, Eugene Garfield, Randy Allen Harris, David L. Hull, Michael J. Rychlewski, and Joseph M. Williams. Not all were sympathetic to our approach, but all helped shape the final product. The first author would also like to thank for their support the University of Minnesota for a Bush sabbatical and two spring term leaves, the Centers for the Philosophy of Science at Pittsburgh and Minnesota, the Institute for Advanced Study at Hebrew University and the Internationales Forschungszentrum Kulturwissenschaften for fellowships, and the British Association for a visiting professorship.

Thanks also go to Rona, Liz, and Emma Harmon for their help in intangible but important ways.

Michael Reidy's contribution as third author is confined to the first three years of our project, years in which as the research assistant of the first author he participated as a full partner in the research that led to this book. He was not involved, however, in the preparation of the final manuscript.

Parts of this book have appeared previously in *The Scientist* ("What's Right about Scientific Writing," vol. 13, p. 20, 1999) and the *Social Studies of Science* ("Scientific Argument in the 17th Century: A Rhetorical Analysis with Sociological Implications," vol. 30, pp. 371–396, 2000), as well as in an exhibition at the Department of Special Collections, Joseph Regenstein Library, University of Chicago ("The Scientific Article: From the Republic of Letters to the World Wide Web," 5 May–21 August, 2000).

CONTENTS

Communicating Science

Introduction

While the first author of this book was in Vienna as a fellow at the International Center for Research in the Social Sciences, he was invited by the director of the Vienna Circle, Frederich Stadler, to present a paper on the development of scientific communication of the Vienna Academy in its earliest years, the decade that succeeded its founding in 1847. Present also were a sociologist, Ulrike Fell, a historian, Mitchell Asch, and a number of graduate students. After the talk, Professor Asch criticized the paper for its stereotyped view of Austrian science, the result of neglecting the contribution of the polytechnics. Professor Fell criticized the paper for its neglect of the social system of the early Academy, especially its silence on the matter of peer review. As the host, Professor Stadler, a philosopher of science, was perhaps too polite to point out that the author of the paper had made no contribution to his discipline. This is a representative anecdote in Kenneth Burke's sense: it seems the fate of studies in the communication and argumentation of science that they should be frequently misunderstood as defective contributions to the history, sociology, or philosophy of science, rather than independent contributions to our understanding of an essential, but otherwise neglected, aspect of what it was and what it is to do science.

Why do we focus on scientific articles[1]? While communicative and argumentative practices are obviously not confined to articles, we have chosen them for three

1. The more popular term today, in English, is probably "scientific paper." For internal consistency, we chose to use "scientific article," in part because of its closer resemblance to the French *l'article scientifique* and the German *der wissenshaftliche Artikel.* Besides, either term is anachronistic when it comes to earlier centuries.

reasons. The first and most important is that articles have become the canonical form for the communication of original scientific results. While this choice may seem "Whiggish" to some, we think the majority of our audience will recognize the scientific article as an important intellectual and cultural phenomenon. Our second reason for our choice of articles is methodological. We have devised a means of gathering a representative sample of scientific articles in English, French, and German—the three most important languages of science—a means that will permit us to generalize about communicative and argumentative practices. In the case of books, no such procedure was available to us; in the case of more informal communications such as letters, e-mails, and conversations, such sampling was even less a possibility. We have also chosen articles over informal communications because of our interest in a special quality of formal communications: they are meant for public scrutiny. Given their public nature, we think the inference is legitimate from their norms to community standards.

In this study, we hope to give our readers an accurate impression of scientific communicative and argumentative practices in each century from the 17th century on, and to account for those impressions in terms of a host of textual features. In addition, we hope to give our readers an accurate impression of the change in these communicative and argumentative practices over time. Finally, we hope to account for this change by means of a selection theory analogous to biological evolution. To describe and to account for our impressions at any one period and over time, we have found the traditional apparatus of rhetorical and linguistic analysis useful. But rhetorical and linguistic analysis is useless in explaining the cause for change over time. To explain change, we use a version of selection theory as elaborated especially by the philosophers David Hull (1988a) and James Griesemer and William Wimsatt (1989). We recognize that such explanations as applied to cultural evolution are currently surrounded by controversy. But while we do not insist that our evolutionary explanation is correct, we do insist that the problem of explaining change is real, and that, since, at the moment, no plausible explanatory scheme exists other than evolution, a refinement of our exploratory attempt seems the only route to explanatory progress.

The Problem

What is the current state of scholarship in the study of the communicative and argumentative practices of science? Writing to Huygens in 1691, Leibniz criticized 17th-century English science for its emphasis on the bookkeeping of nature over the synthesis of factual information into a unified theory:

> I agree with you, Sir, that it is necessary to follow the plans of Verulam [Francis Bacon] in Physics, by adding to them, however, a certain art of conjecturing (*art de diviner*), for otherwise we shall hardly advance. I should be astonished if Mr. [Robert] Boyle, who has so many fine experiments, would not come to some theory of chemistry after meditating so long on them. Yet in his books, and for all the consequences that he draws from his observations, he concludes only what we all know, namely, that everything happens mechanically. (Quoted in Wiener 1951, p. xxv)

In studies of the communicative and argumentative practices embodied in the scientific article, a similar situation prevails. There exist studies of scientific journals, of individual articles, and of groups or sequences of articles. In these studies, observations and opinions abound, but there is little *art de diviner*; methods abound, but there is a want of method in the enterprise taken as a whole. What Alexander George and Timothy McKeown (1985) say of case studies in political science applies to studies of scientific discourse as well: "However interesting and well done in and of itself, each case study tend[s] to pursue rather idiosyncratic research problems and to investigate a set of dependent and independent variables that often [are] correspondingly idiosyncratic" (p. 42). To exemplify this problem, let us look at three approaches: the rhetorical, the philosophical, and the literary.

In our analysis of the rhetorical approach, let us inventory the texts analyzed, and the theories and methods employed by the three most cited books on rhetoric of science: Charles Bazerman's *Shaping Written Knowledge: The Genre and Activity of the Experimental Article in Science* (1988), Lawrence J. Prelli's *A Rhetoric of Science: Inventing Scientific Discourse* (1989), and Alan Gross's *The Rhetoric of Science* (1990).[2] Let us first inventory the texts analyzed by these three. Bazerman analyzes 162 articles and one book. These comprise one article by Watson and Crick, 100 experimental articles from the *Philosophical Transactions,* one article and one book by Newton, 40 articles from the *Physical Review,* and 20 articles by Arthur Holly Compton. Prelli analyzes one book, Patterson and Linden's *The Education of Koko,* an article on memory transfer in flatworms; and the same Watson and Crick article Bazerman analyzes. Gross analyzes 18 articles, and five books in whole or in part. These comprise the article that broke the genetic code, the same article by Watson and Crick that Bazerman analyzes, four articles on zoological taxonomy, short sections from books by Descartes and Boyle, a Copernican astronomical pamphlet, the same book and article by Newton that Bazerman analyzes, a short section from Darwin's notebooks, six articles on biochemistry, and five theoretical papers by Einstein.

To say that this selection is unrepresentative is only, you may say, to state the obvious. The object of study is now a book, now an article. Whatever its source, the text is always in English (or in readily available English translation). The focus is parochial: we hear of the Royal Society, not of the Académie Royale; we analyze the *Philosophical Transactions,* not the *Mémoires* or the *Acta Eruditorum.* Only Gross touches briefly on French science in his treatment of Descartes and German in his treatment of Einstein. Even as a survey of English and American science, the selection is skewed toward physics and biology: chemistry is virtually ignored, as are earth science and astronomy. But the selection of texts is so lacking in method that it would not be much of an exaggeration to say that in the rhetoric of science, science—its actual intellectual topography—is virtually ignored. One last point: these three books seem to fix, not on science, but only on its towering figures—Descartes, Boyle, Newton, Darwin, Einstein, Watson and Crick. The roll call reads like the his-

2. Other important rhetorically oriented books about scientific communication include Myers (1990), Simons (1990), Locke (1992), Halliday and Martin (1993), Moss (1993), and Selzer (1993). See Gross (1996) for a review of the literature in the field.

tory of science found in the introductions to standard school texts in physics and biology.

Let us now turn our attention from the texts analyzed to the machinery of analysis. Prelli refers constantly to Aristotle, Cicero, Kenneth Burke, and—surprisingly—Thomas Kuhn. Despite the anomalous references to Kuhn, neither philosophy nor sociology motivates Prelli's analysis; the driving theoretical force behind his work is rather a synthetic and synoptic view of classical rhetorical theory. Prelli's theoretical stance, purely a product of the tradition of Speech Communication public address, is largely unsuited to capturing what is distinctive about science. This effect is predictable. As long as we treat the texts of science *literally* as a set of classical orations, their authors will seem like Ciceros—inferior Ciceros at that—and not like Einsteins. Like Prelli, Gross claims to use classical rhetoric as his theoretical anchor. Nevertheless, he shifts his theoretical stance now to Roland Barthes, now to Jürgen Habermas, now to Robert Merton, now to Claude Lévi-Strauss, now to Victor Turner. Such methodological and theoretical pluralism may be wisely opportunistic or, to use Dilip Gaonkar's (1993) more pejorative terminology, unwisely promiscuous. At least, Gross analyzes the communicative and argumentative practices of science as uniquely those of science. He does not, as does Prelli, give the definitions of the classical orators and the quantifications of experimental physicists equivalent status. Bazerman states that his "concern for actual practice leads to a smaller role for rhetorical theorists than is usual in rhetorical histories" (p. 15). In fact, in his book these theorists have no explicit role. When theorists do make an appearance, they are, like Robert Merton, sociologists or, like Lev Vigotsky, psychologists.

Let us summarize our critique of these rhetoricians of science of the first generation. First, none of them really makes explicit and appropriately precise what it means for a text to be rhetorical. Bazerman calls rhetoric "the study of all areas of symbolic activity" (p. 6n); Gross refers vaguely to style, arrangement, and invention; Prelli follows Burke: rhetoric is "the suasory use of language as a symbolic means of inducing cooperative acts and attitudes" (pp. 12–13). Given this conceptual fuzziness, we can understand why none among these scholars can move in a principled way from such definitions to a reliable analysis of scientific texts. Second, none of these scholars, save Bazerman, has an inkling of the sampling procedures that would give their generalizations about scientific texts real credibility. And even in Bazerman's case, this insight is insufficient to make any useful generalizations credible through broad-based sampling. Third, none of these scholars, again with the possible exception of Bazerman, addresses the problem of rhetorical change over time. And even Bazerman describes this change only in a sample of limited scope; he does not and cannot explain the nature of this change in a well-motivated way, and he does not try. In a chapter on spectroscopic articles in *Physical Review*, he concludes with the following observation: "The *evolution* of the spectroscopic article over the past century in America reflects the growing knowledge and theoretical character of science and reveals some of the institutional consequences of these changes" (p. 183; emphasis added). Here "evolution" is a metaphor, not a theoretical term.

Marcello Pera's *The Discourses of Science* (1994) is another important book of the first generation. Pera's analysis is philosophical; his central claim is that science is a dialectical process, an interplay of argument and counterargument that incorporates rhetoric as a means of persuasion. This process is mediated through the interaction of three "players": an individual or group making a knowledge claim, the community of scientists judging that claim, and nature. During this process, Pera asserts that "nature reacts to a cross-examination, there is no impartial arbiter, and 'knowing' amounts to the community's *agreeing upon* nature's correct answer" (p. ix, emphasis in original). In order to avoid the charge that science is an irrational enterprise controlled only by the rhetorically most persuasive texts, Pera narrows his definition of scientific rhetoric to logos and focuses on the logic of scientific argument and counterargument. In his model, the community reaches agreement by "finding that view [cognitive claim] that best holds out against criticism" according to a prescribed set of ground rules (p. 130).

There are two problems with Pera's approach. The first is that his examples—Galileo, Darwin, and big-bang cosmology—involve controversies of considerable historical importance, controversies, moreover, with clear winners and losers. We may legitimately suspect that these are not typical, and we know without asking that theory is here being preferred to the equally legitimate enterprise of fact gathering and confirmation. In addition, Pera's model misrepresents the actual discourses of science because it overemphasizes dialectics at the expense of rhetoric. For Pera scientific rhetoric is rhetoric stripped bare: pathos and ethos are of negligible importance, as are style and arrangement, all traditional concerns of rhetoric.

Francis-Nöel Thomas and Mark Turner exemplify the literary approach to communicative and argumentative practices. In *Clear and Simple as the Truth* (1994), they offer their impressions of two styles of expository prose, the classical and the practical. According to their classification, a bird watcher's field guide is typical of the classical style in its transparency to the truth the writer shares with the reader: "The [classical] style is defined not by a set of techniques, but rather by an attitude toward writing itself. What is most fundamental to that attitude is the stand that the writer knows something before he sets out to write, and that his purpose is to articulate what he knows to a reader. The style does not limit the writer's subject matter or efface his individuality, but the writer's individuality will be expressed principally by his knowledge of his subject" (p. 6). The writer assumes the reader is a fellow enthusiast and, of course, interested in such matters as the song of the tufted titmouse or the predatory tactics of the northern shrike. There is no need to convince, cajole, or seduce the reader into reading or even to write as plainly as possible. In contrast, in the practical style, typified by a software manual or legal brief, writer and reader join in a common task:

> [T]he reader has a problem to solve, a decision to make, a ruling to hand down, an inquiry to conduct, a machine to design or repair—in short a job to do. . . . In practical style, the best presentation will allow the reader to acquire timely information with a minimum of distraction because . . . writing is an instrument for delivering information with maximum efficiency and in such a way as to place the smallest possible burden upon the reader, who has other—more important—burdens to bear. (p. 81)

The persuasiveness of these descriptions rests on the typicality of the exemplars. None of the genres Thomas and Turner include under their descriptions of the classical and practical styles has ceased to evolve, but each has reached a stage of relative stability, an evolutionary plateau that permits us to speak with confidence of *the* field guide, *the* software manual.

Thomas and Turner are on safe ground in another respect. In apparent deference to an essentially literary sensibility, they ignore "presentational features" of such texts, features as diverse as headings and illustrations. (We prefer "presentation" to the classical term "arrangement" because we include such features as well as features of organization per se; we will continue to use presentation in this sense throughout the book.) In fact, their generalizations are the more powerful for their *tacit* inclusion of such features—tacit because in a mature genre, such, as an ornithological field guide, they so seamlessly blend in with the running text. Nevertheless, these authors may be faulted for failing to notice this subtle integration. Finally, descriptions such as those of Thomas and Turner are defective in that they are subjective; that is, they rely for their credibility, not on any quantitative evidence, but on the readers' *frisson* of recognition, their sense that the familiar is now more deeply understood for having been placed in an interesting and unfamiliar light.

Our intent in this critique of first-generation work is not to discredit it but to characterize it as the first phase in the establishment of a new field of study, the phase that persuades its audience that a branch of inquiry exists worthy of differentiation from other branches (see also Gross and Keith 1997). This is an exercise in the politics of recognition. In this exercise, the first generation concerned with the communicative and argumentative practices of the sciences has largely succeeded. But in our view this phase is drawing to a close. If this field is to enter a new phase, concerns of method must be more prominent. As a way of addressing these concerns for our project, we have identified three aspects of method: defining the components that make up communicative and argumentative practices in science, sampling the scientific texts that will be the object of analysis, and accounting for change over time.

The First Part of the Solution: Defining What Textual Features to Analyze

As far as we know, Aristotle was the first to isolate the components of style, presentation, and argument for the purpose of analysis. Our work is also indebted to Chaim Perelman and Lucie Olbrechts-Tyteca's *The New Rhetoric* (1969) for an analysis that moves Aristotelian rhetoric a significant step further, integrating its three components more closely. These two latter-day scholars established firm links among argument, which is central to Aristotle's *Rhetoric*; style, which Aristotle regards as largely ornamental; and presentation, which he marginalizes. They also extended the range of rhetorical analysis to include "the human sciences, law, and philosophy" (p. 10). An Aristotelian theory so updated allows us to anatomize the textual components of the communicative and argumentative practices of the sciences. We do not take a stand on alleged defects in Aristotelian theory, in either its original or its newer versions. The most prominent of these is its speaker-centered perspective, so at odds with postmodern concerns, and the neglect of actual communicative effect, which, of course, remains an empirical issue, untouched by classical rhetorical theory. We do not think these points seriously affect the claims we make.

Style, presentation, and argument are the features that scholars of science—rhetoricians, of course, but philosophers and historians as well—regularly select when they analyze scientific texts. In his study of the *Origin of Species*, philosopher Philip Kitcher finds Darwin's style significant in the book's argument. According to Kitcher (1991), part of Darwin's problem "was to soothe potential passions" over its religious implications, and part of Darwin's solution was stylistic: "to deploy the *preferred phraseology* of religious texts and of 19th-century natural theology to advance doctrines that might otherwise seem threatening" (pp. 18–19; emphasis added). In her study of conceptual change in 18th-century chemistry, historian Lissa Roberts (1989) finds that presentation is a symbolic marker of social and conceptual change. She finds her evidence in tables that illustrate the relationships among various chemical substances. She concludes that "by analyzing these tables in terms of their distinct structures of *presentation* . . . we have observed a fundamental shift in chemists' construction and projection of both their discipline and their relation to nature" (p. 131; emphasis added). In his examination of early French experimental articles as reported in the *Mémoires* of the Paris-based Académie Royale, historian F. L. Holmes (1989a) scrutinizes the relationship between argument and creativity. He concludes that "sustained experimentation has an intrinsic chronological structure which makes narrative the natural mode in which to describe it. To incorporate what is salient from the investigative 'story' into a paper *structured as a critical argument* requires transformations that are as central to the creativity of science as are the investigations themselves" (p. 179; emphasis added). This commonality among scholars with diverse interests provides a firm foundation for analyzing the communicative and argumentative nature of the scientific article within the rhetorical tradition.

It would be ill-advised to claim that universally accepted definitions of these textual features exist; we contend only that our definitions do not violate the spirit of the mainstream. Within the rhetorical tradition, style, presentation, and argument are easily and uncontroversially defined. "Style" is our term for any feature of a text whose focus is the syntax of sentences or the choice of words. Preferences for the passive voice and for complex noun phrases are features of syntax; a preference for a highly technical vocabulary is a feature of word choice. In this book we will trace the development of style from its epistolary and essayistic beginnings in proximity to everyday speech to its development as a highly specialized register designed to convey information of great cognitive complexity from expert to expert.

"Presentation" is our term for the ways the text of the scientific article is organized and the ways in which its data are displayed. Citations and headings are features of presentation; so are tables and graphs. Our definition coincides with Aristotle's definition of arrangement, though arrangement's range has been broadened to take into account visual elements beyond Aristotle's scope. In this book we will trace the development of presentation from epistolary and essayistic forms meant to be read from beginning to end to a master finding system designed to promote efficient and opportunistic reading, and dependent on the "reading" of tables and figures as well as text. The stylistic and presentational features combined constitute what we will be calling "communicative."

"Argument" is our term for the actual ensemble of means scientists employ to support their claims. Our focus is on the actual arguments scientists make. We analyze these to determine what, at any one period, counts as a scientific argument. In tracing the development of scientific arguments, we see at first natural philosophers tolerant of a wide range of verificational means, men who rely heavily on the evidence of the five senses and the trust that subsists between gentlemen; in the end we see scientists intolerant of any case that is not closely argued and founded on scrupulously produced experimental evidence, men and women who adhere to a professional code that transcends personal trust.

The Second Part of the Solution: Sampling Scientific Texts

A comprehensive communicative and argumentative history of the scientific article requires a representative sample of texts to which we will apply our definitions. Because of the work of historian of science Robert Gascoigne (1985) and polymath Eugene Garfield (1976), we have a well-motivated ranking of significant scientific journals from the 17th through the 20th century.

Gascoigne (1985) assembled a chronological listing of some 900 scientific journals, from which he ascertained their relative significance by the degree to which each journal was "used as a means of publication by the scientists of the time" (p. vii). For the 17th and 18th centuries, this degree was derived from the bibliographical data in Poggendorff's *Biographisch-literarisches Handwörterbuch.* In the 19th century it was ascertained by analyzing two major periodical indexes, the Royal Society's *Catalogue of Scientific Papers* and the *International Catalogue of Scientific Literature.* From these sources, Gascoigne worked out a ranking of the relative importance of journals from 1665 through the 19th century. One method he used to arrive at the ranking was to compare the listed authors in the table of contents from the journals with the scientists entered into Gascoigne's own *Historical Catalogue of Scientists and Scientific Books.* The more *Historical Catalogue* authors in a given journal over a selected period, the higher the ranking.

Garfield (1976) assessed the significance of 20th-century journals differently. By extensive computer calculations (for mid-1970s technology, anyway), Garfield analyzed the references from the 401,000 articles in over 2,443 scientific and technical journals that were issued during 1974 and tracked by the *Science Citation Index.* Then he ranked the top 206 journals on the basis of total citations received from the more than five million citations in these articles. By exploiting Gascoigne's and Garfield's lists, we are able to ensure that any selected journal in our sample had made a measurable impact on the practice of science.

As our empirical base for the study of style, we analyzed short passages of 10 lines each from the scientific articles appearing in a cross section of the journals given in Gascoigne's and Garfield's lists. We analyzed such passages in almost 200 articles from the 17th century (1665–1700), in approximately 500 articles for each of the next two centuries, and in 600 articles for the 20th century (see appendix A for complete details). These varying numbers reflect problems we had with obtaining periodicals with chronological balance. Within each century, we also selected journals that would give us a fair representation of English, French, and German scientific prose.

The 10-line passages were randomly selected, as were the journal articles in which they appear. In addition, to chart the changing features of presentation and argument during each century, we analyzed a subsample of approximately 100 complete articles selected from among the articles containing the short passages. In sum, we examined short passages in about 1,800 articles for style alone and 430 whole articles for presentation and argument. The range of publications in our sample encompasses

- the elite journals covering the major branches of science (astronomy, physics, chemistry, the biological sciences, and the earth sciences)
- the major languages of Western science (English, French, and German)
- all types of scientific article (methodological, experimental, observational, theoretical, and review)

To the short passages and whole articles, we apply a uniform set of questions, the answers to which comprise our evidential base, the empirical foundation on which we erect plausible generalizations about the argument, presentation, and style in scientific articles over time. These questions, and the hypotheses that motivate them, are detailed in appendix B.

We hope that our method of combining representative examples of style, presentation, and argumentation with their averages derived from our random sample will give the reader both the feel and the range of variation of these aspects of scientific articles, at least as a first approximation. But we hope to do more than that. We hope to give the reader a sense of what it was like to *be* a scientific communicator, say, a German chemist in the early 18th century or a British physiologist in the late 19th century. In each case, we have a man trying to convey an experimental result, in the first by means of a vocabulary of the five senses, in the second by means of a highly developed technical vocabulary. We want readers to see how different were the communicative horizons of these two men, both fully committed to the same task of conveying knowledge of the natural world. We believe that only by a careful analysis of such texts as these will readers develop a sense, albeit a second-order sense, of *being there.*

We have no doubt that more specialized work, focusing on individual features of style, presentation, and argument, will yield more nuanced results than our own. Ken Hyland's *Hedging in Scientific Research Articles* (1998) is an example of the sort of monographs that are needed if real progress is to be made on individual aspects of style. Nor are we unaware that a far more sophisticated use of statistics is possible, as in Dwight Atkinson's *Scientific Discourse in Sociohistorical Context* (1999). Unfortunately, even in their own terms, these monographs are excessively narrow in scope. Both Hyland and Atkinson confine themselves to English, and Atkinson limits himself to a very small sample of articles from a single journal, *The Philosophical Transactions*, whose preeminence probably ended in the 18th century.

Three methodological caveats are in order. The first has to do with data reliability. On the one hand, in reconstructing communicative lineages, we have found that many of the textual characters in our protocol are fairly easy to isolate from the text and to quantify: personal pronouns, proper names, passives, sentence length, abbreviations, clausal density, number of tables and figures, and so forth. On the other hand, not all our rhetorical characters can be readily isolated and quantified, for example, verbal hedges, noun phrases in extremely long sentences, poetic metaphors, and division of articles into sections in the absence of headings. Nonetheless, we can avoid such difficulties only at the cost of creating a model that fails to match our intuitions of what constitutes the communicative. Developing a plausible model is unthinkable if we limit our textual characters to easily quantifiable ones. Whatever the cost, we feel that it is better to have a model that encompasses difficult-to-quantify features, even though this introduces an unavoidable unreliability in our interpretations.

The second caveat concerns our statistical procedures. Our more mathematically inclined readers will no doubt object that we have employed very rudimentary statistical tools: random numbers for selecting texts in the various journals, averages for detecting trends over time, and standard deviations for assessing uniformity. We make no secret of the fact that our results are "soft" compared with actual scientific research, even research analogous to ours such as Atkinson's work on the *Philosophical Transactions*, a rigor precluded by the labor-intensive nature of our work coupled with the size of our sample. Despite these shortcomings, we maintain our work is an advance over earlier studies and rigorous enough to make our generalizations about scientific writing plausible. We also believe it has allowed us to capture, for the first time, how scientists in the Western world have communicated with one another in formal written discourse over the last 335 years. In covering such a long stretch of time, three languages, and so many scientific and technical disciplines, we have had to paint with a fairly broad brush. We are hopeful others will join us in the enterprise of taking a similarly systematic approach to filling in the details on the communicative and argumentative practices of scientists working in various languages and various disciplines and at various times.

Lastly, there is the matter of translation.[3] We have checked our intuitions about the author's intended meaning against those of native speakers and have done our best to get the scientific terminology right. We also searched diligently in secondary sources. But in some cases we were dealing with a science or a technology so obscure and outdated that we are not sure about the terminological accuracy of our rendering. We are reasonably sure, however, that our occasional inaccuracies in this matter have no effect on our conclusions, which, after all, are not about science, but its communication.

The Third Part of the Solution: A Theory of Change

The rhetorical tradition is useless in explaining alterations in style, presentation, and argumentation over time. For such an explanation, it is evolutionary theory to which scholars seem intuitively drawn. According to rhetorician Gross (1990), the style and

3. For the convenience of our readers, we have translated all the French and German passages quoted into English. The textual analysis, however, was done with the original languages.

presentation in Darwin's notebooks embody "a disciplined lack of commitment to the full truth of assertions, a deficiency that enables the *evolutionary* transformations to final theory" (p. 159; emphasis added). In his discussion of Darwin, philosopher Kitcher (1991) "suggest[s] that the processes underlying belief in descent with modification themselves *evolve* during the debate of the 1860s" (p. 16; emphasis added). According to historian Holmes (1989a), "the 'conventional form' imposed on the modern journal article is not a departure from, but the outcome of the long *evolution* of a form that emerged during the late seventeenth and early eighteenth centuries along with the learned journal as the forum for reporting scientific investigations" (p. 165; emphasis added). In these quotations, allusion to theory is not the equivalent of having a theory, but these allusions do all point in the same theoretical direction, even if the authors do not follow their own lead.

There are objections to applying selection theory to cultural artifacts. While some objections are mindless, others are not. In an Amazon.com review, one truculent "reader from Russia" judged that in Gary Taylor's *Cultural Evolution* "the presentation of various evolutionary theories [was] a cheap rhetorical maneuver effected in an attempt to hide a lack of theoretical rigor behind a burlesque of scientific efficacy" (17 October 1998). This is mere rant. But surely it is possible to object that cultural evolution is intentional, while biological evolution is not, and also that while actual biological evolution took millions of years, alleged cultural evolution in the case of the scientific article took less than four centuries.

It is true that the scientific article is a cultural, not a natural, achievement. It did not evolve as species do, without conscious design; by what they said and did, Bacon and Boyle, among numerous others, deliberately influenced the way science was and is communicated. Nor did the scientific article appear by chance. It was a deliberate invention, conceived independently by Henry Oldenburg in England and Denis de Sallo in France during the late 17th century. Not only was the scientific article a deliberate invention; deliberate intervention to alter its course and character has always been possible. In a 1920 editorial, for example, G. C. Fulcher instructed prospective contributors to the *Astrophysical Journal* that "every article . . . however short, is to be preceded by an abstract prepared by the author and submitted . . . with the manuscript" (p. 255). In a subsequent article in *Science* (1921), he encouraged other scientific publications to follow suit, because abstracts "save much time for the scientist not only as a *reader* of current literature but also as an *investigator*" (p. 291). Today, because of Fulcher's encouragement and the evolutionary fitness of heading abstracts in the scientific article, they are as ubiquitous as figures and tables.

But the intentional nature of interventions such as Fulcher's does not bar their evolutionary explanation; evolutionary theory does not exclude intentional action. In the case of conceptual change, for example, it does not matter that two particular scientists, James Watson and Francis Crick, discovered the double helix; in evolutionary theory, the discovery was a consequence of the selection pressures Watson relates so tellingly in *The Double Helix* (1966). In the case of communicative change, Playfair's and Lambert's invention of the line graph at the end of the 18th century also was a response to selection pressure, in this case the avalanche of data produced by European commercial expansion (Tufte 1983, p. 32; Tilling 1975). Creatures are *born*; molecular structures, *discovered*; methods of data presentation, *invented*. The agents for these predicates mark differences important to us, but not to evolutionary theory. Evolutionary theory is a theory of change that is indifferent to individual actions at its most fundamental level of explanation: the struggle for survival among variants subject to the selection pressures of their environments.

An analogy to literature may clarify our point that evolutionary theory can say something true even about actions that are intentional. It takes nothing from Jane Austen's originality as an author to say that she was writing novels in England during the late 18th, early 19th century, that the novel is an evolving genre, and that she must take her place in this evolutionary scheme. Though each element of style and narrative in her work may have been in some genuine sense her deliberate choice, aspects of that selection must always remain that were not personal but general, the consequence, not of being *that* novelist, but of being *a* novelist at a specific time and place. To deny that evolutionary accounts of intentional action are valid, moreover, has unfortunate consequences, as philosopher David Hull (1988a) points out:

> [I]n the *Origin of Species*, Darwin reasoned from the known effects of artificial selection to the possible effects of natural selection. But artificial selection is intentional. Perhaps plant and animal breeders cannot produce mutations at will, but they do consciously choose those organisms to breed that exhibit traits which they find desirable. If reasoning from artificial selection to natural selection is totally illicit, then Darwin's main argument in the *Origin* is one gigantic blunder. (p. 145)

Thanks to recent advances in the biological sciences, breeders of plants and animals can also select for desirable traits "at will" through genetic manipulations in the laboratory. So artificial selection in nature is now doubly intentional (personal communication from David Hull, 1995).

Critical readers might also question whether evolution could possibly be effective on a time scale as brief as the life of the scientific article. But the time span of plant and animal history is not relevant to the cogency of a general theory of evolution, since the pace of evolution is not a matter that can be settled in advance. While we took millions of years to evolve, a great deal of transformation can happen in a Petri dish overnight. In addition, the evolution of cultural objects like scientific texts is more Lamarkian than Darwinian. Convergence of form in the case of scientific articles can be hurried along—and has been hurried along—by disseminating printed instructions to authors on their preparation. Such intervention affects the pace, not the fact, of evolution.

Relying on the work of the philosophers Stephen Toulmin (1972), David Hull (1988c), and James Griesemer and William Wimsatt (1989) in conceptual evolution, we have done our best to isolate the two components that must comprise any evolutionary theory, the selection pressures that create change under conditions of competition, and the units of selection on which these pressures operate. In the case of communicative selection, we identify the scientific article as our unit of selection.

We see it as made up of three suites of features: style, presentation, and argument. In the case of style, we see the quest for an objective and efficient prose as the selection pressure; in the case of presentation, we see the quest for efficiency in reading and searching; in the case of argument, we see the pressure as other arguments, arguments that force the originators to modify or discard their own. In no trend that we describe in the body of this book can we identify the operation of the actual pressures in a specific situation; we can only display their results and speculate as to their cause. We have not an explanation, but an explanatory sketch; we are making conjectures and writing promissory notes. In the final chapter, however, we look at the rapid change in communicative practices that characterize the first decade after the founding of the Vienna Academy of Science in the mid–19th century. In this case, we are able to identify, tentatively, though we think plausibly, an actual selection pressure at work in a specific situation. We think that our examination of this case illustrates the explanatory and heuristic potential of our theory.

Our expository strategy is as follows. In the first chapter, we describe and exemplify the changes in the communicative and argumentative practices of science in their most dramatic form: using a method derived from rhetorical and linguistic analysis, we compare in detail two articles "typical" of the 17th and of the late 20th centuries. We follow this with pairs of chapters, one pair for each century, describing first that century's communicative and then its argumentative practices. In a final chapter, we offer an evolutionary explanation for the changes we have described. To give substance to our theoretical formulations, we use as our example the communicative practices of the Vienna Academy of Science during the first decade after its founding in the mid–19th century. In this case, we see the rapid evolution of communicative practices in the direction of conformity with European, especially with German norms, themselves the product of a more lengthy cultural evolution, a process that maintains communicative efficiency and argumentative efficacy in the face of the increasing volume of information and increasing cognitive complexity.

Conclusion

The scientific article is a developing vehicle for communicating the conceptual system of science and, in the case of argument, a developing means for creating that system. We trace these developments over time in the case of the scientific article by describing its style, its presentation, and its argumentative practices. To do so, we adopt what we consider the most appropriate methods regardless of whether their source is the social sciences, the humanities, or the natural sciences. To create a representative pool of texts spanning four centuries, we have borrowed sampling theory from the social sciences. To analyze those texts, we have adapted the taxonomies of rhetorical theory and linguistics. Finally, to understand change over time, we have adapted selection theory from the natural sciences. Our purpose in drawing upon these diverse methods is to create, not a mixture, but a fusion; not a mélange, but an alloy—a substance that exhibits new and interesting properties absent from any of its constituents.

What sorts of properties might these be? Our focus on science presumes that its communication has intrinsic interest for the simple reason that science has become a privileged cultural formation, the repository of our most certain knowledge of the world, and the exemplar of what it is to be rational. Surely in this case, if in any, the best fit will have been found between communicative needs and communicative methods, within the opportunities and constraints of a natural language. But if some version of selection theory is the best explanation of the cultural development of communicative and argumentative practices in science, it is also the best explanation of these practices in the academy, in business, and in everyday life; indeed, in the general case.

CHAPTER 1

Communicative and Argumentative Development Illustrated

In this chapter, we present in their most dramatic form the changes in style, presentation, and argumentation that scientific articles underwent in their journey from the 17th to the 21st century. We compare the style, presentation, and argumentation of two biological articles written nearly 300 years apart: a 17th-century article on the behavior of juices in different plant species and a 20th-century article on the origin and development of soluble ribonucleic acid, a building block in protein synthesis. We have purposely selected articles so far apart in time to give readers the firmest sense possible of the scientific article as a developing textual entity, characterized by continuities and discontinuities in style, presentation, and argument. It is these developments that we will describe in detail in the pairs of chapters that follow, developments we will try to explain in our final chapter.

The first of our selected articles is Martin Lister's "An Account of the Nature and Differences of the Juices, more Particularly, of our English Vegetables," an observational article published in *Philosophical Transactions* in 1697 and written about 30 years earlier. The second, entitled "Formation of a DNA-Soluble RNA Hybrid and Its Relation to the Origin, Evolution, and Degeneracy of Soluble RNA," is by Howard M. Goodman and Alexander Rich. This experimental article was published in 1962 in the *Proceedings of the National Academy of Sciences of the U.S.A.* In this analysis, we will treat Lister's and Goodman and Rich's articles as typical of their times, assuming that the reader's intuitions match our own. Comparing these articles, we might see many similarities, for example, the relentless focus on the natural world as an object of explanation and the need to argue into place facts and theories about it. Nevertheless, it suits our purpose to emphasize instead the dramatic shifts in style, presentation, and argumentation.

Lister: Communicating Science through Style and Presentation

Today largely forgotten, Martin Lister (1639–1712) was an Oxford- and Cambridge-educated physician and virtuoso who did pioneering work in animal biology and geology (Carr 1973). In keeping with Lister's working philosophy, facts occupy the center of his science, and at the center of his text is a personal narrative of discovery. The focus of the prose style is on Lister himself as well as the things he does or observes in nature, as his grammatical subjects and their verbs testify (in this and subsequent quotations boldface is added for emphasis):

> The 21st of *April,* 1665. about eight in the Morning, I **bored** a hole in the body of a fair and large Birch, and **put in** a Cork with a Quill in the middle; after a Moment or two it [a sap] **began to drop**, but yet very softly: Some three Hours after I **returned**, and it **had filled** a Pint Glass, and then it **droped** exceeding fast, *viz.* every Pulse a Drop: This Liquor is not unpleasant to the Taste, and not thick or troubled: yet it **looks** as though some few drops of Milk **were spilt** in a Bason of Fountain Water. *Vide Philos. Transact.* (p. 381)

This is also a prose constructed largely of simple noun phrases. The subject position is occupied by the pronouns "I" and "it" along with "This Liquor." And the noun phrases in other positions never exceed the complexity of ordinary prose or speech. Also note that the passage is impressionistic ("a fair and large Birch," "very softly," "not unpleasant to the Taste, and not thick or troubled"); contains few quantitative expressions ("about eight in the Morning," "after a Moment or two," "Some three Hours," "a Pint Glass," "every Pulse a Drop"); and concludes with a well-turned metaphor ("as though some few drops of Milk . . . spilt in a Bason of Fountain Water"). Besides these stylistic characteristics, this passage is mostly in the active voice, and it is devoid of technical vocabulary and abbreviations.

Another passage from this same article will bring out other characteristics of Lister's style:

> It [the milk of *Lactuca syl. costa spinosa*] springs out of the Wound thick as Cream and Ropes, and is White, and yet the Milk which came out of the Wounds, made towards the top of the Plant, was plainly streaked or mixt with a purple Juice, as though one had dashed or sprinkled Cream with a few drops of Claret. And indeed, the Skin of the Plant thereabouts was purplish also, perhaps with Veins. Again, in the Shell I drew it, it turned still yellower and thicker, and by and by curdled, that is, the white and thick caseous part did separate from a thin purple Whey. So the Blood also of Animals, whilst warm remains liquid and alike, but so soon as cold, it cakes and has a *Serum* or Whey separated from it. (p. 367)

While simple in certain respects, Lister's is also prose of considerable syntactic complexity, measured by the length of sentences and the number of their clauses.

By modern standards (Flesch 1962), these four sentences are relatively long, averaging 32 words each. Their structure is complex, with three or four clauses per sentence. The first sentence (and the longest), for example, consists of an independent clause followed by a short dependent clause, then an independent clause embedded with two dependent clauses, and finally a subordinate clause—for a total of six clauses.

Whatever its merits for creating an engaging narrative, Lister's descriptive prose lacks the power a technical vocabulary gives: the ability to communicate common patterns well below the surface of the often misleading impressions of the senses. Lacking this linguistic resource, Lister is forced to bring the natural objects he scrutinizes before the eyes of his readers by means of metaphor and simile. But his descriptions evoke nature at the price of systematic understanding; indeed, they evoke precisely because systematic understanding is lacking. This understanding is the gift of the theoretical and phenomenological vocabulary of the mature sciences.

Lister shows some sensitivity to matters of presentation, to helping readers discern the structure of his text. To enable them easily to locate sections of interest, he attempts to make explicit the organization of the article, its sources, and its gist. But neither the author nor his editor proceeds rigorously. Although marginal notes in italic type track the progress of the article's organization, they do so with a certain nonchalance. In particular, these "headings" are not parallel in meaning, mixing properties of juices with the names of plants. And they are not particularly prominent, as they are set in a type size smaller than that of the text. Moreover, at times, the style of the article, instead of working together with the marginal notes to enhance understanding, works against them. For example, a paragraph is accompanied by the marginal note "*Purple Juice.*" But the text only indirectly refers to that key term in the midst of a longish sentence: "And yet I am uncertain what to think of the small **purple** Blebs and Veins, to be observed more or less on all the Hypericum kind, and on the Threads of the Flower, and the Hairs which cover the Leaves of *Rorella*" (p. 365; bold added). The approach toward systemization is casual, rather than systematic.

The article also treats its textual ancestors casually and inconsistently. Citations are sometimes incorporated in his text, sometimes in marginal notes. Moreover, some citations are so general as to appear to be virtually unusable as a guide to actually finding the cited texts. For example, an article is referred to only by citing the journal in which it appears (*Vide Philos. Transact.*), and *V.C.P.A.* is Lister's untranslated code for *Vide* [see] *Catalogus Plantarum Angliae* of John Ray. Clearly, both editor and author imagine an audience of other natural philosophers with similar interests and libraries. In line with this rather casual approach to the transmission of information, the summary that concludes Lister's article is not very informative, recapitulating only the themes, not the content of Lister's observations.

This focus on facts over argument is evident in Lister's introduction and conclusion. The introduction begins by repeating the topic stated in the article's title: "We proceed to set down the Nature and Differences of the Juices of Plants" (p. 365). This initial sentence briefly establishes an intellectual territory. However, Lister's introduction does not establish a niche in that territory, or a means by which his research will occupy that niche—Swales's (1990) norms for an introduction section in a modern research article. Similarly, Lister's brief conclusion repeats his opening statement with slight embellishment, then attempts to shape a research front in which facts will be added, not theories advanced.

Lister: Creating Science through Argument

We are fortunate that Lister was reflective about the method and goals of his science. In a letter to the English botanist John Ray, he reflects on method; in so doing, he makes visible his Baconian working philosophy of science, a philosophy that privileges fact gathering and eschews theory: "For my part, I think it absolutely necessary that an exact and minute distinction of things precede our learning by particular experiments, what different parts each body or thing may consist of; likewise concerning the best and most convenient ways of separation of those parts, and their virtues and force upon human bodies as to the uses of life; all these, besides the different textures, are things subsequent to natural history" (quoted in Lister 1967, p. xxx). This philosophy is fully enacted in "An Account of the Nature and Differences of the Juices": Lister's article moves from individual observations to a descriptive claim about the natural world, and its title reflects a science concerned more with fact gathering and categorization than with theory. In the summary that ends his 1697 article, Lister outlines the same philosophy: "And thus far we have set down our Observations and Experiments, concerning the Juices of Vegetables, both those which appear Coagulate, and also those which are fermentable, and have likewise noted other their respective Natures and Differences. We are in the next place to learn by particular Experiments, what different parts, each particular Juice doth consist of, and by what ways they may best and most conveniently be separated" (p. 383).

Because in Lister's view this systematic fact gathering will issue in unproblematic truths about nature, he can eschew all interpretive problems and the arguments such problems inevitably entail: "Nature will be its own Interpreter in this, as well as in all other matters of natural Philosophy" (Lister 1699, p. 93). To Henry Oldenburg, the respected editor of *Philosophical Transactions,* Lister writes: "I conceive it lesse usefull to Philosophy to dispute, then to deliver faithfully matters of Fact" (Oldenburg 1970, p. 342). And in another letter to Oldenburg, Lister pledges his Baconian faith: "[B]ut let ye Hypothesis be what it will, I am persuaded we shall have very darke & imperfect notions of ye motion of ye juices of Vegetables, untill there tru Texture be better discovered" (p. 417).

Not surprisingly given Lister's faith that the facts will speak for themselves, explanatory talk is rare in this article. At one point, for example, he wants to place gums among coagulating juices: "[Gums] are easily to be dissolved in Fountain Water . . . and do sparkle when put into a Flame; which two Natures **argue** a serous or waterish part in them: Again, put into a Flame, they melt and become as it were Liquid and Ductible; which shews the caseous part in them; and because they will not flame, **it is an Argument** of their leanness and scarcity of Oyl. All three put together **plainly evince**, Gums to be coagulate Juices" (Lister 1697, p. 372; blatantly argumentative terms in boldface).

Our point is not to comment on the thinness of Lister's argument; our point is only to underline the discrepancy between making such arguments and believing nature to be its own interpreter.

When present, moreover, explanations are conveyed in the same language as the effects to be explained, a language largely limited to objects and events perceptible to the senses and interspersed with appropriate hedging, expressing a caution central to the scientific ethos: "And yet I **am uncertain** what to think of the small purple Blebs and Veins, to be observed **more or less** on all the Hypericum kind, and on the Threads of the Flower, and the Hairs which cover the Leaves of *Rorella* in the like manner. I **doubt** much, whether this **may properly be called** an Exudated and Coagulated Juice, **or no?** Our Observations of those of this Tribe, are what follow" (p. 365; hedges in boldface).

The limits of Lister's explanatory strategy have their origin in the limits of his method. The hedges in this passage signal that Lister is speculating, offering a causal hypothesis that "the small purple Blebs and Veins" in the flowers and leaves of certain plants might arise from "Exudated and Coagulated Juice." He pursues this research question further by cutting the adjoining stalk of an "*Androsaemum Hypericoides Ger.*" Finding no vessels that carry a "purple Liquor" (p. 366), he concludes that this evidence is suggestive rather than confirmatory. This ends his investigation on that particular plant species. In the article, such exploratory forays represent Lister's farthest experimental and explanatory reach. At times, he is satisfied with less: "[In the case of *Periclymenum Ger.*] the Purple Juice seems to be a Whey separated from the liquid Gum; but I am of Opinion it's a distinct Liquor" (p. 373).

In the absence of a hypothesis relating to an underlying causal pattern susceptible to experimental confirmation, there is no pressure on Lister to exclude from his article *any* observation related to the juices of English plants. For example, "*Lauro-cerasus,* a beautiful Winter Green, *which we have adopted to adorn our Court Walls with* [italics added], yields a clear Gum very plentifully" (p. 376). Moreover, as Lister adds one observation after another, the modern reader, though presumably not Lister's reader, naturally inquires as to Lister's motivation in any particular case. Why should we be concerned, for instance, that "this Liquor is not unpleasant to the Taste, and not thick or troubled: yet it looks as though some few drops of Milk were spilt in a Bason of Fountain Water" (p. 381)? Why mention those particular properties? Lister never tells us why he decided to examine plant juices in the first place; this is in line with a philosophy of science that considers legitimate any addition to our compendium of facts about the natural world. It is science seen as a museum that, in the ideal case, incorporates every fact about the natural world.

Lister organizes his description of facts on the basis of the apparent properties of vegetable juices, those immediately available to his senses. Juices are divided into coagulating and fermenting types, and coagulating juices into those that are clammy or not, and other sorts. Juices that are clammy are, in their turn, divided into those that break into whey, those that cake, and gums; in their turn, other sorts of juices are divided into stringy and oily. A stream of italicized marginal notes emphasizes this organization: *Juices spontaneously breaking with a Whey; Juices Caking and not letting go their Whey; Gums; Lime or stringy Juice; Oily Juices.* This logic of appearances also dictates the absence of numerical data and, as a consequence, the absence of tables—the only method available in the 17th century for presenting data too extensive to be incorporated into sentence formats (data plots were not invented until late in the next century).

Lister's lack of interest in interpretation, along with his assumption that the workings of nature can be revealed by categorizing and organizing appearances, not only accounts for the virtual lack of substantive arguments in his article, but also points to an unwavering faith in the scope of his method. In effect, his method constitutes an argument against making arguments. His investigatory presuppositions inform Lister's notion of progress as a gradual and systematic unfolding of the facts of the natural world as they appear to the senses, unrelated to theory. It is for this reason that he can present before the public an article gathered from "*some Papers, which belong'd to a Treatise of Vegetation; they were most of them made about Thirty Years Ago*" (p. 365). In effect, Lister believes that what he had discovered as a young man is in need not of revision but of expansion. Accordingly, his belated article is interspersed with queries that ask for more information along the lines of information already gathered: "*Qu.* Whether this Gum comes from the Fruit, or from the Leaves and Stalk? And if from the latter, whether any part of the Tree (as Body, Root, or Branch) will spend it, being purposely Wounded, and in what Season, *& c*" (p. 373). For the purposes of our analysis "*& c*" is the most eloquent expression in this passage; it is synonymous with a science that insists on remaining well within the world of common experience and well away from theory.

There is at least one "argument" Lister does rely on, but it is one that lies outside the bounds of strict logic. To some extent, he relies for his credibility on his status as a natural philosopher, as a physician, and as an English gentleman born into landed gentry and educated at St. John's College, Cambridge. The scientific facts he reports carry authority because he, Dr. Martin Lister, observed them at a particular time in a particular place under particular circumstances. The unique details of time and place and Lister's trustworthiness as an English gentleman (see Shapin 1994), therefore, constitute part of his case. Because Lister is known as a natural philosopher and a physician, his work is associated with the efforts of these two communities of inquirers. In accord with his identity as a natural philosopher, Lister discusses his work in the light of the efforts of other contemporary systematic botanists, the most famous of whom is John Ray; in addition, he associates himself with fellow virtuosos, men such as those he mentions in this article—Robert Boyle and a Mr. Fisher. His membership in the Royal Society, mentioned in his byline, underlines these relationships, which ground his inquiry in an institution blessed by the monarch, Charles II. Despite these relationships, Lister gives little indication that he is immersed in a context of current debate. The 10 citations in his article are primarily distributed according to the needs of plant identification, not argument.

Lister is also a physician. In this capacity, he traces his conceptual and generational lineages back to the ancients, the botanist Theophrastus and the physician-botanist Dioscorides, both of whom he mentions. Accordingly, throughout his article, Lister is alert to the medicinal uses of the plant juices. For example, he thinks of applying to "Narcosis of Opium" an extraction process that has been successful in another connection: "The Whey of *Lact. syl.* will be only dissolved in cold Water, the Curds wholly refusing to mix with it. *Qu.* Whether it will not succeed in other Juices, so as to make good that simple?" (p. 383). This application is consistent with Lister's philosophical commitment to the "virtues and force [of vegetable substances] upon human bodies as to the uses of life" (quoted in Lister 1967, p. xxx). His membership in the College of Physicians, also mentioned in his byline, underlines these relationships, which ground his inquiry in a long tradition of patient care.

Goodman and Rich: Communicating Science through Style

Unlike the prose of Lister (1697), that of Goodman and Rich (1962)reflects a world, and consequently a style, in which objects and events of science have absolute hegemony. In this prose, the facts about the material world that Goodman and Rich regard as relevant are routinely featured in prominent syntactic positions. For example, in the following passage, their use of the passive voice permits the writers to raise "DNA" and then "denaturation" from the object to the subject position, as the boldfaced nouns and italicized predicates make clear:

> The unlabeled bacterial **DNAs** used in this investigation *were prepared* by the method of Marmur.[10] Calf thymus and salmon sperm **DNA** *were obtained* from Sigma Chemical Company and California Corporation for Biochemical Research, respectively. The **DNAs** from the bacteriophages *were prepared* by phenol extraction.[11] Prior to annealing, the **DNA** *was denatured* by heating at 95–98°C for 15 min in 0.015 *M* NaCl, 0.0015 *M* sodium citrate, pH 7.4, and then quickly chilled in an ice bath. **Denaturation** *was followed* by measuring the change in optical density at 260 mμ. (p. 2102)

In this passage, the facts about the material world are promoted by a syntax that favors the passive voice and emphasizes things and abstractions over people as grammatical subject and complement. This is also a prose constructed largely of complex noun phrases (often with multiple modification) that deviate noticeably from everyday speech: "The unlabeled bacterial DNAs used in this investigation," "the method of Marmur," "Calf thymus and salmon sperm DNA," "Sigma Chemical Company and California Corporation for Biochemical Research," "the DNAs from the bacteriophages," "phenol extraction," and "the change in optical density at 260 mμ." In addition, the strong verbs of Lister—"bore," "put in," "drop," "return," "fill," "spill"—have been largely replaced by less vivid ones describing common actions in the laboratory: "prepare," "obtain," "follow." Finally, both "calf thymus and salmon sperm DNA" and "phenol extraction" are examples of fused noun strings, a construction entirely absent from the prose of Lister. Only specialized knowledge can help unravel the latter phrase: does it mean extracting phenol or extracting by means of phenol? The above passage also possesses other characteristics we have hypothesized for contemporary scientific style: circumstantial details and poetic metaphors are absent; technical abbreviations, noun strings, and quantification abound; there is one eponym; and two citations appear as superscripted numerals (of a total of 32 in the article).

Goodman and Rich's technical vocabulary focuses on relationships among sets of allied terms with theoretical import, sets such as "DNA" and "RNA," or "sodium chloride" and "sodium citrate." Unlike Lister, what these scientists see is not only what their eyes register, the sights visible in the laboratory, but also objects and events in the context of previously acquired knowledge. Take the sentence, "The following standard procedure was then adopted: 1 ml of 0.25 *M* NaCl, 0.015 *M* sodium citrate, pH 7.4, contained 45 [micrograms] of heat-denatured DNA and varying amounts of P^{32}-labeled sRNA" (p. 2102). To the knowledgeable, DNA and RNA are abbreviations of the two key molecules in molecular biology and nodes in a network of theory, and the names of the two salts are synonymous with their chemical formulas, formulas that denote the constituents of these salts, their chemical composition, and their stereochemical extension in space. In addition, to those in the know, "P^{32}-labeled" evokes both a chemical substance and a specific technique. It tells the informed that a radioactive form of phosphorus is being used, an isotope valuable because it can be used to track RNA, the dependent variable, in an aqueous solution. All these terms are, simultaneously, the names of the particular qualities of substances Goodman and Rich actually manipulated in the laboratory *and* classes of objects that are part of the causal structure of the natural world. The terms "RNA" and "DNA" have an additional feature: they cross over from chemistry to biology in that their mention also invokes a theory about how living things reproduce and evolve. To use these terms, then, is at the same time to summon up these well-established theories. To the privileged readers for whom this article is meant, there is no implication that the actual series of experiments is its real subject; these experiments are members of a class designed to produce results according to a theory. The issue for Goodman and Rich is never the cataloging of nature, always the cause in nature of laboratory events.

Despite its heavily technical vocabulary, the prose of Goodman and Rich is, in one sense, simpler than that of Lister. Let us look closely at three of their sentences: "The genome in *E. coli* contains a DNA molecular weight equivalent to 4×10^9. Knowing this, and using the molecular weight of *E. coli* sRNA (25,500), we may calculate from the plateau in Figure 3 that there are approximately 40 sRNA sites in the *E. coli* genome. If we assume that there is one site per sRNA molecule, this number provides a direct estimate of the degeneracy of the amino acid code" (p. 2106). The sentences are relatively short—24 words on average. The clausal density of these sentences is greatly reduced from that of Lister. The first consists of a single clause; the second has two clauses and the third sentence, three, with each clause clearly related in meaning and structure to the next. The predicates refer either to relationships presumed to exist in nature ("contains," "are," "is") or to a reasoning process by which nature is revealed ("calculate," "assume," "provides"). Any difficulty in reading arises from the highly technical vocabulary ("genome in *E. coli*," "molecular weight, "sRNA," "degeneracy of the amino acid code") and the assumed knowledge that goes with that vocabulary. This vocabulary is complex but not arbitrarily so. The written language is adapting to the increasing complexities of the allied disciplines of biochemistry and molecular genetics. To the knowledgeable, this prose is relatively straightforward; it employs minimum extraneous detail—each sentence motivated by the authors' stated goal to persuade the reader that DNA is a primary site for the origin of soluble RNA.

Goodman and Rich: Communicating Science through Presentation

Just as fact is given prominence in Lister's presentation, argument is given prominence in Goodman and Rich. Their introduction follows the standard formula Swales discovered. Within the intellectual territory of molecular genetic research (sentences 1–3), Goodman and Rich establish a niche (4–6), and fill that niche (7):

> [1] It has been known for a long time that transfer or soluble RNA (sRNA*) molecules play a central role in the organization of amino acids into polypeptide chains during protein synthesis. [2] Individual sRNA molecules combine with a particular amino acid to produce a complex which is active on the ribosomal particle. [3] Recent experiments[1] make it likely that a sequence of nucleotides in sRNA carry the specificity for determining the position of the amino acid in the polypeptide chain. [4] However, as yet little is known regarding the origin of sRNA. [5] These molecules could arise from DNA in a manner similar to the production of messenger RNA. [6] On the other hand, it has been demonstrated that the sRNA molecule is largely folded back upon itself with a regular system of hydrogen bonding,[2] and this has given rise to the suggestion that RNA may act as a template for manufacturing itself.[2,3] [7] These alternative possibilities have prompted us to carry out a series of experiments in which we look for the presence of a complementary sequence of bases in the DNA molecule by the formation of specific hybrids involving sRNA. (pp. 2101–2102)

Although this article possesses no heading abstract, there is a labeled summary at the end that distills Goodman and Rich's central argument:

> It is possible to form ribonuclease-resistant hybrid complexes between sRNA and DNA. This suggests the existence of a sequence of nucleotides in the DNA complementary to the sRNA. When this complex is formed with an excess of sRNA, the DNA in one *E. coli* genome is saturated with approximately 40 sRNA molecules. If there is one site per sRNA molecule, this suggests that there is considerable degeneracy in the amino acid code. Hybrids have been formed between *E. coli* sRNA and DNA from a variety of bacterial species. Closer relatives form larger amounts of ribonuclease-resistant hybrid than distant relatives. (p. 2108)

Moreover, the brief conclusion that closes the Discussion attempts to shape the niche Goodman and Rich have created in terms of theory over fact: "When experiments of this type are carried out on individually purified sRNA molecules, we will be able to trace the extent of the modifications which have occurred in the course of evolution" (p. 2108). In contrast to Lister, Goodman and Rich appear to understand that "no fact, however strange and curious, becomes relevant except in the context of a genuine problem, and no problem is raised or attracts attention unless it exhibits theoretical implications" (Pera 1994, p. 3).

Unlike those of Lister, Goodman and Rich's organizational cues are used consistently and to good effect in foregrounding their argument and in enabling readers easily to locate and coordinate tables and graphs and sections of text. Separated at the end of their article by the heading "*Summary,*" their précis recapitulates their central argument in a single paragraph. To simplify opportunistic searches for useful bits of method, theory, and fact, a finding system of headings and subheadings is clearly differentiated by italic type. As further aids to opportunistic reading, tables and figures are well separated from text, carefully and uniformly labeled, and always referred to by name in relevant text: "Table I," "Figure 3." Type size is generally uniform, but the article's title and byline are set in larger type for emphasis. On the other hand, the methods and materials section and the figure and table legends are set in smaller type, as is appropriate for subordinate detail. To interfere minimally with reading, citations are referred to in the text only by their numbers in superscript. They are gathered in full at the end, numbered, and uniformly presented. In each case, we are given the journal volume and name—the key information for locating the article—differentiated by typeface: bold for volume number, italic for title of journal cited. To aid anyone unfamiliar with their abbreviations, Goodman and Rich add a footnote at the end with key definitions.

Goodman and Rich: Creating Science through Argument

Unlike the working philosophy of Lister, which he actually recounted, that of Goodman and Rich is entirely implicit. Nevertheless, in acquiring new knowledge, Goodman and Rich share Lister's central empirical faith. They do not, however, share his confidence that the data will speak for themselves: Goodman and Rich's article constitutes an argument meant to redefine the meaning of the dependent variable, RNA. Their central claim is captured in the title, "Formation of a DNA-Soluble RNA Hybrid and Its Relation to the Origin, Evolution, and Degeneracy of Soluble DNA." Before their experiments, it was not clear whether soluble (better known as "transfer") RNA, like its two sisters ribosomal and messenger RNA, derived its base sequences from DNA. Now, as a consequence of Goodman and Rich's experimental program, the formation of a DNA-soluble RNA hybrid has become a new fact of science and, simultaneously, a new part of the meaning of DNA and RNA (Taylor 1965, pp. 493–502). (Notice that the terms "RNA" and "DNA" are flexible enough to incorporate these new meanings, yet rigid enough in denotation to designate consistently an entity that is a permanent part of animate nature. This is what it means to have a scientific vocabulary.)

Goodman and Rich are—even more than their distant ancestor Lister—avid gatherers of fact. While Lister's article is free of numerical information, theirs is replete with it and with tables and graphs, the visual tools for communicating its significance. These data are smoothly integrated into their argument. Unlike Lister, Goodman and Rich realize that interpretations can be wrung from these data only by the power of a sound argument. It is not merely in their discussion section that arguments appear; they argue for the significance of their results even in their results section. Here is a sample passage with its argumentative sinews in boldface:

> A plateau appears as a mass ratio of sRNA to DNA of 0.025 per cent. **Thus,** only a very small portion of the DNA is able to accept an sRNA molecule in hybrid formation. **Furthermore, these results show** that the preparation does not contain ri-

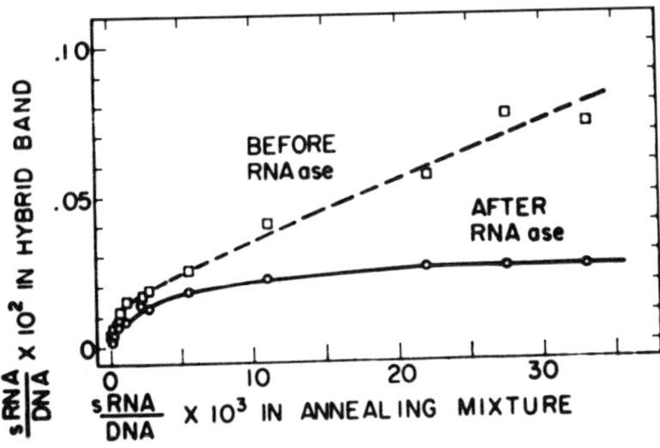

Figure 1.1. Line graph (Figure 3) from H. M. Goodman and A. Rich, "Formation of a DNA-Soluble RNA Hybrid and Its Relation to the Origin, Evolution, and Degeneracy of Soluble DNA," *Proceedings of the National Academy of Sciences,* vol. 48, p. 2106 (1962). Reproduced with permission of authors and National Academy of Sciences.

> bosomal RNA, **since** DNA-ribosomal RNA hybrids contain six times more RNA.[6] **If** cold ribosomal RNA is added to the annealing mixture, **[then] it does not compete** with the bonding of sRNA, **thereby** suggesting that the ribosomal RNA sites are different from the sRNA sites. The genome in *E. coli* contains a DNA molecular weight equivalent to 4×10^9.[13] **Knowing this, and using the molecular weight of *E. coli* sRNA** (25,500), **we may calculate** from the plateau in Figure 3 that there are approximately 40 sRNA sites in the *E. coli* genome. **If we assume** that there is one site per sRNA molecule, **[then] this number provides** a direct estimate of the degeneracy of the amino acid code. (p. 2106)

The key finding here, a plateau on a line graph (figure 1.1), has only the scientific significance that Goodman and Rich bestow upon it by the power of their argument. Moreover, even this line graph has been wrung from nature by the design of the authors' experiments. Indeed, this graph is the simple visible residue of complex laboratory procedures. It is one of eight graphs arranged in five figures that, with one table, take up 20% of the space devoted to the article. Even their experimental design must be considered as the pursuit of argument by means other than strict logic: the apparatus and procedures constrain nature in a manner analogous to the way premises constrain argument. Every scientific move Goodman and Rich make reflects their sensitivity to the reciprocity of theory and experimental fact, of text and visuals, and to the importance of a scientific vocabulary that emphasizes the causal patterns inherent in natural events, such as the link between DNA/RNA and bacterial generation.

Like Lister, Goodman and Rich hedge to fine-tune their arguments to the state of knowledge. The following is from their discussion on the significance of their results (hedges are marked in bold):

> Interpretation of the saturation data in Figure 3 depends upon the extent to which the enzymatic digestion is carried out to completion without denuding DNA stretches of sRNA which should be annealed there. **It is not likely** that this occurs,

> but we have no direct evidence on this point. Bearing in mind these assumptions, we can ask how much reliance may be placed on the calculation of 40 sRNA sites from the data in Figure 3. Although the molecular weight of sRNA is **only slightly uncertain, the uncertainty** in the total amount of DNA in the *E. coli* genome **may be considerable.** Thus, we cannot regard the figure of 40 sRNA sites as a very accurate determination. Nonetheless, **this result suggests** that there is considerable degeneracy in the amino acid code, a finding which is given indirect support from the genetic experiments of Crick *et al.* (p. 2108)

For Goodman and Rich, however, hedging is not merely a tactical epistemological maneuver; it is a verbal marker of their research strategy. Their introduction, already cited for another purpose, traces a path from accepted knowledge to a set of research hypotheses, motivated by recent work and marked by hedges:

> **It has been known for a long time** that transfer or soluble RNA (sRNA*) molecules play a central role in the organization of amino acids into polypeptide chains during protein synthesis. Individual sRNA molecules combine with a particular amino acid to produce a complex which is active on the ribosomal particle. **Recent experiments**[1] **make it likely** that a sequence of nucleotides in sRNA carry the specificity for determining the position of the amino acid in the polypeptide chain. However, as yet **little is known regarding the origin of sRNA. These molecules could arise** from DNA in a manner similar to the production of messenger RNA. On the other hand, **it has been demonstrated** that the sRNA molecule is largely folded back upon itself with a regular system of hydrogen bonding,[2] and **this has given rise to the suggestion** that RNA may act as a template for manufacturing itself.[2,3] **These alternative possibilities have prompted us to carry out a series of experiments** in which we look for the presence of a complementary sequence of bases in the DNA molecule by the formation of specific hybrids involving sRNA. (pp. 2101–2102)

In complementary fashion, their Discussion section traces a path from the results of their experiments to a new set of research questions, a set for which hedges are also the markers of a research strategy.

For their credibility in this rapidly moving field, Goodman and Rich rely not only on a common faith in a science grounded on a reciprocal relationship between theory and fact, but also on their status as respected researchers, working for a respected institution (MIT's Department of Biology) and publishing in a respected journal. As with Lister, credibility is a matter of character, but character has become more fully institutionalized. Goodman and Rich rely also on their position in what Diana Crane calls the "invisible college" and Harry Collins, the "core set." It is this group of researchers that creates the research front in which Goodman and Rich participate. The formation of this front is a communal activity, and the resulting community is far more integrated professionally than that in which Lister worked. The citations, the note added in proof, and the acknowledgments mention Seymour Benzer, Sydney Brenner, Waldo Cohn, Francis Crick, Benjamin Hall, Alfred Hershey, Fritz Lipman, Sol Spiegelman, Gunther Stent, James Watson, Bernard Weisblum, and Maurice Wilkins, all of whom are vital players in the DNA story (Portugal and Cohen 1978). It is fair to say, then, that at a first approximation these form

Goodman and Rich's core set or invisible college. (Paul Doty—who figures in three citations and is named in the byline as having "communicated" the article on 25 September 1962—provides the link between the researchers and publication, since publication in the *Proceedings of the National Academy of Sciences of the U.S.A.* requires sponsorship by an Academy member.) This network of relationships is inextricably part of Goodman and Rich's credibility, however much it is outside the precincts of argument as traditionally conceived.

Conclusion

This preliminary sketch illustrates that, despite the nearly 300 years that separate them, the articles by Lister (1697) and by Goodman and Rich (1962) share a common inheritance. Still, over the intervening years, there has been significant change. In the former publication, we observe a prose style with many of the traditional elements of good story telling: strong verbs in the active voice, first-person narrative, imaginative language, minimal abstraction, little esoteric terminology (except for the many Latin names of plants), and few quantitative expressions or theoretical explanations. In the latter publication, these elements are mostly gone. In both articles, the style, presentation, and argument embody the philosophy of science of scientists that Goodman and Rich share with Lister. However, Goodman and Rich's article reflects a clear, though tacit, acknowledgment of the primacy of theory over data and of the close reciprocity between the two. In addition, there is in Goodman and Rich a closer coordination of style and presentation to communicative purpose.

We must be careful not to to describe these changes in style, presentation, and argumentation as progress, as if Goodman and Rich's communicative and argumentative practices were an "improvement" over those of Lister. Given our eventual choice of evolutionary theory as an explanatory mechanism, such a characterization would be absurd. More consistent would be an explanation of change in terms of plausible selection pressures: increased cognitive complexity, higher standards of proof, and greater volume of data, coupled with a dramatic increase in the number of scientific articles. When we look at Lister in these terms, we see a set of communicative and argumentative practices well adapted to an environment in which a few "natural philosophers" were beginning to turn to the natural world with a new set of methodological tools, obtaining results that could be conveyed by means of a style and presentation only slightly altered from the essayistic, a style presumably common to serious scholarship in the mid-17th century. In the 300-year interim between Lister and Goodman and Rich, individual research projects increase in cognitive complexity, and the standards of proof rise, as does the volume of data required for experimental and observational proof; moreover, in the sciences as a whole, there is an increase in the number of articles (de Solla Price 1961), a proliferation as startling as the overnight increase of bacteria in a petri dish.

Goodman and Rich's is a representative response to these combined pressures (and probably to others as well): what they have to say is more complex than what Lister had to say, and their proof involves more data than Lister's required. This increased complexity and these increased demands led to alterations in scientific style and to an increased reliance on tables and figures. Goodman and Rich also needed to forge arguments designed to survive more searching scrutiny than those of Lister: the community of science had become far less tolerant of argumentative diversity. Finally, in response to the pressure of a high volume of publications in their field, publications to which no one can pay full attention, Goodman and Rich adopted a mode of presentation most likely to get their point across efficiently: the abstract and the claim-staking title are typical of such adaptive mechanisms.

In the descriptive chapters that follow, readers need to keep in mind these cautions about misreading change as progress. In the final chapter, an explanation will be offered for the changes in scientific communicative and argumentative practices over time, an explanation in which the selection pressures we have just mentioned will be prominently featured.

CHAPTER 2

Style and Presentation in the 17th Century

When we watch an old Max Sennett short, we may be amused not only by the antics of the Keystone Kops, but also by their rapid, jerky motions; if so, we are indulging in the pleasures of anachronism. The Keystone jerkiness is a consequence, not of Sennett's desire to please, but of his technical limitations. Only informed hindsight allows us to enjoy exactly what its original audiences enjoyed.

Similarly, in reading 17th-century scientific articles such as Martin Lister's in *Philosophical Transactions* (chapter 1), what we modern readers may take for charm—"a way with words"—is our pleasure in the anachronism arising from the relative absence of a technical vocabulary adequate to the description of the natural world, especially in such "new sciences" as botany. Informed hindsight permits us to see the character of this prose as the consequence of the first struggles among its practitioners to adapt, to a new purpose, a tool of communication and argumentation that had already undergone evolutionary developments in the more expansive format of the scientific book and the more casual style of the learned letter (Kronick 1976; Tebeaux 1997, 1999; Johns 1998).

In this chapter and the next, we examine the communicative and argumentative features of the three preeminent journals of 17th-century science: *Philosophical Transactions, Journal des Sçavans,* and *Mémoires de l'Académie des Sciences* (Gascoigne 1985, p. 93).[1] These three have an important common social bond: each has some

1. The first scientific journals, *Philosophical Transactions* and *Journal des Sçavans,* were both founded in 1665. While the first *mémoires* of the Académie Royale date from 1666, they were not actually published until the 18th century: "The memoirs submitted to the Academy by its members in the period 1666–1699 were, with some exceptions, not published by it at the time (though brief accounts of many of them appeared in the *Journal des sçavans* or similar journals)" (Gascoigne 1985, pp. 4–5).

connection with a scientific society—the Royal Society of London for *Philosophical Transactions* and the Académie Royale for both the *Journal des Sçavans* and *Mémoires.* These neophyte organizations had within their ranks most of the authors, readers, and journal editors of 17th-century science. They also created the social networks needed to establish what constituted acceptable communicative and argumentative practices in science.[2]

No two groups founded at nearly the same time with similar interests could be more different in organization and constituency than the Royal Society and Académie Royale. The Royal Society was a fairly large, loose-knit group of amateurs and "natural philosophers" in and around London—some extraordinarily talented, some with nothing more extraordinary than an above-average curiosity about the natural world. They met regularly to learn about and discuss the latest experiments and observations, as well to witness demonstrations of them. The Society received the blessing of the reigning monarch, Charles II, but depended largely upon members' dues and generosity for its economic survival.[3] The Royal Society secretary, Henry Oldenburg, launched *Philosophical Transactions* in March 1665 as a private venture. His transactions reported on technical news from home and abroad, often sent to him in the form of letters from his many correspondents.

In contrast to the Royal Society, the Académie Royale was closer to what we think of today as a government-funded research institute. Science was the principal occupation of its members, who lived and worked together in Paris under the patronage of Louis XIV, who funded this institution "at a level similar to the annual income of the wealthiest monastery in France" (Stroup 1990, p. 34). The Academy was also deeply involved in the publication of the fruits of its members' labors. During the 17th century, it published two handsome volumes on plants and animals, as well as a large collection of articles on mathematics and physical science, by "gentlemen of the Royal Academy." The first scientific *mémoires* of the Académie Royale date from 1666, but most of these were not actually published until the early 18th century—in the multivolume *Mémoires de l'Académie Royale des Sciences, depuis 1666 jusqu'à 1699.* However, articles by Académie members and summaries of their research did regularly appear throughout the 17th-century in *Journal des Sçavans,* started privately in January 1665 by Denis de Sallo.

Joseph Ben-David (1971) captured a key difference between these two early scientific societies: "[W]hereas the Royal Society was an independent corporation based on membership including amateurs and politicians of science as well as scientists of outstanding accomplishments, the *Académie* was a sort of elevated civil service composed of only a small number of scientists of high reputation" (p. 82). Importantly, the French arrangement had as its purpose "to control science and limit its influence. . . . [T]he empirical and experimental approach of science [was not to be] diffused to politics . . . the norms of universalism of science [were not to be] applied to matters of religion and social estate" (p. 82).

2. There are many excellent historical works on the early journals and scientific societies, including Barnes (1934), Birn (1965), Hahn (1971), Heilbron (1983), Kronick (1976), Laeven (1990), McClellan (1985), McCutcheon (1924), McKie (1948), Ornstein (1928), Stimson (1968), and Stroup (1990).

3. McClellan (1985) notes that in the 18th century the Royal Society did receive governmental funding for "several [large] expeditions and projects that had an immediate bearing on the government's interests in navigation, trade, and colonial expansion" (p. 30).

Given these differences in organization and constituency, we might speculate that English scientific prose would differ from the French in ways that could be traced to the compositional habits of English authors working alone in idiosyncratic ways on a wide variety of subjects. And such turns out to be the case, particularly with regard to some argumentative features we will discuss in the next chapter. Yet, while there are important differences, likenesses between French and English scientific prose outnumber these. As we shall soon show, scientific prose in the 17th century is already well on its way to becoming international.

Sampling Considerations for 17th-Century Articles

Because we are guided by the descriptive statistics we have gathered, we cannot discuss 17th-century scientific prose without first speaking further about our sampling practices (fully detailed in appendix A). In attempting to capture the communicative and argumentative practices of 17th-century scientific articles, we focus our attention on prose written in French and English. In this century, as far as we are aware, there are no published articles in German. And although Latin was clearly an important language for communicating science during this period—the two scientific journals from the German-speaking lands, *Miscellanea Curiosa Medico-Physica* and *Acta Eruditorum,* published articles in Latin in order to reach the widest possible international audience—we have excluded Latin articles. This omission is not meant to slight the significance of the journals in Latin, especially of the *Acta,* which published, among other things, most of the articles in which Leibniz announced and articulated his discovery of the calculus. It is simply that the decline of Latin in the periodical literature is too precipitous for us to make evolutionary comparisons between the 17th century and later centuries. By the late 17th century, Latin was already on the way out in favor of the vernacular, reflecting "a decisive switch from dry and bloodless scholastic erudition toward a mixed scientific/technological literature based upon the experience of the artisan, the practitioner, the traveler" (Cohen 1994, p. 323).[4]

We have also ignored scientific articles written in other European languages—for example, Italian, Dutch, Danish, and Swedish. These omissions are also justified in principle. Despite the major contributions to science of scientists throughout Western Europe, the fact remains that work by investigators in these countries, though often published in their respective vernaculars, was communicated to Europe, and to the world, in one of the major languages of science, not their own.[5]

In this chapter, we describe the essential communicative features of 17th-century scientific prose and discuss its development in the 36 years from the origin

4. Latin never disappears from scientific prose. Along with Greek, it remains a source for names of creatures and diseases; moreover, it never completely stops serving as the language of the learned elite. The really racy passages in Krafft-Ebing's study of sexual psychopathology (late 19th century) are, after all, in Latin, not German.

5. In the 20th century, as science has become a global phenomenon, journal articles in Chinese, Japanese, and Russian also have become significant. We also ignore this literature because our research also depends on comparisons *between* centuries.

of the scientific journal, in 1665, to the beginning of the next century. This gives us a baseline for comparison with later centuries. We make comparisons not only within but also between French and English scientific prose. In making these comparisons for prose style, obviously we must tread carefully. For example, we are fully aware that between these languages the use of the passive voice and dummy subjects is not strictly comparable: in French, the reflexive ("la séparation de toutes ces matières *se fasse* avec . . . ," meaning "the separation of all these materials *is done* with . . ."; 1667-F009)[6] or the pronoun *on* (meaning *one*) is preferred where in English one normally finds the passive voice. But the differences between these two languages do not always make comparisons pointless. For example, they do not greatly affect such stylistic features as evaluative and deviant expressions, poetic metaphors, hedges, quantifying expressions and equations, and citations.

Style in 17th-Century Articles

General Profile

In contrast to the 20th century, we find that the early scientific articles seek to establish credibility more by means of reliable testimony than by technical details, more by qualitative experience than by quantitative experiment and observation in support of theory. Hence, a more personal style is appropriate, and notions of relevance are given a wide berth.

Take this novelistic passage culled from an early issue of the *Philosophical Transactions:*

> I took out 45 *ounces* and better, of blood, out of the *Jugular Vein* of a Sheep, of a lesser size than the former; by which time, the Spectators, as well as my self, found her exceeding faint, and some thought her pass'd recovery, without a supply of blood. Then I convey'd blood from the *Jugular Vein* of a Calf into that of the Sheep for the space of *7 minutes,* when we did believe, by the continuance of a good stream from the Calf, that the Sheep had already received more blood, than she had lost. Whereupon we set her free, and she had no sooner got her liberty, but seeing a Dog near her (which was a Spaniel, that had formerly suffered the transmission of Sheeps-blood into him) she butted with great violence at him three or four times, not appearing at all concern'd at what she had endured in the Experiment. (1667-E003; italics in original)

In this selection on the then-popular topic of experiments with blood transfusion, the author Edmond King relates events in the first person in three complex, loose sentences (average of 4.3 clauses per sentence) of considerable length (average of 51 words). Personal pronouns abound (five of them in the first person, nine in third). There are no passive-voice constructions, no dummy subjects, and no citations linking this experiment to a wider field of research. The mention of "spectators" and the

6. Indicates number assigned to passage from our sample: year of publication (in this case, 1667), language (E = English, F = French, and, in later chapters, G = German), and a code number for article (in this case, 009).

Table 2.1. Averages of Stylistic Features in 17th-Century Passages: Occurrences per 100 Words

	English (n = *100*)[a]	*French* (n = *98*)
Personal pronouns	3.3	2.9
Evaluative expressions	0.2	0.1
Poetic expressions	0.1	0.2
Deviant expressions	0.1	0.0
Suppressed-person passives	1.1	0.2
Objective passives	0.4	0.4
Dummy subjects	0.7	1.1
Hedges	0.2	0.1
Quantitative expressions	1.1	2.5
Citations	0.1	0.2

[a]Throughout the book *n* = number of 10-line passages or whole articles randomly selected. See also table A.1 in appendix A.

parenthetical remark about the Spaniel add to the personal flavor, as does the observation about the sheep's behavior and state of mind after the transfusion.

A passage even remotely as personal as this one is hard to imagine in the 20th century, but a question our sampling method allows us to address is whether this passage is typical of 17th-century scientific prose. The English data, some of which are presented in table 2.1, confirm that this passage is typical from several perspectives. Seventeenth-century scientific prose makes extensive use of first-person personal pronouns and proper names. It is also relatively parsimonious with dummy subjects, citations, and passive verbs—though passive verbs do appear at the rate of 1.5 per hundred words in the English sample. This passage is less rambling in structure than is typical for its time. Typical sentence length averages 60 words, not 51—and typical sentences have slightly more clauses—an average of 5.6 rather than 4.3.

Our data on verb usage (see table 2.2) also suggest that the passage is representative of the 17th century. Of the 13 finite verbs in the passage, six (*to be, find,*

Table 2.2. Ten Most Frequent Verbs in 17th-Century Passages

English Verbs (n = *510*)	*% Occurrence*	*French Verbs* (n = *490*)	*% Occurrence*
to be	22.6%	être (to be)	19.8%
to have	2.4	avoir (to have)	7.5
to make	2.3	voir (to see)	3.4
to observe	2.2	faire (to make, to do)	3.2
to find	1.9	trouver (to find)	3.2
to see	1.8	peser (to weigh)	2.2
to say	1.6	donner (to give)	1.9
to give	1.5	arriver (to happen)	1.4
to seem	1.3	mettre (to place)	1.3
to think	1.3	observer (to observe)	1.2
Total	38.9%	Total	45.1%

think, take, suffer, get) appear among the upper 50% of finite verbs ranked by frequency of use in the English sample. Further, in both the passage and the sample as a whole, the verbs are about equally divided between those relating to actions of people and those relating to the objects of study. A difference worth noting, however, is that the static verbs *to be* and *to have* account for 22.6% of the finite verbs in the sample, but only 8% in the passage. This difference, combined with the complete absence of passive verbs, contributes to a more active narrative style than is normal even for 17th-century English scientific prose.

The Edmond King passage is also atypical with respect to two stylistic features: quantitative expressions and hedges. On the basis of these two measures, the quoted passage would appear to be closer to 20th- than to 17th-century scientific prose. Yet, the three quantitative expressions ("45 ounces," "7 minutes," "three or four times") are not an integral part of any mechanistic or mathematical explanation, but merely contribute circumstantial details surrounding this particular case of blood transfusion. While the exact quantities do not appear to have any particular significance in themselves, they do help communicate the qualitative assertion that the author-experimenter removed enough blood from the sheep to cause faintness, then returned enough to restore its former health. The two hedges ("some thought," "we did believe") add credibility to the impression of a reliable qualitative experience because they convey the message that at least some of the spectators would corroborate the author's visual observations concerning the sheep's health immediately before and after the transfusion.

Despite the very palpable differences between the feel of 17th-century scientific style and its 20th-century counterpart, we find many common features. In both centuries, the prose is relatively impersonal and free of ornament. Our second selected passage, in French and from the end of our chosen period, is less personal and rambling than our English passage, and seems to approximate 20th-century stylistic norms:[7]

> But if one evaporates the urine before it has fermented, one separates from it only a little alcohol and the greater part of aqueous fraction; the other volatile matters, for example, the salt, the oil and the matter of phosphorus, remain there barring the application of considerable heat; and then in order that the separation of all of the matters be accomplished with as much ease as possible, one lays aside to ferment in the cellar for three or four months the black matter that remains after the evaporation of the aqueous fraction. It is not that it is impossible to draw the phosphorus from the fermented urine. Mr. Homberg has done it several times; but the operation is very difficult, and one courts a great risk of not succeeding. (1692-F009)

In this passage, a journal editor (presumably) communicates the gist of chemical experiments with urine performed by Guillaume Homberg, a leading chemist and botanist for the Royal Academy. At first glance this passage has a decidedly modern ring to it: no first-person pronouns, one name, two dummy subjects, one objective

7. For a discussion of such norms, see Bazerman (1988), Atkinson (1999), Halliday (1993a), and Quirk and Greenbaum (1972).

passive, no poetic metaphors, and no statements extraneous to the technical point being discussed. The absence of suppressed-person passive verbs is the result of a general characteristic of the French language that differs from English. In three instances, the author avoids the passive construction and the personal pronoun by combining an active-voice verb with the indefinite pronoun "one" in the subject position (e.g., *on évapore*); in one instance he uses the reflexive "be accomplished" (*se fasse*). These constructions contribute to the overall neutral tone. The passage deviates sharply from modern practice, however, in its preference for qualitative over quantitative expression: "a little alcohol," "the greater part," "considerable heat," "as much ease as possible," "several times," "very difficult," "great risk."

We can say that our second illustrative passage is typical of the 17th-century French style with three exceptions. The French sample has, on average, three times as many personal pronouns and names, 0.75 in the passage versus 2.9 instances per 100 words in the sample. Second, the passage's sentences are substantially shorter than the average, 33.3 versus 51.5 words per sentence in the sample. Third, the passage has no quantitative expressions or equations, compared with the average of 2.5 per 100 words in the French sample.

In modern times, quantification contributes in a major way to the impression of objectivity in scientific prose. But as the above-quoted two passages and our whole sample demonstrate, in the latter third of the 17th century, the data within scientific articles are typically meager and their descriptive complexity is not very far advanced, even in so mature a science as astronomy: the evolving complexities of scientific representation generally prove manageable within conventional syntactic forms and by conventional semantic means.

Personal vs. Impersonal Expression

Despite an occasional liveliness, our lasting impressions are of an English and French prose that is largely objective and impersonal. Although we uncovered examples of evaluative and deviant expressions and poetic metaphors in our sample, we found fewer than one might expect from a prose style allegedly more literary than its modern counterpart (see table 2.1).

Overall, the French sample appears to be slightly more impersonal than the English. In the French sample, only one word or expression in a thousand conveys investigator evaluations or feelings. Evaluations vary: a demonstration is "beautiful" (1668-F014); the author achieves "the success that we hoped for" (1686-F046); the result is "very good" (1693-F070). Investigator feelings vary also: the investigator is "surprised" (1692-F076), "astonished," (1666-F050), "pleased" (1692-F017), or "very persuaded" (1700-F048). Only a very small number of passages—too small to attain mathematical significance—have expressions deviant from standard scientific description. They form no discernable pattern: something is "discovered by accident" (1693-F075); comets promote "the fear of God" (1681-F100); the author poses a rhetorical question (1672-F022).

In the English sample, there are quite a few more passages with evaluative or deviant expressions: enough to create the slightly more personal flavor of English prose style. Evaluations and conventional expressions of feelings parallel the French:

the authors think a publication is not "unseasonable at this time" (1665-E001); an anatomist marvels that "the Artifice of Nature is very extraordinary" (1699-E042). The deviant expressions in English form a pattern; most commonly, they concern extraneous details: Huygens "observ'd Saturn with his Telescope of 22 feet, a little before he came out of France" (1670-E008); in the midst of maritime observations, Stubbs indicates that his ship sailed off course "to avoid the Spanish Fleet" (1668-E010). We hasten to add that these few examples of statements tangential to the science appear to be nothing more than interesting anomalies. We found little evidence that "Fellows of the Royal Society *filled their descriptions* with contingent details of time and place in order to convey the impression that these were actual events, of which the authors were faithful reporters" (Holmes 1989a, p. 165; italics added). Our own general impression is that when there are details of time and place, as is often the case in reports of astronomical observations, they almost always provide information essential to the technical matter at hand.

Our impression of an impersonal style is further reinforced when we consider the use of poetic metaphor in the sample. Ornament for its own sake is wholly lacking in the two quoted passages (1667-E003 and 1692-F009) and in the sample as a whole. We attribute this finding to several factors. One is that, at least since the Renaissance, communicators of new science and technology embraced a "plain style," shunning figures of speech such as metaphor and simile as ornaments to liven up the prose (Tebeaux 1997, 1999). Second, various early commentators on scientific communication openly discouraged excessive use of figurative language—most ardently, Thomas Sprat in his 17th-century manifesto for the Royal Society:

> Who can behold, without indignation, [what] these specious *Tropes* and figures have brought to our Knowledg. . . . [O]f all the Studies of men, nothing may be sooner obtain'd, than this vicious abundance of *Phrase,* this trick of *Metaphor,* this volubility of *Tongue,* which makes so great a noise in the World. But I spend words in vain for the evil is now so inveterate, that it is hard to know whom to *blame,* or where to begin to *reform.* (1667, p. 112; italics in original)

Despite Sprat's open disdain for "this trick of *Metaphor*" and Francis Bacon's similar distrust of "similes and a treasury of eloquence and inanities of that kind" (quoted in Jones 1982, p. 285), we know from many contemporary scholars (to name a few: Leatherdale 1974; Lakoff and Johnson 1980; Lakoff and Turner 1989; Fahnestock 1998) that metaphor and simile—far from being a peripheral literary device outside the realm of poetry and fire-and-brimstone sermons—are central to language and thought, even in the sciences. Indeed, one can easily compile a list of key metaphorical expressions drawn from the history of science: the workings of the universe and clockwork, planetary motion and musical harmonies, Faraday's lines of force and a fluid flowing through thin tubes, the behavior of light and that of waves and particles, the relativity of time and the clock paradox, the structure of the atom and the solar system. In our study, however, we are concerned only with the density of "poetic metaphors" in the selected passages, which turns out to be quite low, even in the 17th century.

The few examples of metaphorical expressions in our 17th-century sample are clearly functional. In our English sample, these are confined almost entirely to biology and earth science and serve to describe features in the natural world in the absence of technical or quantitative terms. A good example of a descriptive use of metaphor, one that will disappear in the wake of a technical vocabulary, is "I observed four sorts of Animals. In the clear part of the Drop were two Kinds and both very small. Some were of the Figure of Ants Eggs" (1694-E013). A good example of a use that will disappear with quantification is "I cut Holes for the Bird's Bill (about as long and as small as a Taylor's Needle)" (1698-E045).

In the French sample, metaphors and similes are confined almost entirely to biology, chemistry, and earth science. They serve to describe features of the natural world in the absence of technical terms, for example, "the most beautiful sea-shells as full of holes as worm-eaten wood" (1666-F010) and "a substance with the taste and consistency of honey" (1676-F062). The following is more elaborate: "[I]t is very difficult to imagine how marine flora, which are as hard as wood or stone, can feed themselves in the sea, especially as there are several who certainly are not at all rooted in place, except perhaps in the first days of their lives. The species of corals and of *Madrepora,* the mushrooms of the sea, *the Tubularia marina, rubra IB* are also as hard as stones" (1700-F040). Even in this elaboration, the metaphors and similes are always functional, never decorative, never a sign of authors striving to show off their literary skills.

Another of our indicators of "personal expression" was whether the verbs signified the actions of persons or of matter. Our English sample consisted of 1,000 verbs, almost equally divided between the two types. In our French sample of 943 verbs, however, we found 56% predicated of the subject of science—nature herself—and 44% of the natural philosophers working with nature. So the French verbs reflect a stronger focus on the objects of nature compared with the English verbs.

To give an example of how verbs work in 17th-century scientific prose, we will discuss two passages that are *atypical* of their respective languages. Our first is from John Wallis's "A Discourse Concerning the Measure of the Airs Resistance to Bodies Moved in It":

> But at what Rate, or in what Proportion, such resistance is; and consequently, at what Rate the Celerity and Force is continually diminished, seems not to have been so well examined. Whence it is, that the Motion of a Projectile (secluding this consideration) is commonly reputed to describe a Parabolick Line; as arising from an Uniform or equal Celerity in the Line of Projection, and a Celerity uniformity accelerated in Line of Descent: which two so compounded do create a Parabola. (1687-E094)

While English scientific prose is more oriented toward the actions of persons than the French, in this passage, nothing much happens and nothing at all happens to anybody. Celerity and force diminish, lines create a parabola.

In the following passage, from "Reflections on the Physics of the Production of Mushrooms in Last Month's Memoir," we see, not the typical object orientation of French scientific prose, but an orientation toward human actions. Tournefort plants and observes; an indefinite "one" feels and doubts:

> But even if one would not feel sure that the *Deer's Tongue* was about to germinate, one could no longer doubt it after the observation that Mr. Tournefort has made.

> Having caused a stalk of this plant to be planted in a deep well, a little above the water, the year after it had produced, on the section of the circumference of this well, he saw many young plants that began their life with a leaf rounder than those of the *Deer's Tongue* that he had had planted, but that were, in the course of time, accompanied by other leaves just like those of this older plant. (1692-F081)

In contrast to the abstract English passage, the object of study, mushrooms, perform concrete actions: they germinate and grow.

Seventeenth-century scientific prose is not only largely objective and impersonal; it is fairly uniform across languages. Our data on verbs, for example, indicate a remarkable degree of uniformity between the two languages, as evidenced by their top ten verbs (table 2.2). Seven of these predicates overlap: *to be, have, make, observe, see, find, give.* The stylistic features in table 2.1 also indicate overall concord between the French and English samples. Only in the case of suppressed-person passive and quantitative expressions is there a real discrepancy; and the latter may be accounted for almost entirely by the higher French interest in mathematics, both pure and applied. We had anticipated greater literary diversity in a genre still in its formative years. This suggests to us that tacit conventions regarding the prose styles for French and English already were in place at the origin of the scientific article, arising in all likelihood from the long-standing traditions of technical book and letter writing. An *international* scientific style was already in the process of maturation by the late 17th century.

By themselves, however, these results tell us nothing about the different literary traditions out of which 17th-century scientific style emerged in England and France: the French apparently leaned toward the order and uniformity of the classical style, as exemplified in expository prose by Descartes's *Discourse on Method;* the English patterned themselves more on freewheeling travel accounts in natural history and the medical case study (Thomas and Turner 1994, pp. 14–19; Daston and Park 1998, pp. 215–253).

Syntactical Complexity

One might legitimately characterize the 17th-century scientific article in French and English as "plain" narrative largely concerned with empirical observations. But although the word "plain" definitely applies when it comes to neutral, inornate language, as we've just demonstrated, it does not apply to sentence structure. By modern standards (discussed in chapter 8), typical 17th-century sentences are quite long and well stocked with clauses. The average sentence length is 60.4 words for our English sample and 51.5 words for the French. The average clausal density per sentence is 5.6 for the English and 4.2 for the French.[8] Nevertheless, the data in table 2.3 indicate that, despite these highly complex, clausally dense sentences, there is a heavy reliance on simple noun phrases, particularly in the subject position. As expected, complex noun phrases dominate the nonsubject position, but even here, simple noun phrases (such as "a Parabola" from 1687-E094) and complex noun phrases with only

8. Interestingly, the clausal density per 100 words for the 17th century is not much different from that for the 20th century: 9.6 (vs. 8.3) for the English and 8.6 (vs. 8.7) for the French.

Table 2.3. Distribution of Noun Phrases of Various Types in 17th-Century Passages

Noun-Phrase Types[a]	*English* (n = *100*)[a]	*French* (n = *98*)
Subject Simple	28.2%	28.8%
Subject Complex	12.0	13.2
Nonsubject Simple	18.6	15.9
Nonsubject Complex	41.3	42.0
Subject Pronouns and Names	25.5	25.3
Subject Multiple Modifiers	5.5	5.5
Nonsubject Pronouns and Names	13.8	7.3
Nonsubject Multiple Modifiers	24.3	26.8

[a]Appendix C defines the terms used in this column and gives an example of the calculations involved.

a single modifier (such as "a Parabolick Line" from 1687-E094) are well represented. By and large, table 2.3 supports the claim that, whatever differences there might be between the style of 17th-century scientific prose in French and English, this cannot be attributed to differences on their noun-phrase structures. Only in the case of nonsubject pronouns and names do we have a discrepancy, which we attribute to the more informal character of English scientific prose.

But a caveat to this claim is necessary. To conform to the counting procedures of Quirk and Greenbaum (1972), we have defined "multiple modification" conservatively as anything beyond a bare header noun and its modification by a single adjective or prepositional phrase. Thus, we have no descriptive statistics of the interesting differences in the length and complexity of multiple modifiers. To illustrate these differences in the noun-phrase structure of the 17th century, we have selected two passages, both from the physical sciences. The English passage, by Robert Hooke, concerns an optics experiment that provides the general reader with instructions on how to "make the Picture of any thing appear on a Wall, Cub-board or within a Picture-frame." The French passage, by Pierre Varignon, relates to a method for the making of water clocks. In both passages, bold type indicates complex noun phrases with multiple modification:

> Opposite to **the place or wall where the Apparition is to be,** let a Hole be made of **about a foot in diameter, or bigger;** if there be **a high Window, that hath a Casement in it,** 'twill be so much the better. Without **this hole, or Casement open'd at a convenient distance,** (that it may not be perceived by the Company in the room) place **the Picture or Object, which you will represent,** inverted, and by **means of Looking-glasses placed behind,** if the picture be transparent, reflect the rayes of the Sun so, as that they may pass through it towards **the place, where it is to be represented;** and to the end that no rayes may pass besides it, let the Picture be encompass'd on **every side with a board or cloath.** (1668-E006)

> For there to be **these 144 equal parts,** it is necessary to have **23 for the first hour of outflow, 21 for the second, 19 for the third, 17 for the fourth, and, finally, 1 for the twelfth,** always following **the natural sequence of odd numbers.**

EXAMPLE II.

XI.* **The acceleration of the water at its exit through the hole O** remaining **the same as in the last example** (art. 8), that is to say, as **the roots of the heights of the surface of the water above the hole,** so that **the curve OVX that expresses them by these ordinates** is still **a parabola whose locus is v = $\sqrt{px}$;** if one now wants **the generated curve FEO of the given vessel,** assume **any conic section whose vertex is within the circumference of O.** (1699-F023)

Both passages have nearly the same number of complex noun phases with multiple modifications. But the somewhat rambling English passage is heavily intermixed with various types of noun phrases, while the mathematical French passage is almost exclusively constructed out of complex noun phrases with multiple modification. Further, while in the English passage the complex noun phrases with multiple modification are relatively brief and simple, those in the French passage are long and carry a heavier semantic burden. Compare "about a foot in diameter, or bigger" with "any conic section whose vertex is within the circumference of O."

The French passage, with its thicket of multiple modifications in both the subject and nonsubject positions, roughly conforms to the general distribution of noun phrases in modern scientific prose, as we shall show in the 20th-century chapter. The more varied pattern of noun phrases in the English passage, however, is more representative of the 17th century. Given the syntactical complexity of both these passages and many others in our sample, we would suggest that the expression "plain style" is a somewhat misleading epithet for 17th-century scientific prose.

Presentation

Scientific presentation concerns features that help readers as they work their way through texts. By the end of the 20th century, features as diverse as titles and citation format have combined to form a master finding system, a visible acknowledgment that scientific articles are meant less to be read than to be mined as a resource for further investigation.[9] This system is, arguably, a response to the exponential growth of the scientific literature. De Solla Price (1961) represents this growth by a rising logarithmic curve with a slope of more than 60 degrees: we start with two journals in 1665 and end with nearly 100,000 three hundred years later. Modern articles are not only more numerous but also longer. Bazerman (1988) documents a doubling in size of the average article in *Physical Review* throughout the 20th century, to about 10,000 words (pp. 162–164).

Presentational features of scientific articles are of two types. There are formal features: headings, thematic titles, and citations. There are also substantive features: introductions and conclusions (table 2.4).

9. This inference has some empirical support. Davida Charney (1993) sums up her empirical investigation of scientists' reading habits as follows: "[T]hey read as is convenient for their own purposes (they read parts selectively and out of order); they weigh the plausibility of claims and evidence; they struggle to understand unfamiliar technical terms; they cheer and get mad." See also Bazerman (1988, pp. 235–253).

Table 2.4. Percentage of Articles with Presentational Features by Language in 17th-Century Sample

	English (n = *50)*	*French* (n = *50)*
Formal features		
Thematic titles	94%	88%
Headings	4	2
Citations	36	34
Substantive features		
Complete introductions	50	24
Complete conclusions	6	4

Since the 17th-century scientific literature was manageably small, and since many articles were meant to be read aloud before a learned audience sharing a curiosity about nature and technology, it is not surprising to find that many articles are quite short and their finding subsystems relatively undeveloped. Nevertheless, these articles exhibit the germs from which such subsystems would eventually arise.

Formal Features

Thematic titles are the norm and offer the reader the best clue to content: "Some Observations and Experiments upon May-Dew" (1665-E102). Indeed, we may get quite a bit more than this; we may get an allusion to the article's central claim: in French, "Observation of a Precise Conjunction of a Satellite of the Planet Saturn with a Fixed Star" (1692-F074); in English, "An Extract of Letters from Dr. John Wallis to the Publisher, 1672. Sept. &c., Concerning the Suspension of Quicksilver Well Purged of Air, Much Higher than the Ordinary Standard in the Torricellian Experiment" (1673-E104).

Headings are few, as is to be expected when articles are, in general, so short. On occasion, however, we see some examples. Detailed headings appear very occasionally in the margin, for example, "2nd *Experiment.* Remarkable anomaly in the descent of water from which all air has been extracted" (1672-F006). We see similar "headings" in footnotes at the bottom of the page (1700-F068). We see sections and subsections numbered in the running text (1699-F067). We see generic headings also: "Remarks" (1699-F067), "Reflections" (1672-F034), "*Experiment 1*" (1696-E103).

Seventeenth-century citations are apparently mere reminders to a small audience of initiates of familiar and mutually possessed books and articles. They are few in number and relatively few articles have them: there are 36% English articles with citations, 34% French. Placement is not uniform. Some citations appear beside, some within the running text. Information included is not uniform. Page number, author, or article title can be omitted and often are. Format also is not uniform. We have "see *Philos. Transact. No.* 198" (1700-E016) as well as "Philosophic-Transactions No

127 page. 653" (1683-E024). Book references are frequently to ancient or standard reference texts: Strabo's *Geography* (1692-F005), the Rudolphine *Tables* (1692-F045). Sometimes we have only the date and name: "of the year 1556, observed by Homelius" (1699-F007). In one case, we have only "after the observation made by Mr. Tournefort" (1692-F081). In neither the English nor the French case do citations provide much evidence of an international scientific network or of a research front to which current scientists are contributing.

Substantive Features

Introductions in only 37% of the sample fulfill Swales's (1990) three steps in a minimal sense, that is, establish an intellectual territory, define a niche in that territory, and then occupy that niche. The following short introduction, by Dodart on plants, covers the first two steps in a single opening sentence: "There is plentiful evidence that plants grow straight up in order to hold themselves up more easily and to bear their fruits; but the question is, not for what end this is done, but how and by what means it is achieved" (1700-F068). This introduction is expository. But introductions are just as likely to be narrative.

More needs to be said about the narrative element in 17th-century French and English science. In an experimental or observational article from the late 20th century, the series of events that constitutes its central design is embedded in an argumentative framework in which these events are meant to represent instantiations of natural laws, a characteristic that renders irrelevant the fact that these events occurred at a particular time or place. In its 17th-century counterpart, however, the narrative is different in tone and purpose. The vivid scene in this introduction to "Observations of a New Comet Made at the Observatory" gives us an excellent picture of the community of astronomers in 17th-century France:

> There now appeared a comet that seemed to be at the end of its cycle, & that one had been able to see several months ago, if the weather had been favorable, but as it is very small, & as it had been occluded for a long time by the rays of the sun, its near neighbor, and then by the moon, which was big, and as, besides that, the sky in these quarters, has been often covered with clouds, one has only seen it recently. The mathematicians of La Flêche saw it from the 16th day of the last month, and they gave the first news of it to Paris. Those of the College of Cleremont, having been informed of it, saw it on the 15th of the same month, & on the notice which had been given of it to the Royal Academy of Science by Father Pardies, Professor of Mathematics at the College of Cleremont, Mr. Cassini has since observed it, as much as the weather permited. (1672-F034)

To call this introduction narrative, however, is not to imply that, as in conventional narratives, the occupants of the subject position are the foci of attention. Clearly, the comet is the star of the show.[10]

10. For that reason, we find Atkinson's (1999) characterization of the early *Philosophical Transactions* as "author centered" (pp. 76–80) to be misleading.

Occasionally, 17th-century conclusions also appear with their modern components in place—reiteration of major points, emphasis on their wider significance, and recommendations based on that significance. At the end of Malebranche's long article on optics, for example, we have all of these components in one form or another:

> Besides it need not be imagined that what I have said of the little spheres of [Descartes's] second element, that far from believing them hard, I see them rather as little vortices of fluid matter, must topple Descartes's *Physics*. On the contrary, my view, if it is true, improves his system in general. Because if my opinion is useful in explaining light and color, it appears to me also a very appropriate way to resolve, in conformity with the principles of this natural philosopher, other quite general questions of physics, as for example, to explain the generation and the surprising effects of fire, as I am going to attempt to do. (1699-F051)

Nevertheless, such elaboration is rare, as we might expect in a time of relatively brief articles (seldom more than 10 pages, sometimes a single paragraph). In our 100 French and English articles taken together, there are only 16 conclusions that mention wider significance, 16 that contain recommendations, and seven that reiterate or add to claims. Only five articles possess all three components. Over half the articles have neither introductions nor conclusions.

Here is an article in its entirety, somewhat atypicial in its brevity, but typical in its minimalistic presentation—in particular, its lack of a context-setting introduction or conclusion other than "nothing certain could be concluded." The passage is by the French savant de la Hire and is entitled "Observation of the Eclipse of the Moon, Occurring the 28th of the Present Month of July":

> The 27th of July, at about nine in the evening, the moon being on the horizon at the same height it would be on the next day at the time of the eclipse, Monsieur de la Hire observed its diameter with a micrometer, and he found it two seconds less than he found it through calculation. He observed again the position of several principal features in order to fix their shape in his mind and to depict the moon in the situation that it would be in during the eclipse.
>
> But the 28th of July, the day of the eclipse, the sky being almost always overcast, it was only possible to observe the moon during the eclipse three times; even then, as the moon only appeared very briefly from among the clouds, he was obliged to make his observations so quickly that nothing certain could be concluded. He observed only the number of the degrees that were eclipsed, not being able to distinguish the features. The shadow of the earth on the body of the moon appeared clearly and sharply contrasted.
>
> At 2 hours, 48 minutes, the moon was eclipsed by 9 doigts,[11] 58 minutes
> at 2 hours, 55 minutes, [the moon was eclipsed] by 10 doigts, 24 minutes
> at 3 hours, 35 minutes, [the moon was eclipsed] by 10 doigts, 28 minutes
>
> These observations have been made with the micrometer. (1692-F041)

11. In astronomy, each of the 12 parallel zones by which one divides the lunar disk to indicate the extent of a lunar eclipse.

In the de la Hire passage as well as our 17th-century sample in general, elaborate subsystems of headings, figures, and citations do not exist.

Visual Representations

At the origin of the scientific article in 1665, several types of visual representation had already reached full maturity: tables of data had long been a staple of the astronomical literature; three-dimensional drawings of anatomical features had attained a high level of technical detail and artistry, as shown by the graphics in the work of Vesalius and Leonardo da Vinci; map making of the earth and the heavens was a long-standing enterprise; and geometric diagrams had been with us since Euclid. Moreover, illustrations of flora and fauna, as in Hooke's *Micrographia* (1665), were on a par with anything produced by graphic artists today. Nevertheless, scientists were just beginning to appreciate the power of visualization as a means of shaping and conveying new knowledge.

In our 17th-century sample of 100 whole articles, only 38 (26 French, 12 English) possess any visual representations at all; there are only six tables.[12] These visuals vary in type—tables of results, three-dimensional drawings of equipment and of objects being investigated, and geometric representations of the operation of natural laws. More important, they also vary in function. This is where their real significance lies: they provide support for the facts and the mechanical and mathematical explanations that are the central topics of argument in 17th-century science. In the next chapter, we discuss scientific argument and visuals at greater length. Here, we concentrate on their presentational features.

Figures are treated variously. Figure titles occur in margins (1672-F006, 1672-F034, 1692-F078) or the bottom of the page (1699-F051, 1700-F068). On occasion they are numbered (in 10 French and eight English articles in the sample). Legends appear only occasionally (in three French and five English articles). But in an article by Dodart, numerous figures are accompanied by extensive legends (1700-F068).

Useful visual conventions seem to be generally observed, for example, the dotted line as an indication of some extrapolation or projection. Varignon uses a dotted line to represent the trajectory of a falling body and the asymptote (1699-F067). Huygens uses it to reveal an otherwise hidden component of his experimental apparatus (1672-F006); Cassini uses a dotted line for the conjectured path of a comet (1672-F034); Molyneux uses it to represent an alternative survey result (1697-E105); Wallis uses it to represent the progressive downward positioning of a tube placed at various angles to a surface (1673-E104). In 17th-century graphics, however, a scale is seldom provided. As a consequence, one is sure neither of the angular distances between "the little stars around Saturn" in Cassini's drawing (1692-F074) nor the size of the tiny "animacules" observed by van Leeuwenhoek under his microscope (1683-E101).

12. Printing technology at this time allowed for text to accompany tables, but engravings were inserted separately (often at the end of the journal issue), and the relative space taken up by illustrations depends on how many fit onto a single plate, not on their importance to the articles they illustrate.

Conclusion

Anyone who has learned a second language knows firsthand how much natural languages differ, yet on our measures targeted specifically to features of scientific style, we find remarkably little difference between, or within, our French and English samples from the 17th century. That style already projects the impression of objectivity. Ornament is largely absent, and there is a movement toward a more impersonal style—one that favors the objects of inquiry over the inquirer. Stylistically, compared with the French sample, the English scores marginally higher on three of the four measures related to personal expression: personal pronouns/names, evaluative expressions, and deviant expressions. The density of the last three measures, however, is not very high in either language. The French sample scores substantially higher on two measures characteristic of 20th-century norms: quantitative expressions and citational density.

With regard to presentational features, we found little difference between the French and English samples. While in no one instance is a master system of presentation fully in place, each of its elements has made an appearance. Scientific visuals—tables, illustrations of objects of study and equipment, and mathematical representations—are conceptually sophisticated and have a real presence in the relatively few articles in which they appear. The elements of a master organizing system also make sporadic appearances: article titles that specify content, introductions that contextualize a research problem, and conclusions that stake a knowledge claim. Citations, headings, and numbered graphics and tables are also found, but only on occasion and without uniform format. The prose is definitely scientific, though it is far from looking like the prose of 20th-century science.

CHAPTER 3

Argument in the 17th Century

On 15 May 1693, in the *Mémoire de Mathématique et de Physique*, there appeared an article by Jean Méry entitled "Observations of Two Fetuses Enclosed in the Same Membrane." The two fetuses were dead, and Méry reflects on the cause of their mortality:

> For if they are separated [each in his own membrane], their umbilical cords cannot interlace; instead, when two fetuses are enclosed in a common membrane, they easily interwine their cords by their movements and consequently suffocate; as actually happened to these fetuses represented here whose cords hindered each other's functions and formed a knot that, having prevented the blood from circulating from the placenta to their vessels, caused their death. (1693-F013)

Méry observes a physiological problem of interest and speculates as to its cause, the immediately preceding events that form a mechanism whose operation leads inevitably to the effect. Clearly, then, mechanical cause is a topic of argument in 17th-century French science. But is the train of Méry's thought typical? Unless this question is answered in the affirmative, this passage can say nothing interesting about 17th-century French science. But the question cannot be answered without the benefit of a representative sample of articles by Méry's fellow scientists. The purpose of this chapter is to analyze such a sample and to draw conclusions from it concerning the nature and development of scientific argument in 17th-century France and England.

Consistent with the spirit of Perelman and Olbrechts-Tyteca's *The New Rhetoric* (1969), we define argument broadly as the ensemble of means that authors employ to make and support their assertions. In particular, we concentrate on how scientists employ argument to establish new facts about the material universe and offer explanations for them. We propose four topics as central to understanding scientific argument in the 17th century. These are based on what we take to be a consensus among scholars who have dealt with scientific communication in the 17th century.[1] While other taxonomies are possible, we take ours as at least plausible:

1. What makes an observation or an experimental result a scientific fact? In the 17th century, there were at least two standards according to which facts were judged scientific. First, a scientific fact was an occurrence in the natural world that was reported by a reliable individual—usually, a member of a scientific society—and was witnessed by one or more such observers. More and more, a scientific fact was a finding resulting, not from naked observation, but from the appropriate use of instruments (telescope, microscope, thermometer, air pump, etc.) combined with methods discussed in item (2).
2. How are the facts generated? Whether in the 17th or 20th century, there are several basic means: observation of objects and events in natural settings, manipulation of natural and man-made objects in artificial settings for experimental purposes, computation or description based on theory, or some combination of these. The fact-generating enterprise of science also entails developing new methods and equipment for improving observations, conducting experiments, and confirming or extending theoretically based assertions.
3. What is the relationship between scientific facts and scientific explanations? In the 17th century, not all scientists were concerned with explanation; many were content with collecting and ordering facts about nature. Scientists interested in explanation, however, realized that their speculations must square in a plausible way with the facts defined according to item (1) above.
4. What sorts of explanation are there? For 17th-century scientists there were two kinds of explanation, both causal: mechanical and mathematical. Sometimes mechanical causes were directly observable. Sometimes they were observable only by their effects. In that case, plausible reconstruction was necessary. But causes might also take the mathematical form of universal laws. These would have a mathematical expression, consistent with the Galilean program, $f = ma$, for example.

In the remainder of this chapter we illustrate these topics and the arguments they typically generate. This survey will give readers a sense of the range of 17th-century scientific argument; it will also provide a sense of the different orientations

1. See, for example, Shapin (1984), Bazerman (1988), Dear (1985, 1995), Holmes (1989a), and Daston and Park (1998, pp. 215–254).

of French and English science in that century, especially with regard to the heightened concern for explanation and theory among the French.

Arguing for Facts

In reading the 100 full articles in our 17th-century sample, one is immediately struck by the *miscellanea curiosa* of new facts about the natural world and its workings. Monsieur de la Voye reports on little worms that eat stone (1666-F010; also in 1676-E082). Lister speculates on the existence of veins in all kinds of plants (1672-E063). Méry describes the physiology of a pelican (1693-F084). Homberg reports on leaflike crystals formed in a flask full of antimony and rainwater (1693-F075) and also on the distillation of phosphorus from urine (1692-F009). Halley calculates life expectancy in the city of Breslaw (1693-E041). Henshaw offers "some observations and experiments upon may-dew" (1665-E102). De la Hire measures the progress of an eclipse of the moon on 28 July 1692 (1692-F045). Hooke provides instruction on how to "make the picture of any thing appear on a wall, cub-board or within a picture-frame" (1668-E006). Cassini observes through his telescope "a precise conjunction of a satellite of the planet Saturn with a fixed star" (1692-F074).

The data for genre in table 3.1 indicate that observation is by far the favorite means of establishing new facts in our 100-article sample. About half this sample presents observational facts exclusively or observational facts buttressed by some theoretical discussion. Also noteworthy is that, of the 71 observational and experimental articles, more than half offer new facts absent any theoretical discussion. We know from Shapin and Schaffer (1985) that English authors from the 17th century, particularly Robert Boyle, "offered the matter of fact as the foundation of proper knowledge" (p. 24). The animating philosophy behind this approach is that theories come and go and are constantly being revised and expanded; facts "mirror nature." For that reason, early researchers such as Boyle offered theoretical explanations of their observational and experimental "facts" only with extreme caution (Daston and Park

Table 3.1. Type of Whole Article in 17th-Century Sample

	English		*French*	
Genre	%	n	%	n
Experimental	12	6	10	5
Theoretical	20	10	12	6
Methodological	4	2	6	3
Observational	36	18	20	10
Observational/theoretical	14	7	34	17
Experimental/theoretical	2	1	8	4
Mathematical	6	3	10	5
Other	6	3	0	0
Total	100	50	100	50

1998, pp. 242–244). This orientation toward observed particulars, however, does not mean that theory is anathema in the 17th-century article.

Of the 100 articles in our 17th-century sample, 53 have some theoretical or mathematical discussion. This interest in the abstract and conceptual appears to be greater among the French than the English articles. True, in our sample, the English were as likely as the French authors to compose purely theoretical or mathematical articles (13 and 11 articles, respectively). Nevertheless, in the English sample, only 8 articles moved from observation or experiment to theory, while in the French sample, 21 articles did so.

Whatever the means of establishing facts, English and French scientists are both concerned about the warrant for them. Clearly, they must meet a higher standard than the opinions and observations of everyday life, if only because authors know their statements will likely receive scrutiny and judgment by an international group of readers with similar interests. In a French passage from 1666, for example, de la Voye carefully modulates his prose to suit his confidence in his insight into insect behavior:

> I have not shown conclusively whether these are the little animals who, near the surfaces of all of the stones near which they congregate, make little round holes and little marks that resemble newly worm-eaten wood; but it seems that way. It would be necessary to examine whether or not these worms have wings, & whether they appear in other respects like caterpillars . . . whether or not they congregate in pitted gypsum, bricks, sandstone, rocks, etc.
>
> You will observe that there are more worms found in the exposed ramparts of the South of France than in those ramparts that are located elsewhere; that those worms that eat stone live longer than those little animals that eat mortar, who survive no longer than eight days: I have observed all of their parts with an excellent microscope. Without this instrument & without a great deal of attentiveness, these parts are difficult to see. (1666-F010; also 1676-E082)

De la Voye is willing to encapsulate hours of painstaking observation under a microscope in a clause—"who survive no longer than eight days"—but is not willing to extend his conclusions even a small step beyond his observations. He has not observed his little creatures on other stonelike surfaces and he will not generalize.

The expectation of plausible warranting did not, of course, eliminate the occasional appearance of unfounded or ludicrous assertions. In the 18th-century *Review of the Works of the Royal Society* (1751), John Hill mercilessly criticized *Philosophical Transactions* for publishing "trivial and downright foolish articles" over the previous century. As evidence, he cited articles on a merman discovered in Virginia and a miraculous plant that heals fresh wounds ("but to touch it, is to be healed"), as well as "incontestible proofs of a strange and surprising Fact, namely, that Fish will live in Water." Not long after Hill's scathing attack, in 1752 the Society established a committee to review articles for publication on the basis of "the importance and singularity of the subjects, or the advantageous manner of treating them" (see also Stimson 1968). Worth noting, however, is that our sample of 100 randomly selected English and French whole articles from the 17th century did not have any obvious examples of ill-advised pieces like those criticized by Hill.

As a means of conveying their degree of confidence in various statements, we know from Myers (1989) and Hyland (1998) that modern scientists hedge. A simple textual feature, barely noticeable to the uninitiated, hedging is their indication that the quality of evidence is being carefully weighed. This feature is present but not prominent in 17th-century scientific prose. As evidence for this claim, we found relatively few hedges in our 200 short passages (see table 2.2): averages of 0.1 per hundred words for the French and 0.2 per hundred words for the English,[2] an appropriately small amount for narratives relying heavily upon personal observations and some mathematics. Typical are assertive sentences without qualifications, for example, "The species of corals and of *Madrepora*, the mushrooms of the sea, *the Tubularia marina, rubra IB* are also as hard as stones" (1700-F040), and "In this equation no more is needed than the substitution of the values of *v* & of *dz*, which will result in *x* & in *dx* of the equations of the given curves *AHG* & *AFK;* & will become that of the curve we are looking for, *BC*" (1699-F067).

Despite the low counts, we found many interesting varieties of 17th-century scientific hedging populating select passages from our sample. In this heavily hedged passage from *Philosophical Transactions* on the existence of veins in all kinds of plants, for example, Martin Lister leaves no doubt that he is speculating about the ramifications of his collected facts (hedges in boldface):

> That **though we seem to be more certain** of the ramifications of the Fibres, wherein those veins are, **we yet are not so,** that those veins do any where grow less and smaller, **though probably it may be so**. That which makes us **doubt** it, is the exceeding smallness of these veins already, even where we might **probably expect** them to be Trunk veins and of the largest size; and being there also in very great Numbers and running in direct lines along the fibre, we **guess**, that one or more of them **may be** distributed and fall off on either hand with the subdivisions of the fibres, and not suffer any diminution in their bulk. (1672-E063)

In a French passage, Méry uses hedges to dramatize the tension the scientist feels between the doubt he must always entertain and the relative certainty he can occasionally attain and enunciate:

> One **cannot doubt** that the small muscles that are attached to the feathers of the skin of the body of the pelican serve to move them in different directions, & that when they move, one after the other, they can make the feathers move in circles. It **certainly looks as if** the fleshy fibers of the down can also create the same movements.
>
> Mr. Méry was not, in the pelican he dissected in 1686, looking for the place from which the air came that filled the cells of the skin, but in 1692 he dissected yet another, in which he viewed it in a manner that **fully satisfied him**. (1693-F084)

In the French sample, unlike in the English, doubt has been expanded to include a set of concerns that focus on instrumental limitations, including that oldest

2. The much lower French average for hedging may reflect inherent differences in the two languages, as well as less concern with the open display of gentlemanly politeness than among the English.

of instruments, the human eye. While Méry's passage on animal physiology parallels Lister's, there is no English parallel in our sample for the following passage of Cassini's, which makes the limitations of naked-eye observations its subject. Cassini's is a second-order skepticism not found in the English sample. Cassini does not merely use hedges; he reflects on hedging:

> Scarcely does one find four or five observations of these conjunctions among all those that have been preserved since the beginnings of astronomy up to the present century: even so **there is room to doubt** whether these four or five apparent conjunctions, **since they were observed only with the naked eye**, are really precise and without any interval. For we now know that, because of light rays that increase the apparent size of the stars, **there are conjunctions that appear to be precise, although they may be nothing of the sort**; the use of telescopes having forced us to recognize that there are considerable intervals between stars that appear to the naked eye to be so completely conjoint that they seem one and the same star. (1692-F080)

English scientists seem to lean more heavily upon reliable testimony concerning new facts about the natural world. In the following English passage, scientific evidence is viewed exactly as forensic evidence would be, the absence of hedges being implicitly justified by the presence of sworn testimony:

> We, the Physicians under-named, do hereby certify, that all the particulars of the Chirurgical operation of extracting the Bodkin out of the Bladder of *Dorcas Blake*, as contained in the foregoing account, are truly and faithfully related, it being perform'd by Mr *Thomas Proby*, Master Chiruregon, with great skill and success in our presence, as witness our Hands, this 22d of *May*, 1695.
>
> *I. Madden* Presid. *T. Molyneux.*
> *Wm. Smith.*
>
> *Dorcas Blake*, of *Fishamble-street*, in the Parish of *St John*[,] *Spinster*, came this day before me, and being sworn on the holy Evangelists, saith that the above relation is true in substance, and that she did swallow the Bodkin therein mentioned, and that the Bodkin now shewed to her is the same that she formerly swallow'd.
>
> *her*
> *Dorcas* **X** *Blake*
> *mark.*
>
> *Jurat coram me decimo die Junii* 1695.
> G. Blackall *Major. Dublin.*
> (It is sworn in my presence, 10 June 1695
> G. Blackall, Sr., Dublin)
> (1700-E110)

In 17th-century science, it was at least an occasional practice to lend credibility to reported facts by mentioning witnesses. In our sample of 100 whole articles, witnessing occurs in articles reporting some unusual observation or especially important experimental results and appears to be more characteristic of the English than the French articles. In the English sample there are five articles citing witnesses: two experiments with animals (1667-E003 and 1696-E014), one physics experiment by Boyle (1676-E021), one trial at Court involving some medication for coagulating blood (1673-E034), and one monstrous birth (1670-E038). Only two French articles mention witnesses: a joint observation by a group of astronomers (1677-F042) and an experimental article read before the Royal Society (1672-F006).

This stronger reliance on personal testimony is further indicated in English scientific prose through an orientation toward human relationships largely absent in the French: witnesses are sworn, observers of experiments are named, readers are invited to repeat experiments. An orientation toward readers is also embodied in expressions that "humanize" the prose to the detriment of its objective stance. When a Fellow of the Royal Society says, "I shall premise some Experiments made many years ago which perhaps may give no less satisfaction unto many of our Experimental Philosophers than they afforded me, when I first made mine" (1674-E072), he is deferring to his colleagues, not expressing doubt.

This emphasis on the importance of human society as an epistemic resource leads to a specifically English credulity not present in the French sample:

> They say [an issue from a male greyhound preserved in spirit of wine] exactly resembled a Greyhound-Whelp, and had on its side a large spot, in the same place as the Dog it proceeded from, had such another; and that with it was voided a whitish mucous Matter, so that the People here will not permit me to question the truth thereof. Mr. Roberts who saw it at first, can best judge what Credit this uncouth Story Merits. But this is certain, That it cost the Dog his Life, to gratifie the Curiosity of some Gentlemen here, who Dissected him, but were disappointed of their Expectations. For my own part, as I am determined *nihil temere credere* [to believe nothing rashly]; so on the other hand, as I dare not pretend to limit the Powers of Nature, I suspend my Opinion, laying only before you what credible Witnesses do assert. (1696-E014)

This passage is of great interest. In it, Halley uses irony—"they say," "permit me," "for my own part," "I dare not"—to distance himself from the credulity of "some Gentlemen." But Halley is judging his amateur brethren, not trying to correct their errors; and, like it or not, they are his brethren. This is a far cry from Cassini (1692-F080), who, in a dialogue with himself, hedges his hedges to hold human credulity hostage to scientific doubt. The attitude is analogous, but the social matrices of French and English science could not be more different.

We depart here briefly from our random sample to address an argument topic of 20th-century science that seems to be largely absent from its 17th-century ancestor: replicability as a check on experimental quality and reliability. We do not mean that experiments are not repeated. In the case of the controversy surrounding Newton's first scientific article (1672)—reporting the optics experiments he carried out in his darkened chamber with a glass prism—the durability of purported facts as indexed by the repetition of experiments is clearly an important topic of argument. But while Robert Hooke and Christiaan Huygens challenged Newton's theoretical interpretation of his experimental results, neither questioned the results themselves. It was not until the letters from Francis Hall (also known as Linus, a Jesuit professor at the English college in Liège) arrived in 1674 that the experiments were performed at the Royal Society, the "house of experiments." Even in this case, the issue was less the durability of purported facts than the official witnessing of Newton's experiments by other Society fellows. In the *Opticks* of 1704, a work just past our period, Newton, in enjoining his readers to repeat experiments, is encouraging them, not to check, but to see for themselves.

The case of Huygens's replication of some of Boyle's experiments with an air-pump, recounted by Shapin and Shaffer (1985, pp. 225–282), is closer to the modern standard. However, it seems to be a notable exception to the rather casual rule. As Shapin and Shaffer note, "even the notion of *verification* itself is profoundly problematic. The Florentines [Accademia del Cimento in Italy] announced that they had verified Boyle's results without needing Boyle's machine" (p. 281). Alan Shapiro (1996) summarizes what we take to be the most accurate view: "The very concept of rigorous and public replication, which is often considered to play a central role in modern science . . . was by no means a standard feature of seventeenth and early eighteenth-century science. . . . [T]he experimental tests of Newton's theory were private, casual, and, by later standards, rather lax in what they took to be either confirmation or refutation" (p. 61).

Arguing Explanations into Place

Our English and French samples differ not only in their manner of establishing new facts but also in their interest in explaining these facts (see table 3.1). In our sample of 50 English articles, 18 made observational claims detached from any apparent explanation and six made experimental claims detached from any apparent explanation. In the French sample, 10 articles made only observational claims, and five made only experimental claims. We thus tallied 24 factual claims independent of causal explanation for the English sample, but only 15 for the French sample.

These bare numbers hint at the differing scientific practices and concerns in each country, but they do not give a firm sense of the flavor of two sorts of 17th-century scientific argument, one presenting new facts, the other providing an explanation for them. To illustrate this difference, we selected two articles: Thomas Henshaw's "Some Observations and Experiments upon May-Dew" and "Extract from a Letter of Mr. Huygens, Touching the Phenomena of Water from which all Air has been Removed."

In the first case, Henshaw subjects May-dew (dew gathered in May and supposed to have medicinal and cosmetic properties) to a series of trials designed, apparently, to ascertain the conditions under which it will putrefy. We say "apparently" because this general purpose is nowhere stated; it must be inferred from a series of loosely connected experiments narrated in no discernible order. The series leads to no conclusion and is preceded by a narrative introduction, not about Henshaw's experiments, but about Henshaw himself, presumably written by the editor of *Philosophical Transactions*: "That ingenious and inquisitive Gentleman, Master *Thomas Henshaw*, having had occasion to make use of a great quantity of *May-dew*, did, by several casual Essayes on that Subject, make the following Observations and Tryals, and present them to the *Royal Society*" (1665-E102; italics in original). Henshaw's experiments are reported in a lively, novelistic style, a mode of representation that leaves their larger purpose unclear. Here is a single sentence vividly weaving together method and results but offering little in the way of explanation: "That having several Tubs with good quantity of *Dew* in them, set to putrefy in the manner abovesaid, and comming to pour out of one of them to make use of it, He found in the water a great bunch, bigger than his fist, of those Insects commonly called *Hog-lice* or *Millepedes*, tangled together by their long tailes, one of which came out of every one of their bodies, about the bigness of a Horsehair: The Insects did all live and move after they were taken out" (1665-E102; italics in original).

In contrast, Huygens's focus is explanation. His *Journal des Sçavans* article in French has three main components: a theoretical introduction that motivates his investigation, a series of experiments designed specifically to answer the theoretical question he poses, and a conclusion that ponders the theoretical impact of his results. His introduction follows the essentials of 20th-century practice. He stakes out an intellectual territory—one of Boyle's research programs—and establishes his niche within it:

> Before communicating to you what I have observed concerning the suspension of water in a vacuum, I want to repeat the experiments, in order to verify the remarks I made at another time and in order to attempt to penetrate to the causes of an effect so surprising. I will first relate my observations and then I will pass to the conjectures I have made to account for them.
>
> The experiments that the illustrious Mr. Boyle performed one day in 1661, with the description of the pneumatic pump, gave me a starting point for examining the matter at hand. In one of these experiments, Boyle put a four-foot glass tube, full of water, in a container or vessel from which the air had been evacuated, the open end of the tube being submerged in another quantity of water, contained in a glass. The air from the container having been evacuated as far as was possible by means of his pump, the water of the tube flowed down into the glass up to the point at which no more than about one foot remained, all the rest of the tube remaining empty of water and of air. He judged with good reason that this height of one foot of water that stayed above the level of that in which the open end of the tube submerged, remained suspended because there remained in the container a bit of air that the pump, being defective in that respect, could not evacuate. (1672-F006)

In the article itself, Huygens occupies the niche his criticism of Boyle creates, providing the reader with a new theory to explain his novel results. In so doing, Huygens challenges Boyle's reasonable inference by completing and reporting on a series of six experiments, each carefully described. Having depicted his apparatus, he launches into a narration about the trustworthiness of his method, a narration that is also a part of his argument:

> But at the end of the month of December in the same year, 1661, having left this water in the vacuum for twenty-four hours (which completely purged it of the bubbles it gives out when fresh water is used) & having filled the vial *C*, I was surprised to see that notwithstanding that I had tried very hard to remove the air from vessel *B*, the water did not descend at all from *C*, which remained perfectly full; I could hardly suspect that there had been any defect in my pump, nor that the vessel *B* was badly blocked; but to be perfectly clear about this, I removed the vial *C* from

> underneath the vessel and after having forced in a small air bubble, I replaced it as before; and having worked the pump, I saw that in the end all the water descended very nearly up to the level of that of glass *D*. That assured me that there had been no defect in the pump, and that the water purged of air remained suspended without descending, although the vessel *B* was completely void of air, or at least as much of it as it was when the fresh water descended from the vial. I made the water descend a second time by inserting into the neck of the vial a bubble so small that it was hardly visible. (1672-F006)

After describing in detail the six interlocking experiments, Huygens concludes with his new claim (the existence of a "matter . . . more subtle than air") and a recommendation for future work to extend his claim:

> Here is another confirmation of our hypothesis of a matter capable of exerting pressure but more subtle than air. Those who would take the trouble to discover up to what point the force of this pressure mounts can do no better than to pursue the experiment with the tubes full of mercury, even longer than those Mr. Boyle used. They will find perhaps that this force is powerful enough to cause the union of the parts of glass and of other sorts of bodies that hold together better than if they were joined only by contiguity and rest, as Mr. Descartes would have it. (1672-F006)

Huygens and Henshaw differ in their goals: only Huygens is interested in explaining the phenomena that experiment reveals. It is significant that the explicit view of the far better known Robert Boyle is coincident with Henshaw's implicit one: Boyle insisted that his "business" was "not . . . to assign the adequate cause of the spring of the air, but only to manifest, that the air hath a spring, and to relate some of its effects" (quoted in Shapin 1994, p. 335). Such a view contrasts with that of Huygens, who designs a series of experiments whose purpose is to test a new hypothesis derived from a reanalysis of Boyle's experimental design.

Because Henshaw makes no claim other than that of fact, he needs no argument apart from the array of relevant data and observations. He describes nature; he makes no attempt to understand its workings. Huygens, who makes a claim about those workings, needs a more robust argument. In satisfying this need, Huygens anticipates the form of the modern scientific article. This form is also an argument: it is meant to recapitulate, not the experimenter's story, but that of the experiment, a narrative that is also a logical progression. This progression justifies a conclusion that contains referents specific to nature, not at all to the laboratory. Huygens's article is not about his elaborate tangle of glassware, but about "matter capable of exerting pressure but more subtle than air." The way in which he structures this argument is clearly consistent with F. L. Holmes's (1989a) assertion that "the 'conventional form' imposed on the modern journal article is . . . but the outcome of the long evolution of a form that emerged during the late 17th and early 18th centuries" (p. 165), the main impetus coming from France under the auspices of the Académie Royale.

Our results in table 3.2 suggest that Huygens's concern for explaining his gathered facts is more characteristic of the French than of the English scientific literature. Forty-six percent of French articles offer explanations, while this is true of only

Table 3.2. Purpose of Whole Articles in 17th-Century Sample

	English		*French*	
	%	n	%	n
Observational	38	19	22	11
Experimental Results	12	6	8	4
Mechanical Explanation	28	14	38	19
Mathematical Rule	4	2	18	9
Mathematical Explanation	6	3	8	4
Making or Improving Equipment	4	2	2	1
Other	8	4	4	2
Total	100	50	100	50

34% of English articles. Nonetheless, both the French and English articles place a healthy emphasis on the search for mechanical causes: of our French sample, 38% offer mechanical explanation; of our English sample, 28% offer the like. On occasion, such mechanical explanations involve entities not visible to the explaining scientist: in Huygens's view (1672-F006, quoted earlier), for example, the action of ordinary air is insufficient to explain the behavior of devices like the barometer in the void created by an air pump. To remedy this deficiency, Huygens hypothesizes "subtle air." But in no English case in our sample does a mechanical explanation depend on speculations like that of Huygens concerning the basic constitution of the physical universe. In any case, both French and English explanations are more likely to be plausible reconstructions of mechanical processes, as in the case of Woodward's conjectures on circulation in plants:

> The reason why in this Proposition I say only a great part of the terrestial Matter that is mix'd with the Water, ascends up with it into the Plant is, because all of it cannot. The mineral Matter is a great deal of it not only gross and ponderous, but scabrous and inflexible: and so not disposed to enter the Pores of the Roots. And a great many of the simple Vegetable Particles by degrees unite and form some of them small Clods and Moleculae; such as those mentioned in H, K, and L, sticking to the extremities of the Roots of those Plant. (1699-E027)

Neither the French nor the English authors in our 17th-century sample show much interest in strictly mathematical explanations, as attested by only seven out of the 100 whole articles possessing them.

In both mathematical and mechanical explanations, physical relationships are invested with causal properties. But only in the latter case must the scientist posit an actual mechanism; in the former case, it is sufficient to offer a formula that either merely predicts or accounts for the behavior of physical objects. In the mathematical case, there need be no pretense that the formula used can actually be mapped onto physical objects or processes. Indeed, the mathematics in this case is less an explanation than a step, one hopes, in the direction of an explanation. Mathematical explanations, of course, can be mechanical also. Einstein's mathematical explanation of Brownian motion is a 20th-century example. In *Discipline and Experience* (1995), historian Peter Dear places mathematical theories in their proper 17th-century context, that of "physico-mathematics." Physico-mathematics acknowledged "that mathematics, and the mixed mathematical disciplines in particular, could yield genuinely causal scientific knowledge of natural bodies and phenomena. . . . True physical causes could still be portrayed as differing from mathematical causes, but such a distinction now worked to the detriment of the former" (p. 170).

A more Galilean approach to explanation also seems to be reflected in our French sample. Varignon's 17th-century attempt to apply the calculus to the problem of free fall is just such an attempt to discover the mathematical "cause" of an important class of phenomena. Varignon chose a long, abstractlike title for his article, "Method for Finding the Curves along which a Falling Body Comes toward or Moves away from the Horizon in whatever Proportion of Times one would Wish and according to whatever Hypothesis of Acceleration might be Supposed, etc." This specifies the explanatory move, a move clearly outlined in the introduction:

> It has already been some time since Mr. Leibniz & the Messrs. Bernoulli found the curves along which a falling body, according to the hypothesis of acceleration established by Galileo, would approach equally from the horizon or from any point in equal times. I also presented to the Academy in 1695 a new solution for the first of these problems without the assistance of the infinite calculus. At the present time, given what this calculus can accomplish when applied to the matter that occasioned my previous article, which only covered equal approaches from the horizon in equal times in accordance with the hypothesis of Galileo, I worked out a general solution for all approaches, in whatever proportion of times one would wish, and also following whatever hypothesis of acceleration one would wish. (1699-F067)

In the following paragraph that forms Varignon's conclusion, intellectual momentum is sustained simultaneously in three ways: (1) the constant link to the Galilean program, (2) the transformations within the calculus that led, finally, to a mathematical explanation of projectile motion, and (3) a logical stepwise motion (indicated in boldface) coordinated at every stage with the mathematical transformations:

> **In effect** (all the rest remaining as above, with RlV parallel to AG) the constant proportion of LR (dx) to RV, **for example**: : $p.\ q.$ will give $RV = qdx/p$; **and thus** $LV = dx/p\sqrt{pp + qq}$ (let $nn = pp + qq = ndx/p$). **But** $RV(qdx/p).\ Rl(dz) : : LV(ndx/p).\ LZ(dt) = ndx/q$. **Moreover,** $Ll = \sqrt{dx^2 + dz^2}$. **Therefore,** the acceleration being generally $v = Ll/dt$, **one would also have** $v = \sqrt{qdx^2 + dz^2}/ndz$ for all conceivable hypotheses of acceleration, **so that** in making $v = \sqrt{x}$ according to Galileo, **one finally has** $\sqrt{x} = q\sqrt{dx^2 + dz^2}/ndz$, which equation is reduced to $dz = adx/\sqrt{nnx - qq}$, whose integral is $z = 2q/nn\sqrt{nnx - qq}$ (let $y = x - qq/nn) = 2q/n\sqrt{y}$, or $zz = 4qqy/nn = 4qqy/pp + qq$, which is still a locus to an ordinary parabola. **This result also agrees** with the doctrine of Galileo concerning the curve that bodies subject to gravity describe when thrown obliquely into the void. **From this article 19 is again deduced** for the case of horizontal projections in which q is infinite. (1699-F067)

In Varignon's conclusion, we see in microcosm the drive to achieve universality in physics by mathematical means. As a consequence of simultaneous intellectual movements, Varignon attains a formula "for all conceivable hypotheses of acceleration," one in agreement "with the doctrine of Galileo concerning the curve that bodies subject to gravity describe when thrown obliquely into the void."

Varignon's Galilean approach seems also to be more typical of French science: 26% of French articles have a mathematical purpose, as compared to only 10% of English articles, consistent with Dear's assertion that "mathematical contributions . . . fitted only uneasily into the Royal Society's [early] work" (1985, p. 159). A more mathematical approach by the French may likewise account for the differences in quantitative expressions and equations found in our random sample of 198 short passages (table 2.1). Our average counts per 100 words for this feature were 2.5 for the French versus 1.1 for the English. This contrast must not be generalized too far, however: Newton, Wallis, and Halley were as Galilean as Huygens or any French researcher.

Tables and Visuals in Scientific Argument

Visual representations also contribute to the argumentative practices at work in our 17th-century scientific texts. Because during this period the technology for reproducing figures (woodcuts, copper engravings, and etchings) was still in its infancy and expensive,[3] it is not surprising to find that, of our 100 whole articles, only 38 have any tables or visual representations. In the following, we give four examples from our French sample of the ways in which 17th-century scientists employed visuals to establish facts and offer explanations for facts.

One simple means of establishing facts is arranging text and data in orderly columns and rows. This simple visual device helps the author (and readers) establish relationships or trends among numerous data. As an example, this table establishes the degrees of rainfall and snowfall by months in 1699, carefully calibrated by a method that Philippe de la Hire is at some pains to describe in detail:

	Lines		Lines
January	11	July	11
February	12	August	18
March	11	September	35
April	36	October	12
May	22	November	9
June	29	December	15

The sum of the heights of the water that fell throughout the whole year is 224 l[ines] 3/4 or 18 inches 8 l[ines] 3/4. (1699-F028)

3. The expense did not impede the production of books that were magnificently illustrated and designed, such as Robert Hooke's *Micrographia: or, Some Physiological Descriptions of Minute Bodies Made by Magnifying Glasses* (London, 1665) and the Accademia del Cimento's *Saggi di naturali esperienzi* (Florence, 1667). For a vivid portrayal of the costs and perils of 17th-century publishing in natural philosophy, see Johns (1998).

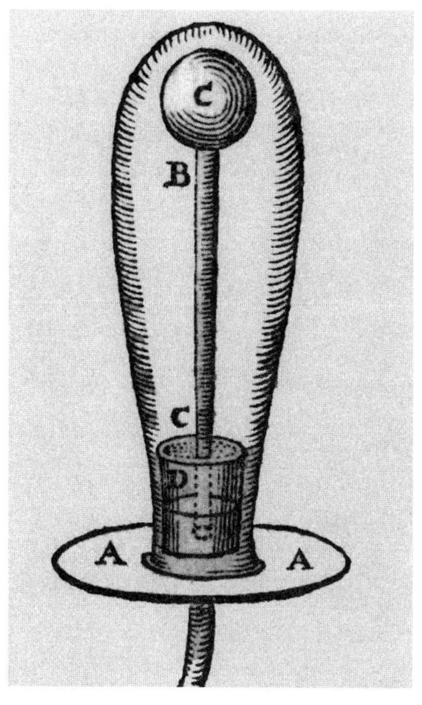

Figure 3.1. Illustration from Christian Huygens, "Extract from a Letter of Mr. Huygens, Touching the Phenomena of Water from which all Air has been Removed" (1672)

The table's single numerical column is clearly labeled by unit of measurement (in French "ligne" and in English "line," a unit equaling 1/12 inch and seldom used today other than by a few botanists). Without any explanation on the part of the author, the reader can thus easily track the precipitation levels on a monthly or even seasonal basis in 1699 or add up the column to check the sum reported by the author in the running text.[4] Such a table is perfectly in keeping with the fact-gathering enterprise of 17th-century science.

Huygens's illustration (figure 3.1) is a typical graphic representation of an experimental apparatus designed to establish facts of nature through laboratory manipulations. Snugly embedded in the text, the stick-figure-like drawing makes use of dotted and solid lines, shading, and labeling and keeps extraneous details and embellishments to a minimum so as to better represent the various experimental components within components. This is not a deeply realistic rendering of an experimental apparatus, as in Boyle's famous engraving of his air pump (Shapin and Schaffer 1985, p. 27), but a simplified abstraction designed better to reveal the apparatus's internal workings. Besides the figure itself, typical also is Huygens's careful explanation of this device in the running text of his article (in lieu of a figure caption), an investigation of the anomalous height of water in a tube under a vacuum created by an air pump: "It is necessary to imagine that the glass denoted *C C* is completely full of water, & that its open extremity dips in the water of glass *D*. Over the top of both is placed the vessel *B*, on whose open mouth is applied a cer-

4. We cannot explain the discrepancy between the sum of the column and the sum given.

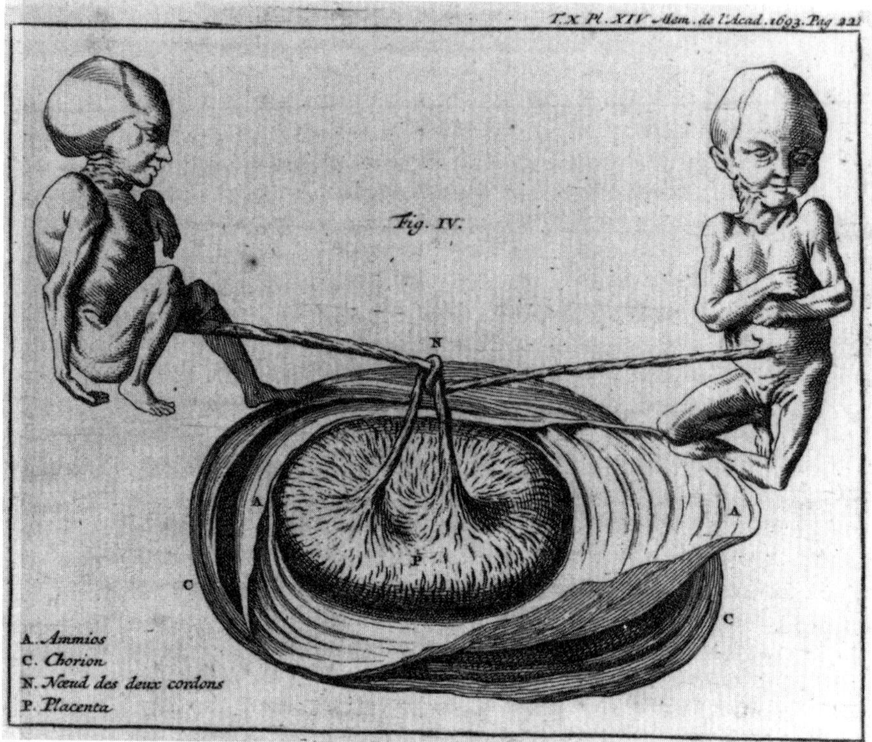

Figure 3.2. Illustration from Jean Méry, "Observations of Two Fetuses Enclosed in the Same Membrane" (1693)

tain soft cement, spread on the plate *A A*, which is pierced by a little hole in the middle, by which the air leaves when one works the pump. When I used fresh water, all of vessel *C* emptied until it was at the level with that of glass *D*" (1672-F006). Huygens is interested in describing the experiment so carefully that through his own words, or through subsequent replication, the fact of this anomalous liquid suspension can be established. The drawing itself gives us no clue, however, as to the mechanical cause for this fact.

Méry's illustration (figure 3.2) of two fetuses enclosed in the same membrane is an example of a realistic drawing of an object of study designed to illustrate a mechanical explanation. Méry observes a problem of medical interest, the death of twin fetuses by strangulation, and speculates as to its cause, a knotting of their umbilical cords. In the accompanying drawing, the visual is clearly at the service of science: each of the technical features—the amnion, the chorion, the placenta, and especially, the knotting of the two umbilical cords—is made visually prominent by means of some combination of contrast, position, and labeling. Moreover, the explanation of the phenomenon—the mechanical cause of the strangulation alluded to in the article—is made visually the most prominent item, placed at the very center of the picture and marked by the letter N. The grotesque yet accurate rendering of the fetuses flanking the knotted cord dramatizes the tragic consequences of this medical phenomenon (the wasting and ultimate death of the fetuses resulting from insufficient oxygen and nourishment through the cord), the human toll of which is outside the bounds of normal scientific discourse. This toll likely includes the demise of the nearly invisible mother, who is visually represented by her scientifically relevant anatomical feature alone.

As our final example (figure 3.3), Varignon's "*fig. 1[premiè]re*" illustrates the close reciprocity between mathematical representations of physical phenomena and their causal interpretation. Here we need not follow Varignon's mathematical argument; we need only keep our eye on the close coordination of the mathematical and its visual representation. First, the author sets the dynamic problem and begins explaining its visual representation:

> Let us begin by looking for a curve *BC* such that, assuming the downward directions parallel between them, a body falling from *A* along this curve departs from the horizon *AD* in such proportion of time as one will wish, whatever hypothesis one may make concerning the speed of the falling body.
>
> After having constructed the vertical *AL* with the horizontals *BH, bh,* asymptotically approaching one another, let us take the ordinates *EH* of any curve *AGH* for the speed acquired by the falls from *A* on *B* or on *E;* let us likewise use the time of fall from *A* on *B,* expressed by the ordinates *EF* of another curve *AFK,* of any sort whatever. Finally, let *AE* = *x*, *EB* = *y*, *&* *EF* = *z*. (1699-F067)

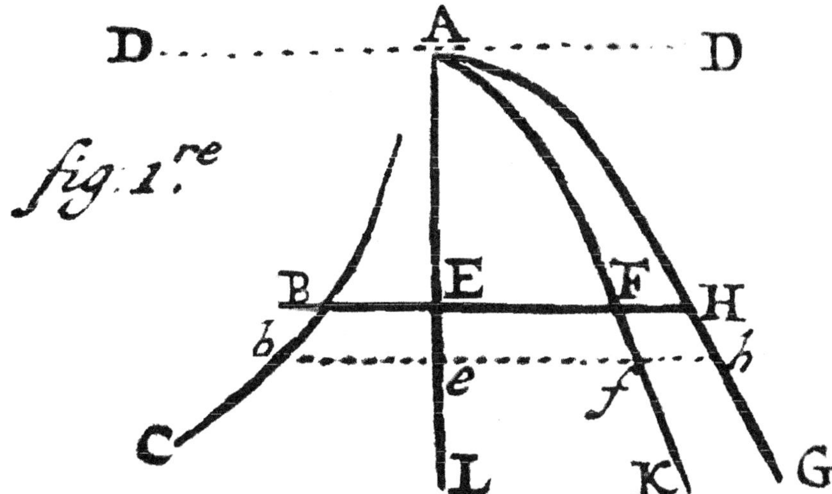

Figure 3.3. Illustration from Varignon, "Method for Finding the Curves along which a Falling Body Comes toward or Moves away from the Horizon in whatever Proportion of Times one would Wish and according to whatever Hypothesis of Acceleration might be Supposed, etc." (1699)

Table 3.3. Function of Tables and Visuals in 17th-Century Sample

	English	*French*
Supports observation	50%	31%
Supports experimental results	8	8
Supports mechanical explanation	8	12
Supports mathematical relation	17	23
Supports mathematical explanation	17	8
Supports equipment building	0	12
Number of articles with tables or visuals	12/50	26/50

Varignon then goes on to apply the then-new calculus to his equations and obtain his solution for the trajectory of falling bodies represented in his figure. His mathematical solution in hand, Varignon gives it an interpretation in terms of "Galileo's hypothesis." From a purely aesthetic point of view, Varignon's graphic is quite plain. Nonetheless, in our sample, it reflects a high point in the reciprocity between visual representations, mathematical equations, causal interpretation, and text.

While our sample of tables and graphics for the 17th century is small (only 38 total articles have them), we report our findings for their principal functions in table 3.3. In general, the functions of the visuals are quite similar for the English and French samples, differing noticeably on only two measures. English articles with visuals are more likely to support observations (50%, compared with 31% for the French), while French articles with visuals are more likely to support the improvement of equipment (12%, compared with none for the English). The most important difference, however, is the heightened overall concern in the French case for the use of visuals (52%, compared with 24% for the English), a crucial element of modern scientific communication.

The Scope of Argument

We want to make a final point concerning, not argumentative practices per se, but their scope. English scientists exhibit a far greater breadth of subject matter than do their Continental colleagues (table 3.4). In the English case, we have one category of article for which there are no French instances: "miscellaneous."[5] The focus of the diverse articles in this category is generally on areas of human inquiry new to scientific investigation: interests are represented that would later become cartography, metallurgy, cultural anthropology, and actuarial science. As a consequence of this broader English interest, the standards of science and the character of its style

5. All of our categories of science are anachronistic with the possible exceptions of astronomy, chemistry, mathematics, and medicine. In applying these categories to the 17th century, we have attempted merely to identify what these men were doing, with no pretense that they would have identified their tasks exactly as such. Much of our terminology must be so viewed, for example, "experiment," "scientist," "professional," even "science" itself.

Table 3.4. Distribution of Articles by Discipline in 17th-Century Sample

	English (n = *100*)	*French* (n = *98*)
Animal biology	16%	16%
Astronomy	12	21
Chemistry	5	11
Earth sciences	6	5
Mathematics	7	10
Medicine	12	0
Physics	16	21
Plant biology	7	13
Technology	2	3
Miscellaneous	17	0

and presentation are applied to a broader range of subjects. Science becomes more a way of looking at the world in general than a way of investigating the natural world, narrowly conceived. Halley's "An Estimate of the Degrees of the Mortality of Mankind, Drawn from Curious Tables of the Births and Funerals at the City of Breslaw; with an Attempt to Acertain the Price of Annuities upon Lives" is a good example of this extension and its communicative and argumentative implications:

> For these Reasons the People of this City seem most proper for a *Standard*; and the rather, for that the *Births* do, a small matter, exceed the *Funerals.* The only thing wanting is the Number of the whole People, which in some measure I have endeavoured to supply by comparison of the *Mortality* of the People of all Ages, which I shall from the said Bills trace out with all the accuracy possible.
>
> It appears that in the Five Years mentioned, viz. from 87 to 91 inclusive, there were *born* 6193 Persons, and *buried* 5869; that is, born per *Annum* 1238, and *buried* 1174; whence an *Encrease* of the People may be argued of 64 per *Annum,* or of about a 20th part, which may perhaps be ballanced by the Levies for the *Emperor's* Service in his Wars. (1693-E041; italics in original)

In this passage of actuarial findings, both Halley's style and his style of argument are indistinguishable from their counterparts in physics, biology, and chemistry.

In contrast, the professional status of French science is manifest in its sharper focus on subjects that are traditionally scientific. A group of scientists who clearly see themselves as astronomers, botanists, chemists, physicists, or mathematicians carry out organized programs of research. Medicine is not among their concerns,[6] nor are they driven by a general desire to create new disciplinary interests by focusing their attention on objects and events hitherto excluded from scientific scrutiny.

6. This finding is a little deceptive in that some of the Académie Royale research in plant and animal biology had an underlying medical motivation. As Stroup points out (1990, pp. 172–173), nearly 30% of the 17th-century Académie members had been trained as physicians or apothecaries, yet the Académie "established its scientific program to be independent of medical research." Also, at this time in France, medicine was already a well-developed discipline with various career tracks available, including academic ones.

The professional status of French science is also reflected in the higher averages for both quantitative expressions and citations, more than double the values for our English sample (table 2.1).

At this point in time, we see little interest on either side of the Channel in publishing news on the application of science to technology. This is an area that will undergo a sea change during the industrial revolution.

Conclusion

In discussing the differences between English and French scientific literature, we have necessarily slighted the many similarities. Most articles in our sample could have been published, with some minor revisions and translation, in the other nation's journal literature; indeed, *Philosophical Transactions* did occasionally publish English and Latin versions of articles by European authors, including such prominent ones as Leeuwenhoek, Huygens, Hevelius, Leibniz, Varignon, and Cassini. Overall, we see the writers of 17th-century scientific prose, whatever their nationality, as addressing an international community of readers engaged in a mutual quest for empirical knowledge of the natural world. Yet our analysis has revealed several trends in argumentative practice that would appear to be national in character.

We have found that, while 17th-century natural philosophers shared a common interest in fact-finding and in explanation, the balance between these two enterprises differed from one shore of the Channel to the other. From words still vivid on the page, we can envision the English gentleman Thomas Henshaw just after dawn on a chilly May morning supervising his servants as they gather quantities of dew for his experiments. We cannot picture the mathematical Dutchman Christiaan Huygens similarly engaged. There is thus a special sense in which Henshaw participates in the great unrealized dream of English science, the dream in Bacon's *New Atlantis* of a museum containing a specimen of every scientific fact. Although the flagship enterprise of Continental science—the Académie Royale—was not uninterested in Bacon's dream, as their early work on animals and plants attests (Dodart 1731, Perrault 1671), their focus on explanation was greater than that of the Royal Society. Furthermore, our French sample placed a heightened emphasis on quantification, visual argument, and use of observations and experimental results as stepping stones to theory.

The relationship between "literary inscriptions" and their sociohistorical context is never a simple one, and the reason behind the differences we have noted presents a puzzle we cannot definitively solve. Only members of the Académie Royale could publish in its *Mémoires,* a practice that skewed its contents in the direction of a small community of academicians. *Journal des Sçavans* heavily relied upon this same limited community for its contents.[7] The professionalization of science on a

7. While translations of articles by Robert Boyle and other English authors did appear in *Journal des Sçavans,* worth noting is that our complete random sample of French whole articles and short passages contains only two authors not members of the Académie Royale (Francine and Bernoulli), neither of them English.

large scale would not take place until the middle of the 19th century, in Germany, when most working scientists were "either university teachers or students, and they worked more and more in groups consisting of a master and several disciples" (Ben-David 1971, p. 108). Nonetheless, the initial professionalization of French science is already evident in the early years of the Académie Royale and the two journals in which its members published their research findings.[8] In contrast, even though closely tied to the Royal Society, the early *Philosophical Transactions* published articles by men[9] both inside and outside that community, including scientific correspondence sent to the editor from seafarers, physicians, world travelers, European savants, and the like. Thanks to its founder and first editor, Henry Oldenburg, *Philosophical Transactions* delivered on the promise of its title page: "Giving some accompt of the present undertakings, studies, and labours of *the ingenious in many considerable parts of the world*" (italics added). And the articles therein favored the reporting of observationally derived facts sans theoretical explanations.

Also worth bearing in mind is that, in the French case, the relationship between professionalization and scientific explanation is not straightforward. It is not that we have, as a direct consequence of this narrowing, a Cartesianism that insists science deliver a material cause, or the Galilean view that the book of nature is necessarily "written in the language of mathematics." Rather, this narrowing—coupled with the talents of such as Huygens and Varignon—opens one set of opportunities for French science while closing off another. While the English are open to "natural science as a model for valid thinking about political, economic, and technological matters" (Ben-David 1971, p. 78), the French pursue a narrower goal with singular intensity. Between this French pursuit of narrower goals and instrumental precision, the path is direct, a concern for such precision being the only means of linking theory firmly to observations and experimental results.

Having established the main communicative and argumentative features of the 17th-century scientific article and the possible influence on them by indirect institutional pressures, we are now well positioned to examine how these features evolved in the subsequent centuries. That is the aim of our remaining chapters.

8. This early professionalization, as well as its financial underpinnings, has been masterfully documented by historian Alice Stroup (1990).

9. Atkinson (1999, p. 102) reports that the first article with a woman listed as author did not appear in *Philosophical Transactions* until 1760, "Effects of a Thunderstorm at Rickmansworth, Herts" by Ann Whitfield. The astronomer Caroline Herschel reported her sightings of comets in several short *Philosophical Transactions* articles published in the 1790s.

CHAPTER 4

Style and Presentation in the 18th Century

The 80th issue of *Philosophical Transactions* features a 12-page article by an up-and-coming young scientist, Isaac Newton—his first scientific publication and the first major scientific article in English. The *Transactions* editor received this article on 6 February 1672 and published it with minor revisions less than two weeks later. The initial reception of Newton's article was largely positive: it had an early impact on thinking about light and color in England and on the Continent, and though hotly contested on many fronts (see Bazerman 1988, pp. 80–127; Gross 1990, pp. 111–128; Westfall 1993, pp. 85–109), it was taken seriously by the prominent natural philosophers in England and Europe. Newton's main contention was that white light, far from being simple, as previously believed, was a compound of all the colors of the spectrum, a compound that could be decomposed by passing white light through a prism and recomposed through reversing that passage in a second prism.

Newton's ground-breaking scientific article begins exactly as one would expect for a formal letter between learned colleagues with an interest in natural philosophy:

> SIR,
> To perform my late promise to you, I shall without further ceremony acquaint you, that in the beginning of the Year 1666 (at which time I applyed my self to the grinding of Optick glasses of other figures than Spherical,) I procured me a Triangular glass-Prisme, to try therewith the celebrated *Phaenomena* of *Colours*. And in order thereto having darkened my chamber, and made a small hole in my window-shuts,

> to let in a convenient quantity of the Suns light, I placed my Prisme at his entrance, that it might be thereby refracted to the opposite wall. It was at first a very pleasing divertisement, to view the vivid and intense colours produced thereby; but after a while applying my self to consider them more circumspectly, I became surprised to see them in an *oblong* form; which, according to the received laws of Refraction, I expected should have been *circular*. (pp. 3075–3076; italics in original)

With a few carefully chosen words, Newton dispenses with the social niceties and places the reader at the site of his experiments, his darkened chamber. This opening passage has a disarming simplicity and even playfulness. Newton's experimental materials are no more than the sun, a wall, window shutters, and a glass prism. And he does not refrain from recording his feelings about his observations: "It was at first a very pleasing divertisement," "I became surprised." Two small illustrations are integrated into the text; with this exception, the article also resembles a letter in its absence of presentational features: one general reference (to "Mr. *Hook* somewhere in his *Micrography*," with no other bibliographic information), no headings, and no tables of data or equations.

The flesh-and-blood recipient and "sir" of Newton's actual letter was Henry Oldenburg, editor of *Philosophical Transactions.* But Newton undoubtedly realized his letter would be read aloud at the next meeting of the Royal Society (it was on 8 February 1672) and would soon thereafter appear in Oldenburg's journal, where it would be read not only by the Royal Society members but also by their international network of correspondents. It is this larger audience Newton addresses in a closing sentence: "This, I conceive, is enough for an Introduction to Experiments of this kind; which if any of the *R. Society* shall be so curious as to prosecute, I should be very glad to be informed with what success: That, if any thing seem to be defective . . . I may have an opportunity of giving further direction about it, or of acknowledging my errors, if I have committed any" (p. 3087).[1]

In this chapter, we hope to show that, in several important ways, Newton's 17th-century introduction and conclusion are paradigmatic of 18th-century communicative practices. That is to say, during the 18th century, we find the persistence of narrative and epistolary conventions, the continued presence of the explicitly personal and social in the communication of science, and a continued tolerance for emotional expression. At the same time, between the opening and closing passages of Newton's article, and many articles from the 18th century as well, the social and the personal fade into the background as the author concentrates on describing and explaining the natural world by means of measurement, calculation, and empirical observation.

Though 17th-century modes of communication persisted, the 18th century was also an age of transition. The two main journals remain the *Philosophical Transactions* of the Royal Society and the *Mémoires* of the Académie Royale (Gascoigne 1985,

1. While this passage echoes the politeness of the opening passage, we know from Newton's subsequent behavior that he really was not much interested in readers questioning his work, only confirming and expanding upon it.

p. 93). But the 18th century was also the golden age of the scientific society, and with their proliferation came a host of other journals sponsored by these societies along with privately published ones (McClellan 1985). By the last quarter of the century, both *Philosophical Transactions* and the *Mémoires* had serious competition not only from scientific books, but also from other journals.

Our 18th-century sample contains nine other journals, listed in Appendix A. Especially notable is the *Observations et Mémoires sur la Physique, sur l'histoire naturelle et sur les arts* (Observations and Memoirs on Physics, on Natural History and on the Crafts), first published in 1773 and also know as "Rozier's Journal" in tribute to its founder Abbé François Rozier. As Rozier eloquently, if brusquely, put it in the preface to the first volume: "We will not offer to idle amateurs purely agreeable works or the sweet illusion of believing themselves to be initiated into science of which they know nothing. . . . We offer this collection to true scientists [*les vrais savants*]" (quoted in McClellan 1985, p. 191). He further asserted that the journal itself would "reject everything that is nothing more than undigested compilation and that is wanting in new and useful views" (quoted in Kronick 1976, p. 143). In Rozier's Journal we thus have a private journal pitched, for the first time, to "the 18th-century equivalent of a professional scientist" (McClellan 1979, p. 440). The general desire for higher professional standards in science and its communication also led to the first great specialty journals, outside of medicine, from France and the German states (Gascoigne 1985, p. 99). Represented in our sample are three specialized journals inaugurated in the last decades of the 18th century: *Annales de Chimie* (Annals of Chemistry), *Chemische Annalen* (Chemical Annals), and *Astronomisches Jahrbuch* (Astronomical Yearbook). In the case of *Annales de Chimie* and *Chemische Annalen,* we have two journals central to the formation of a professionalized chemical community in Europe during the 19th century (Hufbauer 1982, pp. 62–95; Gascoigne 1985, pp. 148–149). We also included in our sample a German-language journal reporting on the applied science of mining and metallurgy: *Bergmanisches Journal* (Miner's Journal), begun in 1788.[2]

With this sign of increased specialization in the last few decades of the 18th century, we might expect to see corresponding changes in communicative features in the direction of 20th-century practice. And we do. Indeed, although meant only for natural history in England, the following generalization rings true about scientific communication as well: "It is virtually a cliché that the 18th century was an age of transition. Nevertheless, like most clichés, it happens to be true. In a very recognizable way, this century started off feeling 'ancient' and ended up looking 'modern'" (Allen 1993, p. 333). While many of the communicative features of 18th-century scientific prose merely repeat 17th-century norms, and while there is much diversity, nevertheless significant trends exist that anticipate 20th-century practices, especially in the case of France, and especially in the area of presentation.

2. The premier journals of German science from the 17th century through the mid-18th century were *Acta Eruditorum* and *Miscellanea Curiosa,* both of which published articles in Latin (Gascoigne 1985, p. 93). Perhaps feeling the need to establish their own communicative identity within the scientific community, German-language journals first appeared in the middle 18th century. For that reason, the first selected passage from a German article in our sample dates from quite late in the century, 1774.

Style

Eighteenth-century scientific style is characterized by the persistence of epistolary and narrative forms, and by the continued intrusion of the personal, especially in English prose. In addition, in the case of our stylistic markers, such as the reliance of personal pronouns and the use of citations, this scientific prose exhibits, despite considerable divergences, some interesting convergences. In some cases at least, it is possible to speak realistically of norms. In addition, in style and presentation, 18th-century scientific prose frequently anticipates 20th-century practice. We will take up each of these topics in turn.

Persistence of Personal, Epistolary, and Narrative Norms: Introductions

Closely linked to past literary and epistolary traditions, 18th-century scientific articles seem the product of a literary education, despite their focus on the material world. To illustrate this tendency, we focus on the beginnings and endings in our random sample of 126 whole articles; we draw upon this suite of introductions and conclusions as the best sites for examining the personal and social elements at work in 18th-century prose style, especially the contrast between the English and Continental.[3]

The introductions of 18th-century scientific articles reflect national differences. Those who write in English persistently employ epistolary and narrative elements,[4] while those who write in French and German frequently anticipate 20th-century norms. Nearly one in three English introductions looks like a letter; nearly one in six starts like a story. Sometimes epistolary conventions are reproduced without alteration:

> *SIR,*
> Being at present at the Point of returning Home, I think myself obliged before my Departure, to return my humble Thanks to that Learned Body of the *Royal Society*, over which you preside, for the Honour they have lately done me, in chusing me a Member; and, to make a grateful Acknowledgement to you in particular, for the many Favours and Civilities, which, according to that amiable Character of Benevolence to all Strangers in general, you have been pleased to bestow upon me.
>
> It is now a Duty incumbent on me to communicate to the *Royal Society* from time to time any thing new and curious, which may fall my way: Therefore I now lay before them a Draught and Description of an *Arithmetical Machine*, which I invented twelve or thirteen Years ago. (1735-E035)

The author, Christian-Ludovicus Gersten, a professor of mathematics at the University of Giessen, conveys to the baronet and president of the Royal Society,

3. In our 17th-century chapter, we included introductions and conclusions among our presentational features because they help orient the reader to what is to come and what is past; we will do so for the 18th-century in its proper place.

4. For additional discussion of the epistolary characteristics of the early *Philosophical Transactions*, see Valle (1997) and Atkinson (1999, pp. 81–84).

Hans Sloane, his thanks for the gift of membership in the Royal Society. To return a gift immediately with a gift would be to turn the newly minted friendship of equals into a commercial transaction, to transform bestowal into barter. The arithmetical machine is, rather, an expression of the obligation incumbent on all members of the Society, even "strangers" from foreign lands, to share their discoveries and inventions with their colleagues.

While one in three English introductions is epistolary, one in six is narrative. Typical is this article on the transit of Venus and the eclipse of the sun:

> The weather, on the morning of the 3rd of June, was so very unfavourable, both at the observatory of the Earl of Macclesfield and also here at Oxford, that there was very little reason to expect that we should be able to make any observation. But here, a few minutes before noon, the clouds began to break, and I was enabled to observe the transit of the Sun's consequent limb over the meridian. At one o'clock in the afternoon, the sky was again overcast, and it rained for some time; but towards three o'clock, the clouds were dispersed, the Sun shone out clearly, and at five o'clock there was hardly a cloud to be seen. The preceding evening was also so very favourable, that the several persons who proposed to make observations of the transit, had an opportunity of adjusting their instruments. (1769-E072)

The case could be made that this description is objective, that it is the state of the weather, not the states of mind of the participants that is in the foreground. But such a reading ignores the reasonable inferences any reader would make concerning those states of mind, the anxiety of the participants, heightened and finally dispelled; objective description and subjective narration are inextricably intertwined.

Unlike its English counterpart, French science eschews epistolary and narrative forms, a position consonant with its early professionalization, discussed in the 17th-century chapters. In our French sample of 54 whole articles, there are only two letters, neither of which conforms to the English pattern. One, on beavers, is identified as a letter, though entirely shorn of epistolary conventions (1704-F129). The other is a letter of transmittal accompanying a translation of an article from the German, a translation made by "an amateur who is taking [M. de Morveau's] course in chemistry" (1781-F447). The epithet implies that de Morveau's readers are the very opposite of "amateurs."

In France, in general, science is business too serious to be an avocation of gentlemen, a seriousness that generally eschews the narrative and epistolary. This seriousness is presupposed in the introduction to an article by the polymath Georges Louis Leclerc, Comte de Buffon, on the origin of colors:

> Although these days many are concerned with the physics of colors, none appear to have made much progress since Newton; it is not that he said the last word on the matter, but that most [French] physicists have worked harder to combat than to understand him, and, although his principles are clear, and his experiments incontestable, there are so few people who have taken the trouble to examine his discoveries in depth, either individually or as a whole, that I do not believe that we can speak of a new sort of colors without at first giving a clear idea of the production of colors in general. (1743-F352)

Clearly, we have here an enterprise devoted exclusively to the progressive understanding of physical phenomena. Indeed, it is the arrest of this progress after Newton, as a consequence of fruitless disputes, that motivates the author's inquiry. Buffon's is a moral fervor in the interest of science: there is throughout no retreat from a strict professionalism.

The three German journals we examined parallel French professionalism. They are all specialist journals; in each case, the targeted audience is clearly those with a professional interest in the subject matter presented: mining and metallurgy, chemistry, astronomy. The impatience with the amateur can be seen in the following *obiter dictum*, a judgment that is all the writer feels he needs by way of introduction: "I can presume as a matter of course that the routine distillation of vinegar is known to every analytical chemist; therefore I can skip it, and turn to the investigation of the consequences of that effort" (1787-G177).

While we have so far represented dominant trends, we would, if we went no further, fail to represent persistent diversity. English introductions can also exhibit an exclusively professional orientation:

> The chief design of this inquiry is, to investigate the nature, origin, and cause, of the permanent colours of opake bodies.
>
> I was led to the pursuit of it, from a persuasion of its utility, to those interesting and elegant Arts, whose object is the preparation and use, of colouring substances.
>
> The discovery of this principle is the foundation, on which alone all the parts and materials of the knowledge relative to those Arts, can be raised and supported.
>
> It should be the office of experimental philosophy, to examine the powers and properties of all the materials, requisite to technical uses. Nor should its views be confined to the theories, which result from those researches, but directed to the practical application of them. (1789-E117)

In this manifesto, the personal and epistolary have been left behind, and narrative has been entirely replaced by exposition.

Equally, French introductions can be narrative in nature, as in this next selection, from Rozier's Journal:

> Caesar, having conquered part of Sequania, directed his victorious arms toward Vesoul. After having taken a favorable position on a hillside dominating the village of Charmois, and having drawn lines of circumvallation according to the usage of the times, the Roman general was constrained to retrace his steps by the obstacle created by the sea of Vesoul to the execution of his plans.* Although it has always been claimed that the momentary outpouring of the source of fresh-water wells was the principal cause that prevented this small town from falling into Caesar's grasp, and that in our day we see such sudden outpourings from this opening producing this same effect, I am far from regarding these observations as equivalent: but because this topic should be the subject of a separate memoir, I will avoid entering into greater detail. The end that I now propose is to make known the phenomenon that produced this opening, and to give the causes that I believe I have discovered.
>
> ---
>
> *These are Caesar's exact words. (1782-F452)

The goal of this article is narrowly scientific: the discovery of the causes of the gap in the earth from which brief, but forceful outpourings of water issue. This goal is framed, however, by a historical narrative, which seems, at first glance at least, to be of equal weight with the scientific phenomenon that is the presumed focus of the author's attention.[5]

Just as English science is not always personal in tone, and French science does not always eschew the narrative and epistolary, German science sometimes sounds an anomalous note:

> Germans were well-known to be the first who dealt with mining and metallurgical technology by reference to fundamental principles. For several years, however, other nations have produced men of our caliber by turning their zealous attention diligently in the direction of this great scientific enterprise. The British lead the pack with an energy, and a strength, so completely characteristic of this nation that perhaps we must turn to this lucky island to find all of the knowledge relevant to these enterprises employed to perfection. (1790-G157)

We see here the anxiety of influence, the mix of admiration and envy meant to motivate those in German-speaking lands to energize lagging efforts by imitating and learning from their English brethren. Motivation of others is the introduction's only purpose; it is impossible to think that such an appeal could survive explicitly in—that such explicitness could be appropriate to—mature communications in science or technology.

Persistence of Personal, Epistolary, and Narrative Norms: Conclusions

The social and personal also rise to the surface in 18th-century conclusions. Our first example is from an article by Patrick Blair entitled "A Continuation of the Osteographia Elephantina," a study of the skeletal structure of the elephant:

> And thus, *Sir*, I have finished my Weak Endeavors: The Undertaking, I doubt [i.e., suspect], will seem bold to some, and rash to others, and the Performance mean. But the many Obligations you have laid upon me, and the frequent Marks of Esteem I have received in your several Letters, made me pass over all Obstacles, Reflections, and Discouragements, when to serve you and your Honourable Society was my only Design. I have rather chosen to address you in a plain and common Stile, than give the least suspicion of Disingenuity in a finer Language; especially since it is History I have written, where Matter of Fact, and not Romance, where Eloquence, is the chief Design.[6]

5. While the subsample of four articles from this journal is far too small for responsible generalization, it is perhaps not insignificant that three of these four exhibit narrative introductions of this sort. It seems as if their authors are addressing an audience whose interests are wider than those of science. This does not contradict, but rather adds a nuance to McClellan's (1985) assertion that "Rozier's Journal was exclusively a scientific journal and was limited to publishing original material in science" (p. 191).

6. In contemporary English syntax: "where matter of fact is the chief design and not romance, where eloquence is."

The Copper Plates, which at my own Charges I have caused to be engraven here, I acknowledge might have been done finer in *London*; but since I had the Original by me, whereby I was able from time to time to correct in the Ingraving what Errors happen'd in drawing the Figures, I rather chose to have them done by me here: And tho' the drafts of the Engraver be cours, yet I have endeavored what in me lay to have the Figures true and wel proportion'd. Wishing all Health and Happiness to your self, Prosperity and Success to your Honourable and Famous Society. I continue,

Sir,
Your most humble, and
most obliged Servant,

From my House at
Dundee, April 27,
1709.

PATRICK BLAIR
(1710-E012)

In this conclusion, no attempt is made to disguise the epistolary nature of the communication, one that epitomizes science as a set of gentlemanly obligations. It is a letter addressed as if by a suppliant to his noble lord, in this case Hans Sloane, President of the Royal Society. Nonetheless, it is no accident that this printed letter in a "plain and common Stile" occurs early in the century, within three decades of Newton's optics article. It is a living fossil.

This is not to say that, later in the century, traditional forms could not survive, adapted to serve new purposes. In this German conclusion, drawn from an article entitled "Preliminary Description of the Establishment and Construction of the New Ducal Observatory in Gotha," the author, von Zach, transforms narrative into science:

> The site and prospect of this observatory is the most beautiful and least visually constrained; with the exception of the Krahnberg and the high towers of the castle, none of the observatories I have seen in my journies in England, France, Italy, and Germany and which were not built on heights, have so unobstructed a horizon, nor air so clear, far from the cross-currents, chimney emissions, and industrial haze that envelop every city. Of course, the wind and weather, and especially the rough north wind, are felt there with redoubled force; for this reason alone the structure is solidly built and the front faces the vast Thuringer forest. (1789-G242)

The conclusion is certainly a description of the site, and it most assuredly includes a compliment to the reigning duke nearly as effusive as Blair's to Sloane. But the details of the description are absolutely relevant to the scientific purpose of the observatory: its potential for astronomical observation is the real theme of this paragraph.

Our next two conclusions turn the personal into the professional; in so doing, they give us an insight into the social and personal dynamics of two very different scientific communities: the French chemists and the German geologists. The first is from an article by Antoine Laurent Lavoisier entitled "Concerning the Combustion of Kunkel's Phosphorous and on the Nature of the Acid that Results from this Combustion":

> Perhaps you will be astonished at the results that I report, different from and for the most part diametrically opposed to those M. Sage has published in various works; I am far from wishing to throw the least doubt on the accuracy of the experiments he has published; I will only remark that, as he has almost always worked with phosphoric acid released spontaneously into the air by the slow disintegration of phosphorous, while I, on the contrary, worked with phosphoric acid obtained by combustion, the difference in the results could stem from this circumstance alone. Moreover, all that I can do is to respond to the Academy concerning the accuracy of the facts that I present to it; to share, if it judges such action appropriate, the laboratory notebooks from which I have drawn these facts, with whatever Commissioners it pleases to name. I would not believe the time wasted that I will employ in redoing my work, when it is a question of dispersing any doubts that could retard the progress of the sciences. (1777-F412)

In this passage, Lavoisier testifies to the bonds of politeness among French scientific gentlemen as firm as those between English scientific gentlemen. These stretch as far as the desire to preserve the dignity and reputation of a scientific rival who has published results "for the most part diametrically opposed" to Lavoisier's; however, they do not extend to the avoidance of confrontation and serious disagreement. While actual witnessing as a persuasive device is by no means absent from 18th-century French science (Licoppe 1997), in this case Lavoisier offers in its stead the virtual witness provided by the evidence in his laboratory notebooks. His concluding sentence is a moral coda, a mantra subordinating the personal to the universal, the vindication of scientists by means of the "truths" of science as revealed through the repetition of experiments.

In the following conclusion, from the German States, no such gentlemanly deference is evident:

> From the announcement, one might reasonably expect that these three letters [that make up the book on which I am commenting] would contain all sorts of interesting intelligence. But because of many personally abusive remarks, what appears therein is so highly unpleasant to read that we are obliged to censure it. From one so scholarly as Herr F[erber], it is so unexpected, and it is so thoroughly disagreeable to normal readers to read the intelligence communicated therein—presumed to be science—in *so slovenly a discourse*, so full of *vague and incorrect terms*. In our report, without Herr F.'s being able legitimately to raise his voice against us for *pedantry* and *quibbling*, we thought it necessary to point to various instances of vagueness and incorrectness, into which he has strayed. Currently scientists have already come so far in *the definition of mineralogical terms* that such uncertainties would create *extraordinary disorder* if they were to run riot and appear in important works; as a consequence, instead of advancing in this science, we would take *several steps* backward. We must conclude this report by not concealing the painful observation imposed upon us by reading this little book repeatedly from cover to cover: that, with increasing years, Herr Ferber *seems more and more to lay bare the weakness of his character*, or more accurately, *of his heart*, for we would rather not speak about defects of mind or knowledge. (1789-G212; emphasis in original)

In this passage, the personal is certainly at the forefront. Herr Ferber's character is attacked; it is regarded as relevant to the scientific issues under discussion, a link between character and performance Lavoisier carefully eschews. But we must not allow these differences between the German author and his French counterpart to disguise the fact that in both cases social norms are used to focus attention on a problem regarded as central to a professionalized science. Just as Lavoisier is concerned with the purity of reagents, the German author is concerned with Herr Ferber's terminological improprieties. His sloppy practices constitute a problem; if they are not criticized, if they happen to prevail, geology in the German-speaking lands will suffer.

Despite these examples of personal and social intrusion, resort to this more literary style is relatively infrequent in all three languages. The intrusion of the personal is also to some extent dependent on field of study: neither in observational astronomy nor in mathematics is it likely. Moreover, in all of these illustrations, though the personal and social intrude in introductions and conclusions, they never obtrude; they never swamp the science in question. Indeed, in the last two illustrations, the social and the personal are alleged to be highly relevant to the conduct of science. Still, in no scientific community are stylistic tendencies strong enough completely to exclude the intrusion of the personal and the social, considered as relevant to the communication of 18th-century science.

Convergences and Divergences in Style

While the examples we have just analyzed give us some sense of the range of possibilities of 18th-century scientific prose, they do not give us any sense of its central tendencies, its norms. To that end, we turn to the 18th-century stylistic data from our sample of 482 short passages, its convergences and divergences. In the discussion of 17th-century style (chapter 2), we emphasized the similarities between the English and French samples. In our sample for the 18th century, covering a much longer time span (1701–1800) and German as well as English and French, divergences became more prominent. Of the 10 stylistic markers for the three languages in table 4.1, seven diverge, while only three converge. These convergences are interesting, however, because they suggest to us that, in all three languages, authors are equally concerned with communicating their degree of confidence in making assertions (they hedge), explaining the natural world through measurement and calculation (they quantify),[7] and contextualizing statements within an existing body of knowledge (they cite).

It is also worth noting that the divergence among the other stylistic markers seems largely French: between German and English, there is convergence on every

7. The averages for quantitative expressions in both samples are the second highest values for the stylistic features we tracked and nearly the same: 2.1 instances per 100 words for the English and 2.2 instances per 100 words for the French. These results make for an interesting comparison with the 17th century. This stylistic marker doubles for the English sample and remains essentially unchanged for the French sample. This finding is consistent with Poovey's (1998) assertion that by the "18th century one could make a case . . . for considering numerical representation the quintessential form of 'useful knowledge'" in England (p. 143).

Table 4.1. Averages of Stylistic Features in 18th-Century Passages: Occurrence per 100 Words

	English (n = *122*)	*French* (n = *217*)	*German*[a] (n = *143*)
Divergence			
Personal pronouns/names	2.4	3.1	2.6
Evaluative expressions	0.9	0.3	1.0
Poetic expressions	0.3	0.1	0.0
Deviant expressions	0.6	0.3	0.2
Suppressed-person passives	1.1	0.3	1.0
Objective passives	0.4	0.4	0.6
Dummy subjects	0.4	0.7	0.4
Convergence			
Hedges	1.3	1.2	1.1
Quantitative expressions	2.1	2.2	2.1
Citations	0.2	0.2	0.3

[a]In this and subsequent tables, the German sample only covers the period 1774–1800.

stylistic marker with the exception of poetic and deviant expressions. The French score noticeably lower on three of the four markers of personal expression (table 4.1, top four rows), the one exception being pronouns/names. And as expected, due to differences in preferred predications, the French sample has fewer suppressed-person passives and more dummy subjects.

In the case of verb frequency, as table 4.2 illustrates, convergence is more evident than divergence, especially in English and French. Still, on the whole, the English and French percentages do not depart much from those of the preceding century. Although some degree of uniformity among languages is evident in the heavy use of the weak verbs *to be* and *to have*, this is much less true in German than in French or in English; nevertheless, five verbs do overlap on the three lists in

Table 4.2. Ten Most Frequent Verbs in 18th-Century Passages

English Verbs (n = *1,280*)	% *Occurrence*	*French Verbs* (n = *2,624*)	% *Occurrence*	*German Verbs* (n = *1,237*)	% *Occurrence*
to be	21.3	être (to be)	18.3	sein (to be)	11.2
to have	2.6	avoir (to have)	5.8	finden (to find)	2.6
to make	2.2	pouvoir (to be able)	4.6	geben (to give)	2.3
to appear	2.0	faire (to make)	3.4	haben (to have)	1.9
to find	2.0	trouver (to find)	2.1	machen (to make)	1.6
to see	2.0	voir (to see)	2.1	enthalten (to contain)	1.3
to give	1.9	donner (to give)	1.9	erhalten (to obtain)	1.3
to say	1.1	devoir (to have to)	1.6	werden (to become)	1.3
to take	1.0	falloir (to be necessary)	1.2	zeigen (to show)	1.2
to equal	0.9	prendre (to take)	1.1	halten (to contain)	1.1
Total	37.0	Total	42.1	Total	25.8

table 4.2: *to be, to find, to have, to give, to make.*[8] Also worth noting is that, in both the 17th and 18th centuries, a mere 10 verbs account for over one third of the verbs in the French and English samples. This suggests to us that, even at this early stage, scientific communication in these two languages was not as "verbally" diverse as one would expect from a literary prose.

Our data also indicate a preponderance of verbs predicated of the subject of science—nature itself—rather than of the scientists working with nature. In the English sample for the 18th century, 47% of all the verbs were predicated of people, 53% of nature; in the German sample, the numbers are 45% and 55%; in the French sample, 39% and 61%. Again, we find that the French seem more focused on the impersonal than are the English or Germans.

We can better view those impersonal and personal strains of 18th-century scientific prose through verbs displayed in situ. As the prose turns to the impersonal and abstract, the typical finite verbs change in response. Three passages illustrate this tendency. The first is from an English article of 1705 (finite verbs italicized):

> I *took* a Bottle somewhat of an Oval form (which I had purposely *caus'd* to be made so, that it might with more ease *Librate* [balance] in Water). It *held* more than three Gallons (but how much we *have* no occasion *to know.*) Into this Bottle I *put* as much Lead as would *sink* it under the surface of the Water, and *was*, when *weigh'd* in that Element, *Ballanc'd* by a small Weight in the Scale on the other end of the Beam. I *chose* to include my Weight, to prevent the Inconveniency of Bubbles of Air, which I *knew* would plentifully *adhere to* and *lurk* in the Irregular Body of the Weight, had it been *fix'd* on the outside, and *must* (I *think*) of necessity *make* an Error in an Experiment which *requires* so great a Nicety as this. (1705-E007)

In this passage, 40% of the verbs are concrete, working in their clauses to express distinct material processes: *librate, hold, sink, balance, adhere, lurk, fix.* In addition, verbs predicated of people are in the majority.

In this next passage, from the French sample, we have an interesting contrast:

> But this explanation, which *appears* plausible enough at first, because it is *based on* principles that cannot be absolutely *denied*, principles that, up to a certain point, *presuppose* only facts already in evidence, *loses* much of its plausibility, and *becomes* almost unsustainable when one *tries* to look deeply into it and to reconcile it with other physical truths which are well *established* and generally *recognized.*
>
> First, everyone *knows* that a substance that is *boiling continues* to boil until completely *dried out*, provided one does not *stop* from applying the amount of heat necessary; that the boiling of water, for example, *continues* until it has entirely *evaporated.* (1748-F361)

The passage contains only a few concrete verbs describing material processes ("boil," "dry out," "evaporate"). In contrast, all but one of the verbs in the initial paragraph of this passage—verbs such as "appear," "base," "presuppose," and "recognize"—

8. The presence of synonyms means that the percentage of verbs in the top 10 is an undercount.

Table 4.3. Percentage of Noun Phrases of Various Types in 18th-Century Passages

Noun-Phase Types[a]	*English* (n = *122)*	*French* (n = *217)*	*German* (n = *143)*
Simple subject	21.7%	27.2%	24.9%
Complex subject	19.0	14.5	12.7
Simple nonsubject	15.3	14.3	22.1
Complex nonsubject	44.0	44.1	40.4
Subject pronouns and names	16.7	23.3	18.8
Subject multiple modifiers	13.1	9.2	6.6
Nonsubject pronouns and names	4.9	5.2	8.7
Nonsubject multiple modifiers	29.3	31.3	20.1

[a]Appendix C defines the terms used in this column and gives an example of calculations involved.

refer back to the abstractions "explanation," "principles," and "truths." These are of human origin, of course, though their individual creators are nowhere in sight. In addition, several verbs are predicated, not of specific individuals, but of the impersonal "one" and "everyone": the personal has become attenuated.

Our third passage crosses a line. Its single verb is *to be*. In all other clauses, even this verb has become a shadow of itself. So have the people making these observations and the verbs predicated of them:

> The beginning of the central occultation *is* at 11:49 P.M. under 250° in longitude and 39° north latitude with the rising of the moon during the day, at the western coast of California. The mean [*is*] at 1:11 A.M. at night under 350° in longitude and 54 1/2° n[orth] latitude in the Atlantic ocean n[orthwards] over the Azores. The end of the central occultation [*is*] at 2:34 at the nocturnal setting of the moon under 58° longitude and 22° north latitude at Mecca in Arabia. This occultation [*is*] visible primarily and for the most part in the evening in North America, over the Atlantic ocean, Great Britain, France, Germany Poland, Italy, Anatolia, Arabia, and Egypt. (1797-G238)

Our data do not permit us to make the case that the dates of these passages—early, middle, and late—have any significance; the kinship between the last two passages and the flavor of 20th-century scientific prose is, perhaps, not accidental, though we cannot say that it reflects the gradual weakening of the verb as a communicator of concrete actions.

While in the case of stylistic features generally, divergence is considerable, in the case of syntax and noun phrases specifically, convergence is the case. As in the English and French samples for the 17th century, the average sentences remain long (55 words) and clausally dense (5.0 per sentence).[9] Also, the relative distribution of noun phrases in both the subject and nonsubject positions remains roughly the same for the English, French, and German samples (table 4.3). As was true for the

9. We have German data only for the last quarter century. Overall, average sentence length is 41.6 words with 3.6 clauses per sentence.

17th century, 18th-century writers favored simple subjects over complex ones by roughly 2 to 1, and complex nonsubjects over simple ones by the same ratio. In both the 17th and 18th centuries, it would appear that simple noun phrases, to some extent, compensate for the long and clausally dense sentences.

Trends in Style

In 18th-century scientific prose, there are trends—trends, moreover that persist (with a few minor exceptions) throughout the next two centuries.

The data in table 4.4 support the following changes in the direction of 20th-century norms:

- Shifts from the scientist to his science, and from subjective to objective prose, are supported by the rise in suppressed-person passives and the decrease in personal pronouns and names, subject pronouns and names, and poetic and deviant expressions.
- A shift from bald to nuanced assertion is supported by the rise in hedges.
- A shift from the individual scientist to the research network is supported by the rise in citations.
- A shift from the reporting of observed particulars to measurements and calculations is supported by the rise in quantitative expressions.
- A shift to the complex noun phrase as the grammatical unit for the conceptual content of the science is supported by the rise in complex noun phrases, accompanied by a decrease in simple noun phrases in the subject position.
- A shift in the direction of syntactic simplicity is supported, as measured by decreasing sentence length and clausal density.

Table 4.4. Stylistic Trends across 18th Century (all three languages combined)

	1701–1725	*1726–1750*	*1751–1775*	*1776–1800*
Up				
Complex subject noun phrases (%)	14.4	16.7	15.8	14.5
Suppressed-person passives (per 100 words)	0.5	0.6	0.7	0.9
Hedges (per 100 words)	0.7	1.6	1.3	1.1
Citations (per 100 words)	0.1	0.4	0.1	0.2
Quantitative expressions (per 100 words)	1.8	1.7	2.4	2.3
Down				
Simple subject noun phrases (%)	26.8	25.2	25.2	24.5
Subject pronouns and names (%)	22.7	20.6	21.5	19.1
Personal pronouns (per 100 words)	2.8	2.9	3.3	2.6
Poetic expressions (per 100 words)	0.2	0.2	0.3	0.1
Deviant expressions (per 100 words)	0.5	0.5	0.4	0.3
Sentence length (words)	60.63	61.31	67.21	46.12
Clausal density (per sentence)	5.5	5.7	6.2	4.1
Clausal density (per 100 words)	9.6	9.5	9.6	9.1

Worth noting, however, is that within the 18th century, the shifts in stylistic markers are fitful and fairly small. Overall, the scientific style used in the late 18th century does not much differ from that used earlier in the century.

Presentation

One of the important communicative differences between Newton's article, discussed in our introduction to this chapter, and the scientific article 100 years later is the more frequent exploitation of presentational features for improved communicative efficiency. These trends can be seen in table 4.5, which divides presentational features into the primarily formal and the primarily substantive. The primarily formal features function like traffic signals, directing reader attention within the text; the primarily substantive features focus reader attention on themselves, informing readers of article content and significance. We can see, as the century progresses, a general increase in presentational features: increases in articles with headings and complete introductions and conclusions. Thematic titles, those that reveal the actual content of articles, decline somewhat, though they remain high throughout the century, as do visuals (tables and figures).

These general trends disguise the diversity among texts in English, French, and German, which is considerable. As we can see from table 4.6, the French sample scores higher than the English or German on all presentational features, with the exception of visuals. Moreover, the much lower percentage of German articles with visuals accounts for the decline in this feature for our sample as a whole (table 4.5).

Formal Features

TITLE AND AUTHOR The modal title of the 18th-century scientific article is thematic and fairly specific, though usually free from technical terminology. Early in the century we have the English title "An Account of an Experiment Made before the Royal Society, Touching the Proportion of the Weight of Air, to the Weight of a like Bulk of Water, Without Knowing the Quantity of Either" (1705-E007). At mid-century,

Table 4.5. Percentage of Whole Articles with Presentational Features, by Half Century, in 18th-Century Sample

	1701–1750 (n = 50)	*1751–1800* (n = 76)
Formal features		
Headings	30%	42%
Thematic titles	76	70
Citations	48	48
Substantive features		
Complete introductions	60	72
Complete conclusions	22	36
Visuals	46	39

Table 4.6. Percentage of Whole Articles with Presentational Features, by Language in 18th-Century Sample

	English (n = 44)	*French* (n = 54)	*German*[a] (n = 28)
Formal features			
Headings	20%	56%	29%
Thematic titles	68	80	64
Citations	45	57	32
Substantive features			
Complete introductions	55	83	57
Complete conclusions	27	37	21
Visuals	41	37	25

[a]German sample only covers the period 1774–1800.

we have the French title "Various Observations Concerning the Raising of Bees" (1754-F377). Toward the end of the century, we have the German title "Concerning the Argento-beryl or Aquamarine" (1792-G162). This last, with its technical terms for a pale-blue transparent gem, is atypical: only 11% of English titles, 41% of French, and 32% of German contain technical terms.

Each of these titles also has the same overall syntactic form: a preposition meaning "concerning" signals that the article's theme will follow immediately.[10] These introductory prepositions include "of" in English, *sur* in French, and *über* in German. They are a form of social signaling, like the handshake in Western cultures: they mark an entrance into the domain of study, in this case, science. This pattern appears in 62% of French titles, 65% of English, and 56% of German.

Despite considerable convergence in title form and content, there is some divergence. Titles range from the minimally informative "News Concerning Avanturino [a sort of Venetian glass]" (1793-G137) to a level of detail approaching that of a modern indicative abstract. Here is an example from an article by Pierre-Simon Laplace:

> RESEARCH *1) on the integration of differential equations concerning finite differences and on their function in the theory of chance. 2) on the principle of universal gravitation and on the secular inequalities of the planets that depend on it.* (1776-F497)

On one occasion, we have a full-blown indicative abstract in the form of a title:

> A CONTINUATION of the
> Osteographia Elephantina:
> OR,
> A full and exact Description of all the Bones of an *Elephant*, which dy'd near *Dundee*, *April* the 27*th*, 1706, with their several Dimensions.
> To which are premis'd,
> 1. *An Historical Account of the Natural Endowments, and several wonderful Performancers of* Elephants, *with the manner of Taking and Taming them,*

10. Sometimes a few superfluous words appear before the preposition, as in "Various Observations Concerning . . ." (1754-F377); often, no words precede the preposition.

2. *A short Anatomical Accounts of its Parts.*

And added,

1. *An exact Account of the Weight of all the Bones in this Subject.*
2. *The Method I us'd in preparing the Sceleton.*
3. *Four large Copper Plates, wherein are represented the Figures of the Stuffed Skin, and prepared Sceleton, as they now stand in the Publick Hall of Rarities at* Dundee; *with the separated Bones of several Views, and other Parts of this* Elephant. (1710-E012)

But these extremes are rare. In our sample, there is only one other instance of a minimally informative title (1784-G252), and titles with a very high level of specificity are few: only 7% of articles have such specificity.

Titles are followed by author designations to which credentials are often appended. But practices diverge widely from country to country. Eighty percent of English articles designate a professional credential or an institutional affiliation, generally membership in the Royal Society, while the French articles seldom mention credentials of any sort, perhaps because in most cases membership in the Académie Royale is assumed and sufficient. In German articles, author credentials are given in 25% of the cases. In no German article is membership in a scientific society given, but we find a wide range of professional and governmental titles, from doctor and professor to inspector and assessor.

Displays of author credentials can be elaborate: "Chief Constable of Zach, Director of the Observatory" (1789-G242) or even "Edward Hussey Delaval, F.R.S. of the Royal Societies of Upsala, and Gottingen, of the Institute of Bologna, and of the Literary and Philosophical Society of Manchester" (1789-E117). But these instances are extreme and rare.

HEADINGS Headings are a far more regular feature of 18th- than of 17th-century scientific articles, increasing by an order of magnitude compared with the preceding century. Moreover, between the first and second half of the 18th century, headings increase by 40%. There is much variety, from a simple series of Roman or Arabic letters (1776-F497, 1767-F394) to five levels of substantive headings (1794-F457).

The following two sets are not typical; they are meant to illustrate the range of possibilities. In the first, the English title carries the substantive burden; the headings are a finding system of general categories:

EXPERIMENTS, *by way of* Analysis, *upon the Water of the* Dead Sea; *upon the Hot Spring near* Tiberiades; *and upon the* Hammam Pharoan *Water*; *by* Charles Perry, *M.D. made on his Journey through the Holy Land,* & c.

EXPERIMENTS (*by way of* Analysis) *upon the Water of* Alphaltis, *commonly called the* Dead Sea.

EXPERIMENT I.

EXPERIMENT II.

EXPERIMENT III.

EXPERIMENT IV.

EXPERIMENT V.

OBSERVATIONS.

(1741-E041)

In contrast, the following French headings combine with the first half of the title to form an indicative abstract of the main body of the article:

> *Memoir on cobalt ammoniate and on the acid contained in the gray oxide of this metal, known as* saffron.
> Of the oxyde of pure cobalt.
> Of the ammoniate of pure cobalt.
> Of the acid removed from cobalt ammoniate and its properties. (1800-F467)

CITATIONS Citations are fairly common in the 18th century. Five out of 10 articles contain them. They are generally incorporated into the text or placed at the bottom of the page: 48% of such articles have citations within texts, while 35% have citations at the bottom of the page. About 12% of the time, both sorts of placement appear in the same article.[11] When citations appear at the page bottom, they are just as likely to appear with an asterisk or dagger as a number.

The format of citations is far from uniform. Page numbers are often omitted; article titles almost always are. In addition, there is almost never an attempt to separate the various segments of the citation by means of italics, small capitals, parentheses, roman numerals, and so forth. In the case of citations incorporated in the text—the most common placement—there is little differentiation in terms of type face or punctuation. Here is a French citation within the text from 1706: "What can be done by means of the method I have published in 1699 for the solution of indeterminate questions, in accordance with what has been said about them in the Memoirs of the Academy in 1702, pag. 231, and in 1703 pag. 162" (1706-F277). From 1748, we have a similar English citation: "Having by your Permission, borrow'd N°. 182 of the *Transactions*, wherein is contained *An Essay towards an Universal Alphabet, by Mr.* Francis Lodwick *F. R. S.* I shall give a brief Account of it; and, in Obedience to your Commands at the last Meeting, endeavour to shew how it may be reduced into less Compass, and set in a plainer light" (1748-E052). Finally, we have the following in-text citation from a 1784 German article: "After this, one must add about 15″ to what will appear in Mr. Nouet's tables in the Connaissance de Temps for 1787, and to what Mr. Oriana gives, in the Milan Ephimerides for 1787" (1784-G252).

While citational format lacks uniformity, in most cases authors provide sufficient citational information to locate the source. Most books have author names and titles. Most journal articles have author names, journal names, and dates.

Finally, while the 18th-century articles seldom have a closely related string of citations in quick succession, we present an outlier illustrating that such organization was within the range of possibility:

> *Caesius*, in his Treatise *de Mineralibus*, p. 601. says, This stone is called *Turcoïs* by *Mylius*, in his Treatise of Minerals; and by *Rueius* in his Treatise of Gems; but *Turca*, by *Caussinus de Lapillis symbolicis. Dė Boodt*, and Dr. *Woodward*,* with other modern Writers, take it for the *Callaïs* of *Pliny. Salmasius*, in his *Plinian. Exercit.* p. 142,

11. Placement in the margins has almost completely disappeared: there are five French, one English, and no German instances of such marginalia.

says, Many have mistaken the modern *Turquoise* for the *Cyanus*, but that the *Cyanus* was transparent like the Saphire; whereas the *Turquoise* is a sort of Jasper.

*Method of *Fossils*. Letters, *p*. 17. (1747-E046; italics in original)

It is unlikely that 20th-century scientists, even geologists or botanists concerned primarily with taxonomical classifications, would have ancients and moderns hobnobbing in citations in so friendly a fashion. But it is not unusual for so many authorities to inhabit the same small space in the 20th century; however, a sophisticated reference system avoids the density and choppiness of the quoted passage.

Substantive Features

INTRODUCTIONS According to Cicero's *De Oratore* (1942), the purpose of introductions is to "attract the hearer straight away" (p. 315); to do so relevantly, the matter of the introduction "must not be drawn from some outside source, but from the very heart of the case" (p. 318). Moreover, "every introduction will have to contain either a statement of the whole of the matter that is to be put forward, or an approach to the case and a preparation of the ground" (p. 320). In modern scientific introductions, these Ciceronian precepts are embodied in John Swales's (1990) three principles: define an intellectual territory, establish a niche in it, occupy that niche. This three-part introduction is far more prevalent in the 18th century than it was in the 17th. Two thirds (67%) of 18th-century introductions follow these principles, if charitably interpreted. The breakdown by language is French, 83%; English, 55%; and German, 57%. Only 26% of the introductions possess none of the three introductory elements.

These data, however, mask the great diversity of our 18th-century introductions, as indicated by the examples quoted at the beginning of this chapter. Given this diversity, no illustration can be exemplary, though the following, from the German, represents a professional strain that is evident in geology, astronomy, and chemistry and will come to dominate most other disciplines in the 20th century:

> In Rozier's scientific journal* there is an excerpt from remarks concerning the so-called analysis of water carried out by Lavoisier, in which Giorgi and Cioni, two physicians from Florence, deny that inflammable air forms when water vapor is passed through glowing iron pipes, and even intend to write a book about it, in which they will contend that this experiment always produces a kind of air which is not inflammable, but is a substance intermediate between common and dephlogisticated air. But these gentlemen have just not replicated the experiment accurately; for I myself, and a number of people as well, find the correctness of the experiment of Lavoisier confirmed through their own experience, even though I am very far from adopting his theory and of finding in his work the correct analysis of water.

*Observations concerning Physics, etc. The y[ear] 1785. The m[onth] of July. (1786-G172)

This introduction replicates Swales's three stages, charitably interpreted. It places its author, Herr Riaproth, at the research front—he cites and reacts to a publication only a year old. His criticism is straightforward—he minces no words; nonetheless, he is neither rude nor rancorous. He asserts without qualification that he has by no means moved over to the anti-phlogistonist camp. If he does so move, he implies, it will be the result of a correct theoretical interpretation of properly done experiments. Presupposed is a science driven by theory.

CONCLUSIONS In the 18th century, article conclusions of one sort or another are frequent, though by no means obligatory: 42% in our sample have no conclusion at all.[12] About 30% approach current norms: adding insight, suggesting wider significance, making recommendations for future research. Of the English sample, only 27% have "complete" conclusions; the numbers are higher for the French and German samples, about 40% each.

Despite considerable variation—a degree of variation represented in the illustrative conclusions at this chapter's beginning—it is possible to find 18th-century conclusions in all three languages that closely approximate 20th-century norms. They do not represent a central tendency; they represent, rather, a tendency yet to become central. The first, in German, by Amberger, is also the most idiosyncratic:

> Because all vegetable acids are decomposed in acetic acid, it has been confidently assumed that the oxalic acid produced from acetic acid is a new substance; its phlogiston binds more intimately with its acidic part; heat or its hidden fire escapes and so forth; but this was a circular argument that current teaching obscured, rather than clarified. I believe it was for the best that we gave this position up, abandoned multiple names for the same substance, and simplified the teaching that concerns the vegetable acids.
>
> But I leave this task to our able analytical chemists, those who have made gains especially in the field of vegetable acids, among whom are Hermstädt and Westrumb, so very distinguished because of their learning and their unflagging diligence. (1787-G177)

In this conclusion, all idiosyncrasy is reserved for the final paragraph: the first is firmly within canonical limits, with its deliberate link to theory, its attempt to influence the future of the field, and its clear indication of a research program as a context for these experiments. In addition, there is an admirable reflexivity concerning arguments previously made, a critique of their logical structure indicative of a community thoughtful about its intellectual practices. In the final paragraph, the personal intrudes: we have deliberate deference to the efforts of two better-known chemists, a candor that would not now be regarded as relevant. This candor allows us to catch a glimpse of a professional community in a stage of rapid maturation and underlines the abiding importance of earned authority in science.

12. This percentage, however, somewhat exaggerates the degree of nonconformity. Two articles are extracts from letters (1719-E020, 1748-E051); three are simple narratives (1740-E038, 1751-E056, 1769-E072); 10 are astronomical observations (1734-E033, 1765-F392, 1774-G247, 1776-G470, 1777-G232, 1780-G227, 1783-G237, 1784-G252, 1787-G257, 1790-G262); three are taxonomical in nature (1711-E014, 1789-G222, 1794-F457). With these articles omitted, only 32% of 18th-century articles lack conclusions.

While the German Amburger displays confidence in his community, especially in its more prominent members, he defers to his betters. Not so George Pearson, the author of "Experiments and Observations, Tending to Show the Composition and Properties of Urinary Concretions." In his conclusion, Pearson defers only to science:

> I have not found the uric oxide in the urinary concretions of any phytivorous animal; but, whether it would be formed in the human animal when nourished merely by vegetable matter, must be determined by future observations. In the mean time, it is warrantable to conclude, from analogy, that it would not, and the application of this fact to practice is obvious; but I now purposely avoid making any practical inferences, until I can, at the same time, state a number of facts I have collected, relative both to concretions and to the urine itself. (1798-E107)

Pearson's caution is driven by his wish to follow his evidence and reasoning to its appropriate conclusions; his self-confidence arises from his membership in a community that justifies the value of his efforts.

Our third canonical conclusion comes from an article by Monsieur Venel, entitled "Memoir concerning the Analysis of Seltzer Water or of Seltz." It is addressed to a community whose primary focus is theory:

> Finally even the synthesis of aerated waters that I will report on in the second part of this memoir complements my proofs; because it is above all the impossibility of synthesizing them in this respect, which has been responsible for the received opinion of the character of the waters.
>
> It only remains for me to examine the essential characteristics of the sort of air contained in the *aerated* waters, to determine more precisely what I understand by its state of *super-abundance*, or of easily disrupted union; but this question will find its place most naturally in the second part of this memoir, after I have dealt with the synthesis of *aerated* waters. (1755-F487; italics in original)

While the introduction and conclusions quoted in this section converge in their seriousness of purpose, they diverge in the goals they set, a divergence not unconnected with national styles of doing science. The German Amburger seems content with existing theory, the English Pearson seems content without theory, the French Venel investigates his chosen phenomenon less for its own sake than for the light it sheds on theory. These are stereotypes, to be sure, but they are stereotypes for a good reason: they contain more than a measure of the truth.

VISUALS AND EQUATIONS While in the chapter on 18th-century argument (chapter 5) we deal with the crucial role of visual representations of different types in substantiating the claims of science, here we treat their relationship to the text that surrounds them and forms their explanatory context.

Tables and illustrations are present in four out of 10 scientific articles in the sample, a figure no different from the preceding century. The average number of such visuals in articles that contain them is 5.1. Whether an article contains one figure or 32 (the maximum in our 18th-century sample), their close integration with text is vital to comprehension; since neither tables nor illustrations display their full scientific significance in isolation, a clear link must be established between them and the words that give them that significance. Sometimes the integration is achieved simply. In a German article, we find the following sentence: "The aerated lime contains 32 parts in a hundred of carbonic acid, and the quantity of the lime precipitated by means of Pottasche and later heated red-hot (after withdrawal of the lime from the lime water) will be as follows" (1794-G192). A table, entitled "Report on the Parts of Coral Moss that have been Identified, with their Proportions," follows immediately.

Sometimes there is a more elaborate reference in the text, one that includes a numbering system: "When we look at the Sky towards the Zenith, we imagine it to be much nearer to us, than when we look at it towards the Horizon; so that it does not appear Spherical, according to the vertical Section EFGHI, (fig. 4) but Elliptical, according to Section eFghi" (1736-E037).

At other times, the burden of this information is too great for the text itself. In the following legend, placed before the illustration at the end of the French article, we have three paragraphs of elaboration: "The first figure, plate 2, represents a section of the two boilers in perspective. One sees at the back, A, D, & C, openings for the taps. Atop, there is a distilling tube, A, B, C, five inches in diameter in the case of A, and whose size diminishes to three inches in the case of C: the length from B to C is five feet . . ." (1779-F442). We stop here to spare the reader's patience.

Equations are easier to comprehend when they are treated, not as parts of the running text, but as units separated visually from that text by white space. This is because only by separation can the meaningful articulation of their elements be easily achieved. In the French case, at least by the eighth decade of the century, equations are almost invariably given this visual prominence. German and English practice varies; equations are just as likely as not to be separated by white space from the text.[13] No equations are numbered.

The difference white space can make, even without numbering, must be seen to be believed. Here is an English passage containing equations:

> In the Miscell. Analyt. a biquadratic, ($x^4 + 2px^3 = qx^2 + rx = s$, of which no term is destroyed) is reduced to a quadratic $x^2 + px + n = \sqrt{p^2 + 2n + qx} + \sqrt{s + n^2}$); and in the second edition of it, printed in the years 1767, 1768, 1769, and published in the beginning of the year 1770, the value of n are found $\frac{\alpha\beta + \gamma\delta}{2}$, $\frac{\alpha\gamma + \beta\delta}{2}$ and $\frac{\alpha\delta + \beta\lambda}{2}$; and the six values of $\sqrt{y^2 + 2n + q}$ respectively $\frac{\alpha + \beta - \gamma - \delta}{2}$, $\frac{\alpha + \gamma - \beta - \delta}{2}$, $\frac{\alpha + \delta - \beta - \gamma}{2}$, and their negatives; and the six values of $\sqrt{s + n^2}$ respectively $\frac{\alpha\beta - \gamma\delta}{2}$, $\frac{\alpha\gamma - \beta\delta}{2}$, $\frac{\alpha\delta - \beta\gamma}{2}$, and their negatives. (1784-E083)

13. As the sample of whole articles contained no equations in English or German articles, the sample of 10-line passages is used here for purposes of illustration.

With this passage, compare a passage in French in which equations are surrounded by white space:

> Let us take as the origin of the coordinates, f, g, h, the very center of the spheroid; let us call a, b, c the three demi-axes which we will assume parallel to the coordinates f, g, h; and let x, y, z be the coordinates of a point of the surface parallel to these axes; the equation of the surface of the spheroid is
>
> $$\frac{x^2}{a^2} + \frac{y^2}{b^2} + \frac{z^2}{c^2} = 1$$
>
> But if one calls R the radius vector appropriate to any point of the surface, one finds
>
> $$\begin{aligned} x &= f - R \sin.\, p \sin.\, q \\ y &= g - R \cos.\, p \sin.\, q \\ z &= h - R \cos.\, q. \end{aligned}$$
>
> (1788-F430)

The alignment of the equal signs in this last series of equations, an alignment with clear cognitive import, cannot be achieved if equations are treated like phrases or clauses and integrated into running text.

Conclusion

We have divided our book into centuries. But this move must be recognized for what it is: a hypostatization. Nothing of significance ends at the end of a century; nothing of significance begins at its beginning. While it is instructive to look at the first century of the scientific article—its first 35 years—it is also instructive to look at its first 135 years—from 1665 to 1800—as a single unit. Each perspective has its value. The first gives us the scientific article at its creation and emphasizes the birth of a medium designed to communicate ever more complex information about the natural world. The second perspective shows us that despite the existence of central tendencies in the scientific literature, there is much variety. Viewed through either perspective—two centuries or extended century—science in the 17th and 18th centuries seems like a moderately successful enterprise, a communicative network of hundreds and, later, thousands united in the enterprise of discovering new facts about the natural world and, on occasion, explaining them from a theoretical perspective.

In this chapter, we track three central tendencies that will remain through the 20th century. First, scientific style moves from the occasionally and overtly social and personal to the mostly impersonal. This transformation is achieved by a wide variety of means: fewer personal pronouns combined with more passive than active verbs, fewer literary expressions of any kind, and a drop in verbs that express the actions of humans as opposed to those of nature. Second, scientific style becomes more nominal than verbal. In this style, the complex noun phrase begins to replace the simple one in the subject position. Finally, presentational features move away from the bare minimum one would expect in a letter or news item. Evident in this transformation are a variety of formal elements for better displaying complex information (headings, figure captions, a numbering system for citations and visuals, etc) and of substantive elements that assist in reader comprehension (introductions that state and contextualize a research problem, conclusions that state and contextualize a new knowledge claim).

In the 18th-century samples we also detect some significant national differences in style and presentation. In general, compared with the English and German samples, the French sample scored lower on our measures of personal expression and higher when the components of a master finding and organizing system were at issue. In other words, the French approached 20th-century norms somewhat more closely than did the English or German samples. This is no accident: 17th-century French science was founded as a small-scale professional enterprise and largely remained so during the 18th century, while English science during the same period maintained a healthy amateur constituency mixed in with the professionals (Gascoigne 1995, Porter 1978). The English practice had the consequence that many of the communications to the Royal Society, and to other English scientific societies as well, were just that—letters directed to a learned group. As letters, their communicative practices were formed, primarily, by epistolary norms and, secondarily, by narrative ones.

Our German sample, which covers only the last three decades of the 18th century, appears, in the aggregate, closer to our English than to our French sample. That finding is perplexing, given that the three German journals in our sample are all specialized ones (chemistry, astronomy, and mining), catering to a professional rather than to an amateur audience. We attribute this apparent anomaly, in part, to a stronger polemical strain among the Germans, as compared with the gentlemanly English or French, but mostly to the fact that the enterprise of communicating science in written German is just getting off the ground and finding its way.

These national differences notwithstanding, in all three scientific communities at the end of the century, newer conventions are emerging and are in the process of replacing the old. But we do not want to leave the impression that there was a steady upward path of scientific communication toward 20th-century norms. Its sometimes hesitant, sometimes meandering path is appropriate to an evolving genre, an evolving vehicle for communication that in part reflects the cognitive and social changes of science in England and on the Continent.

CHAPTER 5

Argument in the 18th Century

In the French *Mémoires* of 1737, there appears an article by Geoffroy and Hunauld, "In which We Inquire Whether Olive Oil is a Cure for Snake Bite." It contains a passage that leads us to question whether our notions of scientific relevance and those of the French Academy coincide, even roughly:

> On September 27 at 3 in the afternoon, the aforementioned la Motte, the apothecary's assistant, a boy with a strong & vigorous constitution, went to the home of an English gentleman, to prepare a snake for a bouillon. When the box containing the snakes was opened, however, all escaped. The boy gathered up five, but the sixth hid on a pot near a terrine heating in the fireplace. This last snake, annoyed by the extreme heat, sprang at the index finger of the boy's left hand, & drew blood. (1737-F342)

The "English gentleman" has some knowledge of medicine and subsequently recommends snake fat as a cure. Whether it works or not is a medical question. But what is the purpose of the narrative details in this passage—the boy's name, his occupation, the date of the event, and its precise hour? The details, it might be said, add credibility to the account. Indeed, they do. But there is a price: the account is so vivid that the story of science seems submerged in the story of the boy. His fate hangs in the balance: did he live or die? And to the extent that this question is uppermost in our minds, we are not focused on the science involved, the presumed goal of the authors. As we know from our sample, such excursions into the personal

Table 5.1. Types of Whole Articles in 18th-Century Sample

Genre	*English* (n = 44)	*French* (n = 54)	*German*[a] (n = 28)
Experimental	14%	17%	10%
Theoretical	0	9	0
Methodological	18	9	4
Observational	30	22	53
Observational/theoretical	12	22	4
Experimental/theoretical	14	6	25
Mathematical	2	15	0
Other	10	0	4

[a]The first German article in our sample of 126 whole articles does not appear until 1774.

are not typical of 18th-century scientific argument, particularly in the French literature.

What, then, are the types of argument being made and the norms of argumentative relevance in 18th-century science?

General Profile

Comparing our data by type of article (tables 3.1 and 5.1), we find no dramatic change between the 17th and 18th centuries. Observational articles, with and without a theoretical component, dominate the pages of journals. Experimental, theoretical, methodological, and mathematical types all lag considerably behind.

There are some changes in the 18th century, however. While the heightened French interest in the abstract and conceptual is clear,[1] the English seem just as concerned as the French with experiments and with moving from observation and experiment to theory. In addition, both the English and French samples reflect a heightened interest in the experimental and methodological; articles also place about equal emphasis on quantification (see table 4.1) and visual argument. So, in general, differences we observed between French and English argument in the 17th century mostly vanish in the 18th century.

New to the last few decades of the 18th century are German-language scientific articles. Here we see two contrasting trends: a very strong orientation toward observation devoid of theory, and a movement from experiment to theory much more frequent than is the case with their French or English colleagues. But a lack of settled orientation might be expected in a scientific community in its early stages of formation.

1. In the French sample, an impressive 52% of articles either are mathematical or have an overt theoretical orientation; the corresponding numbers are 28% for the English and 29% for the German samples.

Table 5.2. Purpose of Whole Articles in 18th-Century Sample

	English (n = *44*)	*French* (n = *54*)	*German* (n = *28*)
Observational	31%	29%	50%
Experimental results	16	15	10
Mechanical explanation	18	13	24
Mathematical rule	5	15	0
Mathematical explanation	5	15	4
Making or improving equipment	20	13	8
Other	5	0	4

The data in table 5.2 on article purpose show a much greater interest in establishing observationally and experimentally derived facts than in explaining. They also reveal a substantial jump in articles whose main purpose is making or improving equipment, particularly among the English. These data tell us that 18th-century scientists argued for facts and argued explanations into place, but the full story requires much closer inspection of individual examples of argument in action, which we do next.

Arguing for Facts

One of the great French scientists and prose stylists of the 18th century, Comte de Buffon, proclaimed that acquiring facts for their own sake was no longer sufficient: "It is necessary to try to rise to something that is greater and more worthy of our time; it is necessary to combine observations, generalize the facts, link them through the power of analogies, and try to arrive at that high degree of knowledge where we can compare Nature with herself in her great operations, and where we can finally find ways to perfect the different parts of Physics" (quoted in Roger 1997, p. 83). Despite this ringing endorsement of theory, many of the rank-and-file scientists of the 18th century simply observe and experiment, eschewing inference. This is especially the case early in the century. The following passage, from one of the Comte de Buffon's countrymen, "Concerning Barometric Observations Made at Paris & Zurich During the First Six Months of 1708," is devoted solely to the establishment of two coordinate sets of facts for two locations several hundred miles apart—barometric readings and wind direction:

> The first of January, the barometer at the observatory read 27 inch[es], 5 lin[es]; the wind was from the south. At Zurich with the same wind the barometer was at 26 inch[es], 3 lin[es], so that the difference between the observatory and Zurich was 1 in[ch], 3 lin[es], the mercury at the observatory being the more elevated. The normal average difference is 1 i[nch], 4 li[nes]. After the first of January, the barometer in both places rose to the third of the month, and dropped until the 10th, a low at Paris of 26 inch[es], 10 1/2 lin[es]; at Zurich, of 25 inch[es], 11 lin[es], which are nearly the lowest readings for Paris as well as Zurich, where it fell around six lines.

> During this time, the wind at Paris was from the south or south-west; at Zurich at the same time it was almost always from the opposite direction, that is, from the north or north-west. (1709-F286)[2]

Although the observations of wind direction and barometric pressure are linked chronologically, no effort is made to find a causal relationship between them or between their differences in Paris and Zurich, though it is presumably the possibility of such relationships that motivates the inquiry. The argument is, simply, one of fact: facts attested to by Scheuchzer, the Swiss observer, and compared by the author, Maraldi, with observations of his own at Paris. These facts are objective; that is, barring errors on the part of the observers, their accuracy is warranted by the instruments designed to measure them and the credibility of the observers.

Viewed in isolation, this passage from a French article on volcanic discharges might seem similar in its avoidance of explanation:

> Mica is another one of the substances found incorporated in this genus of lava, though not as abundantly as in the following kinds. Many volcanoes that have argilo-ferruginous rocks as the basis of all their products, never produce any; such is Etna, among others; & I do not know to what to attribute this absence, mica being common enough in primitive rocks of the same sort. The mica contained in lavas is rarely found alone in its base; it is most often interspersed with some other substance. Lavas of this sort are therefore not very numerous.
>
> The mica of lavas is black or brown; sometimes there are glints of gold or bronze coloring. Most often it is scattered in irregular leaves, more or less numerous, from very small indeed up to an inch wide; on rare occasions, these leaves gather together in order to form parts of a hexagonal prism three to four lines in height. (1794-F457)

Similarities between these two passages certainly exist: the descriptive style, the focus on details ordinary observation might miss. There is also a parallel disinclination to engage in speculation, to go beyond exact description: a puzzling absence of mica is noticed, but no explanation is forthcoming. Despite these similarities, however, the context of the current passage radically alters its import. The article is entitled "Continuation of a Memoir Meant to *Explain* the Systematic Distribution of All Volcanic Products" (emphasis added). The passage cited concerns one volcanic product, "Lavas with mica." This product is, we learn, in "First Order, First Division, First Family." In this genus, it is the "Ninth Species." The recorder is now a systematist in search of an explanation.

A science devoted to recording such facts as these needs to warrant their reliability. At its least reflective, this concern is seen in the practice of witnessing. An article by John Fothergill, "Observations on a Case Published in the Last Volume of the *Medical Essays*, &c. of Recovering a Man Dead in Appearance, by Distending the Lungs with Air," relates an incident that took place in a French street:

2. We might think that for this information a table would be far more perspicuous: its absence makes the point of this passage far harder to discern.

> A Person suffocated by the nauseous Steam arising from Coals set on Fire from the Pit, fell down as dead; he lay in the Pit between half an Hour and three Quarters; and was then dragg'd up; his Eyes staring and open, his Mouth gaping wide, his Skin cold; not the least Pulse in either Heart or Arteries, and not the least Breathing to be observed.
>
> In the Circumstances, the Surgeon who relates the Affair, applied his Mouth close to the Patient's, and, by blowing strongly, holding the Nostrils at the same time, raised his Chest fully by his Breath. The Surgeon immediately felt six or seven very quick Beats of the Heart; the Thorax continued to play, and the Pulse was soon after felt in the Arteries. He then opened a Vein in his Arm, which, after giving a small Jet, sent out the Blood in Drops only for a Quarter of an Hour, and then he bled freely. In the mean time he caused him to be pull'd, push'd, and rubb'd, as much as he could. In one Hour the Patient began to come to himself; within four Hours he walked home; and in as many Days returned to his Work.
>
> There were many Hundred People, some of them of Distinction, present at the time. (1745-E046; italics omitted)

Two facts assist in the reader's assent to this tale of Lazarus raised from the dead: it is the testimony of a French surgeon, and it was witnessed by hundreds, some of whom were gentlemen who would not, out of honor, participate in a fraud.

Serendipitous witnessing, however, was not the only kind; there were invited audiences as well. The Royal Society was an audience for experiments reported in one article (1705-E007). In the German states, G. F. Hilderbrandt also addresses general as well as professional audiences: "Those experiments that I performed only casually before others, I repeated before my professional colleagues." Moreover, in the case of the latter, he increases his credibility by means of audience participation: "Hence for the time being I prepared the nitrogen from niter with the help of two members of my audience, Mr. Pröbsting, a student pursuing the doctorate, and Mr. von Rappard" (1796-G135).

But suppose no witnesses for warranting were available? A French article by Messier entitled "Memoir Containing the Observations of the 17th Comet observed at Paris from the Naval Observatory, from January 18, 1779 to May 17, 1779" illustrates one method for warranting facts in these cases:

> The 27th, weather as beautiful as yesterday, the moon was on the horizon, and the comet appeared in the evening on a course parallel to that of the nebula in Berenice's Hair, which I had discovered February 27, 1777; here is what I said about this nebula in my notebook: "A nebula in Berenice's Hair, which is clearly visible with a telescope: it is more or less round, & does not seem to be composed of stars; its light is dim; this nebula had not risen above the horizon when I discovered it, & I determined its position by comparing it to the forty-second star in Berenice's Hair, of the fourth to the fifth magnitude, following Flamsteed's Catalogue; here is the position, determined for February 27, 1777; its right ascension was $195^{d}\ 30'\ 26''$ & its declination $19^{d}\ 22'\ 44''$ north." (1779-F419)

In this passage, Messier is in effect his own witness; he divides himself in two: his present self, the writer of the article, and his past self, the recorder of the facts in his notebook. His credibility is enhanced because he attests publicly to his avoidance of the distortions of memory.

But not only memory distorts; the sense organs are also culprits—a factor of special concern in 18th-century astronomical observations. In the following passage, from a French article entitled "Observation of the Opposition of Jupiter with the Sun, January 4, 1765; and Corrections that Need to be made in Monsieur Cassini's Tables," a new source of difficulty emerges:

> So little attentive are we to what is happening within us that our sensations appear to us instantaneous; they seem to us to vanish almost as soon as they have been aroused. But these sensations subsist: we sense the burning spark even after it has been extinguished & we believe that we see objects when they have already disappeared; our sensations survive, if the matter can be put this way, for a definite period after the actions that give birth to them; but it is easy to imagine that this effect can cause many errors, some of which can be important. A detailed examination of these errors relative to our different sense organs would doubtless be very interesting, but in this memoir I propose to speak only of those that result from the duration of visual sensations. (1765-F392)

The degree of reflexivity exhibited in this passage represents an advance over that of Cassini in a passage cited in our chapter on 17th-century argument. In the earlier case, the comparative powers of resolution of the human eye and the telescope were at issue; in this case, at issue is the problem that telescopic observation also relies on the human eye with all its defects as an instrument. Moreover, the author recognizes that this truth applies to all of the senses; we must be ever alert to their power to deceive.

In an English astronomical article by Nevil Maskelyne, entitled "Concerning the Latitude and Longitude of the Royal Observatory at Greenwich," we see a further advance in the pursuit of factual reliability, a reflexive account of instrumental difficulties:

> Now the legitimacy of this conclusion depends upon a supposition that both instruments measured the true angle, or that their total arcs were justly laid off, and that the ABBÉ DE LA CAILLÉ'S table of refractions is just. The first indeed has been proved with respect to DR. BRADLEY'S quadrant, but never has been attempted with respect to the ABBÉ DE LA CAILLE'S sextant; for the examination which the Abbé made of his instrument by parts for every 7°1/2 (see Memoires of the Royal Academy of Sciences for 1751 p. 405), could not determine the error of the whole arc, as the differences from the truth might be insensible upon such small arcs, and the examination seems to have been intended to find the differences of these small arcs from one another rather than from the true arc which they represent. (1787-E088)

To be precise is to measure against a standard: a meter stick is capable of more precision if it is divided into millimeters than into centimeters. To be accurate, on the other hand, is correctly to measure the length of a real object (or the force of a real effect). These factors operate independently. In the passage cited, Maskelyne shows his awareness of the problem; it is the basis of his criticism of the Abbé de la Caille. According to Maskelyne, the Abbé's means of obtaining precision was irrelevant to the accuracy of his results; Bradley, on the other hand, used an instrument properly calibrated to suit the problem at hand.

The distinction between precision and accuracy at play in this passage is fundamental if the sciences are to be erected on a factually reliable footing, a footing based on accurate and precise instrumental readings. It is no surprise, therefore, that in the 18th century we find a steep rise in articles concerning the improvement in equipment—500% in the English case, 650% in the French—a rise accompanied by a doubling of tables and visuals supportive of this improvement.

In the case of experiments, as distinct from observations, replicability appears to be the main criterion of reliability, at least later in the century. Take Richard Kirwan's English article "Conclusion of the Experiments and Observations Concerning the Attractive Powers of Mineral Acids":

> Thus, in his first vol. p. 137. [Bergman] says, that 100 grs. of vitriol of iron contains 23 of iron, 39 of vitriolic acid, and 38 of water. But in his treatise *De Productis Vulcanicis*, § 12. he says, that 100 grs. of vitriol of iron contain 24 of iron, 24 of *dephlegmated* vitriolic acid, and 52 of water; and this last calculation scarcely differs from mine, as I assign to 100 grs. of vitriol 25 of iron, 20 of real vitriolic acid, and 55 of water. The difference manifestly arises from the quantity of water still contained in his dephlegmated acid. The most material difference between us regards the quantity of the mineral acids taken up by alkalies; for, according to his and Mr. SCHEFFER'S experiments, they take up more of the vitriolic than of the nitrous, and more of the nitrous than of the marine; whereas, according to Mr. HOMBERG'S, Dr. PLUMMER'S, Mr. WENZEL'S, and my experiments, this does not happen. This difference arises in all probability from the different degrees of evaporation by which the crystals of these salts are obtained; for which reason I did not examine the quantity of the crystals, which must be variable, but that of dry salt, left after through evaporation. With regard to the quantity of earth and metallic basis in different salts, Mr. BERGMAN'S experiments and mine agree almost intirely. (1783-E082)

"Dephlegmation" is the removal of water from substances. If 15 grains of the 39 of vitriolic acid, mentioned in the first sentence, are really water, if the acid is only incompletely dephlegmated, as Kirwan believes, his numbers resolve the problem set by Bergman's inconsistent results. But while those whose analyses agree with his outnumber those whose analyses disagree, he is not describing a democratic process, that is, one in which the majority rules. Replicability is criterial; it shifts the burden away from personal trust. This shift is a crucial precondition of professionalization, because it democratizes science in the sense that the right to vote depends on a demonstration of expertise rather than mere participation. Replication works by comparing the results of various reliable investigators doing the same thing, a likeness guaranteed by methodological rigor. That is Kirwan's point: he implies that, properly replicated, his experiment will always turn out his way.

In the French "New Observations concerning the Nature & Saline Properties of Zinc, in its Metallic Form, or Reduced in Lime," De Lassone also recognizes some of the complexities of methodological rigor in his chemical experiments:

> On one part of zinc in iron filings, I poured six parts of volatile alkali in solution, freed from sal ammoniac by fixed alkali; this saline solution was completely saturated. In the flask from which I had drawn it, there surfaced a considerable amount

> of concrete volatile alkali, & I had taken care to use it just after it had been prepared in my laboratory: the activity and the surprising [*surprenans*] effects of this solute that will soon be revealed depend crucially on its complete saturation, its concentration, & its use immediately after its preparation, when it still possesses all its subtlety, its strength, and its energy, that without these absolutely necessary conditions, one never obtains the results I am going to describe, and that I have demonstrated by repeated and varied tests. (1775-F409)

By asserting that methodological rigor is central to the epistemology of experimentation, and by extending the concept of rigor to encompass the state of his reagents, De Lassone has turned late-18th-century chemistry into a science in the 20th-century sense. We see this criterion reflected in German chemistry as well: "When chemical experimentation is considered, one of the most important requirements in each case is the complete purity of the reagents needed" (1796-G161; similar statement in 1789-G179).

It is as a consequence of this increased rigor that De Lassone earns the right to call his results "surprising." They are surprising in a quite ordinary sense for science, the sense in which all interesting experimental results are surprising—sometimes to the experimenter who did not expect them, always for readers for whom they must be news. Surprise, of course, was always a criterion of interesting science, but in the modern era, beginning in the last quarter of the 18th century, science domesticates and democratizes surprise.

The professionalization of trust is evident in these illustrations. There is a definite movement toward a new set of criteria that will become fully operational in later scientific arguments. In the 18th century, this movement is represented by a rise in the standards for reporting and systematizing observations and warranting experimental results.

Arguing Explanations into Place

In "Experiments concerning a Mineral related to Potassium Ferrocyanide; Especially Concerning its Relationship to Baryta, and to other Earths," Stouth makes what seems at first to be a dismissal of the descriptive as a subject of scientific inquiry:

> The "wet way" is one of the most useful chemical discoveries with everyday applications, particularly by those who work in metallurgy. For the mineral kingdom, in so far as the knowledge of its substances is limited only to features visible to the naked eye, can give an experienced miner, metallurgist, or eager student of nature no more than a hint of important discoveries; however, in no way can the examination of externals lead to conclusions worthy of science. (1787-G148)

This is not, on careful reading, a denigration of descriptive mineralogy and geology; rather, it is a programmatic statement about the quest for *chemical* knowledge relevant to geology. The "wet way," the reactions of reagents in solution, is, according to Stouth, the only path to this knowledge; appearances are, at best, an index to underlying *chemical* structure.

Throughout the 18th-century sample, such causal analyses crop up regularly, for example, explanations of temperature variations in terms of wind direction (1725-F315), cardiac function in terms of the structure of the heart (1752-F369), earthquakes in terms of subterranean water pressure (1760-F061), volcanic action in terms of the combined action of fire and water (1793-G213). In all of these instances, cause operates by means of immediate physical contact: the wind sweeps the hot air away, the structure of the heart constrains cardiac circulation, the water's action lifts the earth, water and fire account for volcanic action.

Despite these likenesses, there are significant differences among this class of causal-mechanical explanations, as the following two geological passages illustrate. In the first, from a French article, entitled "Description of a Small Extinct Volcano whose Summit is Under the Village & Chateau of Montferrier," the past is reconstructed from present evidence:

> The eruption of the Montferrier volcano was limited to the same terrain as the hillock; everything indicates that it did not last long and that it was not repeated; it is on the western side that the most considerable streams of dense lava are found. I saw two of them about ten or twelve meters wide. The dense lava that cooled on the north side occupies a far narrower space; this lava, to which the term *basalt* properly applies, is the product of the eruption at its greatest force; it crossed whatever matter was first spewed out, and covered it; this first matter is gravelly & often lacking a definite structure. (1779-F420)

From the facts on the ground, the author, Joubert, infers that there was only one eruption, that it took place in two stages: one during which the volcanic matter was gravelly and formless, and another, more powerful, during which basalt was formed. In this passage, the object of study has shifted from the phenomenon to its origin. As a consequence, the phenomenon itself has changed its nature: it has become evidence for a geologic event that, in the nature of things, cannot be directly experienced. Still, this passage is not causal in any deep sense. It does not aspire to universality: it concerns not volcanoes, but *this* volcano. Moreover, it does not purport to explain the phenomenon at its most fundamental level.

Contrast Joubert's limited strategy of causal-mechanical explanation with that of the following passage from our German sample:

> It seems in fact that the great force of these ancient volcanoes depends on this circumstance: that frequently water, which penetrated to their seat of fire, increased the ferment in it, without completely putting it out, the returning flood surprising the still glowing lava, and permitting a normal accumulation, which a sudden cooling caused.
>
> The development of my views, the collection of facts that could make them more probable, the application of the causes on which I am working to countless individual circumstances, would require a large volume. (1793-G213)

This reconstruction of the mechanical cause of vulcanism is highly speculative, to say the least. What evidence is there for the internal ferment? Nonetheless, the author is well aware of its speculative nature; that is the point of his promise of more research. Although we have reason to be skeptical about such pleas (so frequently excuses for the shortcomings of current research), we recognize that his hypothesis will gain credibility only by means of the program he proposes; further, even were his program no more than a verbal gesture, its mention indicates that the community in question values, not description only, but also causal explanations at the deepest level, explanations that are both universal and fundamental.

Causal-mechanical explanations are not limited to geology. In a biological article entitled "Observations on the Aesters [the genus of which house flies are a species]," Bracy Clark, the scientist whose research is being reported in the third person, concludes that he has found the "lungs" of the insect:

> Among the features that the dissection of the larvae presented to him, he noticed the impressive branching of their tracheae, which seemed to be injected with mercury, although they contained only air. From these vessels stem not less than ten principal trunks that meet at a common reservoir; these are without a doubt the lungs of the insect &, considered as such, they have a volume proportionally far greater than that of the respiratory organs of any other animal. If this was indeed their function, one might well be taken aback [*s'étonner*] by the received opinion, which attributes to respiration the production of animal heat; because assuredly these larvae, living among high temperatures already, have no need of an organ dedicated to producing heat; and this organ disappears when they pass into the states of chrysalis & of adult insect. (1798-F458)

The respiratory system of this insect, Clark infers, is not used to maintain its body heat. Its environment requires no such system; moreover, in its transformation to chrysalis and to fly, the larva loses this system altogether. But if the respiration system does not regulate body heat in fly larvae, one can no longer blindly assume that it has this function in other insects. In proclaiming this result, Clark claims that those who believe "received opinion" ought not to be merely surprised; they should be astonished, taken aback (*s'étonner*); in the root sense, they should be thunderstruck. Unlike the surprise in the passage by De Lassone analyzed above (1775-F409)—expressed by a different word in French, *surprenans*—to be astonished in this case is to signal a serious criticism of the reasoning power of previous anatomists and physiologists as they form explanations that are fundamental to their discipline.[3]

Of course, just which level is "fundamental" varies legitimately from discipline to discipline. In the chemistry passage below, Pfepenbring shows his awareness of this important principle. He is concerned with the action of coal in the purification of reagents, specifically the removal of phlogiston from various substances by heating:

> "In my opinion, when it works, coal-dust operates mechanically, certainly not chemically" [thus Professor Klaproth]. I confess I believe that, on the contrary, it oper-

3. Clark's article is also an attempt by a *veterinary* surgeon to assert the value of comparative anatomy, to assert that his conclusions are salient when matters of general physiology are in question. Perhaps his lower professional status accounts somewhat for the edge of aggressiveness he displays toward his opponents.

> ates chemically. If coal operated mechanically, then all bodies could be purified for the most part by treatment with coal without being roasted over and over, indeed to the fullest extent possible. But in fact, e.g., potassium acetate, various other salts and liquids, can be purified only then, or rather the process of dephlogistification is guaranteed to succeed only if the coals are fully roasted over and over. This in my opinion is a chemical operation. The more coals themselves are freed from phlogisticated parts, the more capable they are of again drawing phlogisticated parts to them. (1792-G149)

Pfepenbring's argument concerning whether the process is mechanical or chemical is straightforward: since coal enables dephlogistication, and dephlogistication is a chemical process, coal functions chemically in these reactions. The distinction is vital: it asserts that chemistry is a separate science in that it has its own class of fundamental explanations, very different from the fundamental explanations of physics or geology.

Although Pfepenbring differs from Professor Klaproth on fundamental matters, he shares with his fellow scientist a reliance on a fundamental theoretical entity, phlogiston, as a way of explaining an experimental result. What is the nature of such theoretical entities? For elucidation, let us look at an article by Klaproth, "Concerning the Denial of the Generation of Inflammable Air [hydrogen] from Steam and Iron, etc." In this article, he employs two theoretical explanatory entities: caloric, the principle of heat, and phlogiston, the principle of inflammability:

> The aqueous vapour is, so to speak, supersaturated with pure caloric, which happens when it is driven through substances heated until they glow, from which at the same time the inflammable principle cannot be taken; as a consequence, no inflammable air [hydrogen] is formed, but only ordinary dephlogisticated air [oxygen]. Messrs. Giorgi and Cioni have also erred in this regard; they did not heat their iron tubing until it was hot enough. It follows that the phlogiston in the iron did not free itself sufficiently, and this escape is exactly what would have happened had they directed the aqueous vapor only through heated tubing of clay or glass. (1786-G172)

Klaproth is in search of what went wrong with the experiment that is his focus. Only then will he be able to demonstrate how to proceed correctly and obtain the desired result. The key, he says, is procedural: Giorgi and Cioni have not heated the iron to a temperature high enough to precipitate the caloric from its supersaturated state. So precipitated it can, in its turn, allow the inflammable principle, phlogiston, to act. As a consequence, inflammable air, or hydrogen, is released, rather than dephlogisticated air, or oxygen. Phlogiston and caloric have for Klaproth an explanatory force: they allow him to make an argument. Without their aid, he has no means of interpreting Giorgi and Cioni's experiment; without their aid, the experiment has no proper scientific meaning.

Caloric and phlogiston may be fruitfully compared with "mutual attraction," a fundamental force susceptible to mathematization. In 1789 there appears in the German *Astronomisches Jahrbuch* a piece by Gerstner entitled "Concerning the Needed Improvement in the Observations of Uranus, Owing to the Mutual Attraction of Saturn and Jupiter, with the Aim of Having a More Accurate Calculation of the Constituents of its True Elliptical Orbit." The article, which appeared originally in French, and is therefore an expression of interests common to both scientific communities, concerns the use of Newtonian attraction to account for the motions of the newly discovered planet Uranus:

> Owing to these mutual alterations, which the calculation of the perturbation in the elliptical path of this planet reveals, a process that also works in reverse, I thought it a good idea once more to perform this calculation, and will now calculate the constituents of the planet's orbit, according to the method of de la Place.—At the same time, I looked into whether perhaps the mutual influence of Jupiter and Saturn itself did not produce some anomalies in the path of the new planet. It is clear in advance that from the existing observations it will not be possible to fix all of the anomalies with exactitude while nevertheless this calculation teaches us everything that Newtonian attraction can say about the movement of this planet, and what in any event must have come to pass, if we would really have had the observations of several centuries before us, and had wished to shed light on their anomalies. (1789-G223)

As did Klaproth, Gerstner wants to explain a phenomenon by means of theory, in this case a theoretical force, mutual attraction. The difference is that this force can be translated directly into the language of mathematics, creating a description that applies to a wide range of phenomena: the relationships among bodies that create the planetary orbits and, in particular, the anomalies in those orbits that result from the fact that Uranus's orbit is perturbed by the masses and consequent attractions of Jupiter and Saturn. The translation into mathematics allows Gerstner to argue that his result would have been the same whether he took his measurements now or had relied, counterfactually, on accurate measurements from the past centuries.

We see this same explanatory strategy within a Newtonian framework in a French article by Clairaut entitled "Memoir concerning the Apparent Orbit of the Sun around the Earth, Taking into Consideration the Perturbations Produced by the Actions of the Moon and the Principal Planets." In this case, however, the universality of the result as a consequence of mathematization is even more clearly emphasized:

> *Comparison of the preceding formulas with those that have been given.*
>
> When we now compare the value of *A* from § I and that of *B*, which results from § II, with the values that we find for these quantities (*p. 30* of Mr. Euler's treatise), we will see that, in limiting *n* to a multiple of 4, & in changing the series of the cosines into that of the cosines [sines?], which amounts to no more than taking it in the opposite sense, we will see, I say, that my expressions revert to those that this author has arrived at only by induction & without demonstration.
>
> An advantage of the preceding formula is in the universality of the construction that it achieves, a universality such that we can apply it to the functions of *t* more complicated than the one we have treated until now. In the case in which the law of the function is not even given algebraically, in those cases in which the curve which one expresses is only represented by several points, our manner of solving the series is as easily applicable. (1754-F375)

Induction from observation has a well-defined role in Clairaut's science: it is a heuristic aid only, employing the astronomical data to discover the general laws whose mathematical character permits derivation and demonstration. Subsequent to the formation of these general laws, this same range of data tests their truth; induction, having already served its purpose, is discarded as a method. This shift in relative importance permits Clairaut to say that universality is "an advantage" of his methods; rather, we would say, it is *the* advantage.

Clairaut uses a second phrase of interest: the final three words "as easily applicable." He does not mean that his mathematics are easy; he means, rather, that to do the science he does, astronomers will have to learn the appropriate mathematics. And not only astronomers: 18th-century mathematization is not confined to astronomy and optics (1767-F394), their traditional homes. We find it in chemistry (1794-G165); we find it in the physics of impact (1726-F317), the motion of water (1730-F327), and spherical motion (1790-E095); we find it in probability (1789-E091) and in economics (1789-G220). The increasing penetration of mathematics into scientific argument rings the death knell of the scientific amateur.

The use of theoretical entities and forces in constructing the arguments that count as scientific explanations leads to an interest in their alleged properties, but not, paradoxically, in their reality. This is not to say that 18th-century scientists do not believe in this reality, only that its discovery and specification are not, generally, their tasks. Given the means of investigation available at the time, it was perhaps best that they held such matters in abeyance. This studied disregard eventually deepens into a skepticism about the reality of fundamental theoretical entities such as atoms, a skepticism that persists until the early 20th century, when the mathematical, observational, and experimental tools became available that would reveal the reality of such entities.

Arguing with Tables and Figures

In article after article, 18th-century arguments reach a point at which words will no longer suffice; only a table, a likeness, a schematic, or a mathematical depiction will do. Among the 53 articles with visuals in our subsample for this century, 42% have tables; 30%, likenesses; 32%, schematics; and 23% depict mathematical relations. These are not merely illustrative; they all have roles crucial to argument.

Our examples illustrate the range of possibilities for establishing a fact, making a prediction, and proffering an explanation. Our first example is a likeness (figure 5.1), an engraving of a shell found attached to a beached whale. The illustration has all of the realism of the Dutch school; the object even casts a shadow. But as science the visual is defective in two respects, considering the avowed purposes of its English author. He wants to describe not only the outside of this shell, but also its inside. Speaking of the prominent striated tubes, he says: "All the Tubes are hollow in the inside, making cavities betwixt the Lines, both simple and branched, which compose them. They arise from the Orifice in the middle of the inner part of the Shell, and proceed toward the sides of it" (1706-E008). In this case, words alone must

Figure 5.1. Engraving of a shell found attached to a beached whale, from an English article published in 1706

serve: the artist does not depict what the author describes; he cannot do so and be true to the artistic conventions he deploys.

The situation is only slightly better in the case of the shell's external details. While depicted, they are not differentiated by labeling or by sufficient visual contrast; consequently, the eye must sort them out from the complex configuration of which they are an integral part. It is no easy task, for example, to identify the arms of the animal inhabiting the shell: "There is a cavity betwixt all of them, in which the *Cirrhi* or Arms of the Animal are probably placed, tho in this subject they stood in the middle of the upper part of the shell, with their ends contracted as the Figure showeth them; for the upper Orifice is deeper than the lower. They were altogether within it, but we raised them with the Leg of a Compass to the posture that they appear in the Figure" (1706-E008).

Readers have more visual acuity than we if they can immediately discern, between the two upraised claws, a set of crossed arms, the one laid over the other. Such difficulties have epistemic implications: the credibility of this illustration as science rests squarely on the close coordination of visual depiction and verbal description.[4]

4. Further hampering the "reading" of this figure is an accidental factor: owing to 18th-century printing limitations, it is only one figure on a plate not paginated with its article, a plate that contains another figure illustrating another article. This latter figure, as it happens, visually overwhelms the smaller illustration of the marine specimen.

Regardless of deficiencies, however, this illustration largely serves its central scientific purpose: it is an argument of fact; it establishes the existence of the creature it depicts. Nevertheless, it cannot be said to be an "improvement" over the illustration of the strangled fetuses that we used as our 17th-century example; clearly, the quality of scientific illustration still depends heavily on accidents of talent, rather than on a set of well-established conventions.

Our remaining examples illustrate the tendency of visual representations "to become more formalized and theory-laden in the course of time" (Rudwick 1976, p. 183). Our first such example, an English table, also establishes a fact: the longitude of an island off the coast of Brazil, calculated by means of an eclipse. To obviate any criticisms concerning the accuracy of the observations from which he will derive his data, Captain Legge calibrates his watch, then sends one of his officers with a second telescope over to the island of St. Catherine's, so the observations made on shipboard may be checked against those made ashore, and their combined result compared with those from the Greenwich Observatory. Between Greenwich and Brazil there is a difference of six minutes, an error accounted for by the haze at the horizon, masking the eclipse's beginning from the Captain and his ship's officer. The way in which the two sets of data appear on the page facilitates their comparison and highlights the small but significant difference between them:

> This Eclipse was observed at the Island of *St. Catherine*, on the Coasts of *Brasil* and the Captain places said Island in Latitude 27°30′. Mr. *Gael Morris* calculated the said Eclipse; and the Middle of it, apparent Time, at *Greenwich* was,

		h.	′	″
		11.	44	50.
By the Captain's Observations, supposing the Beginning Exact, }		8.	27.	30.
Difference of Meridian		3.	17.	20.
	= 49°	20′		
		h.	′	″
The End of it, by Calculation at *Greenwich*}		13.	06.	57.
——— by Captain *Legge's* Observation		9	50.	00.
Difference of Meridian		3.	16.	57.
	= 49°	14′		

(1741-E042; italics in original)

After taking these measurements, we learn, Captain Legge lost his way "attempting to pass Cape *Horn*." Why? Because his map contained serious errors, which can be corrected now that the exact position of St. Catherine's has been established beyond a doubt: "By comparing the Longitude at *St. Catherine's* as above settled, with *Senex*'s Maps, the Coasts appear to be placed about 6 Degrees too much Eastward and if the other Parts of *America* about the Cape are laid down as faultily in the Charts, this Error will probably account for [Captain Legge's] misfortunes."

Bruno Latour's (1987) remarks about centers of calculation seem pertinent in connection with this example: he thinks of such things as eclipse measurements, tables that determine meridians, and maps derived from these tables as "stable, mobile and combinable elements that allow a centre to dominate foreign lands" (p. 224). Applying Latour's observation to the quoted passage, we can envision the long arm of science advancing from eclipse calculations to inference, from inference to cartography, from cartography to British sea power, and finally, from British sea power to imperial control.

Our next visual example, from the German states, shifts from the establishment of facts to their prediction. It is a series of 10 representations of the occultation of the stars by the moon. These are not likenesses; rather, they are schematic depictions of only the scientifically relevant details—the phase of the moon and the position of the relevant heavenly bodies. The moon is not realistically depicted. It is a simple ellipsoid, its phase represented by blackening its unlit portion. The visual as a whole has a title, and each representation is carefully labeled. The representation we have chosen (figure 5.2), the second from the left in a row of six similar representations, illustrates "the conjunction of the moon and Venus on the afternoon of 31 August." The beginning of occultation is labeled "IV:32"; its end, "V:15":

> On the 31st of August Venus will be obscured for the most part by day in Greenland, on the Atlantic, in Great Britain, Spain and Portugal, France, Germany, Italy, Turkey, Asia Minor, Arabia and Egypt. At Berlin the entrance is at the moon's dark eastern rim at 4:32, two hours after the moon has reached its height in the sky. At 4:53 Venus is at the center of the moon nearest to 13′ n[orth], and at 5:15 Venus' exit begins at the moon's illuminated westerly edge. (1780-G227)

Note that the first verb in the passage is future tense: these are not astronomical observations but predictions, depictions of events that have not yet happened; they are fully the creatures of a theory of the motions of the moon and Venus. They do not merely illustrate the author's argument; they enact it.

Our next example shifts from establishing and predicting facts to explaining them. In "An Experimental Inquiry into the Cause of the Permanent Colours of Opake Bodies," published in the *Memoirs of the Manchester Literary and Philosophical Society*, Edward Hussey Delaval examines and finds wanting Newton's conjecture in the *Opticks* that reflected light is the "true reason" for all colors, including the colors of opaque bodies. His is not, according to Delaval, an argument against authority. Newton recognized his idea as a conjecture, subject to experimental proof. Delaval thinks that experiment supports rather a different "law," the law that the color of opaque bodies has transmitted light as its cause. Indeed, he asserts that transmitted light is the cause of all sensations of color.

His experimental apparatus is simple indeed, a collection of small flasks with rectangular bodies and long cyclindrical necks filled with different-colored liquids. The liquids in these flasks can serve as a convenient, easily manipulated experimental model for all colors because "for the most part, the tinging Particles of liquors, or other Transparent Substances, are extracted from Opake Bodies [and] the Opake Bodies owe their colors to those particles in like manner as the Transparent Substances do" (1789-E117).

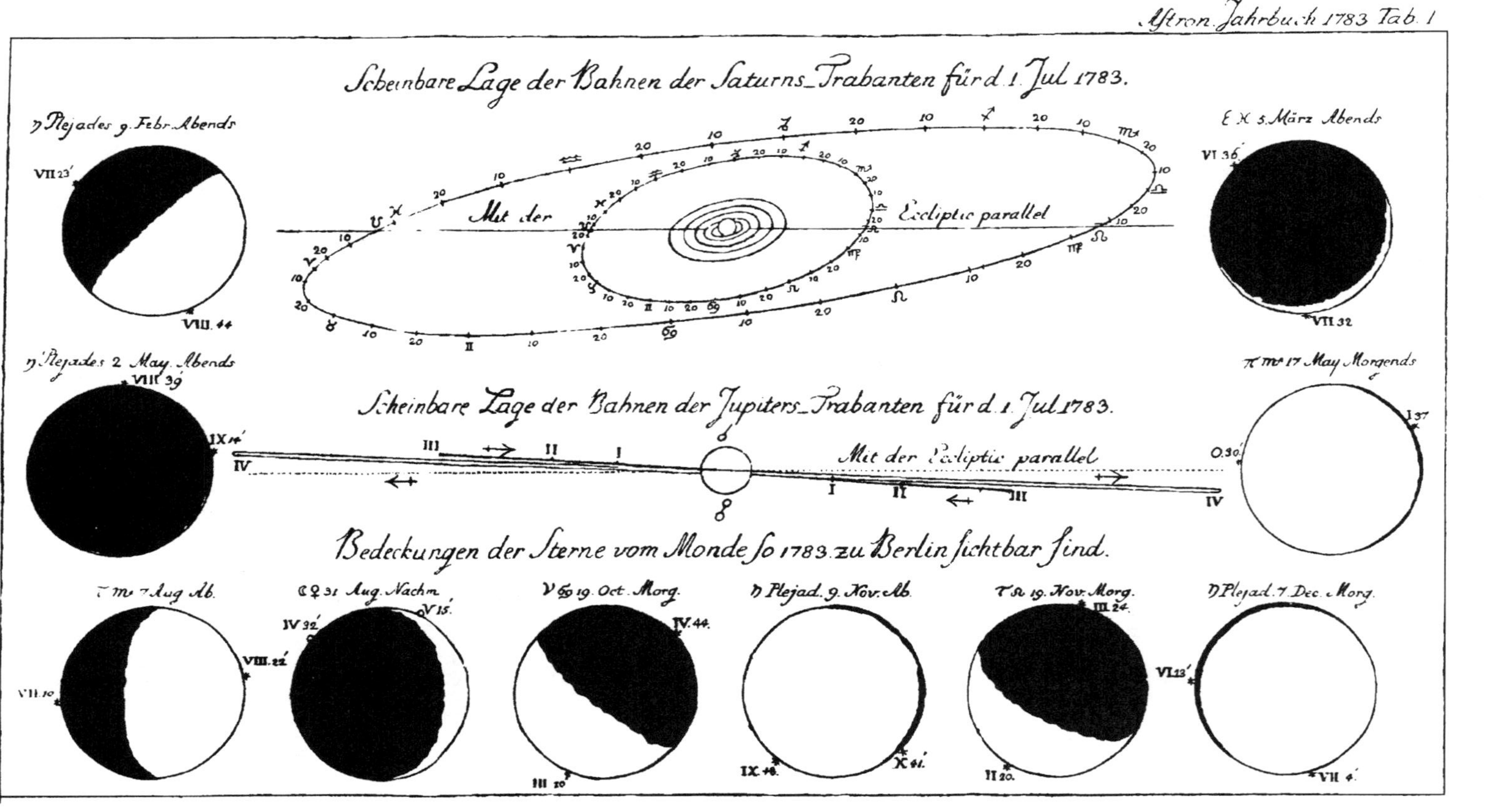

Figure 5.2. Illustration of "the conjunction of the moon and Venus on the afternoon of 31 August," from a German article published in 1780

Figure 5.3. Illustration of a flask from Edward Husse Delaval, "An Experimental Inquiry into the Cause of the Permanent Colours of Opake Bodies" (1789)

In the realistic depiction of the flask (figure 5.3), the neck and body are labeled A and B. Three of the four sides of the body of the flask are painted black; only the fourth side and the neck of the flask are transparent. The flasks are filled with various colored liquids and are placed sequentially at right angles to a window, and "in every instance, that part of the liquor, which was contained in the neck of the vials, exhibited its colour distinctly and vividly, but, that portion, which was in the body of the vials, and which was viewed through the uncovered side, *exhibited no colour,* but was *black*" (1789-E117; italics in original). To Delaval, this means that transmitted light is the only cause of sensations of color. His summary is followed by a confirming table, 68 instances in which transmitted light was one vivid color or another, while what Delaval calls "incident light" produced only black. Through this series of experiments, we have taken a journey from Newton's apparent conjecture to its experimental disconfirmation, an explanatory journey parallel to Captain Legge's factual journey from observation to cartographical revision.

Our final visual example relates to the mathematization of physics. In "Remarks Concerning the Movements of the Planets and, Principally, that of the Moon," de la Hire shows that Kepler's theory of the motion of the moon leads to error, an error traceable to a mistake in the calculation of its eccentricity. In a pair of diagrams, the Frenchman de la Hire contrasts his method with Kepler's and suggests a generalization of his findings to the other planets and their satellites. We reproduce the

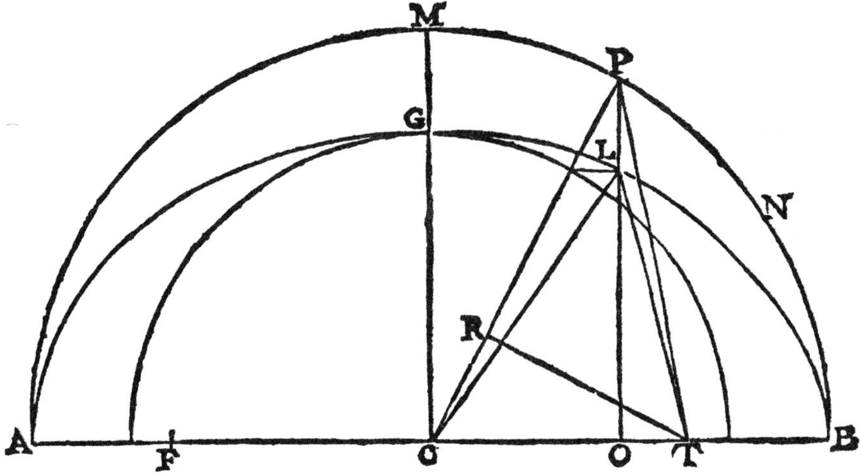

Figure 5.4. Diagram from de la Hire, "Remarks Concerning the Movements of the Planets and, Principally, that of the Moon" (1710)

first diagram of the pair, the exposition of Kepler's theory (figure 5.4). The accompanying text reads:

> Let line *ACB* be the larger axis of the ellipse *AGLB* and its smaller axis *CG*, & one of its foci be point *T*. Let the planet be on *L* in its elliptical orbit. If from the center *C* of the ellipse & for the radius *CB* one describes a circle *APB* & that at the point *L* one takes the ordinate *PLO* perpendicular to the axis *AB*; and having drawn the radius *CP*, one will have, in accordance with the properties of the ellipse, *PO* | [is proportional to?] *LO* || [is proportional to?] *CB* or *CM* | *CG*. But also one knows that the circular segment *OPB* is to the elliptical segment *OLB* || *PO* | *LO* or || *CB* | *CG*; that is why if one also takes *PT*, the triangle *TPO* being to the triangle *TLO* || *PO* | *LO*, it follows that the circular arc *TPB* will be | to the elliptical arc *TLB* || *PO* | *LO* || *CB* || *CG*. (1710-F290)

De la Hire's geometric representation depicts Kepler's theory, while his contrasting representation depicts his own, preferred because "Kepler's hypothesis, although very plausible, cannot be maintained for the moon, and it is very likely that it would not suit the other planets better" (1710-F290). These contrasting visuals do not merely illustrate de la Hire's argument; they are at its center. In a sense, they *are* his argument.

None of these visuals is in any way innovative. The application of Euclidian principles to motions of the heavenly bodies, for example, is as old at least as Ptolemy. Nor do we see in the 18th century any "improvements" over the 17th; the realistic rendering of the shell is actually inferior to our example of the knotted cord of twin fetuses from the 17th century (chapter 3). Moreover, we found no evidence that the major 18th-century graphical invention, the line graphs invented independently by

William Playfair in England and Johann Heinrich Lambert in Germany (Tilling 1975), had filtered down into the everyday scientific article: in our entire sample, tables remained the only means for displaying data outside straight text.

Arguing in Applied Science

Historians of 18th-century science have long debated the influence of science on technology, the orthodox view being that this influence was slight. Nevertheless, without for a moment denying technology its own history, independent of that of science, it is possible to argue, as do D. S. L. Cardwell (1972, 1980) and F. L. Holmes (1989b), that a great deal depends on one's definition of science. If, for example, we fix our attention solely on the chemical revolution led in France by Lavoisier and insist that to discover such influence one must "trace the course of [a] significant theoretical concept from abstract formulation to actual use in industrial operations" (Gillispie, quoted in Holmes 1989b, p. 87), then we will find little or no influence. If, on the other hand, we ask if there was significant interaction between science and the practical arts, then our answer will differ. In one case Holmes analyzes, the production of soda on a large scale, we find that efforts toward that goal "fitted within the framework set by Duhamel [de Monceau]'s investigation of the alkali in sea salt" presented to the Académie Royale in 1737 (p. 101). Moreover, this connection between French science and French industry was encouraged by the French government, whose "prime consideration," as Rappaport (1969) states, "was the strengthening of the French economy so that ultimately France might become as self-sufficient as possible and a major exporting nation as well" (p. 128).

In the German states, the link between science and practice in chemistry is also evident. As early as 1718, we have chemist G. E. Stahl's statement that "rational chemical knowledge" will improve medications, mineral processing, distilling, brewing, and "many other generally useful things" (quoted in Hufbauer 1982, p. 8). Practice goes beyond this programmatic statement. Among 65 prominent German 18th-century chemists, medicine and mining are the two most frequent occupations; the situation is similar if we look at the subscribers to Crell's journal, *Chemische Annalen* (Hufbauer 1982, pp. 153–224). Sciences other than chemistry are also implicated. In the 18th century, the German states were the leaders in founding schools of mines designed to provide "a first-class engineering education based on mathematics, mechanics and related sciences" (Cardwell 1972, p. 479). The case of German physicians toward the end of the century, as Broman (1995) makes clear, was parallel: they were in the process of redefining themselves in terms of "a new discourse that made the relationship between theory and practice the compass of professional identity" (p. 870).

In a similar vein, Margaret Jacob (1997) has shown that English harbor construction, canal building, and steam engine installation depended crucially, in some instances at least, on a relatively sophisticated knowledge of mechanical principles (pp. 187–207). In addition, Larry Stewart (1986) has demonstrated the intimate involvement of Newton's apostles "in commerce and industry" (p. 192). Finally, Robert

Kargon (1977) has shown that the Manchester Literary and Philosophical Society was founded expressly to promote the interrelationship between science and the practical arts. In 1781, the Society's founding year, Thomas Henry, eventually president of the Society, wrote: "[T]he misfortune is that few dyers are chemists and few chemists dyers. Practical knowledge should be united to theory in order to produce the most beneficial discoveries" (quoted in Kargon 1977, p. 9).

This sentiment is reflected directly in two articles in our sample. Of his inquiry, the English Delaval says that his purpose, the investigation of permanent colors in opaque bodies, is governed by utility, the feeling that the discovery of their "nature, origin, and cause" will help those in industries that impart such colors to manufactured goods, for "it should be the office of experimental philosophy, to examine the powers and properties of all the materials, requisite to technical uses. Nor should its views be confined to the theories, which result from those researches, but directed to the practical application of them" (1789-E117).[5] Similarly, in the German "Experiments Concerning a Mineral Related to Potassium Ferrocyanide" (1787-G148), chemistry is positioned as an enterprise equally useful to the seeker of knowledge and the seeker of profit: "an experienced miner, metallurgist, *or* eager student of nature" (our emphasis). The strict demarcation between pure and applied, so evident in the 20th century, does not seem to exist in the 18th; indeed, the distinction between pure and applied does not appear to operate at all: applied science differs from pure only in its focus.

This link between science and technology has a corollary, which has not, to our knowledge, been noticed, one that is vital to our purposes: applied-science articles deviate in no essential way from the argumentative standards evident in pure science. Our first illustration of this likeness, "Mineral System of Inspector Werner, Published with the Permission of C. A. S. Hoffman," appeared in the German periodical devoted to mining and metallurgy, *Bergmanisches Journal*:

> It seems almost unnecessary to say that Inspector Werner, in classifying minerals *completely by their chemical composition,* in so far as it is known with some reliability, has been concerned about not having been misunderstood precisely on this point, extraordinarily, one might almost believe, indeed deliberately, notwithstanding his various *clear* and *explicit* explanations in this case. But how contradictory and how unreliable are current chemical investigations of minerals will be seen very clearly from a table in the process of completion, one that will appear likewise in one of the next issues of this journal. (1789-G222; italics in original)

Despite its practical orientation, this article represents an impressive attempt to classify minerals into genera, familae, and species according to chemical principles. It may be usefully compared to a French geological article of the same period, "Continuation of a Memoir Meant to Explain the Systematic Distribution of All Volcanic

5. It is no accident that this article was published in the second volume of the *Memoirs of the Manchester Literary and Philosophical Society,* a volume that also contained a proposal for a course of lectures that would pay special attention to mechanics and chemistry "because of their intimate connection with our manufactures" (quoted in Kargon 1977, p. 11).

Products" (1794-F457), discussed above. In the French case, the principle of classification differs: it is phenomenological. Nonetheless, two geologists, one "pure" and the other "applied," establish a geological classification in analogous ways, at roughly the same time. It is, we think, a sign not only of the interpenetration of standards in pure and applied science, but also of the unity of purpose in the case of two geological communities, the German and the French.

Our second selection comes from Boucherie's "Memoir in Response to that of M. Prozet of the Academy of Science of Orleans, Printed in the French *Journal of Physics* Last December, Concerning Sugar Refining." This article deals with a contentious problem in the chemistry of the industry:

> But how can we account for Mr. de Morveau's opinion concerning the molasses reported by Mr. Prozet at the time of the formation of the cane juice? Could it be to support the claim that the acid, in combination with the cane juice, yields a product no different from that which the sugar supplies without distillation? Let us see if in this case the presence of this acid will prevent the sugar from crystallizing.
>
> I poured a half ounce of syrupous acid (1) into a solution of a pound of Orleans sugar and I brought all to a boil. The syrupous acid was volatilized during evaporation, an effect easily apparent by its smell, and I obtained by cooling a crystallization as abundant and as perfect as the same sugar could provide without the addition of acid. The crystals were only contaminated by a bit of empyreumatic oil[6] which was found joined to the acid.
>
> ---
>
> (1)The proportion of acid that I used can be presupposed neither in the cane juice, nor in the raw sugar, since it would necessitate a quantity of strong lime over and above that which the sugar producer and refiner employs, given that twenty-four grains of lime are necessary to saturate three hundred grains of syrupous acid. (1778-F454)

In this passage, we see in action a program of empirical research closely linked to sugar production. Its research question is clearly enunciated: "Let us see if in this case the presence of this acid will prevent the sugar from crystallizing"; the answer is arrived at by cautious experimentation in no way different from the norms Kirwan presupposes in his purely scientific "Conclusion of the Experiments and Observations Concerning the Attractive Powers of Mineral Acids" (1783-E032) discussed above. Like Kirwan, Boucherie regards as crucial the relationship between the weight of experimental evidence and the plausibility of empirical claims.

In the next passage, though we move from the empirical to the theoretical, a parallelism between argumentation in pure and applied science is fully sustained. In "A Disquisition on the Stability of Ships" (1798-E108) Atwood's goal is to reduce the danger of ships capsizing by increasing their stability. Although Atwood's concerns are practical, his are the methods of mathematical physics: his model for ships is "an extended wedge perpendicularly placed." The problem of stability is thus re-

6. "Empyreumatic oils are liquid oils that are (a) acid, (b) are soluble in ardent spirits [ethyl alcohol], (c) do not retain the taste and odor of the substance from which they are obtained, (d) have a taste and/or color of burnt organic matter" (Eklund 1975, p. 26).

duced to one of statics, and the methods used, which lead to the conclusion that ship design must be radically altered, are those of its geometry:

> GZ is the measure of the vessel's stability, when inclined from the upright through the given angle MOI. The demonstration follows. Through E, draw ET perpendicular to ΓP; and, through G, draw GR parallel to ΓP; let the parameter of the curve be denoted by *p*.
>
> By the construction, LX:LI::LI:LF::tang. MOI to rad.
>
> therefore— LX:LF::tang.^{2} MOI:rad.^{2} and
>
> LX:4LF::tang.^{2} MOI: 4rad.^{2}
>
> By the properties of the curve,
>
> LX:XV::XV :4LF
>
> wherefore— LX:4LF::LX^2 :XV^2.
>
> But— — LX::4LF::tang.^{2} MOI: 4rad.^{2}
>
> therefore— LX^2: XV^2::tang.^{2} MOI:4rad.^{2}
>
> and— — LX:XV::tang. MOI:2rad.
>
> or, since LX = 1/2XN
>
> 1/2XN:XV::tang. MOI: 2 rad.
>
> or— — XN:XV::tang. MOI:rad. but by
>
> the construction, XN:XV::tang.XVN: rad.
>
> consequently tang. XVN is equal to the tangent of MOI to the same radius; and therefore the angle XVN is equal to the angle MOI, or the given angle of the vessel's inclination from the upright. (1798-E108)

While it is true that Atwood's mathematics are relatively unsophisticated compared to the mathematics of Gerstner and Clairaut in a pair of astronomical articles discussed above (1789-G223, 1754-F375), in all cases it is the nature of the problem, not the skills of the scientists, that determines the choice of method. Gerstner's and Clairaut's models of planetary motion are, necessarily, dynamic and therefore are best attacked with calculus. Atwood also knows calculus—he uses it for another purpose later in his article. But, since he believes that the resistance of the water is irrelevant to ship stability, he can legitimately treat the problem as one of statics. From his point of view, he is merely adjusting his mathematics to the problem at hand.

Our final example compares visualization as an argumentative device in pure and applied science. For this purpose, we pair an illustration from the German "Concerning Several Principal Defects of Various Iron Mines in Germany" (1790-G157) with one from a "pure science" counterpart, a German astronomical article analyzed above (1780-G227). In the applied science article, a series of improvements in metal smelting is suggested, one of which concerns the shape of blast furnaces and the sources of air used to fan their flames: "For these, and other reasons, I would design a blast furnace with either two intake openings or, if of a larger size, four; as to the structure itself, give it a nearly oval shape, pretty much as in the drawings below. That the efficient use of the space and, above all, the efficient running of the whole, must be performed by so-called ventilation-managers, which are equipped with a regulator, goes without saying" (1790-G157). The two diagrams that follow are of the simplest sort—a child could have drawn them (figure 5.5). But not only are they perfectly adequate to their purpose, they are also at least as sophisticated as

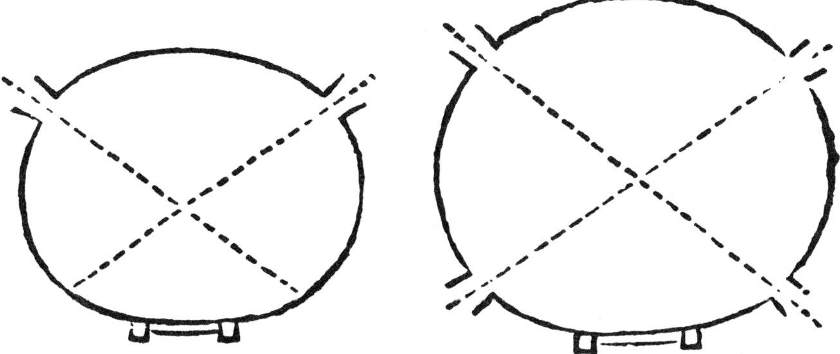

Figure 5.5. Diagrams from "Concerning Several Principal Defects of Various Iron Mines in Germany" (1790).

the astronomical depiction analyzed above, concerning the lunar occultation of Venus. In each, shape and relative size are depicted, as well as other crucial details: in the one case the relative positions of Venus, in the other the currents of air (by means of dotted lines). An interesting difference also emerges. While in the astronomical engraving the draftsmanship is superior, the mining drawing is superior in that it acts as a extension of the text, visually and cognitively integrated, in the manner of Leonardo in his notebooks and, of course, in the manner of 20th-century scientific illustrations (Tufte 1983, p. 182).[7]

Our examples are meant to demonstrate that, at least in the applied-science articles from our 18th-century sample, the influence of science and the standards of science on technology are everywhere evident. Not only are articles on pure and applied science near neighbors in the scientific journals, they are also virtually indistinguishable in the arguments they make. In our view, the argumentative indistinguishability reflects a social and cognitive situation where scientists and artisans are distinguishable less by the criteria by which they measure their achievements than by the sort of problems on which they focus their attention.

Conclusion

Rather than contrasting argumentation in the 18th century with the period 1665–1700, we might have fused the last 36 years of the 17th with the 18th century as a single period, punctuated at each end by revolutionary developments in science. At the beginning of this extended period came three major revolutions: two, in mechanics and optics, are the work of Isaac Newton; the other, the invention of the

7. The astronomical engraving cannot work in this way, in part, because the limitations of 18th-century printing meant that engraving of this sort had to be gathered into single comprehensive plates, generally interleaved at the end of volumes.

calculus, is the work equally of Newton and Gottfried Leibniz. Toward the end of this period, we have another major revolution, the new chemistry of Antoine Lavoisier. Between these two revolutionary periods, we have science as usual, though to be sure, science sometimes of signal importance. A period of scientific activity cannot be lightly dismissed that includes Georges Louis Leclerc Buffon, Carolus Linnaeus, Stephen Hales in biology; Jean le Rond D'Alembert and Leonhard Euler in astronomy; Joseph Black and Karl Wilhelm Scheele in chemistry; Benjamin Franklin in electricity; and John Harrison in technology. Despite the impressive achievements of these men, however, the period from about 1700 to 1775 may still, without excessive distortion, be characterized as one of consolidation and altered emphasis.

A long period of relative stability is also evident in scientific argument. On the whole, 18th-century argumentation is not greatly different from its 17th-century counterpart. The emphasis in all three languages is firmly on establishing facts of observation, with the French sample also showing a robust interest in the mathematical and theoretical not nearly so evident in English or German. Visual representations also support authors' efforts to establish facts of observation by means similar to the 17th century, primarily tables of data and realistic drawings and schematics of natural and man-made objects.

In the last quarter century, however, something significant seems to happen in both science and its arguments for new facts and explanations. As the reader may have noticed, most of our examples of 18th-century argument come from this period: our bias and that of many historians, in fact, coincide. We are also attracted to the last quarter of the century as a time when chemistry altered forever; geological uniformitarianism emerged as a viable theory; electricity and paleontology became sciences; the first specialized journals emerged in the natural and physical sciences; and applied science, fueled by the industrial revolution, began its rapid upward growth.[8]

In scientific argument during this same quarter century, we note a rise in the standards for reporting and systematizing observations and warranting experimental results. This change comes about because of several combined trends: improvements in the accuracy and precision of astronomical observations, more sophisticated systematizations of biological and geological classification, and a greater concern with methodological rigor in experimentation. Explanations also changed as a result of the penetration of mathematical argument into many different branches of science and the emergence of causal explanations particular to particular sciences, for example, phlogiston in chemistry and mutual attraction in physics. Finally, visuals during this period not only depict and record new facts; they also represent calculationally based predictions and embody theories, largely by means of geometric diagrams and schematics. But the last quarter of the 18th century, so interesting to us and to historians, is not typical of the whole.

8. See, for example, Garber (1999), Kronick (1991), Porter (1978), and Wolf (1939).

CHAPTER 6

Style and Presentation in the 19th Century

At the founding of the British Association for the Advancement of Science in 1831, William Whewell suggested that membership be restricted to those "who have published *written papers* in the memoirs of any learned society" (quoted in Stimson 1968, p. 215). He wanted to exclude as members those who were not, as one critic of the Royal Society put it, "labourers in the vineyard" of science. This linking of journal publication with the scientific profession led to an influx of individual articles primarily aimed at subject-matter experts. It also spawned the first specialty journals in natural history and physical science from Germany, France, and England, including *Archiv für Mikroskopische Anatomie* (Archive for Microscopic Anatomy), *Journal de Pharmacie et de Chimie* (Journal of Pharmacy and Chemistry), and *Transactions of the Entomological Society of London.* In addition, during the 19th century, the number of scientific journals rose, not just steadily, but very steeply (Houghton 1975, p. 101). In de Solla Price's (1986) well-known plot of total number of scientific journals (p. 8), there are fewer than 10 journals by 1700, about 100 by 1800, and 10,000 by 1900.[1]

Hand in hand with this outpouring of new scientific journals came the professionalization of science on a wide scale within the countries represented by our

1. As de Solla Price (1986) acknowledged, these data depend on how one defines a "scientific journal." Moreover, his logarithmic plot, created in the 1960s, extrapolates to 900,000 new journals founded between 1950 and 2000. While we know of no recent count of scientific journals, that growth rate seems highly implausible. Still, our point here is only that an explosion of scientific journal publication occurred in the 19th century.

sample.[2] Of course, professionalization does not happen overnight, or even in a single century; when we use the term "professionalization," it is thus important to keep in mind Helge Kragh's (1998) observation that "[w]hereas a profession is a relatively static entity, professionalisation is inherently dynamical. It is a process, not a state" (p. 339).

Professionalization created new identities for the scientist, nurtured and reinforced by such social factors as the proliferation of societies for the special sciences in England and the Continent, the creation of chemical research institutes in Germany,[3] the founding of the British Association for the Advancement of Science (and its equivalent in America), and the reform of the Royal Society of London. So rapid and irreversible was this change that Edward Schunck, a student of the great German chemist Justus von Liebig and a very productive research chemist, could say in an 1889 address before the British Association: "The marvelously rapid progress of chemistry during the last twenty years has made it difficult for the most industrious cultivator of the science to keep abreast of the knowledge of the day, and for a *dilettante* like myself one may say it is next to impossible. I confess myself painfully conscious of my defects in this respect" (quoted in Kargon 1977, p. 147). More and more, specialization and professionalization excluded from the readership of the scientific literature the self-instructed enthusiast for whom science was a part-time occupation or hobby, in favor of individuals institutionally trained at an advanced level and earning their living by means of science alone.

Despite the growing separation between amateur and professional in many disciplines, the scientific article of this century stubbornly refuses to look like its late 20th-century counterpart. This chapter will show that many of the articles in our sample reflect a general avoidance of the highly technical: sentences are weighty without being weighted down with complex noun phrases consisting of multiple modifiers, equations, and quantitative expressions. Moreover, the burden of keeping current with the literature in one's field still does not seem to be particularly onerous, as least judged by the citational density. Finally, there is only the beginning of a movement toward the modular arrangement of parts so prevalent today. Still, our data also show the style and presentation inching toward 20th-century practices: style becoming less personal and varied, and presentation, more formalized. We view this movement toward uniformity and formalization as a sign that the science professional is replacing the science enthusiast in ever increasing numbers as both reader and author.

2. For historical background information on French science, we consulted Ereshefsky (1997, 1999), Rothschuh (1973, p. 151), Lesch (1984), Appel (1987), Silliman (1974), Fox (1992), Fox and Weisz (1988), Lundgreen (1988), and Crosland (1992). For German science, Homberg (1998), Rothschuh (1973, pp. 151, 292), Nyhart (1995), Beer (1958), Boig and Howerton (1952a,b), and Nye (1996). For British and American science, Kargon (1977), Cannon (1978), Christie (1974), Rudwick (1985), Oldroyd (1990), Secord (1986), MacLeod (1996), Rothschuh (1973, pp. 305–306), Crosland (1995), Blum (1993), and Kevles (1978).

3. In particular, the chemical laboratories of Justus von Liebig in Giessen and Frederich Wöhler in Göttingen.

The Implied Audience

Perelman and Olbrechts-Tyteca (1969) define the audience for the modern scientific report as follows: "The scientist addresses himself to certain particularly qualified men, who accept the data of a well-defined system consisting of the science in which they are specialists. Yet, this very limited audience is generally considered to be really the universal audience, and not just a particular audience. He supposes that everyone with the same training, qualifications, and information would reach the same conclusions" (p. 34).

This is the only audience addressed by current science; it is, most emphatically, *not* the only audience addressed by 19th-century science. Nineteenth-century readers of the same journal can be addressed as scientists per se or, more generally, as professionals who happen to be scientists; as those interested more in pure science, or more in its applications; as professionals within a specific discipline, or anyone with a general interest in science.[4]

Our first readership division is between those interested in science as a discipline and those interested in it as a profession. We see in the same journals, for example, original research reports addressed to scientists as scientists, appearing side by side with scientific "news," transcripts of discussions at meetings, and speeches of welcome to scientific societies, addressed to scientists as professionals. While in the 20th century the latter items will be segregated from those that are strictly scientific—they will appear, perhaps, in a proceedings volume or in a special section of a journal—in the 19th century they were more readily interspersed among scientific reports. In *Annalen der Physik* (Annals of Physics), we have "A Calculation Concerning Garnerin's Air-Trip in Berlin, How It was Carried Out and How It Was Planned along with Herr Hermstädt" (1804-G025). In *Ornithologische Monatsshrift* (Monthly Journal of the German Society for the Protection of Birdlife), we have an article commenting on the avian exhibits of the British Museum (1891-G065). In the *Bericht über die Versammlung Deutscher Naturforscher und Ärzte* (Proceedings of the German Society of Scientists and Physicians), we have a speech of welcome by the Baron Jacquin, Royal Imperial Counselor and Professor of Chemistry and Botany (1832-G180). The introduction to this last, equally about science and the intrusion of the outside world, must serve for the rest:

> Highly esteemed, most honorable gentlemen, colleagues and friends!
>
> For the tenth time the natural philosophers and physicians of the German-speaking nations find themselves gathered together in friendship to discuss seriously, to consult and to enlighten one another, concerning the state of natural knowledge and its possible practical application to pharmacology. For nine consecutive years this meeting had been held in various northern and southern German states successfully and without interruption, up until the first shock of the dan-

4. Almost none, however, is addressed as the recipient of a letter; epistolary conventions have by now disappeared from scientific articles with the exception of two English articles from the first quarter of a century (1801–E150; 1822–E175).

> gerous and swift appearance of a most terrible sickness [the revolutions of 1830–31],[5] at this time still little understood, which, causing changes in the atmosphere, not only in the greater part of Austro-Hungary where it began, but almost equally in the great part of northern Germany, put obstacles in the way of our meeting in Vienna. (1832-G180)

A second readership division contrasts those more interested in the science itself with those more interested in its applications. In the 20th century, articles on pure and applied science often do not share the same journal space; in the 19th century, they frequently do. This division is illustrated by the difference between an article entitled "Survey of Some Discoveries Concerning Carbon Bonds, Some New, Some Already Known" (1832-G145) and one entitled "Note on Opium, and its Composition Using Various Procedures for Obtaining it from White Opium Poppies (Papaver somniferum Linné)" (1801-F177). The introduction to an article on lightning rods may be taken as typical of a central concern with the improvement of technology. It turns Swales's tripartite introduction to its own purposes: its territory, the application of electrical principles; its niche, the protection of property from lightning; the candidate for that niche, an improved lightning rod:

> Although it has already been a hundred and one years since lightning rods were introduced by the famous Benjamin Franklin of Philadelphia, they are unfortunately too little valued in this day and age. A chief reason for this neglect might be attributed to their cost, although this trifling expenditure cannot account for the reluctance of well-off owners of property to insure the safety of their home and hearths, nay, their lives by this expedient. But it is not only the absence of good sense that characterizes the criticism of this important device; it is also the superficial way in which this technology is currently understood and applied. Hence, the exact description contained in this article might not be supererogatory. (1853-G095)

The target for this editorial-like introduction is clearly any reader with an interest in the practical application of science.

A third readership division contrasts an audience of scientific professionals with one of general readers possessing an interest in science and technology; it is marked by the difference between an article entitled "Concerning Naphtha and Dulcified Spirits" (1801-G170) and one entitled "Acetylene, The New Illuminant" (1899-E005). While in the 20th century general audiences warrant separate periodicals devoted to "popular" science, in the 19th century such separation was clearly incomplete. In the same year, 1877, we have in *Science* an article entitled "The American Whale Fishery: 1877–1886" (E065) and in *Chemical News* an article entitled "On the New Metal—Gallium" (E001). The introductions to these articles look like those common in journalism, with its "hook" and its passion for the anecdotal:

> If half-a-dozen years ago our most able chemists had been told that it was possible to obtain a gas from a piece of builder's lime producing a light more brilliant than

5. See Brose (1997, pp. 153–163).

electric light and cheaper than paraffin, the statement would have been received with a smile of derision or pity. Such, however, is one of the most wonderful recent discoveries of applied science. Like so many other important inventions, this was the result of an accident, during some experiments made by Mr. Henri Moissan, the eminent Parisian chemist, to whom all honour is due, not only for his discoveries, but because it is his custom, without seeking reward, to throw them open for the benefit of mankind. (1899-E005)[6]

Despite its kinship with journalism, this introduction reproduces a schema analogous to that of Swales: the territory is the wonders of applied science; the niche, public lighting; its current inhabitant, at least conjecturally, acetylene.

These reader dimensions mark boundaries that are somewhat artificial: What is pure science? What is technology? What is a professional reader? What is a general reader? Moreover, the range of readership depends, to some extent, on where we draw the line between science and nonscience. *Science Gossip* is included in our sample: is it a scientific journal? But we need to notice that, wherever we draw the line, the range of journal readership in the 19th century is far wider than in the 20th: in our sample, nearly 25% of the articles are outliers by modern standards.

Style

Uniformity

We have kept track of the finite verbs in our sample passages to test our hypothesis that there is a general shift from verbal to nominal elements and that, as a consequence, predicates will be relatively colorless, that is, will exist near the top rung in a ladder of abstraction.[7] We also have a second hypothesis concerning the verbs in scientific prose. We posit a shift from verbs predicated of people to those predicated of matter and material objects, a prose centered on the science rather than the scientist. For the 19th century, as we shall show, both hypotheses are supported by the data.

Table 6.1 speaks to our first hypothesis. In each case, where two figures are presented, the first is the 18th century, the second is the 19th; when one figure is presented, there is no 18th-century counterpart. In addition, the first total is not the total of the figures before the slash, but of all the figures for the 18th century:

6. "Scientific journalism" is largely absent from our French sample. It is worth noting, however, that the French were at the forefront of disseminating the latest scientific research to the general public. Up to its demise as an elitist institution during the French Revolution, the Académie Royale des Sciences published summaries of its *Mémoires* in the annual *Histoire;* starting in the early 19th century, the *Annales de Chimie et de Physique* provided that same service, as did several learned journals and newspapers. The French *Moniteur,* founded in 1800, is the first newspaper to publish "stories" about scientific research for the public written by scientists (for further details, see Crosland 1992, chap. 8).

7. Contrast verbs like "to wreck," "phosphoriscieren," and "vibrer," all of which pick out unique actions, and are, not coincidentally, unique in our sample.

Table 6.1. Ten Most Frequent Verbs in 18th- and 19th-Century Passages

English Verbs (n = *1,651*)[a]	% *Occurrence*	*French Verbs* (n = *1,096*)	% *Occurrence*	*German Verbs* (n = *1,815*)	% *Occurrence*
to be	21.3/26.1[b]	être (to be)	18.3/20.6	sein (to be)	11.2/17.4
to find	2.0/2.8	avoir (to have)	5.8/3.8	erhalten (to obtain)	1.3/1.6
to have	2.6/2.5	faire (to do; to make)	3.4/1.9	geben (to give)	2.3/1.4
to appear	2.0/1.4	former (to produce)	1.5	haben (to have)	1.9/1.3
to make	1.3	trouver (to find)	2.1/1.3	werden (to become)	1.3/1.2
to observe	1.2	voir (to see)	2.1/1.2	zeigen (to show)	1.2/1.2
to seem	1.2	donner (to give)	1.9/1.1	enthalten (to contain)	1.3/1.2
to become	1.0	présenter (to present)	1.0	scheinen (to seem)	1.1
to form	1.0	paraître (to appear)	0.8	bleiben (to remain)	1.0
to give	1.9/1.0	dire (to say)	0.7	finden (to find)	2.6/1.0
Total	37.0/39.5	Total	42.1/33.9	Total	25.8/28.4

[a]These totals are for 19th-century verbs.
[b]The first figure is for the 18th century, the second for the 19th.

The degree of uniformity in the use of abstract verbs is remarkable: six verbs overlap on the lists: to be, to find, to have, to give, to appear, to seem.[8] There are also interesting increases compared with the last century; there is an increase in English and German totals and an increased use of "to be" in all languages.[9]

We also compared the percentages of verbs that referred to the subject of science—nature itself—and to scientists themselves. Our hypothesis was that a shift away from the person would be evident. The expected preponderance is confirmed. In the English case, 39% of verbs were predicated of people, 61% of nature; in the German case, the numbers are 35% and 65%; in the French case, 37% and 63%. In all three languages there is an increase compared with the last century in the preponderance of verbs relating to matter and material objects, though in the French case the rise is slight.

Mere numbers, however, do not give us the flavor of prose in which predicates differ so markedly. Here is the first of three illustrative passages:

> The whole, uncovered in a earthenware recepticle, immediately *fermented*; four days *sufficed* to develop the aroma of true oriental opium.
>
> I *kept back* a part for future use, and *thickened* the other by heating it to no more than 40 degrees. This extract *retained* a very faint odor of laudanum; it *was* a mixture nearly equivalent to that of commercial opium, minus the odor and gas driven off by the heat. (1801-F177)

This French passage from 1801 has a mix of verbs: specific actions side by side with more abstract verbs. The effect is similar in the following German passage of

8. Moreover, the number of verbs in the top 10 is an undercount, since virtual synonyms abound. In English, if we add "see" to "observe" we get 36 or 2.2% of instances; in German if we add "erscheinen" to "scheinen," we get 34 or 1.9% of instances; in French, if we add "regarder" and "observer" to "voir" we get 27 or 2.5% of instances.

9. We cannot explain the drop in the French totals, indicating an increase in the variety of verbs employed.

1854, though here there is a shift toward the abstract—while two out of six verbs in the first passage are specific, in the second, the ratio is only three out of eleven:

> It [the mouth] *is lined* with dark-granular cells, which *move* like cilia.
>
> Within the system for evacuating liquid waste, one *distinguishes* two canals (*d*), which *begin* at the rear with unobstructed openings and *stretch* through the entire body up to the front, twisting and turning many times in their passage and at the head *seem to loop* in and out each other.
>
> In the head one *sees* very few little corpuscles circulating in the empty space between—the worm equivalent of blood corpuscles. Such a manifestation *seems* rare in the Turbellaria: at least Oskar Schmidt explicitly *notices* (in "Fresh-Water Rhabdocolerae Flatworms," page 12), that in the species he *examined* he *found* no "blood or chyle corpuscles." (1854-G070)

This final passage, from an English article of 1897, shows a definite shift toward the abstract end of the verbal spectrum. Not a single verb specifies an action:

> It *is* in regard to the relation between this massive variety, which *corresponds* most closely to the type described by Zirkel, and the porous form, that my field observations *are* unfortunately so imperfect. But little of the massive rock *was seen* and then nothing *was observed* to indicate that the two types *belonged* to different flows. On this account, and from the chemical identity of the two rocks, I *am* at present *inclined* to regard the leucite of Zirkel's report as a part of the same flow that *is* predominately a more or less vesicular sanidine-leucite rock, described in succeeding pages as *orendite.* (1897-E070)

While these passages, which come respectively from 1801, 1854, and 1897, give us the feel of a language whose conceptual burden is gradually shifting from the predicate to the noun phrase, our data support only the hypothesis that we are likely to see *any* of these patterns in *any* decade of the century.

Uniformity is also evident in the case of the varieties of noun phrases shown in table 6.2, a uniformity equally evident in the last century, as the figure before the

Table 6.2. Distribution of Noun Phrases of Various Types for 18th- and 19th-Century Passages

Noun-Phrase Types[a]	*English* (n = *122/188*)[b]	*French* (n = *217/122*)	*German* (n = *143/214*)
Simple Subject	21.7/26.3	27.2/25.1	24.9/25.1
Complex Subject	19.0/17.3	14.5/14.5	12.7/15.2
Simple Nonsubject	15.3/12.8	14.3/12.2	22.1/19.9
Complex Nonsubject	44.0/43.7	44.1/48.3	40.4/39.8
Subject Pronouns and Names	16.7/19.0	23.3/21.4	18.8/17.7
Subject Multiple Modifiers	13.1/8.8	9.2/7.1	6.6/8.0
Nonsubject Pronouns and Names	4.9/5.3	5.2/5.2	8.7/7.4
Nonsubject Multiple Modifiers	29.3/27.6	31.3/35.0	20.1/23.3

[a]The first figure is for the 18th century, the second for the 19th.
[b]Appendix C defines the terms used in the column and gives an example of the calculations involved.

slash indicates. The differences among languages are generally small, an interesting result considering the considerable syntactic differences between French and English and the enormous ones between these two languages and German. This suggests that an international style of science may in some respects have preceded the internationalization of the late 20th century.

Convergence

Nineteenth-century scientific prose shows trends that persist from the 18th century and that will continue to persist into the 20th. These trends concern two sorts of convergence. Although there is no convergence across languages in sentence length and clausal density, there is a uniform reduction in both, as shown in table 6.3. Table 6.4 shows a convergence across languages in reduction in relative standard deviations of seven of 13 measures and virtual stability in an additional two. This indicates that on these measures not only was scientific prose relatively uniform among languages, it was also becoming more uniform as the century progressed.

Table 6.5 demonstrates a different sort of convergence, one in the direction of 20th-century norms. On the one hand, complex noun phrases increase; on the other, personal pronouns and evaluative, deviant, and poetic expressions decrease. The first trend betokens a prose in which noun phrases carry more and more of the cognitive burden; the second, a prose that is becoming impersonal and "objective." When we look at sentence length and clausal density, convergence is even more remarkable (table 6.6).

These changes may be illustrated by means of two passages from French physics, the first from 1819, the second from 1886. These passages are *not* typical; they are meant to give the reader the feel of three contrasting communicative tendencies: (1) the movement toward a syntactic simplicity that stems from decreased clausal density and sentence length, (2) the movement that copes with complexity by increasing the conceptual load on the subject noun phrase, and (3) the movement toward the appearance of objectivity that stems from the reduction of personal pronouns, evaluative and deviant expressions, and an increase in abstract and impersonal predicates. The first passage comes from an article that appeared in the

Table 6.3. Average Sentence Length and Clausal Density across Languages in 19th-Century Passages

	1801–1825	*1826–1850*	*1851–1875*	*1876–1900*
Sentence length				
English	41.46	37.08	38.89	31.69
French	51.87	59.55	40.31	33.10
German	40.72	45.04	38.48	35.00
Clausal density (per sentence/per 100 words)				
English	3.24/8.5	3.07/8.1	2.97/8.0	2.59/8.4
French	4.12/8.5	4.05/07.4	2.86/7.4	2.62/7.7
German	3.46/8.6	4.19/8.7	3.16/8.6	2.63/7.9

Table 6.4. Relative Standard Deviations for Stylistic Features across Centuries

	17th Century (n = 198)	*18th Century (n = 482)*	*19th Century (n = 524)*
Personal pronouns	87%[a]	82%	100%
Evaluative expressions	250	200	225
Poetic expressions	300	400	300
Deviant expressions	300	225	500
Suppressed-person passives	180	157	155
Objective passives	250	260	200
Dummy subjects	190	160	175
Hedges	250	125	157
Quantitative expressions	320	155	180
Citations	700	300	300
Clausal density	57	62	71
Sentence length	55	60	59

[a]Ratio of the standard deviation divided by the mean, multiplied by 100.

Journal de Physique, de Chimie, D'Histoire Naurelle, and Des Arts (Journal of Physics, Chemistry, of Natural History and of the Practical Arts) in 1819:

> Mr. Paradisi, an Italian scientist, has undertaken on the same subject, research that seems to have been directed toward the real point of view of the theory. In making a rectangular sheet of glass vibrate by very small successive strikes of a bow, he recognized that the nodal lines first formed curves that, in his opinion, were semicircles radiating from the sides of the rectangle, one of which had its center at the

Table 6.5. Stylistic Features over Time: Occurrences per 100 Words

	1776–1800	*1801–1825*	*1826–1850*	*1851–1875*	*1876–1900*
Trends					
Complex subject noun phrases	14.5	14.0	15.9	16.1	17.0
Complex nonsubject noun phrases	42.1	42.2	44.9	41.6	44.2
Nonsubject multiple modifiers	25.0	26.1	29.6	26.1	28.5
Simple nonsubject noun phrases	18.8	17.4	14.9	16.0	13.9
Subject pronouns and names	19.1	20.3	18.0	19.5	18.3
Nonsubject pronouns and names	7.3	6.8	6.0	6.2	5.5
Deviant expressions	0.3	0.2	0.0	0.1	0.1
Evaluative expressions	0.8	0.5	0.4	0.5	0.3
Poetic expressions	0.1	0.1	0.0	0.0	0.0
Personal pronouns	2.6	2.6	2.3	2.0	2.0
Citations	0.2	0.2	0.2	0.3	0.3
No trends					
Suppressed-person passives	0.9	0.8	0.9	1.0	1.0
Subject multiple modifiers	8.9	6.4	9.2	8.0	8.6
Objective passives	0.5	0.4	0.4	0.3	0.5
Simple subject noun phrases	24.5	26.4	24.3	26.4	24.9
Dummy subjects	0.5	0.3	0.4	0.5	0.5
Hedges	1.1	0.6	0.6	0.8	0.8

Table 6.6. Sentence Length and Clausal Density: Average and Standard Deviation

	1801–1825	*1826–1850*	*1851–1875*	*1876–1900*
Sentence length				
Average	44.23	46.15	38.98	33.32
Standard deviaton	26.23	31.71	19.11	13.47
Finite clauses (per sentence/ per 100 words)				
Average	3.57/8.5	3.75/8.1	3.04/8.2	2.61/8.1
Standard deviation	1.93/2.4	3.69/2.7	1.43/2.4	1.14/2.1

> place where the bow had been applied. In pursuing the experiment, he saw the semicircles gradually undergo a change in shape, with the assistance of which their curvature diminished, and they turned in the end to a symmetrical collection of straight lines, of which one, directed parallel to the longer sides of the rectangle, was divided in half, and the others were parallel to the shorter sides. (1819-F193)

This second, contrasting passage is from an article that appeared in *Comptes Rendus* in 1886:

> One may even add that this irritant action is the more intense the more elevated the atomic weight of the halogenous body enclosed in the nitrile. The monochloritated acetonitrile ClH^2-CAz is an active agent in reddening skin, but does not produce blisters, at least not after temporary contact; the mono-iodated acetonitrile ICH^2CAz, on the contrary, is a powerful caustic and causes very painful burns. Because of this, it is a very unpleasant compound to handle. Likewise, it provokes tearing, which becomes more noticeable in moving from derived chlorides to derived iodides.
>
> Finally, the presence of nitrogen increases the ability of halogenous bodies to react with the elements with positive valences. (1886-F119)

With its average sentence length of 46 and its average finite clausal density of 4, the first passage is more akin to 18th-century norms; in contrast, the second passage, with its average sentence length of 29 and its average finite clausal density of 2, is more akin to norms of passages in the 20th century. In addition, in the first passage the ratio of simple to complex noun phrases is 3 to 1; in the second, in contrast, it is 1 to 1.2; moreover, multimodified phrases such as "the mono-iodated acetonitrile ICH^2CAz" have no parallel in the first passage. Finally, the second passage is clearly more impersonal: science rather than the scientist is in the subject position, a shift readily apparent in the contrast between the initial words in each passage: "Mr. Paradisi, an Italian scientist," in the first, "one," in the second.[10]

Considerable uniformity and convergence bespeak a community with communicative practices that are steadily becoming more homogeneous. But this convergence toward 20th-century norms is not the whole picture: though we see articles

10. Our counts are based on the French originals.

toward the end of the century that approximate current norms, the flavor of 19th-century scientific prose is remarkably similar, in many respects, to that the 18th century. Moreover, even relatively large changes in such measures as sentence length and clausal density need not result in a prose that is definitively perceived as in another register. We can experience this bifurcation without altered perception if we compare two passages, one an exemplification of 18th-century norms, the other, of the norms of the 19th century. Here is a French passage of 1725, from "Second Memoir on the Purely Analytical Measurement of Angles":

> These examples contain a new method of division, which seemed to me simpler and smoother in operation than the old ones, either those that consist in operating on high factors (in which case it is necessary to construct, by addition and simple doubling, the small table of the eight first multiples of these factors), or those in which the given factors are of only inferior numbers, in which case one can manage without the small table of multiples. I have always proposed to banish absolutely, or as far as it is possible, trial and error in arithmetical and algebraic computations, by reducing them all to simple addition and subtraction. (1725-F316)

Compare with this a German passage of 1857, from "Concerning the Melting- and Boiling Point of the Members of Several Triads":

> In four cases (Na, Pb, ZnCl, Se) the modification is positive, in two (As and Cr) it is negative. In one of the latter (Cr) and probably also in one of the former cases (ZnCl), the modification is so clear that the average melting point exceeds the limits set by both the others. Since the displayed table demonstrates seven others beside these, in which the average melting-point always lies between those of the two outlying members, one may, in accordance with every probablility, only rarely draw a false conclusion, if one takes the latter as a rule and counts such triads as positive or negative merely from their two known members. (1857-G029)

The differences are clear. In the first passage, all the sentences have suspended constructions; in the second, this is true only of the last sentence. In the second passage also, the sentences are shorter and their average clausal density is less. Although there are two personal pronouns in each passage, there is a significant difference in stylistic demeanor between the first-person pronoun in the first and the third-person impersonal pronoun "one" (German "*man*") in the second. There is also a difference in the verbs used: a verb like "banish," denoting a very specific action, would not be at home in the second passage. Nonetheless, only a zealot would proclaim that these passages *feel* different. Despite the century and a quarter that separates them, they seem contemporaneous; moreover, either would be comfortably at home in any 21st-century journal.

Presentation

In presentation in 18th-century articles, we see a movement toward 20th-century norms of scientific communication: an increase over the previous century in all cat-

Table 6.7. Percentage of 18th- and 19th-Century Articles with Presentational Features, by Half Century

	1801–1850 (n = *50/53*)[a]	*1851–1900* (n = *76/51*)
Formal features		
Headings	30/43	42/53
Thematic titles	76/87	70/84
Citations	48/58	48/67
Substantive features		
Complete introductions	60/91	72/80
Complete conclusions	22/21	36/24
Visuals	46/42	39/55

[a]18th-century figures are reported before the slash.

egories except complete conclusions (table 6.7; 18th-century figures are reported before the slash). In all categories except for complete introductions and thematic titles, we also see an increase between the first and the second half of the 19th century.

Another perspective, one that contrasts English, French, and German practice, brings out interesting discrepancies that these combined totals obscure. Table 6.8 shows that these increases in table 6.7 are due in large part to English and German communications, a consequence, we think, of the late professionalization of their sciences as contrasted with the French.

Having surveyed some general trends, we will now examine these formal and substantive features in detail. Our investigation will support the claim that, while uniformity and convergence are general, there is considerable variation; that, while there is movement toward the master finding system of the modern scientific article, this movement is not as marked as one might have expected if a gradual upward curve toward modern organizational patterns were our hypothesis.

Table 6.8. Percentage of 18th- and 19th-Century Articles with Presentational Features, by Language

	English (n = *44/37*)	*French* (n = *54/25*)	*German* (n = *28/42*)
Formal features			
Headings	20/49	56/60	29/40
Thematic titles	68/84	80/96	64/81
Citations	45/68	57/44	32/69
Substantive features			
Complete introductions	55/81	83/72	57/97
Complete conclusions	27/14	37/16	21/33
Visuals	41/52	37/40	25/50

[a]18th-century figures are reported before the slash.

Table 6.9. Percentage of 18th- and 19th-Century Titles in Canonical Form

	1701–1800 (n = *126)*	*1801–1900* (n = *104)*
English	65%	41%
French	63	68
German	56	62

Formal Features

TITLE AND AUTHOR Like its 18th-century counterpart, the modal title of the 19th-century is thematic and fairly specific; but, unlike its 18th-century counterpart, it is very likely to contain technical terminology. At the start of the century we have the technically specific English title "On the Specific Gravity of Sea Waters, in Different Parts of the Ocean, and in Particular Seas, with Some Account of Their Saline Content" (1800-E165). At midcentury we have the technically specific French title "Note on the Hypotrophy of the Spleen and the Alteration of the Blood, Consisting of a Rise in the White Corpuscules" (1854-F112). Toward the end of the century, we have the technically specific German title "Concerning the Electromotoric Effect of Selenium Heated until it Glows, Discovered by Mr. Fritts in New York" (1885-G040).[11]

These three titles have the same overall syntactic form, signaled by a word meaning "concerning": "on," "sur," "über." These are a form of social signaling that mark an entrance into the domain of science. The trend is shown in table 6.9. In German and French at the end of the century, the percentage of titles in this form is so high that talk of a norm would not be out of place. Moreover, deviations from this norm tend to signal communication of a sort different from research: "Ornithology from the British Museum" (1891-K065) is science news in German; "Fuel and Heating Systems" is a German summary and commentary on research findings (1891-G085); "The Radiation of Electrical Energy" (1892-G105) is a German précis of a lecture; "The Invertebrate Ureter " (1894-G110) is the title of a German dissertation; "Bloodless Surgery on Ordinary Nasal Passage Polyps" (1898-G045) precedes a transcript of an interchange among German physicians.

French and German scientists in the 19th century seem more anxious than did their 18th-century counterparts to display their professional credentials along with their titles: a membership in a scientific society, a medical degree, a university appointment. This trend is reflected in table 6.10. The spread of science from capital cities to the periphery may account in part for this general increase: scientists need no longer know one another personally. For example, an atypically expansive title

11. There is also a definite diminution compared with the last century of titles that are relatively uninformative, from 24% to 13%. This contrast suggests increased professionalization.

Table 6.10. Percentage of 18th- and 19th-Century Articles with Author Credentials

	1701–1800 (n = *126)*	*1801–1900* (n = *104)*
English	80%	62%
French	6	56
German	25	79

from the German states suggests the need of provincial scientists to locate themselves firmly on a professional map:

(From the physiological institute at Breslau)[12]
Concerning the Reaction of Cow's and Mother's Milk and Their Relationship to the Reaction of Casein and Phosphate.
By
Georg Courant
Assistant Physician at the Royal University Woman's Clinic in Breslau
(1891-G035)

More typical of German credentialing is "by Prof C Nägli" (1861-G135). French and English credentialing is also typically sparse, for example, "By M. Rozet, Officer in the Royal Corps of Geographers" (1825-F207) and "By Francis R. Japp, F[ellow of the].R[oyal] .S[ociety]." (1891-E045).

HEADINGS Nearly half of 19th-century articles have headings. This is an increase of 30% compared with the last century. Between the first and second half of the century, headings increased by 18% and substantive headings increased by 37%. Throughout this century, substantive headings are clearly preferred, generally by themselves, far less frequently in combination with general headings.

The following sets of headings illustrate the range of possibilities:

Set 1. Title and General Headings (German)
Concerning the Spontaneous Decay of Sweetwater Polyps Together with Several Remarks on the Succession of Generations.
Observation of 15. December
Observation of 16. December
Observation of 17. December
Observation of 18. December
Observation of 19. December
Observation of 20. December
Concluding Observations
Clarification of the Table (1860-K125)

12. Breslau is now Wroclaw in Poland about 150 kilometers east of Dresden.

Set 2. Title and Substantive Headings (English)
ON QUERCUS FISSA, *Champion,* IN REFERENCE TO THE DISTINCTIVE CHARACTERS OF QUERCUS AND CASTANEA . . .

1. *It may be included in Quercus.*
2. *It may be separated as the type of a genus.*
3. *It may be referred to Castanea.* (1863-M0120)

Set 3. Title with General and Substantive Headings (French)
Note on a case of primitive interstitial myocarditis, in a chloro-anemic woman of 23. Death caused by gangrene of the extremities and cerebral deterioration. Aphasic. Autopsy. Embolism of the left sylvian, of the tibal on the same side and of the pedicle of the right side. Infarction of the kidneys. Atrophy of the arterial system. Intracardiac clots, the consequences of myocarditis.

Current condition.—
10 January.—
12 January.—
15 January.—
22 January.—
31 January.—
6 February.—
8 February.—
AUTOPSY. *Heart.*
Right lung.
—Left.
Liver.
Stomach.
Spleen.
Right kidney.
—Left.
Intestines.
Uterus.
Brain.
Prefrontal section.
Pediculo-frontal section.
Frontal section.
Parietal section.
Pediculo-pariental section.
Occipital section.
Lower limbs.
Microscopic examination.
COMMENTS. (1880-A102)

In set 1, the title carries all the substantive burden; the headings are a finding system of general categories. In contrast, in set 2 the headings combine with the first half of the title to form an indicative abstract of the main body of the article. In set 3, along with the detailed title, there are general and substantive headings that allow the article to be read opportunistically. This anticipates the master finding systems of late-20th-century counterparts.

CITATIONS Six out of 10 articles contain citations, as compared with 5 to 10 in the preceding century. Citations are still incorporated in the text, but with increased frequency they are placed at the bottom of the page: 60% of articles place them there, as contrasted with 42% in the preceding century. When citations appear at the bottom of the page in English and German articles, they are occasionally numbered; this is the invariable practice in French articles. In one instance only are citations represented, as in the 20th-century, by consecutive numbers in the text, numbers whose key is a "Works Cited" list at the end of the article (1894-G110).

The format of citations is far from uniform. Page numbers are often omitted; article titles almost always are. Two practices are well entrenched: the abbreviation of such words as "page" and "volume," and abbreviation of the titles of periodicals. In addition, in marked contrast to the preceding century, there is almost always an attempt to separate the various elements of the citation by means of italics, small capitals, parentheses, roman numerals, and so forth. For example, from 1800 we have a citation within the text: "Messieurs Landriani and Van Marum (*An. de Chimie*, Tom II, p. 270)" (1800-E180). From 1854, we have the following in-text citation: "Dugès discovered (Annal. d. scienc. XXXVI) in the fall of 1830" (1859-G070). From 1893, we have a raised footnote number in the text at "From a revision of this work published by the scientist Mr. Henri J. Osborn"; at the bottom of the page, we have the corresponding number and the note, "*Rev. Arg. de Hist. Nat.*, I, para[graph] 4, p. 218, August 1891" (1893-F217).

In all cases, despite much variation, there is information sufficient to locate the source. Moreover, there is more information than in the preceding century, especially in the case of article citations. In the 19th century, article citations contain an average of 4.2 reference elements—author name, article title, journal name, and so forth—up from 3.5 in the last century, an increase of 20%.

In the 19th century, clearly, it has become increasingly important to convey the sense that the literature has been searched, and that no relevant article has been omitted. Nevertheless, it is no more difficult to read the texts of scientific articles because, more and more, citations are tucked out of the way, at the bottom of the page; moreover, it is easier to read the citations themselves because their elements are, more and more, subject to visual separation.

Substantive Features

ABSTRACTS In our sample of 19th-century scientific articles, though abstracting is an occasional practice, we find no heading abstracts as such, no informative summaries that follow the title and precede the main text of articles. In two cases, we have substantial abstracts of papers apparently read in full at scientific meetings, a form invented by the Académie Royale des Sciences in their 17th- and 18th-century *Histoires*. In the *Proceedings of the Royal Society of London*, we have the abstract of a paper entitled "On a New Series of Compounds containing Boron" (1863-E060). Similarly, in the *Comptes Rendus*, we have an "*extrait*" entitled "Absorption of Gas by Iron Wires Made Red-Hot and Dipped in Dilute Sulfuric Acid, during Wire-Drawing Operations" (1874-F132). In the 19th century, as in earlier centuries, the main textual clues as to article substance remain informative titles and headings.

INTRODUCTIONS As table 6.7 shows, most 19th-century articles open with a complete introduction as defined by Swales (1990). Yet we must not conflate 19th-century introductions with their 20th-century counterparts: the different audiences discussed at the beginning of this chapter are the source of considerable diversity. We choose three sample introductions to illustrate this diversity as it pertains to significant differences within the audience for serious science.

In the early 19th century, the French chemist Gay-Lussac wrote an article in *Annalen der Physik* entitled "Remarks Concerning the Precipitation of Silver by Means of Copper." The original is a translation from French into German, so, for our purposes, it has the advantage of representing French as well as German practice. It begins:

> Most chemists believe that the precipitate that is formed when a strip of copper is placed in a solution of silver nitrate is an alloy of both metals, and it is therefore impossible to obtain pure silver in this way. This is correct if in the process one takes no special circumstances into consideration. If, however, one pays attention to the timing and to actual causes, one can easily obtain silver that is free from all of the precipitated copper. (1812-G160)

While there are signs of its authorship in a preprofessional period, for example, the reference to the beliefs of "most chemists," a vagueness that will eventually be replaced by specific citations, the article is clearly addressed to disciplinary adherents. Moreover, the article's emphasis is not merely empirical, but theoretical: we cannot obtain an authentic result unless, its author states, we focus on "timing and . . . actual causes." Along with these signs of disciplinary maturity, we see illustrated Swales's schema for scientific introductions. While the intellectual territory is largely presupposed—a characteristic omission where the members of research groups are well known to each other and are working on a set of common problems—the niche in which new knowledge is to be placed is clearly marked, as is Gay-Lussac's niche-occupying candidate, an improved method for the precipitation of silver out of a silver nitrate solution.

Let us compare this introduction with one from England, from three-quarters of a century later. The article in question, on taxonomy, is from *The Zoologist* and is entitled "A Few Words on European Bats." It is by the Right Honorable Lord Lilford, a Fellow of the Zoological Society:

> Prompted by your remarks in the last number of "The Zoologist," and by the excellent plate of the Greater Horse-shoe Bat, I venture to offer to your readers a few notes on those species of the order of Cheiroptera which I have met with in the European region. I may mention that I took up the study of Bats in the summer of 1870 and in a few days discovered that five species are tolerably abundant in the neighbourhood of Lilford and that at least two more, which I have not been able satisfactorily to identify, are occasionally to be met with in the northern division of Northhamptonshire. I have no work of reference at hand except Lord Clermont's "Guide to the Quadrupeds and Reptiles of Europe," so I adopt his arrangement and nomenclature. From the habits of the European Bats a close study of the animals in their natural state is almost impossible, but to my mind most attractive; I have no pretense to any special knowledge on the subject, and my only object in thus addressing you is the hope that my notes may induce some of your readers to turn their attention to this comparatively little-known branch of Zoology, and give us the result of their experiences in your Journal. To those who have as yet paid no attention to Bats, it may be useful to mention Dr. Dobson's exhaustive British Museum Catalogue of the Cheiroptera as the standard English work on the subject. (1887-E095)

Swales's paradigm in this case is as strictly followed as in the Gay-Lussac example, but how different the result from its much earlier embodiment! In each passage, a territory is presupposed, a niche prepared and occupied. But the natural history article is addressed, not to professional others, but to fellow enthusiasts, "readers" with whom Lord Lilford is having a chat about a topic of mutual interest, the habits of European bats. This is not a formal research report for experts, but a "few notes" by someone with, by his overly modest admission, no "special knowledge of the subject." Even its references to the literature attest to the amateur status of the author[13] (the first citation is to a book the author happens to have "to hand") and of the audience (the second citation is to a work about whose existence a professional would not need to be reminded).

The first passage is aimed at chemists interested in the extraction of silver; the second, to an audience whose avocation is the study of bats. We can see this difference in emphasis clearly when we contrast the use of "impossible" in these two introductions. In Gay Lussac's case, nature is responsible for the difficulty, and there is nothing even an expert chemist can do to change it: "[I]t is therefore *impossible* to obtain pure silver in this way" (emphasis added). In Lord Lilford's case, the word is attributed to the efforts of students of nature like Lord Lilford himself, who by due diligence can overcome the observational difficulty posed by nature: "[A] close study of the animals in their natural state is *almost impossible*, but to my mind most attractive." In the first case, we have the kind of authoritative, neutral statement we expect from an expert; in the second, the enthusiasm of the devoted amateur hoping his enthusiasm will rub off on others.

These introductions by Gay-Lussac and Lord Lilford represent two audiences for science that persisted from the 17th through the 19th century: professional and amateur. They also represent two geopolitical orientations, the one standardly Continental, with a strong tendency toward professionalism; the other, standardly English, persistently bent on preserving amateurism. This is not to say that English science is dominated by amateurs, only that if we see an example like Lord Lilford's article, it is more likely to be English than Continental.

This divergence, however, should not be emphasized to the point of obscuring the considerable convergence in communicative practices between England and the Continent. Our sample includes seven articles in observational astronomy from 1825 to 1844. While all three of our languages are represented in this group, their communicative uniformity transcends national and linguistic barriers. Here is the introduction to "The Solar Eclipse of 8 July 1842," an anonymous contribution to the *Bulletins de l'Académie Royale des Science et Belles-Lettres de Bruxelles* (Bulletins of the Royal Academy of Science and Belles-Lettres of Brussels). Foremost in the author's mind is his firm sense of membership in a community concerned with accurate astronomical observations reaching back to antiquity. In this close-knit international community, there is no need to remind fellow astronomers of the intellectual territory all mutually inhabit:

> *Brussels.*—The sunrise on the morning of the eighth was very beautiful; it heralded the most favorable conditions for the event to be observed. However, clouds, driven rapidly by a south wind, spread over the sky, which was almost entirely covered sev-

13. The word "amateur" perhaps does not do justice to Thomas Littleton Powys Lilford, president of the British Ornithologists Union from 1867 to 1896 and a leading authority on birds in his region. One of his articles on birds was cited by Charles Darwin in *The Descent of Man* (chap. 4). Lilford is a good example of the devoted amateur who makes a serious contribution to local knowledge in natural history.

> eral moments after the beginning of the eclipse. The sky continued covered during the whole of the eclipse, the phases of which it was possible to observe only during those rare intervals when the cloud cover parted. It was during one of these intervals that the final moments of the eclipse could be viewed; and luck alone was thus responsible for two most important astronomical observations that were made, those at the beginning and the end. As to observations relevant to physics, it was necessary to abandon them entirely. (1842-F142)

There is a final point to be made: during the next century, the scenic introduction reporting the weather conditions for astronomical observations will vanish from the pages of the scientific literature, as will the folksy address to fellow students of nature, while Gay-Lussac's austere introduction for "other chemists" will become the gold standard others will follow in all disciplines. And it is no coincidence that chemistry during the 19th century was, arguably, the most "professionalized" of the scientific disciplines.

CONCLUSIONS In the 19th century, conclusions of one sort or another are frequent, though by no means obligatory: 22% of articles in our sample have no conclusions at all. This percentage, however, somewhat exaggerates the degree of nonconformity. Two articles without conclusions are abstracts (1874-F132, 1863-E060); the absence in these cases is hardly surprising. Moreover, six of the articles without conclusions are taxonomical, no more than expanded lists (1857-G050, 1854-G070, 1855-F107, 1889-F167, 1848-E025, 1846-E135); three are mere observations (1825-G115, 1875-E055, 1834-E110); two are simple narratives (1891-G065, 1801-G025); one is an extract from a letter (1801-E150). With these articles omitted, only 10% of 19th-century articles lack conclusions.

By and large, 19th-century conclusions approach current norms: adding insight, suggesting wider significance, making recommendations for future research; 24% do all three, by and large in the order we designate as canonical. In the following late conclusion, for example, from an 1891 article in *Zeitschrift für Angewandte Chemie* (Journal of Applied Chemistry), "Fuel and Heating Systems," all components are present in the canonical order strictly interpreted:

> Then the combustibility requirements of A. Bauer were cited, whose results do not deviate fundamentally from the Dulong formula; concerning the carrying out of the experiment, there was no more accurate information. So long as nothing exact was cited concerning the execution of the experiment, whether and especially how the product of combustion was investigated, nothing can be said of the degree of accuracy attained. If they are indeed actually correct, at this time they show merely that for this test the Dulong formula comes near to the truth. Next (that is, as soon as the Annual Report is ready) more will be said. (1891-G085)

Such a conclusion reflects professionalism: a common disciplinary formation to which individual researchers will continue to contribute.

Detailed summaries at the end of articles are infrequent (1891-G035, 1898-G045, 1807-G190, 1894-G110, 1838-F127). But when they do appear, they look familiar to modern readers. This conclusion appeared in the *Annalen der Physik* at the end of an article entitled "Several Incidental Thoughts Provoked by Experiments Concerning Heat"; in all respects it is a model for the summary-type conclusions in the 20th century:

> The conclusion of this article is that, to clarify the phenomena of heat exchange, one needs no special caloric, whose existence is beforehand associated with many difficulties of various sorts. One need only assume that positive heat is really nothing other than the positive oscillating expansion of the ponderable materials within the scope of everyone's experience; equally, negative heat is nothing other than the oscillating contraction of such materials, in so far as their masses were by this means neither increased nor reduced. One must have always before one this proposition only: that the now greater, now lesser expansion of various materials, containing heat energy of whatever degree, depends on the now stronger, now weaker cohesion and gravitational force among its parts. (1807-G190)

As was true for introductions, 19th-century conclusions more than occasionally depart from the purely scientific, deviating into the personal and the polemical, a practice virtually unknown in the late 20th century. In these roles, they can be the vehicles for telling stories, making excuses, and indulging in sarcastic attacks. Publishing in the *Proceedings of the Royal Society of London*, the Englishman E. J. Stone concludes an article on magnetical observations of the earth with the following personal narrative: "I arrived in Namaqualand on April 9, by the Union steamship 'Namaqua,' [its captain] Captain Barker, reached Port Nolloth [on the Western coast of South Africa], on my return, on the evening of Wednesday, April 29, but did not sail until Wednesday, May 6, reaching the observatory on Saturday, May 9" (1875-E055). A personal note is also struck by another Englishman, H. F. Hance, with a closing apology for the quality of his work about plant taxonomy, published in the *The Journal of Botany*. His excuse is that he is in Hong Kong, "at nearly the edge of the civilized world":

> Were I more favorably located, with access to extensive herbaria and libraries, I have no doubt that I might have illustrated and enforced the arguments adduced above by examples both more numerous and more striking; but I may plead my habitat "in ultimo fere orbis angulo," to use the words of Thunberg, and with nothing but my own library to fall back upon, some excuse for whatever defects or oversights may be observed in this paper. (1863-E010)

The personal can also turn polemical, as in the conclusion to a German article that appeared in the *Neues Jahrbuch für Mineralogie* (New Yearbook of Mineralogy) entitled "Concerning the Extinct Volcanoes of the Rhenish and the Eifel Regions, Especially in Reference to Dr. Hibbert's History of the Former." The author, Herr General van der Wyk, has nothing good to say about Dr. Hibbert's work, which he attacks with venomous gusto:

> In chapter 30, page 229 the writer develops for the fourth time (compare pages 16, 75, 188) his theory of the direction of the current of this stretch of water that flows from Bingen onwards in a southerly direction. The sketch that accompanies this

> theory, whose arrows are designed to make things convincing, does not fail again (!) to make his point. He must have very little confidence in his readers' memory, since he considers such repetition necessary. Therefore I welcome this remark (page 231): *But our history now draws near to a close.* Here I break off; the rest, whatever little captures our attention before we reach page 261, is of no great interest to geology. (1836-G130; emphasis in original)

VISUALS AND EQUATIONS Visuals are very frequent. They are present in half the articles. In articles that contain them, their average number is 7.4 (excluding the one article with 73), an increase compared with the preceding century.

Thirteen percent of articles have equations, also an increase compared with the past century. While in only two cases are equations numbered as in modern practice (1886-F212, 1886-F222); in all cases after 1812, they are separated by white space from their surrounding text; that is, equations are treated as elements deserving special visual prominence.

Close integration of tables and figures and their texts is evident. As in the preceding century, most tables and figures are numbered. Nevertheless, there is an interesting change: in the second half of the century, the use of legends for figures increases nearly eightfold. While this increase needs to be treated with caution—the numbers in the subsample are quite small—it is certainly suggestive of greater systematization.

Our three illustrations of visual-textual integration come from the last two decades of the century, a time when printing practices permitted the easier integration of visuals and text. Full communicative advantage is taken of this technical advance. In our French example, we have in the text "I have traced in *fig.* 1 opposite a certain number of these curves for the values of C between 0°, 2, and 4°"; on the opposite page we have a figure, labeled "Fig. 1" at the top, with the following legend at the bottom: "Curves of raw coefficients of the lowering of C/P" (1886-F222). In our German sample, we have the text "In table I the results of this series of experiments are given." Just below, we have a table with its number and title above it: "Table I. Reaction of the Cow's Milk" (1891-G035). In our last, American illustration, we have the text: "Figure 4 shows a transverse section of one of these primary divisions or carpels which well indicates the position of the ovules (*a*), the funiculus (*b*), the placenta (*c*), and the ovarian cell (*d*)." The figure follows just below, and then the following legend: "Figure 4.—Transverse section of one of the carpels of Yucca pistil: *a*, ovule; *b*, funiculus; *c*, ovarian cell; *d*, fibro-vascular bundles; *f*, fibro-vascular tissue; *g*, primary dissepiment × 9 [magnified nine times]" (1882-E105).

We reserve the next chapter for a discussion of the substantive features of 19th-century visuals.

Conclusion

Stylistically, 19th-century scientific prose appears to more closely resemble its 17th-century origins than the highly compressed, neutral, monotonal prose of the late 20th century. The implied audiences include both the avid amateur and the no-nonsense professional. And the personal, openly polemical, and journalistic remain vital elements within this literature. Yet we do not mean to imply that movement in the direction of 20th-century style is not evident. For example, our German and English samples become more like the French in terms of impersonal expression. Moreover, in all three languages, sentence length and clausal density drop to a level fairly close to the levels we find in the 20th century. Further, despite the great diversity of scientific journals represented in our 19th-century sample, our data suggest movement toward a homogeneous communicative style.

We also have a master presentational system approaching maturity. Its primarily formal elements meaningfully separate and coordinate the various communicative units in scientific texts: title and author credits, headings, equations segregated from text, visuals provided with legends, and citations standardized as to format and position. Simultaneously, elements that are primarily substantive orient the reader: introductions prepare readers for what is to come, while conclusions summarize what has passed and, occasionally, propose what ought to happen next.

CHAPTER 7

Argument in the 19th Century

Concluding his article on European bats, Lord Lilford asked the readers of *The Zoologist* for more research on the subject, not because of any particular problem, but because of its past neglect:

> In conclusion, I may mention that, besides the species mentioned above as occurring on our islands, I find that Lord Clermont (on the authority, as I suppose, of Thomas Bell, "Brit. Quad.") admits six other species, viz. *V. Bechsteinii*, Desm., *V. Leisleri*, Desm., *V. discolor*, Desm., *V. Daubentonii*, Desm., *V. emarginatus*, Desm., and *Plecotus brevimanus*, Bonap.*; but the simple truth is that few English zoologists have studied, or at all events published the results of their studies on our Bats, and if my meagre remarks should induce any of your readers to turn their attention to this subject, I will hope that we may shortly have the benefit of "more light." (1892-E095)

Our concern is not so much with the words in Lord Lilford's text as with its asterisk. That mark directs the reader to an editorial comment at the bottom of the page: "*Plecotus brevimanus* Jenyns, is now generally admitted to be merely the young of *Plecotus auritus*, Linnaeus. The nomenclature here adopted from Lord Clermont's 'Guide to the Quadrupeds and Reptiles of Europe' (1859) stands in need of considerable revision, and cannot be regarded as authoritative at the present day." Here, relegated to a footnote is a genuine research problem: the need for a "considerable revision" of Lord Clermont's nomenclature. And that revision likely will only come to fruition as a result of efforts by a "professional" zoologist with a deep knowledge of animal taxonomy, not just any reader of *The Zoologist*.

We will not dwell on the history of this editorial transaction; we are interested only in the communicative result that makes visible the tension between two views of science, the amateur and the specialist. This tension is at the root of much of the variety of 19th-century science, and of 19th-century scientific argumentation as well.

The arguments we analyze in this chapter provide ample testimony of this variety. Scientists are still very much in the business of establishing new facts about the natural world, though, as the century wears on, the evidence required in support of new factual claims increases and the need for explanation arises, on occasion from *within* the fact-gathering enterprise rather than as part of some larger explanatory scheme. There is still, of course, a well-differentiated explanatory enterprise, though the differentiation among explanations in different disciplines, begun in the late 18th century, becomes more clearly marked.

Despite the variety of explanatory goals and their supporting arguments, as the 19th century progresses increasingly more complex argument becomes a unifying force, a common bridge from observations and experimental results to responsible theorizing, whether in the pure or in the applied sciences. There is a gradual shift from description to explanation in many of the sciences, and a consequent increase in the complexity of their supporting arguments, an increase especially evident in those arguments that integrate texts and visuals. It is this trend toward complexity that will eventually exclude the amateur from serious science.

General Profile

Table 7.1 shows the distribution of article types in our 19th-century sample of complete articles (our data for the 18th century are included before the slash for ease of comparison). As was the case in the 18th century, observational articles reign supreme in all three languages, and the French still show a strong overall interest in the theoretical and mathematical. Unexpectedly to us, the percentages of experimental articles in the French and English samples actually decline between the 18th and 19th centuries. Only the German sample reflects some gain in experimental articles, as well as purely theoretical ones, a finding consistent with the impression that

Table 7.1. Type of Whole Articles in 18th- and 19th-Century Samples

Genre	*English* (n= *44/37*)[a]	*French* (n = *54/25*)	*German* (n = *28/42*)
Experimental	14%/8%	17%/8%	10%/22%
Theoretical	0/0	9/4	0/12
Methodological	18/14	9/4	4/7
Observational	30/41	22/32	53/29
Observational/theoretical	12/13	22/36	4/12
Experimental/theoretical	14/13	6/8	25/16
Mathematical	2/3	15/4	0/0
Other	10/8	0/4	4/2

[a]Numbers before slash, 18th century; after slash, 19th.

Table 7.2. Purpose of Whole Article in 18th- and 19th-Century Samples

	English (n = *44/37*)[a]	*French* (n = *54/25*)	*German* (n = *28/42*)
Observational	31%/43%	29%/32%	50%/26%
Experimental results	16/5	15/8	10/26
Mechanical explanation	18/24	13/36	24/34
Mathematical rule	5/3	15/12	0/7
Mathematical explanation	5/0	15/4	4/0
Making or improving equipment	20/16	13/4	8/7
Other	5/9	0/4	4/0

[a]Numbers before slash, 18th century; after slash, 19th.

German science moved into the front ranks of physical science during the 19th century (Nye 1996, pp. 6–12).

Table 7.2 shows many more 19th-century articles offering mechanical explanations for the acquired facts. Indeed, in the French and German samples, mechanical explanation[1] has dethroned straight observation as the main purpose of scientific articles. Also, in the German sample we find the balance shifting for the first time toward experimental results over observations—a trend that will accelerate during the next century in the samples for all three languages. As in the 18th century, the English sample has outstripped the others in articles about making or improving equipment, an important enterprise if experimental results and observations are to gain in accuracy and precision.

Arguing for Facts

Just as in preceding centuries, scientists argue facts into place throughout the 19th, though the nature of the case they make alters as the century progresses. Early arguments have, as might be expected, an 18th-century look: qualitative description is the ground of factual reliability. But there are differences. In our 19th-century sample, there is no reliance upon witnessing in the reporting of observations and experiments, and no resort to a reflexive concern with the accuracy of instrumentation or the purity of reagents. From this neglect, we should infer, not a lack of interest, but rather a sense that these matters are mostly settled, or in any case are no longer the subjects of scientific discourse.

Early in the century, we have, in chemistry and geology, claims for the existence of facts supported, not by measurements of any sort but, in the 18th-century manner, simply by the evidence of the senses. In an article in *Berlinisches Jahrbuch für die Pharmacie* (Berlin Yearbook of Pharmacy) entitled "Concerning Naphthene and

1. We use the term "mechanical" here in the very broadest sense of the word, meaning any principle for how things work that is not mathematical. Later in this chapter, we will differentiate between mechanical explanations that have some basis in the workings of a machine and those that do not, such as evolution.

Dulcified Spirits,"[2] Georg Wilhelm Friedrich describes an experimental result in terms of sight, color, smell, and taste: "The residue, which remained in the retort, I distilled now by itself, and was greeted with an acidic liquid, which consisted of a sulfurous acid combined with some acetic acid, on which swam numerous drops of a yellowish oil which sink in water, an oil usually made use of under the name Oleum vini. Through rectification, this oil becomes bright yellow, and is spicy to the taste and sweet to the smell" (1801-G170). Especially at a time when technical terminology is not uniform—when a substance is *usually* called "Oleum vini"—it is understandable that chemists should convey their results by means of complex phenomenological descriptions. There seems no better way of conveying chemical identity.

Early geological claims can be similarly phenomenological. In the *Journal für die Chemie, Physik und Mineralogie* (Journal of Chemistry, Physics and Mineralogy), in an article entitled "Concerning an Aerolite that Fell to Earth at Lissa," Dr. Reuss describes a meteorite in phenomenological terms parallel to those of Friedrich:

> [The crust] displays numerous large and small depressions and bumps such as contact with a soft, elastic body makes, as when one presses or kneads it with one's finger. As a whole, indeed, the crust feels smooth, only here and there is it somewhat rough. The meteor stones themselves are conglomerate masses; they all have a light, ash-gray color and a very small-scale fine grained structure. In all directions, they are shot through with extremely small lumps or veins, whose maximum width might be 1/2 to 3/4 of a line, and which exhibit very small and finely sprinkled metallic grains, generally the yellow of brass, but occurring in silver-like or copper-red colors here and there. (1807-G175)

In this description, despite its isolated single measurement, the feel, color, and mass of the meteor stone predominate.

Taxonomy has a similarly 18th-century flavor, a sense that amateurs as well as professionals are welcome. In a *Philosophical Transactions* article entitled "Experiments and Observations on Certain Stony and Metalline Substances, which at Different Times are said to have Fallen on the Earth," Edward Howard parallels the German chemist and geologist in his passion for sensual re-creation. Nevertheless, he supplements this re-creation, as the rest of the article also makes clear, with a concern for chemical composition. Yet, in this early 19th-century article, we are still well within the orbit of 18th-century geology:

> This stone was in a perfectly entire state; consequently, its whole surface was covered over with the black crust peculiar to all stones of this kind. As the stone was of a small size, it became necessary to sacrifice the whole of it to the investigation of its nature. Its grain was coarse, similar to that of stones from Benares; in it might be perceived the same gray globular bodies, the same kind of martial pyrites and the same particles of iron in the metallic state. The proportion of these last was much less than in the stone from Yorkshire; but rather greater than those stones from Benares. (1802-E170)

2. "Dulcification" is the process by which the acidity of a solution is neutralized.

In this next passage, from the end of the 19th century, we are in a different world, one in which the amateur is not as welcome. In an article appearing in the *Bulletin, Société Botanique de France* (Bulletin, Botanical Society of France), "Lichens of Cantal and Several Neighboring Departments Collected in 1887–88,"[3] Hue places species firmly in their genuses, for example,

> 189. **Lecanora veronensis.** *Acarospora veronensis.* Mass. *Ricer. Lich. crost.* p. 29. *C.*—Saint-Flor—on the basalt.
>
> This lichen is like the one Massalongo described, a specimen of which has been sent to the Museum; it differs from it only in that its little apothecia (width 0.2–3 millimeters) are not always solitary in the little squama of the thallus; one sometimes sees two, very rarely three or four of them. The paraphyses are slightly septated in the Museum specimen and they are not here. The spores, very numerous in these thecae that are 0.10–11 mm. in length by 0.020–25 mm. in width, are 0.0025–45 mm. long and 0.0010-.15 wide. (1889-F167)

Here, in contrast to the previous three passages, science is a matter of careful comparison based on accurate and precise measurement of objects described largely by means of a specialized technical terminology. In this passage, the lichen species exists as a range of features deployed in rigorously determined taxonomic space.

Even within a factually oriented enterprise, the need for explanation may arise, as it were, of its own accord. Such is the case with the selection that follows, from chemistry. Despite its factual nature, because his claim relies on chains of inference, Herr Vogel regards it as contestable. Because of this, he is obliged to argue. In this passage, the coexistence of "calcium chloride and magnesium sulfate" in mineral water is in question. The author has serious doubts about this coexistence, despite the opinions of "many chemists of our time":

> I am very far from denying the possibility that these salts, dissolved in a large quantity of water, could exist together; however, for this really to be so, it must be proved by means of an experiment still to be devised.
>
> Even assuming for the sake of argument that the calcium chloride is only incompletely decomposed by heat and evaporation of water by means of the magnesium sulfate, that at the same time this latter salt exists in great excess in the water seems to me to argue against all experience. (1815-G150)

In this passage, the author deftly argues against the received opinion that the substances coexist in the same chemical environment; he does so by adverting to a received opinion of a higher order, the necessity of careful experimentation as a test for claims.

We also see factually driven explanation in the case of four articles in observational astronomy published from 1831 to 1844. Each shows a heightened concern for instrumental and observational accuracy. This concern is not an occasional topic for reflection and argument, as in our 18th-century examples, but a matter of routine, especially in a field in which there is a necessary reliance on instruments for

3. "Cantal" is in the Auvergne region of France.

observation and measurement. Two articles deal with the quality of instrumentation: one with the effects of warmth and humidity on the running of an English astronomical clock (1840-E100), the other with the geometrical optics of a new German sextant (1844-G010). An article in French discusses the limits that meteorological conditions place on the accuracy of astronomical observations (1842-F142). The remaining article in this subset is the most interesting; it reveals with clarity a natural transition within the descriptive enterprise from instrumental accuracy to explanation with a theoretical base. In this English article, factual discrepancies impel their explanation:

> An error discovered by M. Santini in the constants of the variation of the daily motion brought the two results much nearer; but a difference still remains between the observed times of the perihelion passage in 1826 and 1832, such as would arise from a resisting medium. Toward ascertaining this point, M. Santini has recomputed the perturbations caused by *Jupiter* with the values of the mass given by Laplace and by Professor Airy. (1834-E110)

These astronomical articles also bespeak a European science; in particular, they exemplify an international enterprise with a common set of high professional standards.

Arguing Explanations into Place

Table 7.2 shows that articles whose purpose is mechanical explanation increased in varying degrees in all three languages. Even early in the 19th century, descriptive geology is giving way to its explanatory counterpart. In a French article concerning a geological survey of the Ardèche River, Rozet offers strong arguments that a natural bridge was not a result of water erosion:

> Several people have claimed that the arch of the bridge of Arc was the result of erosion caused by the water of the Ardèche. It is enough, in my opinion, to have examined the scene in order to be convinced of the contrary view; in the first place, the interior surface of the arch not being at all smooth, cannot have been created by a substance capable of wearing stone away; thus, not only has the water not created the arch, it has not enlarged it either. If the rock of Arc ever blocked passage of the river, a like effect would have occurred six hundred meters further on. Opposite the village of Chames, the valley is bisected by a rock similar to that of Arc. At one time, water passed over it, as everything indicates. But finally a cataclysm occurred on the left, which opened a passage to the river, which presently makes a large detour in this place and in examining the rock that it uncovered, one sees not even the beginning of a trace of perforation.
>
> Now I say that the bridge of Arc is only a cavern, and I am going to prove it by exemplification. (1825-F207)

In this passage, while Rozet is sensitive to a range of geological forces that form a causal relationship with current geological features, his argument by strict analogy assumes a particular cause can be read off from a particular constellation of effects.

His is an appeal merely to look at the facts, but the facts, as it turns out, are only such when seen through the lens of a particular explanation of their origin.

Chemistry also manifests an early theoretical turn. An article in German, entitled "Ideas Concerning Acidity and Alkalinity in Relation to the New Discoveries of Davy," is wholly theoretical, arguing for a lawlike relationship between the ability of bodies to oxidize and their oxygen content:

> The nearer the substances in this table stand to oxygen, it could be said, the more oxygenating (?) (*plus oxigénque*) they are; and from this it follows that oxygenicity (?) (*oxygénicité*) is the property of these substances of having an acid antagonism in relation to others, one that gives it to the bonds, which they [the bodies] enter into with these [bonds], and oxygen itself is chiefly the oxygenating substance (*la substance oxygénetique, par excellence*). From the preceding, it follows that the oxygenicity of substances must be the smaller, the greater their oxidizability (*oxydabilité*). (1810-G195; French and question marks in original)

These explanations are purely chemical; no material substratum is involved, though, of course, one is presupposed. It is an ontology, not of things, but of relationships among things. In this selection from the early 19th century we also have signs of the internationalization of chemistry: we are reading the German translation of a French article by an Italian; also, and more important, we are witnessing the incorporation of the new French chemistry into the German chemical community (Hufbauer 1982).

Our last three examples, from the biology and physics of the last quarter of the century, are each motivated by the deep-seated belief that theoretical argumentation is a routine expectation. The first selection, by Frederick W. Mott, is from the article "Results of Hemisection of the Spinal Cord in Monkeys." Mott's question is precisely what inferences are permissible from one in a series of experiments on monkeys:

> The clip is fixed on the sole of the right foot which is paralyzed by the hemisection of the right side of the cord. The impulses which travel up the posterior roots, and posterior columns of the same side, arrive at cell (*c*); the channel of least resistance is by the nerve process which this cell gives off to the hemisphere of the *opposite* side, by which connection it reaches the hemisphere on the *same* side. Sensory impressions received in the right hemisphere are referred to impressions coming from the left foot. Consequently, the animal projects the sensation received from the right foot to the left foot, and it believes the cause of irritation is there until undeceived by repeated fruitless endeavours at removal and by visual correction. Whether this explanation be the correct one or not, it seems to me to support the view that the path of least resistance for some sensory impressions, *e.g.*, tactile and muscular, passes up the same side of the cord, and inasmuch as the same phenomenon of Allochiria was observed in the high hemisection of the 3rd cervical segment as in the mid dorsal, upper dorsal, or lower dorsal regions, we must conclude that main decussation does not take place till above the 3rd cervical. (1892-E020)

Mott's argument takes the following form. First, there is a narrative of experimental procedures and observations, understandably unhedged; for example, "The clip *is fixed*" and "The impulses . . . *arrive* at cell (c)." This is followed by an explanation that is equally unhedged and, one might consequently think, equally certain: the animal reacts as it does just because of its surgical alteration. But just as the skeptical reader might begin to object to this perhaps unwarranted certainty, the author retreats to a weaker claim, signaled by an elaborate hedge: "Whether this explanation be the correct one or not, it seems to me to support the view that. . . ." If this view is correct, as the author firmly believes, then "we *must conclude*" that the nerve impulses mainly cross only above the third cervical vertebra of the spinal chord. As in the passage quoted above, concerning the coexistence of "calcium chloride and magnesium sulfate," the author recognizes that his claim is only as strong as the argument he makes, an argument carefully modulated to its audience's notion of legitimate scientific inference from experimental results.

A passage from the *Proceedings of the Biological Society of Washington* shows that the passion for explanation has crossed, not only into physiology, but into biology proper:

> The peculiarities which I [the author C. V. Riley] have endeavored to present to you are full of suggestion, particularly for those who are in the habit of looking beyond the mere facts of observation in endeavors to find some rational explanation of them; who, in other words, see in everything they observe significances and harmonies not generally understood. The facts indicate clearly, it seems to me, how the peculiar structures of the female Pronuba [moth] have been evolved by gradual adaptation to the particular functions we now find her performing. With the growing adaptation to the Pronuba's help, the Yucca flower has lost, to a great extent, the activity of its septal glands; yet coincident with it we find an increase in the secreting power of the stigma. This increase of the stigmatic fluid has undoubtedly had much to do with originally attracting the moth thereto, while the pollinizing instinct doubtless became more and more fixed in proportion as the insect lost the power or desire of feeding. (1892-E105)

With the single phrase, "mere facts of observation," we have a measure of how far we have come from a time when such facts, and, possibly, their systematic arrangement, might legitimately constitute the main thrust of a scientific discipline. For Mr. Riley, deciphering the "significances and harmonies" behind the facts is the real work of science.

Our final example of the shift to explanation is from German physics. Its author, the inventor W. Siemens, enthusiastically proclaims he has discovered

> an entirely new physical phenomenon, which has the greatest scientific consequences! The result of my experiments is that a potential difference originates in the region of the illumination of the gold-leaf between it and the ground-plate, a potential difference that, to all appearances, is proportional to the strength of the illumination and that persists unaltered so long as the illumination lasts. Because dark heat-rays do not have an electromotoric effect, the assumption of a thermoelectric effect is excluded from the explanation of the phenomenon. Mr. Fritts presumes that the light waves that penetrate the selenium are directly converted into electrical current, and that the proportionality between the current strength and the luminous intensity confirms this. This effect is exhibited within the bounds of experimental error in results compiled in the following table. (1885-G040)

In this, as in the previous selection, we are squarely in the midst of an explanatory enterprise. But there is an important difference. For the biologist, evolution is an explanatory scheme; it is a matter, as it were, of connecting the dots of observation to those of theory. In the case of the German author, in contrast, we find ourselves at the edge of a research front, his exclamation point merely underlining the depiction of a "Eureka!" moment, one in which experimental observation and theory, always in dialectical tension, significantly interact. A new phenomenon defies explanation within existing thermoelectrical theory, forcing on the researcher the interesting burden of an alternative explanation, one in which the strength of the current will be proportional to the strength of the illumination, as measured in footcandles. Herr Siemens's excitement is infectious, or is meant to be.

Thus far, we have spoken as if all 19th-century arguments were cast in a language distinguished from the ordinary only by its use of specialized terminology and its inferential explicitness. But mathematical argument also plays a part in 19th-century science, though it can hardly be said to be predominant (e.g., see low counts of mathematical explanation and rules in table 7.2). Still, there is deviation from our 18th-century sample, in which only one article, in French, used equations outside of pure mathematics and the traditionally mathematicized fields of observational astronomy and optics (1726-F317). Fourteen percent of the articles in our 19th-century sample make use of equations, as compared with 10% in the 18th century; more important, these applied articles indicate that fields outside the traditional ambit have realized at least some of the potential of representing physical quantities in equations. For example, we find equations describing the mathematical regularities of crystals (1826-F172); ground temperature as a relationship between two determining constants and the sine of the latitude (1829-G155); the oscillation of the earth, given the latitude and the mean temperature (1833-E145); the time of vibration of a magnet on the South African coast (1875-E055); kinetic energy in the hydrodynamics of hydraulic motors (1886-F212); and the influence of degree of concentration on the freezing point of solutions (1886-F222).

The equations of 19th-century science instantiate Leibniz's dream of a notational system so transparent to the underlying structures of the natural world that to solve its equations is to display nature in action. Here is an example concerning the speed of sound through a column of liquid:

> Let D be the thickness of a liquid, k the length of a cylindrical column of this liquid at a known pressure, the small reduction of this column for a given increase in the pressure P. If one designates the speed of sound by a, a will be given by the following formula:
>
> $$\alpha = \sqrt{Pk/D_{\varepsilon}}$$
>
> Now, given this law, one takes for P a pressure equal to the specific gravity of 76 centimeters of quicksilver. As a consequence, one has:
>
> $$P = (0^{\mathrm{m}}, 76)\ g.m.$$ (1828-G020)

Equations are not only mathematical. Chemical formulas appear as early as 1832. Here, for example, is a formula for oil of ethylene: $Cl^5C^2 + 3ClH + 6\ CH^2$ (1832-

G145). But it is not until some 30 years later that an actual chemical equation appears in our sample,[4] the equal sign a signal that mathematical principles are being applied:

$$\underbrace{2B\begin{cases}O\\ O + 3\left.\begin{matrix}C_4H_5\\ C_4H_5\end{matrix}\right\} O_2\\ O\end{cases}}_{\text{Boracic ether.}} + \underbrace{Zn_2\begin{cases}C_4H_5\\ C_4H_5\end{cases}}_{\text{Zincethyl.}} = \underbrace{2B\begin{cases}C_4H_5\\ C_4H_5\\ C_4H_5\end{cases}}_{\text{Boric ethide.}} + \underbrace{6\left.\begin{matrix}C_4H_5\\ Zn\end{matrix}\right\} O_2}_{\text{Ethylate of zinc.[5]}}$$

(1862-E060)

These mathematical and chemical formulas exist at a point in the scientific spectrum directly opposite the phenomenological descriptions of the early century. They are part of a shift toward explanation that is international in scope and that includes within its range sciences as diverse as geology, chemistry, physiology, biology, and physics. Just as these sciences differ, so do the kinds of explanations they profer and prefer. These differences, moreover, are not unrelated to the larger social forces that shaped the research enterprise first in Germany and later in the rest of Europe and America: "[L]argely thanks to the German universities of the late 18th and early 19th centuries which developed the form of the modern research university, the separate disciplines which had emerged by the end of the 18th century out of the traditional pursuits of natural philosophy and natural history were to be absorbed back into the transformed structures of 19th-century university life" (Gascoigne 1985, p. 580). While the increased importance of the explanatory role in science does not delegitimatize such enterprises as taxonomy, it does change any purely descriptive enterprise from a wholly sufficient to a merely necessary condition of doing science. What once might have been the goal of much scientific argument is becoming, in a plurality of cases, its raw material.

Arguing with Tables and Figures

Tables and figures are indispensable to 19th-century science, whether they are depictions of relationships visible in nature, such as those between insects and plants, or relationships in nature not visible to the naked eye, such as crystalline structures and geological sections. They may depict relationships posited by a theory, such as Hertzian electrodynamics, or they may be tables and visuals organizing masses of data in support of lawlike relationships. In both the 18th and 19th centuries, nearly half the articles contain at least one visual. But in the 19th century, compared with the preceding one, the average number of tables and figures per article with visuals rises from 5.1 to 8.7.[6] Of these, the majority are tables; nearly 6 in 10 visual-bearing

4. As was the case with the line graph (discussed below), there appears to have been a considerable lag between important communicative innovations and their widespread adoption. In both cases, this did not happen until well into the 20th century.

5. This seems to be an example of the "rational formula" developed according to type theory (Crosland 1978, pp. 322–327).

6. This average is not far from that of the 20th century, though in the next century nearly all articles except very short ones have some visuals.

articles have a table. Typical among the figures are a depiction of a cyst in the heart after autopsy, supporting a factual claim in physiology (1855-F107), and a series of photographs of spinal sections of monkeys supporting a claim in neurophysiology discussed above (1892-E020). There are also four illustrations of experimental equipment or arrangements, and one map.

The examples of tables and figures we have selected for extended comment illustrate the cognitive possibilities of visuals, not their routine use during the period. In each case, the table or figure not only is part of the argument, a fact generally true in the case of 18th-century visuals, but also is heavily theory-laden: it bears an explanatory burden. Our geological illustration uses a stratigraphic section to suggest a mechanical cause; our biological illustration employs a plant section to support a theory of coevolution. Our first physics example—a set of tables—establishes the existence of a phenomenon that defies explanation according to current theories. Our second example from physics actually embodies a theory—Hertzian electrodynamics. Our final example, from chemistry, is a line graph—the sole instance of a line graph in our 19th-century sample. It communicates relationships among patterns of data that support a lawlike physical relationship.

Our earliest example of a scientific visual comes from geology, an article from the *Proceedings of the Geological Society:* "On the Sandstones and Breccias of the South of Scotland of an Age Subsequent to the Carboniferous Period" (1856-E115). Of Haskins's illustrations of stratographic columns we will focus on the fifth and last: "Section near Dumfries, from Lochar Moss (S.E.) to the River Nith (N.E.)" (figure 7.1). This carefully labeled and oriented geological section depicts the strata of sandstones and breccias, each laid down in the same period of geological time, then

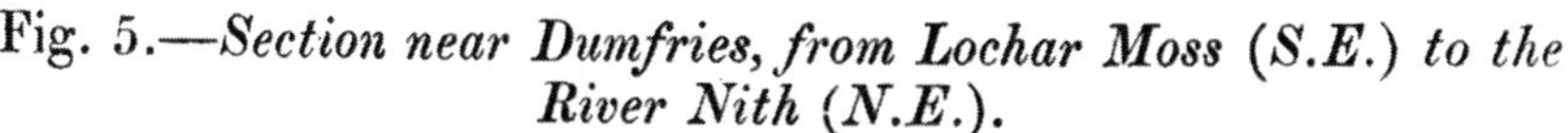

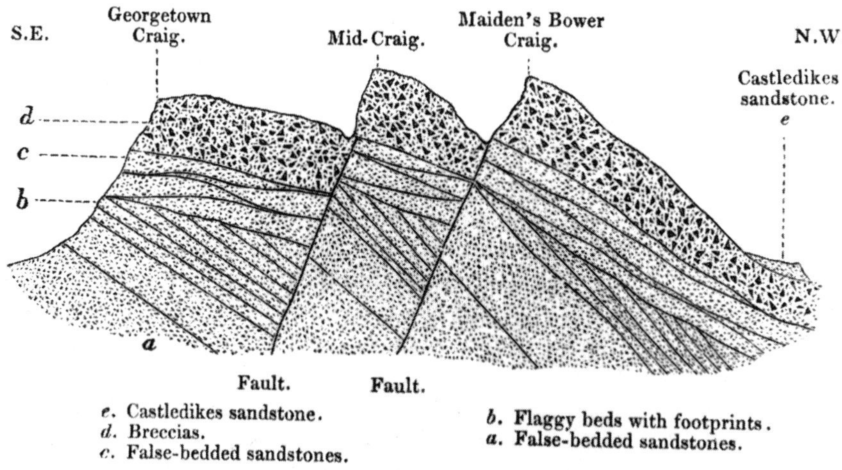

Figure 7.1. Illustration (figure 5) from Haskins, "On the Sandstones and Breccias of the South of Scotland of an Age Subsequent to the Carboniferous Period" (1856), titled "Section near Dumfries, from Lochar Moss (S.E.) to the River Nith (N.E.)"

subsequently the subject of geological forces that created the two vertical faults clearly marked at the figure bottom.

Haskins focuses on two features that occur just above a stratum where fossil traces have been discovered. The first consists of "[undepicted] singular markings, which, at first sight, are so remarkable that there is a difficulty in knowing what to make of them. They consist of sunken impressions on the upper faces of the beds. These markings are in some cases somewhat rhomboidal in form, with sharp angles. In other cases, they have a rib-like appearance; sometimes, they are sinuous, and at other times they are cylindrical." The second feature, also undepicted, consists of "pitted hollows. . . . [T]he length of these impressions is about 3/4 of an inch, and their breadth about 5/12 of an inch, so that they have a form approaching to oval. They have a deeper impression on one end than the other, which gradually thins out; and these deeper impressions are all in the same direction on one surface."

The author records his initial inference as to the cause of these two features. In the first case, he conjectured that they were floral remains, or perhaps the effect of a small rill; in the second, he guessed that the hollows were an effect of rain drops. In both cases, he acknowledges, he was mistaken. In the first case he defers to a friend who provides the "correct explanation . . . a unique form of dessication-cracks, produced on mud which, in consequence of exposure to solar rays after the crackling, has curled up at the edges in some instances; and this curling has sometimes proceeded so far as to cause the mud to assume almost the form of a hollow cylinder, into which sand has afterward been poured." In the second case, it was Sir Charles Lyell who "had an opportunity of examining this quarry" with the author and suggested as the correct cause "the splashing of spray driven almost horizontally on a muddy shore." These suggestions represent improvements because they can be combined into a plausible story of mechanical causation at a time when these sandstones formed the surface of the earth: "If the singular marking already alluded to be the result of desiccation, and if these irregular oval markings owe their occurrence to spray, then we have on these ancient shores proofs of a hot sun's rays falling on a muddy beach, and proofs of the lashings of the sea by a violent wind which drove the tops of the foam-crested waves in the form of spray on this old beach." Those inclined to acknowledge the strong social influence on scientific explanation might note some resemblance between this scientific description and its siblings in romantic novels of the period in question. But the romantic flourishes should not detract from the author's relentless focus on causal explanation.

His explanatory interest, moreover, conforms to the shift, noted by Rudwick (1976) after the third decade of the 19th century, from a visual language of geology suggestive of structures to one suggestive of causes. The section itself "is a kind of thought-experiment in which a tract of country is imagined as it would appear if it were sliced vertically along some particular traverse of the topography, and opened along that slice in a kind of cutting or artificial cliff" (p. 164). The appearance of sections in geological articles is coincident with the formation of geology "into a self-conscious discipline" (p. 166). By the 1830s the visual language of such sections formed a set of conventions "that were generally accepted and widely understood not only by practicing geologists but also by the wider audience for geology" (p. 172). By the 1850s, these visual conventions would be put in the service of "theory-dominated observation" (Secord 1986, p. 248).

Biological illustration can be equally theory dominated, equally focused on explanation. A suite of five figures from C. V. Riley's "Some Interrelations of Plants and Insects," published in the *Proceedings of the Biological Society of Washington,* supports a coevolutionary theory of the relationship between moths and the yucca plant, the thesis being that, while "upon a superficial view, this little moth shows nothing very peculiar . . . the female . . . shows some remarkable structural peculiarities, which admirably adopt her for the functions she has to perform, for she must fertilize the plant, since her larvae feed upon the seeds" (1892-E105). Riley's five figures tell a causal story, a coadaptation in which the moth pollinates the yucca in exchange for a place to deposit its eggs. The first figure illustrates the female anatomy; the second and third figures illustrate the female gathering pollen, depositing her eggs within the flower of the *Yucca filamentosa*; the fourth and fifth figures show the anatomy of the pistil on which the moth in the third figure has alit, and the position of the moth's eggs as they lie within that pistil.

We reproduce the fifth figure in this suite (figure 7.2). Each drawing that forms a part of this figure illustrates the relevant structure of the pistil, the position of the egg, and the physical distortions the egg creates in its floral surroundings. In the first depiction, the egg is labeled *b*; in the second, reading from left to right, the egg con-

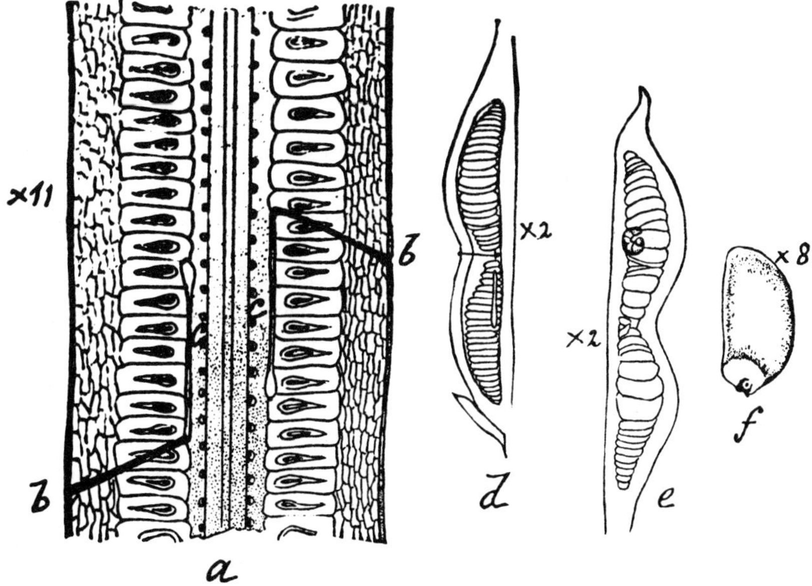

FIG. 5.—*a*, longitudinal section of pistil of *Yucca filamentosa*, showing (*b*, *b*) punctures of Pronuba, and (*c*, *c*) the normal position of her eggs in the ovarian cell; *d*, section of a punctured carpel 7 days after oviposition, showing the egg yet unhatched and the manner in which the ovules in the neighborhood of puncture have been arrested in development so as to cause the constriction; *e*, section of an older carpel, showing the larva above the original puncture; *f*, a seed 13 days from oviposition, showing young larva at funicular base—enlargements indicated.

Figure 7.2. Illustration (figure 5) from C. V. Riley, "Some Interrelations of Plants and Insects" (1892)

Strom umgewandelt werden und dafür spricht in der That die Proportionalität der Stromstärke mit der Lichtstärke. Diese ergab sich annähernd durch die in der folgenden Tabelle zusammengestellten Versuche

Lichtstärke in Normalkerzen	6.4	9.9	12.8	16.8
Stromstärke	18	30	40	48
Quotient	2.8	3	3.1	2.8

Die Lichtstärke wurde mit einem Bunsen'schen Photometer gemessen, die Stromstärke durch die Ablenkung eines empfindlichen Spiegelgalvanometers.

Als das Goldblatt der Beleuchtung durch die südöstliche Seite des wolkenlosen Himmelsgewölbes ausgesetzt wurde, während die Sonne selbst durch benachbarte hohe Gebäude verdeckt war, ergaben sich die in der folgenden Tabelle zusammengestellten Messungen.

Beobachtungszeit:	$9^h 37^m$	$10^h 5^m$	$10^h 30^m$	11^h	$11^h 35^m$	12^h	$12^h 30^m$	1^h	$1^h 30^m$	2^h	$2^h 30^m$	3^h	$3^h 30^m$	4^h
Ablenkung des Galvanometers:	190	196	209	223	250	250	244	245	249	228	188	173	172	108

Es ergiebt sich aus denselben, dass die elektromotorische Kraft der Selenplatte von Morgens 9 Uhr 30^m bis Mittags 11 Uhr 35^m ziemlich gleichmässig zunahm, dann während zwei Stunden mit einigen Schwankungen

Figure 7.3. Page from W. Siemens (1885), including the article's two tables

stricts the ovules in the direction of the arrow and arrests their development, a definite cost of coevolution to the plant. In the penultimate illustration, the moth larva is clearly visible in the upper left quadrant; in the final depiction, we see the young larva at the base of the seed. These illustrations depict coevolution of plant and animal in action.

Our next two examples are from German physics at the end of the century. In the first case, the foundation of Siemens's experimentation and theorizing is an electromotive phenomenon first noticed by Charles Fritts, an American physicist. In the second case, we have a German summary of an English lecture on Hertzian electrical theory. When we speak of the theory-ladenness of the visuals of the two articles, we are speaking, not of German, therefore, but of international physics.

In Siemens's case (1885-G040), the article's two tables work together to establish the existence of the phenomenon in need of explanation (figure 7.3): "[T]he electromotoric effect of the selenium heated until it glows." Siemens is confident "that the light waves that penetrated the selenium were directly converted into electrical current, and that the proportionality between the current strength and the luminous intensity confirms this." It is this relationship that his first table supports: the ratio of light intensity in footcandles to the current strength is constant (allowing for experimental error). We can read off this result easily across the bottom row of the table. There is a complication in this argument, however: the experiment may have been influenced adversely by its exposure to indirect sunlight. To eliminate the possibility of a refutation arising from this quarter, Siemens takes galvanometer readings throughout the day, readings given in his second table on the same page. They show an independent pattern, unrelated to the pattern of the phenomenon in question. The experimental result stands; it is real.

But why is it significant? Siemens himself provides the answer: "[W]e are faced here for the first time with the direct conversion of light energy into electrical energy." What is the cause of this new phenonemon? He does not know. He knows only that, "because dark heat-rays do not have an electromotoric effect, the assumption of a thermoelectric effect is excluded from the explanation of the phenomenon." As a consequence of this ignorance, "fundamental experiments must still be carried out." To further the argument, then, we need further experiments, as well as additional persuasive visuals like figure 7.3.

Our next example does not so much suggest as embody a lawlike relationship in physics. The illustration serves as a concrete manifestation of a theory. The article, "The Radiation of Electrical Energy," appeared in *Elektrotechnische Zeitschrift* (Electrotechnical Journal). It is a synopsis of a lecture by Fred. T. Trouton, who asserts that "the study of these electrical waves, although relatively new, is of exceptional importance to electro-technology" (1892-G105). To explain to his audience the experimental and theoretical groundwork for these important new developments, Trouton uses four line drawings. The first illustrates an experimental setup; the other three embody the theory that explains the experiment. We reproduce the third visual, a depiction of the behavior of electrical waves (figure 7.4). This drawing shows a cable, one end of which is attached, the other free. The dotted lines represent the movement of the cable set into motion in the manner of a skip rope in a children's game. The inference is not that electrical waves behave like a skip rope, but that the skip rope accurately depicts the behavior of the waves:

> If we fasten a rope at one end and swing the free end, a wave moves along the rope, up to the point where it is fastened, from which, furthermore, a new wave returns in the opposite direction, one that represents the reflection of the first wave. Our continued contemplation of the uniform swings of the rope and the reflections of various waves eventually produces the insight that there are points on the rope at equal distances from each other and that remain at rest; these points, at which the generated and reflected waves meet, we call junctions, while the swinging parts lying between these, we call flanks; the distance from junction to junction is equal to half the wave-length and gives us, together with the duration of the swing, a means by which the speed of propagation of the waves may be calculated. (1892-G105)

Fig. 7.

Figure 7.4. Line drawing (figure 7) from Fred. T. Trouton, "The Radiation of Electrical Energy" (1892)

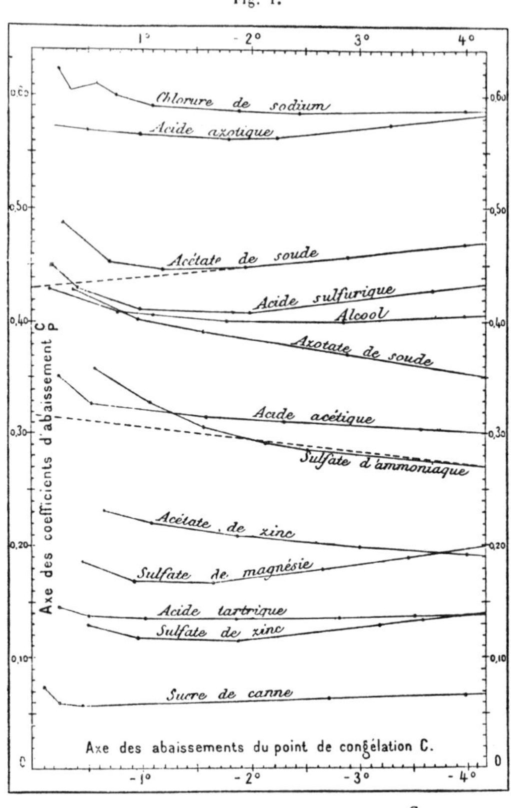

Figure 7.5. Graph (figure 1) from F.-Ma. Raoult, "Influence of the Degree of Concentration on the Freezing Point of Solutions" (1886)

The exact coincidence of diagram and theory is emphasized by a final formula: the velocity of wave propagation is calculated by means of the wavelength, shown in the figure, and the duration of vibration. Trouton is persuading his audience by displaying the simplicity and scope of a theory. His depiction of his theory should be compared to that of de la Hire, illustrated in chapter 5 on 18th-century argument. De la Hire is rationalizing the changes in lunar position in terms of geometry, a rationalization that may be traced back at least as far as Ptolemy. Trouton's task is analogous, though applied to a new class of phenomena.

A last example comes from French chemistry. In the *Annales de Chimie* (Annals of Chemistry), F.-Ma. Raoult published an article entitled "Influence of the Degree of Concentration on the Freezing Point of Solutions" (1886-F222). The author is concerned with the relationship between the freezing point (C) of a solvent and the weight (P) of a dissolved substance (figure 7.5). In his figure, these relationships for 13 substances can be compared. Raoult's goal, however, is not to depict data relationships but to extend theory; he explains the commonalities that the line graphs make clear: the parallel lines by Blagden's law, the rising and falling of the rectilinear portions of the curves by modifications of that law, and the nonrectilinear portions "by an initiation of the chemical or physical break-up of the dissolved molecules." The line graph depicts, not data relationships, but lawful relationships between the weight of a dissolved substance and the freezing point of its solvent.

The late appearance of this line graph, unique in our 19th-century sample, does not jibe with Tilling's (1995) conclusion concerning the development of these visuals: she asserts that by the late 1850s "graphic presentation became a popular technique" (p. 208). But whether Cartesian graphs—one of the staple representations of 20th-century science—were frequent during the last half of the 19th century as Tilling states, or infrequent, as our data seems to reveal, there is little question of their power in depicting relationships among data. What is being communicated in a line graph such as Raoult's is not merely a congeries of facts; it is a new fact, something that the individual data points presented in a table cannot have conveyed. Tilling quotes the 19th-century philosopher of science William Whewell to good effect:

> But the Method of Curves not only enables us to obtain laws of nature from *good* Observations, but also in a great degree, from Observations which are very imperfect. . . . The regular curve which we thus obtain, thus freed from the casual errours of observation, is that in which we endeavour to discover the laws of change and succession.
>
> By this method, thus getting rid at once, in great measure, of errours of observation, are obtained data which *are more true than* the individual *facts themselves.* The philosopher's business is to compare his hypotheses with facts, as we have often said. But if we make the comparison with separate special facts, we are liable to be perplexed or misled, to an unknown amount, by the errours of observation; which may cause the hypothetical and the observed result to agree, or to disagree, when otherwise they would not do so. If however, we thus take *the whole mass of the facts* and remove the errours of actual observation, by making the curve which expresses the supposed observations regular and smooth, we have the separate facts corrected by their general tendency. We are put in possession, as we have said, of something more true than any fact itself is. (p. 209; italics in original)

With Cartesian graphs, we thus have a communicative tool with genuine heuristic potential. They contribute to the process of discovery in that they help scientists detect "change and succession" in data that might not be otherwise apparent. They also contribute to scientific argument by representing lawlike relationships in the form of correlations, for example, as x increases y decreases. In the data- and theory-driven science of the next century, Cartesian graphs will come to dominate scientific visualization.

Our series of visuals illustrates the impossibility of basing any conclusions about 19th-century scientific communication on words alone. In Haskins's article, realistic line drawings embody and suggest explanations; in Riley's, they support theory. In Trouton's, a geometric figure actually depicts a lawlike relationship; in Raoult's, a line graph supports its modification. In Siemens's, tabular data suggest a theoretical direction, a new research program. The series also illustrates the development of visuals as vehicles of scientific communication: we see old devices—such as geometric diagrams, line drawings of objects, and tables—applied to a wide range of argumentative ends; we also see the first appearance of new kinds of visuals—the line graph and chemical equation.[7]

Arguing in Applied Science

The reciprocity between argumentative practices in pure and applied science, noted in chapter 5 on 18th-century scientific argument, is a trend continued and amplified in the 19th century. Two parallel statements are worth our scrutiny in this regard, one from Justus Liebig, the other from Lyon Playfair. In 1840, in an argument for the expansion of academic chemistry in Prussia, Liebig promised that "when one knows the principles and laws of science, the applications will be found easily, they will come of themselves" (quoted in Homberg 1998, p. 68). In 1851, Playfair wrote: "If England still continues to advance, it will not be from the abundance of her coal and iron, but because, uniting science with practice she enables her discoveries in philosophy [i.e., science] to keep pace with her aptitude in applying them" (quoted in Kargon 1977, p. 134). This similar point of view is no accident: Playfair was Liebig's student and the application of chemistry to industry was as important in England as it was in Germany. And not in chemistry only. In this German selection from near the end of the century, a summary of a lecture on Hertzian electrical theory is concluded by its practical application, ship-to-shore communication:

> As an improvement, the author proposes two alternate radio lines to provide for direct current and by this self-same means to cancel the radios' alternating magnetism, immediately after the emergence of the current; when the condensor is turned on a certain resonance period is obtained.
>
> Together with appropriate receivers, a more powerful beam of electrical waves transmitted from the coast could be used to signal the passing ships, a use uninfluenced by clouds—in contrast to the now usual application of electrical beams.
>
> The future promises a series of highly important technical applications for electrical waves. (1892-G105)

A similar link between pure and applied science is evident in England and France.

To emphasize this link is not to assert the absence of a division of labor between the pure and the applied, or to broadcast the falsehood that technological advance depends on the advance of its basic science counterpart. The history of technology undermines such claims. Nevertheless, we see in our 19th-century sample a recognition that scientific explanation and technological control can be reciprocal activities; we also see the colonization by the sciences of such industries as mining, dyeing, papermaking, and agriculture. Nor is professionalization limited to pure science only; it permeates applied science as well, as the example of the German chemical community abundantly illustrates (Beer 1958; Hufbauer 1982; Homberg 1998; Kargon 1977; Wetzel 1998).

7. The photograph entered the realm of scientific visuals in the late 19th century, though none appears in our sample until the 20th century.

The applied-science articles in our sample have two general purposes: the manufacture of practical devices that embody scientific principles, and the improvement of such fields as agriculture or mining by means of the application of scientific principles. Over 15% of our 19th-century sample falls in one of these two categories. In the first half of the century, we have articles on opium manufacture (1801-F117), balloon flight (1805-G025), potatoes as a source of bread flour (1818-F202), a pantograph (1822-E080), and mining (1835-F137). In the last half of the century, we have articles on lightning rods (1853-G095), water transportation in India (1857-E140), an English cross-channel tunnel (1870-E085), wire manufacture (1874-F132), dyeing (1874-G100, 1885-F117), American whale fishing (1887-E065), English tobacco cultivation (1891-E35), and ship-to-shore communication (1892-G105).

That the professionalization of science meant the application of the same standards of argumentation to both pure and applied science is supported by our sample. As the century unfolds, in applied, as in pure science, we see increasing sophistication in the production and interpretation of effects along with an increasing concern with the inferences permissible from observations and experimental results. In this passage from applied chemistry, the focus is the absorption spectra of chlorophyll dyes:

> Indeed, a more exact investigation leads to the surprising result that this yellow dye possesses a spectrum almost exactly like the spectrum of chlorophyll, which differs from this only in the relative absorption amounts of the positions corresponding to the chlorophyll bands, and as a result the hypothesis is supported that this yellow dye represents only a slightly deviant modification of chlorophyll, which is generated by means of the respiration of plants in the dark, and for which I suggest the name "Etiolin."
>
> This is recognized as soon as the investigation is extended to wider limits of the concentration of solutions and thicknesses of light-penetrated layers. (1874-G100)

This passage may be usefully compared with that of Mott on neurological experiments with monkeys discussed above (1892-E020). In both cases, the experimenter is concerned with the level of permissible inference in pursuit of lawlike relationships. In both cases, conclusions are carefully hedged so that they reach no further than the evidence can safely take them. The final explanation of an experimental result is made to depend on further experiments, in the Mott case tacitly, in this case explicitly.

Mathematical arguments and inferences also appear in applied science. Here is a passage from an article entitled "Law of Kinetic Energy in Hydrodynamics and its Application to Hydraulic Motors." There is no question that we are in the realm of mathematical physics

> In assembling the homologous elements of S and S'' one thus will have:
>
> $$\frac{S' - S}{\Theta} = L\Theta + \frac{S'' - S}{\Theta} = L\Theta + \Sigma m\left(\frac{p' - p}{\Theta}\right)$$

here p and p' correspond to the center of gravity of m at the two times; the pressure has varied like a function, either of t, or of x, y, z, coordinates of the center and functions of t. One therefore has:

$$p' - p = \left[q + \left(\frac{dp}{dt}\right)\right] + \Theta + \text{etc.}$$

the following terms having Θ^2 in factored form and q being the expression (2) or

$$\left(\frac{dp}{dx}\right)\frac{dx}{dt} + \left(\frac{dp}{dy}\right)\frac{dy}{dt} + \left(\frac{dp}{dz}\right)\frac{dz}{dt},$$

which corresponds to the center of gravity at the first period of time. (1886-F212)

As in the example from physics discussed above (1828-G020), mathematics is here an integral part of scientific argument.

Nor is applied science behind in the use of visuals as an integral part of arguments. In the following selection, from a French article by Girard and Pabst, "Concerning the Spectra of Absorption for Several Dyes," we have not only a meticulous analysis of the spectra of various dyes, but also a visual (figure 7.6) that provides evidential support for the assertions made in this passage:

> Fuschine displays an extremely clear and intense band of absorption, visible in very dilute solution. Sulfo of fuschine or its sulfo-conjugated derivative exhibits the same band a little displaced toward the red and in another separate band at the beginning of the blue. The two bands disappear under the influence of an alkali, coloring the solution red. The green of methyl, or dichloromethylate of trimethylrosaniline, exhibits a spectrum very close those of green malachite, derived from tetramethyl of diamidotriphenylmethane, and of brilliant green, which differs from green malachite in the substitution of four ethyl radicals at the methyl site; it is a direct homologue, but the spectra of these two homologues resemble each other very much. (1885-F117)

This passage of applied science may be usefully contrasted with that of Raoult on the relationship between temperature and solubility discussed above (1886-F222). In the applied case, the comparative spectral data "can show the chemist the way to follow, and in doubtful cases confirm the results of his trials" (1885-F117). In contrast, Raoult's results provided evidential support in the form of a line graph for "the laws relative to the molecular lowerings and tested their generality . . . [with] an expected precision" (1886-F222). Despite their differences, there is in both articles a close and reciprocal relationship between visually depicted data and the credibility of scientific claims.

Conclusion

Nineteenth-century science is increasingly dominated by a passion for factual precision, coupled with systematization, and leading more and more to carefully artic-

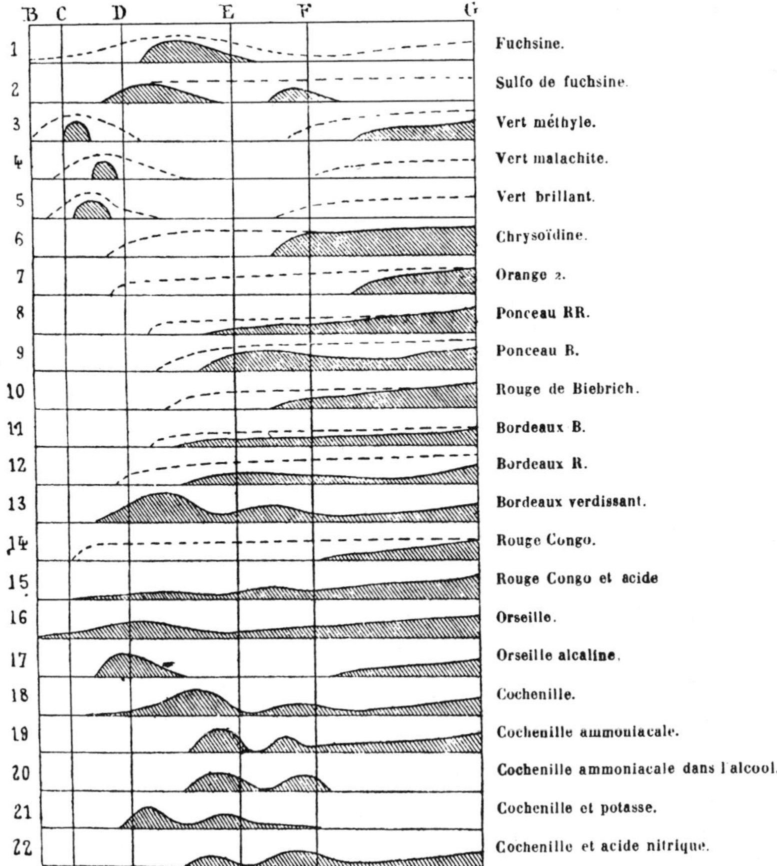

Figure 7.6. Illustration from Girard and Pabst, "Concerning the Spectra of Absorption for Several Dyes" (1885)

ulated theorizing. Taxonomy, for example, becomes the science of the classification of living matter: the Linnaean binominal describes exactly the conceptual space occupied by the species in question (Ereshefsky 1997, 1999). In describing his lichens, therefore, Hue (1889-F167) carefully measures and compares; his reputation depends on the accuracy of his identifications.

While he does not theorize, while taxonomy remains a descriptive science, its results can nevertheless form the ground of theory, as in the case of Riley's article on the coevolution of moths and yucca plants (1892-E105). While in biology theory can on occasion use taxonomic data, in another historical science, geology, the whole enterprise undergoes a shift from description to theory, from a science of facts to a science of causes. In the cases of physics and chemistry, the move is steadily in the direction of turning qualitative into quantitative facts and in creating a permanent reciprocity between experiment and theory. Such reciprocity exists also in physiology, a biological science; the issue is not whether a science is or is not biology or physics, but whether it is ripe for colonization by experimental methods coupled with carefully articulated theorizing.

But there is no sense in which the various sciences are converging on a single theory that would explain the whole of nature; rather, each science develops explanatory structures appropriate to its enterprise. There are chemistry explanations, geology explanations, physics explanations, biology explanations. As the sciences develop, they diverge rather than converge. Chemists are concerned with the nature of the elements and the ways in which they combine to form compounds; geologists, with the description and causal history of the physical features of the earth. Physicists focus more and more on the mathematical description of relationships among fundamental entities and fundamental forces. Biology becomes, not a science, but a federation of sciences, a collection of very diverse enterprises from taxonomy to physiology to evolutionary theory. We have here, not the division of labor within a single enterprise, science, but a loose coalition of enterprises with less and less conceptually in common.

Despite these differences, however, there are argumentative procedures common to the sciences; all are engaged in turning observations and experimental results into scientific facts. Early in the century, this task is accomplished by accurate phenomenal description; later, the same task is accomplished by accurate measurement using ever more precise scientific instruments. All of the sciences are also moving toward the explanation of facts by carefully articulated theorizing. In each case, it is argument that forms this bridge that links fact to theory by exploring the limits of scientific inference in a given situation. This task is routinely accomplished in a special register of ordinary language distinguished not only by its technical terminology but also by its inferential explicitness, an explicitness that often requires not only verbal but also visual language. At times the overriding need for explicitness also requires the use of an artificial language: mathematics. These developments occur equally in the pure sciences and in their applied counterparts.

CHAPTER 8

Style and Presentation in the 20th Century

In the chapters on earlier centuries, we touched upon the effects on scientific prose of the formation of scientific societies and research institutes, the emergence of journals restricted to ever more narrow specialties, and the professionalization of science on a small scale in France during the 17th and 18th centuries and on a much larger scale in Germany, France, and England during the 19th century. Particularly important in the 20th century has been the hyperspecialization and global professionalization of science (Menard 1971). This has spawned a truly international network of authors, readers, publishers, and editors that supports the annual production of hundreds of thousands of articles in thousands of journals aimed at a discourse community for whom terms such as "renormalization," "Fissurellidae," "paratolylsulfonylmethylnitrosamide," and "mRNA" can appear without definitions, and mathematical equations without apologies.

A brief history of *Physical Review* will illustrate the remarkable fecundity and mutation rate of specialized research information in the 20th-century literature. A Cornell University physicist, Edward Nichols, launched this journal in 1893, and it came under the aegis of the American Physical Society in 1913 (Kelves 1978, pp. 77, 94). It is the second-most-cited journal in Garfield's 1976 list of "Significant Journals in Science." Initially, it contained full-length research articles along with brief communications and book reviews. The six issues covering 1894 are 747 pages long and have a scant 20 articles and 20 short contributions and book reviews. Between 1900 and 1960, the number of articles published per year doubled approximately every 15 years; it doubled again between 1960 and 1965, to over 2,000 articles and about 14,000 pages. In 1970, the *Review* was subdivided into four parts, issued as separate journals: A, general physics; B, solid state physics; C, nuclear physics; and D, particles and fields. Part A alone for that year is longer than all of *Physical Review* for 1947. Division of Parts A and C into five subsections each occurred in 1975. In 1993, the *Review* gave birth to yet another offspring: E, statistical physics, plasmas, and fluids, and related interdisciplinary topics. At present, Parts A through E annually fill up tens of thousands of information-rich pages housing several thousand articles composed for and by the 40,000 members of the American Physical Society worldwide. Yet, though it is an order of magnitude greater than all of the articles produced in the 17th century, it represents but a tiny fraction of the world's scientific literature in the 20th.

Along with the rampant specialization and mass production of scientific articles have come attempts to legislate standardization, as reflected in the proliferation of style sheets and manuals seeking to promote explicit communicative norms. As early as 1909, the U.S. Geological Survey assembled a slim volume of "suggestions to authors of papers" submitted for its publications,[1] and a 1917 issue of *Astrophysical Journal* carried a page of instructions for its contributors. In 1925, Sam Trelease and Emma Yule published one of the first general style manuals, *Preparation of Scientific and Technical Papers*, and the first edition of Robert Day's influential *How to Publish and Write a Scientific Paper* dates from 1979. Over the last several decades, many discipline-specific style manuals have arrived on the scene under the patronage of scientific societies and related organizations, including the American Chemical Society (first edition, 1967), American Institute of Physics (1951), Council of Biology Editors (1960), Association of Official Analytical Chemists (1963), American Medical Association (1964), and Society for Industrial and Applied Mathematics (1993).

What we have found in tracking the communicative features in our 20th-century sample, particularly with regard to the presentational features, is more and more convergence catalyzed by codification in various documents on preparing articles for publication.[2] Stylistic and presentational homogeneity has also arisen from the pressures created by the institutionalization of the gatekeepers of science, peer reviewers and editorial boards, as 20th-century authors have tailored their manuscripts in expectation of, and in direct response to, critical comments by these groups.[3]

1. According to the foreword, the U.S. Geological Survey also issued a pamphlet on their preferred style in January 1888 (see U.S. Geological Survey 1916).

2. With regard to matters of "style," most style guides primarily concern themselves with good housekeeping issues such as whether or not a space goes between the temperature value and °C.

3. There exists an extensive body of recent literature relevant to modern scientific style and presentation written by scholars from many different disciplines, including Atkinson (1999), Bazerman (1988, pp. 153–253), Berkenkotter and Huckin (1995, pp. 27–44), Gopen and Swan (1990), Gopnik (1972), Gunnarsson (1997), Hagge (1997), Halliday (1993a), Hoffmann (1988), Locke (1992, pp. 87–133), Martin and Veel (1998), Myers (1989), Selzer (1993), Suppe (1998), Swales (1990, pp. 110–176), Van Maanen (1988, pp. 45–124), and Wilkinson (1991). Anyone interested in learning about the actions behind the printed words should consult Fleck (1979), Galison (1987, 1997, 1998), Gilbert and Mulkay (1984), Holmes (1991), Hull (1988c, pp. 111–276), Johnson and Coates (1999), Knorr-Cetina (1981), and Latour and Wolgar (1986).

Style

Our stylistic analysis for the 20th century is based upon 600 ten-line passages randomly drawn from 35 significant scientific journals listed by Garfield (1976) and six from Gascoigne (1985). Because of our method of selecting articles in this century (see appendix A), this random sample is primarily written in English (about 80%), and the focus of this chapter and the next thus rests upon English scientific prose. This is in keeping with the fact that English has become the international discourse of science (Garfield 1998, Watson 1985), which involves not only a specific language but also a suite of stylistic features. Indeed, at no other time in the long history of the scientific article has one language, what Halliday (1993a, 1998) aptly calls "scientific English," so dominated its communications. Even the four German and three French journals in our sample turned to publishing summaries and whole articles in scientific English during the later part of this century, and that includes *Comptes Rendus,* the principal organ of the French Académie des Sciences. The adaptation of English to reach the widest possible audience has extended well beyond Europe. In the early 20th century, when the Japanese scientific community launched several new specialized journals, their editors chose English in the hope of tapping into the large potential audience beyond their small island (Montgomery 1996, p. 326).

We first treat English scientific style, then briefly compare it with French and German.

Embracing the Objective

Modern scientific style has been adapted from a natural language where people are the central characters occupying the subject position to a specialized discourse where things and abstractions have become the foci of attention. Somewhat to our surprise, by the 20th century, our principal indexes of this "objective" style—passive voice and dummy subject—have reached a point of evolutionary stability, as reflected by the data in table 8.1.

Here is a fairly typical example of English scientific prose dominated by the passive voice, with one instance of the dummy-subject construction (bold type used for emphasis):

> This finding contradicts the conclusions of Klein et al. [1987] based on Voyager observations. How can this discrepancy **be explained**? **Is it caused** by differences in

Table 8.1. Averages Measures of Objective Style in 20th-Century English Passages ($n = 486$): Occurrences per 100 Words

	1901–1925	*1926–1950*	*1951–1975*	*1976–1995*[a]	*1901–1995*
Suppressed passive	2.0	1.9	2.2	1.8	2.0
Objective passive	0.6	0.5	0.5	0.6	0.5
Dummy subject	0.5	0.5	0.4	0.4	0.4
Hedges	2.1	2.2	2.3	2.2	2.2

[a]Our text sampling occurred in 1995.

> the measurements, one set of measurements presumably being in error? The question **is not easily answered** because of the different ways in which the data **are analyzed** by the Pioneer and Voyager investigators. Thus **it is** not possible to compare figure 5 with the corresponding Voyager measurements. (1990-E475)

Even though the authors are trying to explain two sets of data in apparent conflict, they keep the prose objective and impersonal by relying upon the passive voice and keeping the key players out of the important subject position. It is thus not a matter of *us* versus *them*, but abstract entities in contention. This neutered style leaves the impression that the authors wish only objectively to evaluate and explain the available facts, not participate in an intellectual donnybrook. As Bazerman (1998) put it: "[W]hile science-in-the-making is deeply contentious, science-once-made appears co-operative and harmonious, as traces of division are excised within a narrative of progress towards current belief, taken as true" (p. 17).

In our 20th-century English sample, the average suppressed-person passives per decade is about two instances per 100 words. That's a 25% increase over the 19th century—a sizable jump to be sure, but not as great as one might expect based on the complaint that the passive voice is the main ingredient of the present-day opaqueness and impersonality of scientific prose (e.g., Stratton 1984, p. 422). In fact, looking at the averages every 25 years throughout the 20th century, we found *no significant change* in frequency of the passive over time. Surprisingly, the average for the last quarter of the 20th century is more than 10% below the first quarter. Our results thus do not support Alvin Weinberg's (1967, p. 54) conjecture that scientific prose suddenly turned "impersonal, literal, passive" around 1920 as a result of "big science" and the dramatically increased influence of government institutions on scientific research. As we have shown in earlier chapters, these attributes long preceded the widespread involvement of governments and industry in scientific research.[4]

The results in table 8.1 indicate that, throughout the 20th century, the use of dummy subjects has also remained steady. According to Killingsworth and Gilbertson (1992), "This convention aids nominalization and the passive voice in the attack on personality" (p. 134). We thus expected the more frequent appearance of dummy subjects as scientific prose turned more impersonal. Contrary to this expectation, the average in table 8.1 (0.4 per 100 words) is the same as that for the 19th century and about half the average for the 17th century. We must conclude from this finding that the dummy subject has not contributed to the increasing impression of objectivity and impersonality over time. Yet, it has been a consistent ingredient in scientific prose from the very first articles and remains so to this day. For example, the American physicist Arthur H. Compton uses the indefinite *it* to begin four sentences in only two paragraphs: "It follows from Eq. (2)," "It is of interest to notice," "It will be seen that," "It is clear, therefore, that" (1923-E147). Compton's (probably unconscious) strategy here is to exploit *it* to draw the reader's attention to the text that follows these opening phrases. So what Rodman (1991) refers to as the "anticipatory *it*" can do more than occupy dead space within sentences and does not entirely deserve the designation "dummy subject." The indefinite subject *there* can also serve that same anticipatory purpose.

4. Further supporting this claim, we note that our percentages of English verbs referring to the actions of nature over persons did not change from the 19th to the 20th centuries (about 62%).

Hedging

Our average count for hedging in the 20th century, a healthy 2.2 instances per 100 words, even exceeds that for suppressed-person passive and is nearly a factor of four higher than the 19th-century count.[5] Hedging is so carefully woven into the fabric of the modern scientific article because authors nearly always wish to "suggest the possibility" (1975-E309) or "show a trend" (1920-E206) or sketch a "rough picture" (1931-E138) and also politely criticize the research of others (Myers 1989, Hyland 1998). The typical impression projected in our sample passages, then, is not one of invincibility or impersonal authority or absolute truth ("This is so" or "They are wrong") but of tentativeness ("This probably is so" or "They might be wrong").

Here is a passage from an article on the genetics of the fly *Drosophila melanogaster* where the author hedges each assertion:

> **It seems obvious** that experiments with large continuous cage populations **may suggest** the nature of the influence of certain environmental agents on the genetic factors of natural populations, beginning with some of the genetic factors already under investigation. At the same time **it should perhaps be emphasized** that in a natural population the combination of important variables and effective agents **is probably** so complex that **only very general** applications can be made of the findings from studies of artificial cage populations. (1954-E156)

Such hedging fills both stylistic and argumentative functions. Stylistically, its function is to communicate doubt within the constraints of a prose where the absence of the personal automatically conveys the impression of authority and assurance. The more impersonal the prose, the greater the pressures for hedging to counterbalance the appearance of absolute certainty. Argumentatively, the function of hedging is to avoid the most common of counterarguments, the charge of overclaiming, and to help the reader gauge the author's epistemic commitment in establishing scientific facts and explanations.

Shunning the Personal

Anyone reading the modern scientific literature for the first time will readily notice the near absence of those resources of language by which poets, novelists, literary essayists, and so forth, formulate a "personal" voice. Gross (1990) has put his finger on why that is so: "[S]cientific prose . . . generally excludes . . . any device that shifts the reader's attention from the world that language creates to language itself as a resource for creating worlds" (p. 43). This style is purposely designed so that the author's individual voice remains subservient to the presentation of a new knowledge claim and its accompanying evidence, sometimes to the point of cold-bloodedness: "The undisturbed animal with extended tentacles is quickly grasped back of the tentacles before it has time to retract. The oral end is then immediately dipped into a solution of nitric acid and paralyzed" (1943-E172).

5. Another quantitative sign of the increased importance of hedging in the 20th-century sample is use of the verb *to suggest.* This hedging verb only appears once in our 19th-century English passages, but it is the tenth most frequent verb in the 20th century.

Table 8.2. Average Measures of Personal Style: Occurrences per 100 Words

	1901–1925	*1926–1950*	*1951–1975*	*1976–1995*	*1901–1995*
Pronouns/names	1.0	1.0	1.2	1.0	1.1
Evaluative expressions	0.4	0.2	0.1	0.1	0.2
Poetic metaphors/similes	0.2	0.1	0.1	0.1	0.1
Other deviant expressions	0.2	0.1	0.1	0.1	0.1

In our stylistic analysis, we sought roughly to gauge the personal expression in the selected passages by counting the personal pronouns and proper names, poetic metaphors, evaluative expressions, and other expressions departing from plain scientific discourse. Table 8.2 shows that all these measures were on a generally downward slide during the 20th century, as technical language and painstaking description have largely elbowed out what little personal language remained at the turn of the century.

In our 20th-century English sample, the overall representation of persons in the form of personal pronouns or proper names averages one instance per 100 words, 50% of the 19th-century average of two. The use of pronouns and proper names has decreased substantially (and the passive voice increased) over the last four centuries because the objects and processes of the natural world, the methods and materials of the laboratory, and abstract nouns have increasingly occupied the subject position. According to Bruno Latour (1992) in his analysis of Louis Pasteur's prose, scientific prose works on "two narrative planes: one in which the narrator is active, and one in which the action is delegated to another character, a nonhuman one" (p. 141; see also Riley 1991, p. 247). Over time, the balance between these two narrative planes has steadily drifted to the nonhuman one.

One of the principal devices for creating a distinctive literary voice is poetic metaphor and simile, "a way of conceiving one thing in terms of another" (Lakoff and Johnson 1980, p. 36). While they are relatively few and far between in our English sample (overall average of only 0.1 instances per 100 words), we did uncover at least some metaphors and similes: "a family of theoretical curves" (1982-E012), "honeycomb texture" (1975-E119), "three sets of wave trains" (1918-E049), "three units of strangeness" (1969-E275), "the first mother liquor" (1911-E229), "fruitful application of the disorder models" (1948-E436), "slit-like nostrils [of the white rhinoceros]" (1905-E195), "the richest of our May [meteor] showers" (1908-E194), "grape shot effect" (1959-E258), and "tailor-made impurities" (1982-E184). We even discovered an extended simile, though only one: "Each particle [neutral micelle in soap] is like a pair of military hair brushes, in which the bristles represent the hydrocarbon chains of the molecules arranged parallel to each other in sheets. . . . The two backs of the brushes on the outside represent the hydrate layer and the unionised electric double layer" (1925-E182).

As was true for earlier centuries, the metaphors and similes are nearly always functional and only minimally decorative. Other personal expressions in our sample include "this I recall pleasantly" (1920-E173), "curious separation" (1974-E063), "somewhat of an enigma" (1978-E289), "to depart seriously from reality" (1949-E359), "is plagued by" (1988-E273), "if in such speculative realms we may speak figuratively" (1934-E375), "beautiful pink-flowered *Predicularis sylvatica*" (1918-E426), "the exotic possibility" (1981-E331). Ironically, these good examples of a personal style are examples of "bad" scientific prose, or in less pejorative terms, they are science on holiday. That is because if they were far more pervasive they would be counterproductive in communicating science effectively.

Managing Cognitive Complexity

By far, the greatest evolutionary change in the 20th century has occurred in our measures related to cognitive complexity. As science has grown more theoretically and methodologically complex, its grammar has adapted by adding substantially to the complexity in its noun phrases and by deployment of specialized literary devices (such as fused noun strings and abbreviations) aimed at compactly conveying technical messages to small groups of highly trained readers in a specialized research field. These findings are consistent with Halliday's view (1993a, 1998) that the "nominal group" evolved as a grammatical resource "for constructing scientific reality as a world of logical relations among abstract entities" and the material universe (Martin 1998, p. 6).

Table 8.3 summarizes our English noun-phrase results for the entire 20th century and compares them with those acquired for the preceding three centuries. A dramatic shift in use of noun phrases is readily apparent. From the 17th through the 19th century, simple noun phrases outnumber complex ones in the subject position by about two to one, while for the 20th century, the reverse holds. In the nonsubject position, complex noun phrases greatly outnumber simple ones in all four centuries, but the ratio is between two and three to one in the 17th through 19th centuries and almost eight to one in the 20th. The greatest change occurs with the complex noun phrases having multiple modifiers. From the 17th to the 20th century, they increase by a factor of six in the subject position and nearly double in the nonsubject position.

Several scholars have proposed explanations for the function of the typical noun phrases in modern expository prose. Perelman and Olbrechts-Tyteca (1969) note

Table 8.3. Percentages of Noun Phrases of Various Types, across Centuries, in English Passages

Noun-Phrase Types[a]	*17th Century (n = 100)*	*18th Century (n = 122)*	*19th Century (n = 188)*	*20th Century (n = 486)*
Subject				
Simple	30%	22%	26%	14%
Complex	12	19	17	33
Pronouns/names	14	17	19	9
Multiple modifiers	4	13	9	24
Nonsubject				
Simple	19	15	13	6
Complex	39	44	44	47
Pronouns/names	3	5	5	1
Multiple modifiers	19	29	28	35

[a]Defined in Appendix C.

that the rhetorical effect of the noun phrase is "to make a statement [appear to be] timeless and, in consequence, beyond the limits of subjectivity and bias" (p. 182). And as pointed out by Quirk and Greenbaum (1972), as well as Halliday (1993a, p. 60), the practical advantage of noun phrases is that scientists can compress a complex thought or phenomenon into a "single semiotic entity," which they can then deploy as the subject or complement of a sentence, as appropriate to the unfolding argument.

In practice, the complex noun phrases of 20th-century science tend to demand serious decoding abilities on the part of readers, as illustrated in this fairly typical passage on the molecular biology of plants: "**Degreened *y-1* cells** contain **the same level of translatable LHCP mRNA in the light or dark at 38°C.** Thus, **the disparate kinetics of accumulation of LHCPs shown in figure 2a** could result from **selective inhibition of translation of LHCP mRNA or subsequent rapid degradation of most of the newly synthesized polypeptides**" (1989-E324). This passage is made up almost entirely of complex noun phrases with multiple modifiers (in bold). Close reading shows these phrases to be inhabited by objects prepared in the lab ("y-1 cells," "LHCP mRNA," etc.), conditions of nature reproduced in the lab ("light," "dark," 38°C), nominalized processes ("accumulation," "inhibition," etc.), and finally, qualities of these objects and processes ("degreened," "newly synthesized," "rapid," etc.). Contrast that with the 1668 optics passage quoted in Chapter 2 ("Opposite to the place or wall . . . ," 1668-E006). Its noun phrases contain no nominalized processes, and the nouns themselves name objects from the world of everyday experience: "wall," "room," "Picture," "Looking-glasses," "Sun," and so on. No quantitative analysis is needed here to detect the shift in noun-phrase structure and content. In passages such as 1989-E324, readers are immersed not in a thicket of clauses, as they might be in 17th- or 18th-century scientific prose, but in rather the complex noun phrases of otherwise syntactically simple sentences.[6]

A unique characteristic of English scientific prose is strings of noun modifiers, also the result of what Halliday (1993a) refers to as "a steady drift towards the nominalizing region" (p. 67). In this grammatical form, essentially nonexistent before the 20th century, "bulb containing a condensed filament" gets shortened to "condensed filament bulb" and then combined with other noun modifiers to form "500 W condensed filament bulb" (1949-E335), meaning "bulb containing a condensed filament and possessing a rated capacity of 500 watts." Our quantitative results show this grammatical form definitively on the ascent throughout the 20th century, the averages almost quadrupling (table 8.4).

6. We do not present our verb census data for the 20th century because the results do not much differ from those of the 19th century. Apparently, the dramatic shift in complex noun phrases did not strongly affect verb usage. Indeed, six English verbs overlap on the top 10 lists for all four centuries we have covered (*to be, find, give, have, make, see*). New to the 20th century are *to show, obtain, use, suggest.* These verbs arise from the increased emphasis on analyzing data and using different instruments and methods to obtain them. At the other end of the verb usage spectrum, we found a small percentage (5% of total) of what we would call "technical verbs" not evident in earlier centuries (*to aerate, clone, centrifuge, collimate, decarboxylate, electroelute, endocytose, granitize, hydrolyze, ionize, isomerize, metabolize, metastasize, oxidize, protonate, solubilize, translocate*).

Table 8.4. Average Measures of Compact Style: Occurrences per 100 Words

	1901–1925	*1926–1950*	*1951–1975*	*1976–1995*	*1901–1995*
Noun strings	0.9	1.4	2.5	3.3	2.2
Quantitative expressions/equations	2.9	3.1	3.3	2.9	3.1
Abbreviations/eponyms	0.7	2.0	3.0	4.4	2.7
Citations	0.3	0.8	1.5	1.8	1.2

These noun strings are convenient and even necessary devices for communicating technical information concisely. Take the expression "15-day-old mouse embryo dorsal root ganglia" (1977-E299). The "dorsal roots" consist of nerves that penetrate the spinal cord from the back and convey sensory information to the central nervous system from the skin, viscera, and other peripheral organs. The "dorsal root ganglia" are the collection of cell bodies in those sensory nerves. The dorsal root ganglia taken from mice embryos are a favored research subject because, though they can be removed from the animal before neuronal maturation begins (presumably after the embryo is 15 days old), the maturation processes continues unabated in a culture dish, where researchers can more easily experiment with them.[7] The noun string "15-day-old mouse embryo dorsal root ganglia" thus forms an incredibly information-rich phrase. By this means, scientists can build complex noun phrases with multiple modifiers to the left of the central noun. Still, such communicative efficiency comes at a cost: the possible misreading or confusion from having dropped the syntactic clues the reader may need to readily comprehend the semantic relationships within a noun string. And of course, the longer the train of noun modifiers, the more likely that confusion will occur.

Like noun phrases and noun strings, quantitative expressions, abbreviations, and citational density add further "levels of abstraction" to scientific prose, making it even more challenging to grasp for the uninitiated. The next passage appears in an astronomical article reporting calculations on the nitrogen content in a star called "ν Indi":

> The opacity sources allowed for were H, H^-, He^-, Mg I and Si I (Travis & Matsushima 1968), electron scattering and Rayleigh scattering by H and H_2.
>
> The six-colour photometry of Kron, Feinstein & Gordon (1966, unpublished) and measurements of neutral and ionized lines indicate that the effective temperature of ν Indi is lower than that of the Sun by between 0.10 and 0.15 in θ_{eff}, where $\theta_{eff} = 5040/T_{eff}$. The curve of growth analysis of the star, to be discussed in detail in a later paper, yields [Fe/H] $= -1.0$ for $\Delta\theta_{eff} = 0.10$ and [Fe/H] $= -1.2$ for $\Delta\theta_{eff} = 0.15$. (1970-E372)

By our count, this short passage has eight quantitative expressions, nine abbreviations, and two citations. Moreover, this is not a prose for the technically squeamish,

7. Thanks to Lee Eiden (National Institutes of Health) for attempting to explain to us the meaning of this complicated noun string.

drawing as it does from the disciplines of astronomy, chemistry, physics, and mathematics. Clearly, we are in an entirely different rhetorical universe from that envisioned by Bishop Sprat in the 17th century: "preferring the language of Artizans, Countrymen, and Merchants, before that, of Wits and Scholars" (p. 113).

Table 8.4 shows our calculated averages for these complexity-enhancing factors. The averages for quantitative and mathematical expressions started nearly 50% higher than the 19th-century average and remained fairly stable throughout the 20th century. Given the privileged position quantification holds in modern scientific prose, this plateau may at first glance appear odd. But as we shall soon show, the surge of data in scientific articles has resulted in their migration from straight text to tables and figures.

Of all the stylistic features we counted in the short passages, technical abbreviations of words ("H" for hydrogen and enthalpy, "m" for meter) and expressions ("mRNA" for messenger ribonucleic acid) exhibited the most robust growth, a sixfold increase. Like fused noun strings, abbreviations have increased over time as one mechanism for coping with the increasing cognitive complexity of the various sciences. They also, however, make an already information-laden discourse even more dense, as in the following sentence, fairly typical of an article in molecular biology from the late 20th century: "The *ftsZ* gene . . . was expressed at a higher level in the absence of cAMP, as measured with an *ftsZ::lacZ* fusion, but the amount of protein per cell . . . was independent of cAMP, suggesting that *ftsZ* expression is regulated by the cAMP-CAP complex" (1988-E311; italics in original).

We also found a substantial rise in citational density, reflecting a more complete immersion of articles within diverse argumentative contexts and further intensifying the information load carried by scientific prose. As shown in table 8.4, citational density begins surprisingly low, an average of only 0.3 in 1901–1925 (exactly the same value as for our 19th-century sample), then increases markedly over the last 75 years to the point where one or two citations appear every 100 words on average.

We believe the sudden jump in citational density reflects not only an important communicative change, but a social one as well. By means of diligent citation practices, the various scientific communities reward their members for having made their research public. Put in economic terms (Franck 1998, 1999), citation reflects the intellectual payment from one researcher to another for having provided information that can be employed in a productive way. Moreover, the more citational attention a particular researcher receives, the more likely he or she will receive a promotion, additional research resources and funding, publication in the elite journals, and other perks so important to a productive career. This system of rewarding attention helps ensure that the knowledge-manufacturing machine of the 20th century runs with reasonable efficiency and productivity.[8]

8. To explain further, Franck's (1998) *Ökonomie der Aufmerksamkeit* (Economy of Attention) may be summarized as follows. The primary input of scientific production is attention devoted to doing research; the primary output is the research itself. Publication establishes intellectual property; citation is the prescribed way of acquiring the license to use someone else's product. Through publication, scientists petition for attention in competition with others—the success of which is measured, roughly, by the number of citations that appear to their work over time. Citations are valuable for this purpose because,

Decreasing Syntactical Complexity

Fog indexes commonly use sentence length as one of their measures of the readability of written prose. By that measure, scientific prose does not fair particularly well. The average sentence length for our 20th-century English sample is a substantial 28 words, with 2.2 clauses per sentence. This value is consistent with the average words per sentence in modern scientific prose reported by others (Bazerman 1988, pp. 167–169; Harmon 1992a; Bostian and Hollander 1990). While a sentence length in the mid 1920s may appear high compared with, say, newspaper writing, it is not unreasonable for a genre communicating a complex message to a highly trained group of readers (Flesch 1962, pp. 119–130). In fact, our results also show a definite shrinking in average sentence length over time, from 33 words in 1876–1900 to 30 words in 1901–1925 to 27 in 1976–2000, while the clausal density has remained fairly stable at a little over two per sentence. Moreover, this decline has been in progress since the 17th century, when the average sentence length was more than double, 60 words, with more than five clauses per sentence. From similar findings derived from the last 100 years of *Physical Review*, Bazerman concluded, and we agree, that the "data support neither of two related folk beliefs concerning contemporary style: an increase of sentence complexity resulting from an influx of German speaking scientists, and a loss of syntactic control resulting from the general loss of command of the English language" (1988, p. 168).

To go a step further, we propose that, while modern scientific prose has continually grown more challenging to read because of the lexical difficulty associated with its increasingly complex and compact noun phrases (see also Hayes 1992),[9] it has also become easier to read because of its declining sentence length and number of clauses per sentence. As an example, the last displayed passage (1970-E372) has an average sentence length slightly above the norm, 31 words, and clausal density of only 1.6 per sentence, and poses no serious syntactical barriers to penetrating its content, yet its lexical difficulty is considerable.

in pursuit of their own interests, scientists will pay attention only to information that enhances their productivity. When they give credit for this, they create a trail of citations. This trail constitutes the scientist's income; it is converted by the social system of science into that most precious of commodities, a scientist's reputation. As a consequence of this economy of attention, as a consequence of market forces, science is a self-organized system. It is also an intelligent system: "If a mechanism is thus operative in the scientific economy of attention that allocates the attention in the service of the maximization of knowledge, science, as a social system, deserves to be called intelligent" (Franck 1998, p. 20).

9. In an article called "The Growing Inaccessibility of Science," Hayes (1992) quantified lexical difficulty (using international English-language newspapers as a standard for comparison) in research articles from 12 scientific journals spanning the past 145 years. He found a similar steady climb in lexical difficulty for each journal studied. To illustrate how lexically complex articles have become, we need only note that the 1990 articles in *Science*, *Nature*, and *Cell* scored from 28 to 38, while *Discover* (popular science) scored −4.7 and, for comparison, "adult American fiction" (presumably not Thomas Pynchon's novels), −19.3. The articles from scientific journals existing in 1900 scored from −5 to 7, essentially the equivalent to that of newspaper international journalism. Hayes's study confirmed what just about everyone who reads the literature knows intuitively: the contemporary scientific article is written by specialists in a language meant for fellow specialists. The Hayes study, however, does not really tell us much if anything about the "accessibility" of scientific prose for its intended audience. We believe the principal barrier to comprehension is not learning a language in the dictionary sense, but learning the science behind that language.

French and German Styles: A Brief Encounter

The diachronic trends in the English sample related to objectivity, cognitive complexity, and syntactical simplicity remain the same for both French and German, but to widely varying degrees. For example, even though the French sample has, on average, far fewer passive verbs and more personal pronouns/names than do the English and German samples, it still projects a style every bit as "objective."[10] To illustrate, we translate a short French passage from a theoretical article on the spectra of inorganic compounds; the passage has one personal pronoun and one passive verb: "In working out the reflections in polarized light on a face parallel to the axis, **we distinguish** the modes of the ordinary beams (modes E_u) from those of extraordinary beams (modes A_{2u}). The first terms [in an equation] **are put** in resonance for an electric vector field perpendicular to axis A_4, and the second, when this vector is parallel to it" (1974-F491). Similarly, the German sample contains almost no fused noun strings, yet German, in contrast to French or English, permits fusing of words into information-loaded single words and complex noun phrases, such as *langkettige Carbonsäureester* (which translates as "long-chained carbon ester," 1973-G563), *Zellwandregeneration* ("cell-wall regeneration," 1976-G564), and *Tunnelkontakten ultrakleiner Kapazität* ("ultra-small-capacitance tunnel junctions," 1992-G560).

Uniformity of Style

Table 8.5 shows the relative standard deviations for our stylistic features when our stylistic data are lumped together for the three languages. Compared with the 19th-century data, the relative standard deviations for the 20th century increase somewhat for three of our four markers of personal expression (table 8.5, top). For all other measures, the trend is downward, reflecting the very high degree of stylistic uniformity in 20th-century scientific prose.

Presentation

In all disciplines and in all three languages covered by our sample of 20th-century complete articles, the scientific article has grown an abstract that immediately follows the title and byline, developed a routine three-step introduction, become increasingly concerned with setting the intellectual context by referencing, added a list of citations and acknowledgments as a ready means of crediting others, and evolved a sophisticated finding system that employs headings and different font sizes, graphic legends and numbers, numbered references and equations, and so forth. By the second half of the 20th century, we find relatively little variation from these presentational norms, as table 8.6 indicates. Overall, these measures have helped improve communicative efficiency, in partial compensation for the growing conceptual and semantic complexities of the subject matter and the purposeful narrowing of the intended audience.

10. For a comparison of French and English style in general, see Vinay (1995).

Table 8.5. Relative Standard Deviations for Stylistic Features

	19th Century (n = 524)	*20th Century (n = 600)*
Personal pronouns	100%[a]	138%
Evaluative expressions	225	267
Poetic expressions	300	370
Deviant expressions	500	380
Suppressed-person passives	155	94
Objective passives	200	158
Dummy subjects	175	156
Hedges	157	90
Noun strings	—	111
Technical abbreviations	300	124
Quantitative expressions	180	107
Citations	300	168
Clausal density	71	38
Sentence length	59	33

[a]Ratio of the standard deviation divided by the mean, multiplied by 100.

Table 8.6. Profile of Changes in 20th-Century Organizing and Finding System: Percentage Occurrence of Features across Century

	1901–1925	*1926–1950*	*1951–1975*	*1976–1995*
Title				
Specifying claim	24%	30%	22%	40%
Specifying theme	62	70	68	50
General	14	0	9	10
Abstract	14	22	81	95
Introduction				
Three elements	62	71	73	85
Two elements	29	24	24	15
One element	9	3	0	0
None	0	5	0	0
Conclusion				
Three elements	19	9	13	15
Two elements	33	13	27	30
One element	24	26	14	15
None	24	52	46	40
Headings	86	79	90	100
Numbered figures with titles	33	54	86	100
Numbered tables with titles	43	46	68	47
Numbered equations	14	33	41	40
Complete references[a]	71	83	100	100

[a]Each reference includes basic bibliographic elements (authors, journal or book titles, volume and page numbers, publisher, year of publication, etc.) in uniform format.

We ascribe the growing presentational uniformity in the scientific article, at least in part, to the rising tide of style manuals and instructions to authors, such as the following from the *Journal of the American Chemical Society*:

> It will be of great assistance to the Editor's office if the style, arrangement, and orthography of the manuscripts are made to conform to the usages of the Journal as exemplified in recent issues. . . . Authors should arrange their textual material in clearly defined sections which separate experimental descriptions and results from discussion and conclusions. . . . *References* to the literature . . . should be numbered in one consecutive series. . . . Figures should be numbered in series and the caption, if short, placed below the diagram. (American Chemical Society 1959)

So in the latter half of the 20th century, authors of scientific manuscripts face both the general social pressure to conform, present since the very first scientific articles, and the specific pressure to conform to a rule or guideline. Both are in the interest of communicative efficiency; both are at the expense of personal expression.

Front Matter

While not a traditional concern, the front matter forms a small communicative outpost of enormous importance. The title announces the article's main theme or the gist of the central claim. The byline establishes the authors' professional standing within the scientific community. The abstract concisely states the article's key points. Together, these three elements act as a screening device, enticing some readers to want to read more, signaling to others they might want to direct their attention elsewhere.

About 30% of our 20th-century titles from our 100-article sample contain the gist of the article's central claim: "On a Method of Making Visible the Paths of Ionizing Particles through a Gas" (1911-E209), "Delayed Propagation of Solar Cosmic Rays on September 3, 1960" (1961-E122), "The *Avena* Geo-Curature Test: A Quick and Simple Bioassay for Auxins" (1975-E346), and "Dynamics of an Arrangement Made from Two Tunnel Junctions with Ultrasmall Capacitances and Supraconducting Electrodes" (1992-G522). By far, the most frequent style of title (about 65%), however, refers to the article's main theme without offering clues as to the central claim: "Notes on Diseases of Trees in the Southern Appalachians" (1913-E428), "Crystal Structure of Titanium and Chromium" (1925-E129), "Cell Wall and Peroxidase-Isoenzyme Synthesis in Isolated Protoplasts of *Nicotiana tabacum* L." (1976-G518), and "Ambipolar Diffusion of a Collisional Plasma Diffusing through an Inhomogeneous Magnetic Field" (1982-F488). In contrast to earlier centuries, we found only 5% of our French and English titles starting with a superfluous preposition, all from the early 20th century (1906-F487, 1907-F497, 1911-E209, 1923-F489, 1934-E375). This syntactical form of title, however, remained strong in our German sample (41%), as exemplified by the following title in *Annalen der Physik*: "On New Phenomena Related to Haidinger's Brush and Its New Explanation" (1988-G521).[11]

11. Our work is not about making predictions, but we will go out on a limb and predict that this style of title will vanish in German during the next century, just as it did earlier for the English and French.

We could discern no significant change in title style over time until the last quarter century, when claim-type titles increased from about 22% to 40% and thematic ones declined from 68% to 50% (see table 8.6). This finding is consistent with the data of Berkenkotter and Huckin (1995) showing a recent rise of more informative titles.[12]

Following the title comes the byline reporting author names, institutional affiliations, and date of manuscript receipt (these details also sometimes appear at the end of articles and in footnotes). The byline does give us a somewhat different look into science as a social practice. We calculated an overall average of just under two authors per article in our whole-article sample (maximum, five authors). This fairly low number makes us question whether "big science" isn't a misleading generalization for contemporary practice. The evidence from our entire sample of authors per article and from the content of article titles makes it appear that scientific communication has been for several centuries, and remains today, largely the product of an individual or very small group trying to solve a limited problem within a larger research field.[13]

All but two bylines in our English sample and all in the German sample give the authors' affiliations with a research institution, another sign of the professionalization of science. With two exceptions, *not* reported are advanced degrees or memberships in scientific societies; readers now assume all authors possess such credentials. One of the exceptions, significantly from early in the century, is rich with biographical and circumstantial details, and reads "Hugh Ramage, B.A., A.R.C.Sc.I., St. John's College Cambridge. / Communicated by Professor G. D. Liveing, F.R.S. / Received November 7,—Read November 28, 1901" (1902-E222). The 20th-century norm is name, organizational affiliation, and sometimes, details about the original manuscript's history: "T. J. Kennett, L. M. Bollinger, and R. T. Carpenter / Argonne National Laboratory, Lemont, Illinois / (Received June 16, 1958)" (1958-E121). Only 30% of the French bylines follow the English and German norm, the remaining 70% presenting the author names by themselves. This relative lack of concern over author credentials is consistent with French practice dating back to the 17th century, though French bylines from the last few decades appear to conform to the English norm.

Not surprisingly, nearly three-fourths of the research institutions listed in the English-article bylines were located in the United States, United Kingdom, Canada, or Australia. Other countries represented include Chile, France, Germany, Switzerland, Japan, the Netherlands, Russia, and Sweden, lending further support to the claims that English is the international language of contemporary science. No such

12. Curiously, our sample also had no instances of the headline-style or literary title meant to attract reader interest and actively encouraged in some style manuals (e.g., Society for Industrial and Applied Mathematics: Higham 1993, p. 70). They certainly do exist, notably, "A Cosmic Book of Phenomena" for a recent cosmological article (Peebles and Silk 1990) and "The Spandrels of San Marco and the Panglossian Paradigm" for an evolutionary biology article (Gould and Lewontin 1979). But these crop up infrequently. We view this infrequency as yet another manifestation of the "objective" style, shunning personal expression.

13. This is in no way meant to minimize the importance of big science projects generating articles with anywhere from 10 to over 100 authors, such as those in high-energy physics and the mapping of the human genome.

internationalism was evident in the bylines of our French articles, although our German sample includes authors from China and Switzerland.

Another piece of information displayed is the date of manuscript receipt, official acceptance for publication, or presentation at a scientific meeting (included in 60% of our sample before 1950, 93% after). This reflects the increasing importance of establishing the exact date of discovery as a means of settling potential priority disputes. Although this practice dates back to the 18th century, it is not until the 20th that it became a routine feature.

After the byline comes the abstract, a device for featuring the article's essence up front. These summarizing passages normally report the authors' major knowledge claims and the methods by which they derived them. Typical is "Hexokinases of *Drosophila melanogaster* [a species of fly] were investigated by starch-gel electrophoresis. A hexokinase is present in both sexes during earlier stages of development, but it persists only in male adults. In addition, in this species there is a testis-specific hexokinase which is first observed during the pupal period" (1967-E179). The first abstract in our sample dates from 1923, but not until the latter half of the 20th century do abstracts appear with any regularity. As shown in table 8.6, only 14% have abstracts in the first quarter of this century, 22% in the second, 81% in the third, and 95% in the fourth. This makes the abstract a norm only in the last half of the century. We believe the abstract evolved to replace the long, descriptive title at the article's beginning and the summary at the article's close (half the titles in our 17th-century sample specified the article's major claim, but less than a third in the 20th-century sample).

Introductions

A 1925 article read before members of the U.S. National Academy of Sciences opens with the informal, breezy style of a prepared speech: "I wish to thank the Local Committee of the Academy for the opportunity of presenting to you my views concerning the history of the recent fauna of Siberia and High Asia. These views are the result of studies based in part on my field work in the Kirghiz Steppe, in southern Siberia and in N.W. Mongolia" (1925-E159). This courteous first paragraph addresses a particular audience: the flesh-and-blood academy members sitting before Peter Sushkin as he read his "views" aloud, 27 April 1925. We modern readers can easily imagine the dozen or so audience members, amateurs and professionals, sitting side by side as the Russian guest speaker reads his paper.

But this paragraph is unique in our 20th-century sample and more representative of earlier centuries, when a large share of articles were first read at regularly scheduled scientific meetings attended by three or four dozen at most and then printed in a journal. More typical are the first three sentences from an *Annales de Chimie* article:

> In a preceding article, I reported a theory on the formation of mercurammonium iodides, based on the verification of limited and reversible reactions and on the measure of equilibrium states that correspond to them. Since then, I have undertaken a series of experiments with the goal of determining in what measure the formation of mercurammonium chlorides and bromides conforms to this theory. It fol-

lows from this study that, besides strikingly exact analogies, the chlorides and bromides present differences from the iodides. (1932-F488)

This French author addresses a group of imaginary chemists, colleagues eager for clues on how to conduct their own research. Despite the two first-person pronouns, the voice is cold and distant. There is no sign here (or elsewhere in the article) of any attempt to reach a diverse audience, as we saw in the introductions quoted for earlier centuries.

Both introductory paragraphs conform to Aristotle's observation that "[t]he most necessary and specific function of the prooemion [introduction] is this: to make clear what is the 'end' [telos] for which the speech [is being given]" (Kennedy 1991, p. 262). Yet, the introduction to the scientific article delivers much more than this: it typically defines a research territory, establishes a limited research problem within that territory, and then gives some hint as to how the author solved the problem (Swales 1990). The data in table 8.6 indicate a steady shift toward Swales's three-step introduction: we found all three elements in 85% of the 1976–1995 subsample and at least two of the three elements in all articles in our 20th-century sample, a significant quantitative difference from the sketchy introductions of the late 17th century and even from the more fully developed ones of the 19th. And there is a qualitative difference from earlier centuries as well: the typical modern introduction more precisely and elaborately inserts the article's claims within the context of current disciplinary research and debate. Absent for the most part are epistolary or other personal elements we found in earlier centuries.[14]

The typical introduction in the 20th-century sample of whole articles fits well with Swales's (1990) three-step formalism. The first step establishes the status quo in the research field under study, for example, "The injury of plants occasioned by winter conditions has been a subject of great interest and importance to plant breeders and agriculturists" (1930-E322) and "It is well known that the atoms of a molecule are the seat of vibrational movements that describe the normal modes" (1974-F491). Particularly in the second half of the 20th century, this step often involves a brief review of the most recent literature. The great majority of references cite earlier work less than 10–15 years old (Price 1986, p. 110) and provide only "those details that help to structure the problem and show how the pertinent earlier concepts and findings lead to the question [or problem] addressed in the present paper" (Wilkinson 1991, p. 100):

> Since the first reports on the magnetic properties of $Fe_{80}B_{20}$ glass [1,2], binary Fe-B metallic glasses have received growing attention . . . for their attractive properties [3] as well as for the fundamental insight they afford into the nature of the glassy state [4–9]. This insight has been particularly rich when physical properties are studied as a function of composition in the series $Fe_{100-x}B_x$. Laminar-like behavior has been observed in the coefficients of thermal expansion [10] as well as in the Curie temperatures [5, 10], the structural behavior [5] and the spin-wave stiffness constant [6]. (1979-E127)

14. There is only one remaining trace of the epistolary tradition: some journals (e.g., *Nature* and *Physical Review Letters*) still call short articles "letters" even though they no more resemble letters than do their longer brethren.

Those first three sentences cite 10 references documenting 15 separate literature sources, all dating within three years prior to the article's publication. This contextualizing of the research article within a research front, haphazard in earlier centuries, has become standard operating procedure in the 20th century.

In the second element of Swales's introduction, the author stakes out a niche by acknowledging a contradiction, inconsistency, or gap in present knowledge or by offering to build upon a neglected, undeveloped, or misunderstood topic. Swales's second step is key to any introduction because that is where authors establish the problem they will subsequently claim to have solved, at least in part, for example, "J. J. Thomson's classical theory of the scattering of X-rays, though supported by the early experiments of Barkla and others, has been found incapable of explaining many of the more recent experiments" (1923-E147) and "Virtually nothing is known about the molecular bases of this spatial and temporal regulation [of *E. coli* cell division], and no specific regulatory functions have been clearly identified" (1988-E312). As these two examples indicate, the typical scientific article attempts to solve only well-formed, smaller problems within subdisciplines in "an unending attempt to create the conditions for new work, to find gaps or instabilities in existing structures" (Montgomery 1996, p. 57). These problems do not arise in the everyday world we all inhabit. A scientific problem is not a personal quandary such as how to fix a broken window or rid one's home of rodents, but rather the "Genetic Determination and Enzymatic Induction of Tyrosinase in *Neurospora*" (1960-E078). Scientists fashion such problems out of the conflicting or inadequate knowledge claims within their own research fields.

More often than not, Swales's third step simply states the article's purpose or aim: "This communication deals with the conditions which cause secretion of the pituitary gland to meet the needs of the animal economy" (1923-E125). In 16 articles, half of which are German and almost all of which are from the second half of the 20th century, there is a variant of this—the third step ends with a detailed summary of the author's main contention, which serves as a kind of secondary abstract:

> Here we report a UGA suppressor activity in rabbit reticulocytes which produces a β-haemoglobin readthrough protein. A purified rabbit reticulocyte $tRNA^{Trp}$ dramatically enhances UGA suppression in the reticulocyte lysate. Furthermore, evidence is presented which strongly suggests that the UGA suppressor activity is active within intact reticulocyte cells producing very small amounts of the β-haemoglobin readthrough protein. This is the first demonstration of naturally occurring readthrough in a non-viral system. (1980-E193)

Our data also suggest a congruence between the order in which Swales's three steps are presented and the predominance of the abstract that became evident in our sample from the 1950s onward. The arrangement preferred by the end of the 20th century delays telling the reader what the article is actually about, Swales's third step, until the very end of the introduction. That could be a serious compositional weakness, especially in a long introduction. But in articles containing an abstract, the third step is usually related in the first few sentences of the abstract itself, so authors feel no great urgency to repeat essentially the same information to open the introduction. We believe this helps explain why we find greater diversity in the ordering of the introduction's elements before 1950: only 50% of introductions in our sample from that period follow Swales's order, but 70% from after 1950 do so.

Conclusions

Rhetoricians since antiquity have observed that speeches normally end with a concluding statement that presents the author's resolution of the problem defined, or at least implied, in the introduction. In the words of Aristotle: "The starting point [of the recapitulation] is [for the speaker] to claim that he has performed what he promised, so there should be mention of what these things are and why" (Kennedy 1991, p. 281).

The conclusion to the scientific article offers more than that. Like Swales's three-step introduction, the scientific conclusion can be broken down into three components: (1) original claims derived from having occupied the niche or solved the problem defined in the introduction, (2) wider significance of those claims to the research territory, and (3) suggestions on future work to validate or extend the original claims. The first element ensures that readers who read from front to back will finish the article with a reasonably clear notion of the author's chief claims. The second element places these claims within the context of current disciplinary debates. The third element makes a case for the continuing value of the authors' research program. The conclusion also marks the authors' last opportunity for their new claims to gain the approval of their peers.

To view all three elements at work, we selected an example from a French earth sciences article involving fieldwork in the Aquitaine basin:

> The principal results of this study show that the observed deformations have a tectonic origin [*first new claim*]. This deformation, less than 500,000 years old, would have staggered at least the formations close to the surface by a total vertical component of 1.4 meters . . . [*second new claim*]. A plausible hypothesis, in order to explain the whole of these deformations, is to propose a seismic origin with segmentation of a major fault toward the surface . . . [*wider significance*]. These data must be compared with the existing geophysical data pertaining to petroleum, in order to know more precisely the geometry of the underlying structures in the sedimentary covering . . . [*future research*]. (1994-F500)

This passage, however, is not representative of actual practice. The three steps of the conclusion are not nearly so ingrained in the typical modern article as are Swales's introductory steps, as is evident from table 8.6. Overall, 13% of the 20th-century article conclusions had all three elements, 26% had two elements, and 19% had a single element, for a total of only 58% with a separate conclusion section of any kind. This latter figure is roughly the same as for the 18th-century sample and substantially lower than the 78% for the 19th century. The data in table 8.6 also show that the percentage of articles without conclusion sections doubled after 1925. We attribute this trend to the rise of the heading abstract at the same time. In effect, the abstract can make a final concluding statement redundant.

Citations and Back Matter

Unlike speeches, scientific articles in the late 20th century really conclude not with the conclusion, but with two types of credits: references to past literature cited in preceding text and acknowledgments. Like the abstract, both of these components became a routine part of the scientific article in the second half of the 20th century, though both existed well before that time.

Typically, through the use of consecutive numbers or an author-date system, the listed references are linked to some relevant statement in the preceding text. The average number of such citations appearing throughout the main body of the modern scientific article attests to their 20th century prominence (see Garfield 1996): the averages per article are 26 for experimental, 12 for methodological, 18 for observational, 35 for theoretical, and 309 for review.[15] Clearly, the review article far outstrips the other types with regard to average citational counts. This is no great surprise given that a review article is an individual evaluation of the quality of the published literature at some research front, rather than a report of original research.

Analysis of our 20th-century data for all five article types combined shows the average citational counts throughout the scientific article increasing over time. Further, with the increasing number of citations, the references they contain come to form a section unto themselves. Before 1950, only 18% of our articles close with reference lists, but 84% do so after 1950. And the basic format has definitely been standardized. For a journal article, that means listing author names, journal name, volume number, page number, and year of publication—with the inclusion of the article title and journal issue number as optional. For a book or book chapter, the standard presentation is author names, book title, publisher and city, page numbers if appropriate, and year of publication.

Just as is the case for graphical and tabular presentations, citational numbers are visually segregated from the main text in such a way that the important information they contain does not impede reading. Here is an example from the *Annales de Chimie*: "By two different methods, Mr. Violle was led to conclude that the probable mean temperature of the solar surface was between 2000° and 3000°C. ([1])" (1906-F487). The superscript number in parentheses acts like an abbreviation: it stands for "VIOLLE, *Comptes rendus*, t. LXXVIII, 1874, p. 1425 and 1816; t. LXXIX, 1874, p. 746; t. LXXXII, 1876, pp. 662, 727 and 896." This text appears in a footnote clearly segregated from the main text. Actually incorporated into that text, the full citation would have inhibited reading, especially for those not interested in the bibliographic details. Even the citation itself is modularized: note its use of typeface and punctuation to create borders between information modules that might otherwise be hard to separate visually. The author name is in caps and small caps, the year of publication is surrounded by commas, the volume numbers are in uppercase roman numerals and preceded by the letter *t* for "tome [volume]," the page numbers are preceded by the letter *p* for page, and the semicolons separate the different articles being cited in the same journal by the same author. The 41 other citations in this article

15. Citations are also distributed throughout the modern scientific article, not bunched together in the introduction as typical in earlier centuries. We counted an average of 21 citations in the first third, 15 in the middle third, and 15 in the final third.

follow similar stylistic principles, as do the citations in other articles in the same journal during the early 20th century. Indeed, the citations in all of our 20th-century articles follow similar conventions of typeface and punctuation, though they vary somewhat from journal to journal and even within a journal over time.

Sometimes immediately preceding the reference list is an acknowledgment section, whose purpose is to give credit to those people or organizations who directly or indirectly provided support but were not directly involved in the work. About 58% of our 20th-century English sample carry acknowledgments (but only 24% of the German sample and only 6% of the French sample, for reasons we do not understand), with the total percentage increasing from only 33% before 1950 to 77% after that time. This list typically includes funding agencies, technicians who helped carry out experiments, and other scientists who donated materials, were consulted during the course of the research, or reviewed a draft of the manuscript.

We conjecture that the discrete acknowledgment section arose because of the growing complexity of work arrangements, even though science itself has largely remained the work of small groups (as we inferred from the average number of authors per article). The rise of the acknowledgment section may also reflect the democratization of scientific culture, just as in movie credits, where even technical advisers and electricians get an acknowledgment. Strictly speaking, these are not communicative matters; rather, they are verbal traces from which one can infer social arrangements.

Finding System

The finding system in the modern article consists of headings and subheadings, as well as numbered equations, numbered figures and tables with captions, and citations tagged within the text by means of either numbers or author and date in parentheses. Nearly all of the articles in our sample from the last two quarters of the century contain headings, citations, and figures; over half also have numbered tables, and over one-third, numbered equations (table 8.6).

Of all these features, headings are by far the most important in terms of tracking article content. By the last quarter of the 20th century, all articles in our sample possess both general and substantive headings. While their average per page decreases slightly from 0.8 in the first 25 years to 0.6 in the second, there is a sizable increase in the last half of the century, to 1.1 in the third quarter and 1.5 in the fourth. Over the whole century, substantive headings outnumbered the general by almost three to one.

In our whole-article sample, the widespread use of numbered tables, figures, and equations reflects not only the equal attention given to the visual and the verbal in the modern scientific article, but also the high value placed on mathematization and quantification. In 1994, for example, there appeared in *Zeitschrift für Physiologische Chemie* (Journal of Physical Chemistry) an article entitled "The Calculation of the Fractal Dimension of Several Porous Solid Fuels from Nitrogen Adsorption Isotherms." In it, the following paragraph appears, in which words, pictures, and fractal mathematics form an integrated whole:

> But for the identification of such a substance a single measurement procedure of independent characteristic value is sufficient, the fractal dimension that Mandelbrot introduced [1]. While in the case of the distribution of the size of the pores their specific volume is represented as dependent on their diameter, the surface-fractal dimension is characterized by the roughness of the outer surface and the walls of the pores over a wide area in the interior (Illustration 3). From the fractal dimension for the sorptive molecules of each size, the specific surface of a porous, or rather, a finely divided substance can be calculated.
>
> The fractal dimension of the surfaces d_{fs} of a flat surface is equal to the topographical dimension d_t
>
> $$d_{fs} = d_t = 2. \tag{1}$$
>
> The fractal dimension of a rough surface may be accounted for by
>
> $$2 < d_{fs} < 3. \tag{2}$$
>
> It also lies between the integral topological fractal dimension of a surface, $d_t = 2$, and that of a body, $d_t = 3$. (1994-G585)

Not surprisingly, our data support the increased primacy of mathematics in the 20th century. Overall, 47% of the sample has at least one equation. The average number of equations in these articles is about 35. Four articles have more than 50 equations. In our samples from the earlier centuries, only about 10% of the articles had at least one equation, and of those few had more than a handful of equations.

In the 20th-century sample, quantification is evident not only in the verbal text (as discussed under Style above), but also in the visual representations. More than half the articles in our 20th-century sample have numbered tables of data (average of five per article), a near doubling from the preceding century. Also, more than half have numbered graphs of data (average of five per article), compared with only one graph in our entire 19th-century sample! All figures have numbers along with the captions, as do all but about 15% of tables.

We can best illustrate how the modern finding system works with two examples. The first, Doucet's methodological article in *Journal de Physique* (1967-F495), has a thematic title ("Propagation of Ionic Waves Excited by Impulsion in Ionized Rare Gases") with general headings at the beginning and end, and three substantive headings between them:

> Abstract
> Introduction
> Propagation of a Perturbation of Density
> Direct Detection of the Ionic Wave
> Determination of the Coefficient of Adiabatic Compression
> Conclusion

The title, abstract, and headings all work together to facilitate the tracking of intellectual content. This article also has 10 figures, eight of them graphs and the other two schematics of experimental arrangements. Each figure is numbered, has a caption, and appears shortly after its first mention in the text. Three numbered citations appear in a list at the end, and their corresponding numbers occur in brackets within the main text eight times: four in the first third, once in the middle third, and three in the last third. This tracking system for the verbal and visual elements is typical of 20th-century practice.

More elaborate than the norm is Jacobson and Lark's experimental article in the *Journal of Molecular Biology* (1973-E310). It has a thematic main title followed by a claim-staking subtitle ("DNA Replication in *Escherichia coli*: Evidence for Two Classes of Small Deoxyribonucleotide Chains"). It also has a complex system of two sorts of headings: general headings that segment the overall argument and substantive headings that reveal its detailed anatomy:

Abstract
Introduction
Materials and Methods
  Bacterial strains
  Growth media
  Chemicals
  Enzymes and substrates
  Measurement of cell number
  Pulse labeling of DNA
  Extraction of DNA
  Sucrose gradients
  CsCl gradients
  Preparation of DNA fractions for phosphates and kinase treatment
  Preparation of [γ-^{32}P]ATP
  Treatment with alkaline phosphatase and polynucleotide kinase
  Determination of ^{32}P-labeled 5′ ends
Results
  Incorporation of thymidine into small pieces of DNA
  The number of small deoxyribonucleotide chains
  Base composition of 5′ terminal deoxynucleotides of short chains of DNA labeled with polynucleotide kinase
  Cesium chloride centrifugation of DNA containing short pieces
  Size of small deoxyribonucleotide chains
  Accumulation or loss of small deoxyribonucleotide chains in ligase or *dnaG* mutants of *E. coli* K12
  Chromosomal location of pieces labeled by ^{32}P
Discussion
Acknowledgments
References

The italicized general headings are the standard components of the modern experimental article; the laundry list of subheadings form a précis of the "Materials and Methods" and "Results" sections. Materials and methods, however, are not strictly confined to the "Materials and Methods" section. In the "Results," there are 11 graphs and 6 tables, each of which is accompanied by a lengthy paragraph or two on materials and methods, positioned at the bottom so that they can be easily accessed or easily skipped; plainly, this article derives a large measure of its authority from the authors' having employed appropriate materials, methods, and instruments in combination with sound experimental design and data analysis. It also derives its authority from its close acquaintance with the large body of knowledge on the mechanism of DNA replication. Accordingly, under the heading "References," there are 51 citations: 32 linked by an author-date notation to the first third, 3 to the middle third, and 16 to the last third.

Making Arrangements

In classical rhetorical theory, "arrangement" is the name for a speech's gross anatomy. Arrangement concerns the order of the components of the author's argument (Kennedy 1991, pp. 257–282). Guided by this order, and the logical links among the different components, the readers infer the strength and uncover the weaknesses of the author's key claims. Aristotle's typical arrangement for a speech consists of four parts: introduction, statement or claim, argument or proof, and epilogue. The present-day scientific article possesses a somewhat different basic structure: introduction, methodology, results and discussion, and conclusion. In this arrangement, Aristotle's statement or claim appears as part of the introduction, and the middle two parts communicate the author's argument or proof. Ancillary to these main parts are what we have called the front matter and back matter. In outline form, then, the canonical arrangement is as follows:

- Front Matter
  - Title
  - Byline
  - Abstract
- Introduction
  - Establishment of research territory
  - Creation of niche within that territory
  - Occupation of niche
- Methodology
  - Procedures used to occupy niche
  - Materials used in carrying out procedures
  - Theoretical principles and assumptions behind procedures
- Results and Discussion (separate or combined)
  - Experimental or calculated results in text, tables, or figures
  - Comparisons of results (baseline vs. altered state, experimental vs. control, theoretical vs. experimental)
  - Interpretation of significance of results and comparisons
  - References to previous research for purposes of criticism or support
  - Refutation of criticisms that might jeopardize the main knowledge claim and concession of possible weaknesses in the interpretation or research design

Conclusion
- Main claims derived from having occupied niche
- Wider significance of those claims to research territory
- Suggestions for future work to validate or expand upon claims

Back Matter
- List of literature cited
- Acknowledgment of assistance provided during writing or research

We have already discussed at some length the introduction and conclusion sections, along with the front and back matter. In the next chapter, we turn our attention to the middle sections—methods followed by the results and discussion—which convey the crux of the authors' argument.

It is important to bear in mind that the particular arrangement outlined above is a norm in the English sample only, and even there it is far from ubiquitous. Overall, about 63% of our 20th-century sample in English follows this arrangement or slight variations on it. We found two alternative arrangements worth mentioning. The first appears in the *Journal of the Chemical Society* and *Journal of the American Chemical Society* during the early part of the century (1903-E230, 1929-E136, 1930-E137). It consists of two main parts. The front half distills the essence of the discovery and its intellectual context, with minimal technical details. The beginning of the second half is signaled by the only major heading, the adjective "Experimental" or noun "Method," which reports the experimental methods and results in some detail. In essence, the first half works like a short essay or extended abstract for chemists in general; the second half offers the technical details of interest to the experts in the field.

In the second alternative, while front matter, introduction, conclusion, and back matter are in canonical order, the middle is divided into subsections motivated by subject matter. For example, a review article on insulin in body fluids has three subsections: "Insulin in Bile," "Insulin in Lymph," and "Insulin in Other Body Fluids" (1974-E063).

The canonical form of the English sample does not hold for our German and French samples. Over 70% of German and French articles follow a variant form. In the typical German article, there are essentially two sections: an introduction that also expounds theory, where relevant, and an experimental section that includes methods, results, and discussion. A number of the chemical articles in our French sample more resemble small books than articles, even possessing a table of contents divided into *chapitres*. In general, however, French articles follow the second alternative described above. Even though less than 30% of the French and German articles conform to the canonical form preferred by those writing in English, the components listed above remain the primary ingredients of articles in all three languages.

Conclusion

In our 20th-century sample, we have found that sentences are shorter and syntactically simpler than those in samples from earlier centuries; that is, they have fewer clauses per sentence. At the same time, the information-carrying content of the sentence has grown because of the increasing use of complex noun phrases with multiple modifications in the subject position, noun strings, abbreviations, mathematical expressions, and citations. Within this quantitative, highly compressed style, the material universe commands center stage. One sign of this occurrence is the relatively high counts for passive voice in English scientific prose—the voice that places things and abstractions in the subject position. Other signs include the low occurrence of personal pronouns/names or other forms of personal expression, as well as the frequent appearance of verbs more often conveying the actions of nature over people. These generalizations about modern scientific style largely hold true across article type, discipline, and language.

One of the more remarkable features of the modern scientific article is its elaborate finding system of headings, graphic legends, numbered citations, numbered equations, and so on. This master finding system also allows scientist-readers to navigate more easily among the diverse components of the article; they can thus extract the desired bits of theory, methods, results, and conclusions without necessarily having to read the text from front to back.

The apotheosis of this master finding system is the scientific article in electronic format on the World Wide Web. This system has made the scientific article an ideal candidate for early "webification" with relatively minor adjustments to the current presentational practices. A solid majority of the journals from our 20th-century sample now produce both hard-copy and Web-based versions of their articles. Indeed, we would not be surprised if, by 2025, nearly all new scientific articles appear on the Web first.

CHAPTER 9

Argument in the 20th Century

To do science is to assert that a fact or a theory is true of the natural world and to defend that assertion. We call such assertions "knowledge claims." Any assertion is open to challenge: even for a statement as apparently innocent as "It rained today," the question can always be asked, what is your evidence? In our terminology, however, a knowledge claim is an assertion *explicitly* open to such challenge, one for which its author *must* offer appropriate evidence. In other words, an argument must be made. Watson and Crick, writing in 1953, could not simply state "the structure of the DNA molecule is a double helix" and be done with it. They had to construct an argument meant to convince their discourse community that their alleged fact was credible; they pulled this feat off with flair in their now-famous *Nature* article. In Randy Allen Harris's words (1997), "[S]cientists argue, in private, in public, in the pages of journals and books. They sway and are swayed. That's how they do science, far more profoundly than by staring into beakers or out of telescopes. What issues forth, as data, as theory, as law, is the residue of the strongest communal arguments they can muster."

Of course, Harris's assertion is just as true for the 17th as for the 20th century. So what has changed in terms of scientists' arguments? As we shall discuss in this chapter, it is no longer sufficient to string together an array of facts describing what the observer did, saw, or measured; one must argue them into place by pulling together a multimedia collage of words and pictures exhibiting methods used to acquire facts, new facts derived from those methods, theoretical explanations for the facts in the light of past published research, and visual evidence in support of the facts and explanations. The ultimate goal of this multimedia presentation is to mount an argument so strong that the authors' discourse community will have to acknowledge the importance of the research problem posed, and to welcome the authors' solution "into the discipline's domain of putative knowledge" (Suppe 1998, p. 384), preferably manifested by frequent positive citations or financial support for future research projects. And in contrast to the 17th and 18th centuries and much of the 19th century, the universal audience for this information is a small circle of specialists who have passed through the rigors of a science education and research apprenticeship and are working in a related field at a scientific institute or university science department.[1]

In what follows we will discuss four topics we believe central to understanding modern scientific argument: method, explanation, visualization, and arrangement.

METHOD The typical scientific article in the 20th century is experimental and includes some engagement with theory—not the theory-free observational types more prevalent in earlier centuries. Whether experimental or observational, with or without explicit mention of a theory, most 20th-century articles have a section set aside for discussing the research methods used. If these methods worked in the past, the tacit argument goes, they should work in the present and future. Many of these methods have a lineage dating back several decades, if not longer, and are codified in textbooks such as W. S. Jevons's *The Principles of Science: A Treatise on Logic and Scientific Method* (1874), R. A. Fisher's *The Design of Experiments* (1935), and D. J. Finney's *An Introduction to the Theory of Experimental Design* (1960). This of course does not rule out the possibility that the authors somehow misapplied these methods, or erred in some other way. Also, in those instances where the authors have invented a new method, the burden of proof is on them to establish its credibility.

EXPLANATION What counts as a legitimate argument has constantly risen in step with the theoretical and methodological evolution of science. As in preceding centuries, the authors seek to establish new facts about the natural world and explanations for them. In the 20th century, however, facts in the form of quantitative representations are almost always preferred over their qualitative siblings, and almost all authors offer some kind of mechanistic or mathematical explanation for their facts, an explanation appropriate to their disciplinary orientation. And the argumentative strategy for establishing facts and explanations typically revolves around comparisons of data sets.

VISUALIZATION In contrast to earlier centuries, modern scientists almost always make their case not only with words but visual representations as well—particularly Cartesian graphs, an invention of the late 18th century, and photographs, frequently of microscopic objects imaged with an electron microscope, a technique developed in the 20th century. With some exceptions, modern visuals are no longer realistic drawings of natural objects or research equipment.

1. As always, there are exceptions. Readers of the medical literature, for example, often include nonspecialists with an interest in the latest research on a particular disease and its treatment, usually for personal reasons.

ARRANGEMENT The various arrangements discussed in chapter 8 give a logical framework (or at least the appearance of one) to the overall argument. In closing this chapter, we examine two physical science articles from our sample with the intent of illustrating how arrangement and other communicative features work in the service of argument.

General Profile

In the 20th-century scientific article, we find a greatly increased emphasis on establishing facts and explanations by means of experiment as opposed to observation. As shown in table 9.1, experimental articles in the 20th-century sample of whole articles greatly outnumber observational ones—the reverse of the preceding centuries.

It is instructive to briefly examine the typical content of basic article types (experimental, observational, theoretical, methodological, and review) and their various relationships. Experimental articles recount the manipulations of natural objects in artificial settings such as research laboratories. They provide the empirical information essential for the continued conceptual evolution of science. On the other hand, observational articles describe natural objects collected or studied outside the laboratory. They involve such activities as describing a new hummingbird or fossil or measuring the spectrum of a star; they do not primarily involve manipulating natural objects under controlled conditions. Observational articles complement the experimental; they exist because part of the task of science will always involve describing the natural world outside the laboratory. As modern cosmology and paleontology demonstrate, some phenomena that interest science will always be closed to direct experimentation.

Despite these sizable differences in content, the 20th-century observational article in our sample differs little in argumentative style from the experimental one. As we show below, whether in the laboratory, observatory, or field, modern scientists gather and analyze quantitative information produced by their specialized instruments of measurement. Of the 10 observational articles in our 20th-century sam-

Table 9.1. Types of 100 Whole Articles 20th-Century Sample

Genre	%
Experimental	16 (13)[a]
Theoretical	12 (6)
Methodological	10 (9)
Observational	2 (34)
Observational/theoretical	8 (18)
Experimental/theoretical	43 (13)
Mathematical	0 (2)
Review	9 (1)

[a]Data for the 19th century are included in parentheses for comparison.

ple, seven report quantitative measurements made by research instruments, not the naked-eye observations of a student of nature in the field or observatory, as one would typically find in the 17th or 18th century.

Less than a quarter of our sample is primarily theoretical or methodological. Theoretical articles focus on explaining the natural events discovered through experiment or observation, often suggesting tests that might confirm the explanations. They offer the new conceptual variations necessary for the continued evolution of science. Unlike the other types, methodological articles do not make new claims about the natural world but present new means for facilitating and creating experiments, testing theories, and improving observations. They are about the tools used to create new science.

Curiously, the percentages of theoretical and methodological articles in our 20th-century sample differ little from earlier centuries. But that finding is deceptive. The considerable importance of method and theory to 20th-century science is readily apparent by examining the contents of our 69 experimental and observational articles. Overall, 85% of them make some explicit mention of theory, and 80% have a discrete methods section.[2] We will discuss these two major contributors to scientific argument in greater detail shortly.

A type of article almost entirely new to our sample is the scientific review. Such articles describe and evaluate the recent claims in a field; they usually make no major claims about the material universe not contained in previous articles. While their primary purpose is to interpret past science, not invent new science, they serve an indispensable function—winnowing the fit from the unfit among the other major types. They constitute a second tier of peer review, one more selective than the first.

This taxonomy represents a simplified version of article types; in practice, many articles are a blend of the different types. The data in table 9.1 reflect our choice of the predominant types.

Methodology and Argument

In spite of the exalted place given to theory in the modern scientific enterprise, only 5% of our 20th-century articles have a distinct section set aside for theory (not counting the 12% strictly theoretical articles), while 42% have distinct methods sections (not counting the 10% strictly methodological articles). A reasonable question to ask is why so much more attention is devoted to method.

As we see it, the basic argument in the modern scientific article is not much different from that of other intellectual discourse communities (legal, philosophical, political, literary, etc.) in that it involves defining a research problem or posing a question up front, then making claims or offering solutions based on the gathered evidence. When all is said and done, readers either buy the argument or they don't. What distinguishes the arguments of science is the use of a scientific method for solving the problem. By "method" we do not mean *the* Scientific Method so hotly

2. See Bazerman (1988, pp. 153–186) for a description of the growing integration of theory into experimental articles using spectroscopic techniques in the period 1893–1980.

contested in philosophical circles (Pera 1994, pp. 13–29), but the whole panoply of research equipment and techniques for querying nature that have evolved over the centuries: from Hooke's compound microscope for examining small objects like fleas and snowflakes to the Hubble telescope for exploring celestial matter in the far-flung corners of the universe; from the calculus used by Varignon to solve celestial problems to the renormalization used by Feynman to solve subatomic problems.

In contrast to earlier centuries, nearly all experimental and observational articles in the 20th-century sample are methodological in the sense that they have a space set aside for explaining how the authors adopted new or well-established methods to their own research ends. This research equipment and these techniques permit scientists to construct new problems and thereby fabricate new factual and explanatory claims. The first paragraph of an article on insulin in body fluids, by J. R. Henderson, suggests as much for a specific method (boldface added for emphasis):

> Yalow and Berson (115, 116) described the **first measurement** of a hormone using the **technique** of immunoassay and thus introduced a powerful **new method** to endocrinology. Insulin was the hormone **so measured**, and **its measurement** provided a **new approach** to the understanding of human diabetes. **The technique** has been extended to **measurement** of many other polypeptide hormones and has allowed concentrations of 10^{-7}–10^{-11} g/ml to be reproducibly estimated. (1974-E063)

By means of repetition in the critical first paragraph, Henderson drives home the high value that he places on method and measurement.

The continual evolution of discovery-manufacturing methods is as important to the evolution of science as is its conceptual-theoretical evolution. In the words of sociologist of science Randall Collins (1998):

> The rapid movement of research equipment [this includes mathematical techniques as well] from one modification to the next is the key to the mode of rapid discovery in which scientists take so much confidence. . . . The genealogy of equipment is carried along by a network of scientific intellectuals, who cultivate and cross-breed their technological crops in order to produce empirical [and theoretical] results that can be grafted onto an ongoing lineage of intellectual arguments. (pp. 870–871)

Modern scientists constantly develop and interchange their methods to quantify more and more properties at ever greater precision and speed.

In our 20th-century sample of whole articles, we discerned an increase in the rigor and level of detail of methodological sections. In the earliest, the authors present their methods within a traditional narrative:

> In 1921 simple experiments on the rate of growth [for organisms living in polar waters] were carried out in 7 fathoms of water close to Anser Island in Klass Billen Bay, Spitsbergen, by the biologists of the Oxford Spitsbergen Expedition, and mainly under the direction of Mr. Julian Huxley and Mr. A. M. Carr Saunders. The present writer had hoped to carry out the experiments under their personal supervision, with the promised help of Dr. Hoel of the Norwegian Fishery Board, but circumstances nullified these arrangements.

> Two pieces of apparatus were used—a galvanised iron-wire network cage . . . was tarred and moored to the bottom of the sea after putting a large number of dried oyster shells inside it; and a floating tarred wooden raft with strings of shells attached was anchored in the sea near the cage. The apparatus was put in the sea on June 27,1921; the raft and shells were inspected by Mr. Huxley on July 16, and—owing to the illness of Mr. Carr Saunders—finally hauled by Mr. R. W. Segnit, geologist, and Capt. Johannesen on August 24, 1921. (1923-E192)

This passage is more typical of earlier centuries, deriving at least some of its authority from the circumstances of time and place and the individuals involved. In the second early example, also typical of preceding centuries, methodological details appear to be fairly sketchy, little more than hastily scribbled notebook entries on animal physiology:

> PROTOCOL 1. Dog, male, 20 kilos cerebro-spinal fluid, collected as follows:
> A. Normal fluid.
> At 11.50, 3 c.c. 1% $Te(CH_3)_2Cl_2$ given.
> B. Fluid collected from 11.50 to 11.55
> C. " " " 12.20 " 12.30
> D. " " " 12.50 " 12.60
> E. " " " 2 " 2.10 (1923-E125)

More often, particularly in the latter half of the 20th century, we found the methods details expressed in a formulaic cookbook style relaying, in elaborate technical detail, the materials and procedures carried out in the laboratory or observatory, that is, in a special place reserved for scientific work:

> Cultures were grown for 4 days at 25°C on a modified Fries medium ("low-S" medium) containing 0.06 mM sulfate (Horowiz & Shen, 1952), or on Vogel's medium N (Vogel, 1956) modified to contain this amount of sulfate. For certain experiments a "high-S" medium, containing 8 times as much sulfate, was employed. Routine assays of tyrosinase activity were carried out in crude extracts in 0.1 M sodium phosphate buffer, pH 6. (1960-E078)

These detailed descriptions of method give argumentative weight to the quantitative result and to mathematical and chemical equations that are the products manufactured by the research. In such "highly conventionalised accounts of what the authors did in their laboratories in the course of producing their empirical results" (Gilbert and Mulkay 1984, p. 51), the specifics of time, place, and persons involved are considered superfluous, as are statements of "rationale or discussion of choices" (Swales 1990, p. 170). Instead, we find operations performed by hidden agents on materials prepared and stored in the modern scientific laboratory. In this literary no-man's-land, the authors generally keep hidden from sight the test tubes, beakers, Petri dishes, pipettes, stirrers, furnaces, bottles of chemicals, and other commonplace paraphernalia of the laboratory.

It would appear that underlying these painstaking details concerning methods and materials is the implication that readers knowledgeable in the field could replicate them (Katz 1985, p. 31). But in practice replicability as a check on veracity is seldom an issue (Neufeld 1986) outside controversial knowledge claims such as "cold fusion." In any case, these details are seldom if ever precise enough for replication, absent telephone calls, e-mails, and laboratory visits. Nevertheless, the methods section remains an essential step in the scientific article's overall argument—providing evidence that the authors followed some scientific method in the laboratory or field. As in the case of the realistic novel, the methods details prompt readers not so much to act as to imagine events whose reenactment legitimates the narrative of the article as authentic. Their real importance lies in the fact that, if the knowledgeable reader judges the methodological details as a plausible strategy for solving the problem stated in the introduction, then that reader will likely view the article as authentic science.

In the disembodied world of the modern science, there is no place for the mention of witnesses of experiments or observations, a not infrequent rhetorical tactic of the 17th and 18th centuries. That practice has long since gone extinct, though a botanical article in our sample does briefly call upon the testimony of expert witnesses: "[S]everal nurserymen in Minnesota have expressed the opinion that the canker caused by this fungus [*Cytospora chryosperma*] is one of the greatest factors with which they have to contend in growing ornamental poplars" (1940-E123). In no instance, however, does an author in our random sample even hint at the actual witnessing of an experiment or observation by others.[3]

To replace trustworthy witnesses, an elaborate peer review system has emerged (Burnham 1990), a system that leaves no overt verbal traces in the final article itself other than the rare mention of reviewers in the acknowledgments section, but definitely does shape the final text since few articles get published without some changes in response to comments from journal referees and editors, as well as friendly colleagues. This review system does not certify the impartiality and truthfulness of all the claims in refereed articles, as sometimes naively assumed, but it does provide the reader with some tacit assurance that the results are a consequence of the application of appropriate methods to appropriate objects in the natural world.[4]

Facts and Their Explanation

In contrast to earlier centuries, the emphasis of 20th-century science is fixed firmly on establishing explanations for the gathered facts (table 9.2). For example, in a *Nature* article from the late 20th century, molecular biologists Geller and Rich reported a mechanism related to polypeptide chain synthesis. Their article's abstract serves as a good example of the orderly march from method to fact to explanation that is the hallmark of modern scientific argument. While the language is techni-

3. Witnessing, however, is still occasionally called upon to resolve a controversy when the repeatability of an experiment or observation is at issue.

4. Nearly all research projects over the past several decades go through extensive reviews in order to obtain and retain funding. In that sense, even articles in publications without official peer review have had at least some of their content peer "reviewed."

Table 9.2. Purpose of 100 Whole Articles in 20th-Century Sample

Purpose	%
Observations	4 (34)[a]
Experimental results	13 (14)
Mechanical explanation	49 (31)
Mathematical explanation	23 (1)
Mathematical rule	0 (7)
Improving equipment or techniques	11 (9)
Other	0 (4)

[a]Percentages for 19th-century articles are given in parentheses for comparison.

cal and compacted, we think the gist of that three-part movement clearly shines through:

> A $tRNA^{Trp}$ was purified from rabbit reticulocytes which suppresses the UGA termination codon of β-haemoglobin mRNA [*method*]. Evidence is presented that the β-haemoglobin readthrough protein is found in reticulocyte translations and intact cells [*new fact*]. Some natural readthrough proteins perform essential functions; they are synthesized through suppression of UGA or UAG but not UAA termination codons [*mechanical explanation*]. (1980-E193)

Even in the 20th century, however, fact-driven narratives have not entirely vanished. About 17% of the articles in the sample present observational or experimental results without an accompanying mechanical or mathematical explanation. One such fact-based narrative is, in essence, a weather report from the Cheltenham Magnetic Observatory on magnetic storms observed over the period April to June 1936. Here is one of its four similar paragraphs: "*June 8–9*—A minor disturbance occurred between 17^h GMT June 8 and 24^h June 9. Conspicuous was a rapid decrease in horizontal intensity of 70 gammas at 6^h on June 9, immediately followed by a rapid increase of 56 gammas. The last third of the disturbance consisted of short-period fluctuations" (1936-E469). We think it at least plausible to assume that some explanatory theory, though unspecified, motivates these reported measurements and gives them meaning and relevance for the intended audience. In similar 17th-century passages, no such theory need be waiting in the wings.

Establishing Facts

In our journey from 17th- to 20th-century science, what counts as a "fact" has gradually become transformed. From the 17th century into the 19th, the reported facts were typically what Mary Poovey (1998) has called "observed particulars." In the 20th century, in contrast, we find scientists routinely manufacturing new facts by means of experimental measurements and calculations. In the words of Poovey, "numbers have come to epitomize the modern fact" (p. xii). Perelman and Olbrechts-Tyteca (1969) came to a similar conclusion several decades earlier: "In contemporary natural [and physical] sciences, facts are increasingly subordinated to the possibility of measurement, in the broad sense of that term. The natural [and physical] sciences display a resistance to any observation which cannot be fitted into a system of measurement" (p. 102). We find evidence for these assertions in just about every article from our 20th-century sample. Qualitative sense impressions no longer count for much in establishing new facts. Quantification rules in all scientific disciplines, even botany and geology.[5]

But qualitative assertions are not always relegated to the wings, especially earlier in the century. One of the exceptions to the drive toward quantification in our sample is a botanical article of 1913. In it, Arthur Graves diagnoses the diseases of trees in the southern Appalachian mountains as would a physician. Examine this passage, written almost as though the author feared that his observations and assessments, if made too strongly, might not hold up in court under a malpractice suit:

> **Judging from** the manner in which this fungus appears on the living branches, the writer is **inclined to the belief** that it is a faculative parasite, for, as already intimated, besides its frequent occurrence in the long discolored strips surrounded by the healthy bark, it often entirely envelops the smaller, terminal twigs, which are quite dead, **apparently** as a result of its attack. On the other hand, it is **quite possible** that its attack is of a secondary: i.e., preceded by injury to the branches from drought, cold, sun-scald, etc. (1913-E428)

Throughout Graves not only offers observed particulars on the diseased trees and their symptoms, but also explains why he thinks the diseases occurred, a subject of considerable interest to his patron, the U.S. Department of Agriculture, Forest Service. For evidence, Graves's facts rely upon his botanical expertise, as demonstrated by his vivid descriptions of plant diseases he personally observed; these are supplemented by results from microscopic examination of select specimens in the laboratory. Also contributing to the impression of professional expertise are Graves's 32 citations of the botanical literature in three languages, with 25 of them taken from foreign-language (French and German) publications.[6]

But the primary means of establishing 20th-century facts is argument by comparison: "[A]rgumentation could not proceed very far without making use of com-

5. We do *not* mean to imply that collecting specimens in the field and then fitting the observed particulars into some taxonomy has completely vanished in the 20th century—far from it. But the relatively few professionals and many amateurs pursuing such research have, perhaps unfortunately, become second-class citizens within the larger scientific community. For an example, see Johnson and Coates (1999), a book that describes the tribe of researchers and collectors involved in studying the diverse group of butterflies known as "Nabokov's Blues."

6. Contrast this reliance on European citations with an article appearing in the French *Journal de Physique* some 70 years later (1982-F496), where seven of the 10 references are to English-language publications.

parisons, where several objects are considered in order to evaluate them through their relations to each other" (Perelman and Olbrechts-Tyteca 1969, p. 242). For contemporary scientists, the "objects" compared are usually data sets; this mainly involves comparisons between previously published and new results, or between experimental results and theoretical calculations, or between experimental or observational results obtained by different methods.

More typical of the 20th century, therefore, is the following experimental article from the physical sciences; exemplified are the combined drives toward quantification and comparison. In it, Patterson reports the crystal structures for titanium and chromium using the newly invented method of X-ray diffraction. Patterson's new knowledge claim has little to do with the structures themselves, accurately reported a few years earlier, but with "slightly" more precise measurements of these metals: "For chromium (98.8 percent) a body-centered cubic structure, with α_o = 2.872A, is found; for titanium (99.9 percent) an hexagonal close-packed structure, with α_o = 2.951A; axial ratio c = 1.590. These structures are of the type previously assigned by A. W. Hull, but differ slightly in numerical values" (1925-E129). Patterson's new facts conform to an ethos in which precise, comparative measurement holds a privileged position.

Maringer and Manning also employ a quantitative comparison to reconstruct the thermal environment through which a meteorite had passed on its way to the earth (1960-E386). After borrowing a meteorite from the U.S. National Museum in Washington, D.C., the authors measured its hardness as a function of depth near its surface, which had been altered owing to aerodynamic heating as the meteorite entered the earth's atmosphere. As a control, they then took an inner segment of the meteorite not altered by aerodynamic heating and measured its hardness as a function of temperature. Comparing the two data sets in graphical form, they reconstruct "the thermal gradient which at one time existed near the surface" as the meteorite made its descent toward the earth.

Modern statistical analysis evolved, in part, as a means of better comparing quantitative data sets. In two articles in astronomy from our sample, the major factual claim rests on a statistical argument. For the first, the astrophysicist van den Heuvel reported his discovery of three new magnetic stars through the "130-inch telescope of Lick Observatory" (1971-E433). His argument in favor of that new fact involved a detailed analysis of the spectrograms produced by "thirteen peculiar A stars and one metallic-line A star." On the basis of data extracted from the spectral plates, he computed each star's magnetic field by a standard calculation. He then defined a star as magnetic if it "showed on more than one occasion a magnetic field strength with an absolute value of three probable errors or more." Three of the fourteen analyzed stars met that statistical criterion, and that justified his claim for having "discovered" three new magnetic stars. In another astronomical article, K. K. Ghosh employed a statistical argument to resolve conflicting reports over the variability in the spectral emission lines from a Be star called η Cen (1989-E374).

In these and other fact-based articles from our sample, the authors propose no underlying mechanical or mathematical explanation tying together their new facts. In some cases, explanations are irrelevant; in others, that is left for other researchers or a later publication by the same authors.

Establishing Explanations

As indicated in table 9.2, nearly three-fourths of our 20th-century articles specify mechanisms or mathematical explanations, more than double the percentage for the 19th century. Virtually half of these articles offer a mechanical explanation for the facts, an explanation appropriate also to a particular disciplinary formulation. Of course, only by the broadest definition of mechanism are these figures accurate: "the fundamental physical or chemical processes involved in or responsible for an action or reaction, or other natural phenomenon such as organic evolution" (*Merriam Webster's Collegiate Dictionary,* 10th ed.). By this definition, the following explanation would count as mechanical, though obviously it is a carefully nuanced analysis couched in terms of electrical forces and mathematical equations governing their behavior:

> When the conductivity of the electrons of the oxides is restricted, one should expect that, at the location of the thin layers, the electrons will tunnel through the potential threshold. At the same time there arise the variable equations for the electron current, a variability dependent on whether the voltage U is zero or smaller or, respectively, larger than W/e. In each case, there arises a rule in the form of (17), though the potential dependence does not agree with Eq. (18). The quantitative analysis of these equations is indeed unsatisfactory, because the calculated electron current at these thin layers is clearly always greater than the experimentally observed current intensity. It is still not possible to decide, whether the decline in the current intensity of the oxygen development is traceable to a potential drop in the oxide caused by the restricted electron conductivity of the layer or to the decline the surface activity. (1970-G561)

But mechanical explanations can also be more conventional. An early-20th-century geological article in French from *Comptes Rendus,* for instance, moves in straightforward fashion from a detailed description of French geology to an explanation of the formation mechanisms of different rock structures. Here is a representative explanatory paragraph: "The graphitic bands of Berric and Morbihan have an identical structure, but it is not particular to them, for we find it again without appreciable modifications in those of the crystalline ξ^2 schists of Sarzeau-Guérande and in those of the X schists of Belle-Ile. There is thus evidence for all of them having the same formation mechanism" (1907-F497). In this paragraph and elsewhere the author argues by comparison from facts, established presumably by chemical analyses and naked-eye and microscopic examinations,[7] to their cause. In short, substance *x* appears identical to substance *y*; "there is thus evidence" they have the same cause. Furthermore, if we already know the cause of *x*, that of *y* is probably the same. A geological article from the late 20th-century, also in French, follows the same argumentative pattern to establish the origin of an observed "Quaternary tectonic deformation" in the Aquitaine Basin of France (1994-F500).

We also find the crossover of mechanical explanations from one discipline to another. An article in *Zeitschrift für Physiologische Chemie* (Journal for Physiologi-

7. We say "presumably" here because this short article has no detailed methods statements.

cal Chemistry), "Concerning the Adsorption Heats of SO_2 and C_3H_8 with respect to $NaCl$ and of C_3H_8 and C_2H_6 with respect to Decomposed $KMnO_4$," applies the mechanical explanations of physics to a chemical process:

> Through the chemosorption, these active centers [of catalyzation] are so extensively called upon that, by means of the adsorption-isothermals employed, an absorption is induced that is for all practical purposes pure—it results from the least-formation of gas and the reversibility of the retro-curves. The observations allow us to infer a chemosorption by means of those adsorption-isothermals, which does not occur until after the heating of the powder; a surface still not in touch with SO_2 seems to form a gas less strongly, as a consequence of this chemosoption, than a powder that has already come in touch with SO_2. (1932-G586)

Mechanical explanations in our sample come from all disciplines and corners of the globe. In most cases, as expected, the explanation rests on some form of comparison. In an article read before the U.S. National Academy of Sciences (1925-E159), the Russian scientist Peter Sushkin argues for his mechanistic explanation of the fauna in Palaearctic Asia by "grouping together different species having the same distribution, and by taking into consideration their ecology, the amount of their structural differences, and the facts of palaeogeography." Chilean scientists Balazs and Agosin (1968-E256), by comparing test and control groups of houseflies exposed to the insecticide DDT, reveal a mechanism explaining the enzyme changes produced by this insecticide. In a French study, D'Arci and three coworkers (1988-E311) at the Institut Jacques Monod conduct experiments confirming the various lines of previously published evidence that "cyclic AMP (cAMP) and its receptor protein (CAP) may regulate certain aspects of cell division." In a geological article from Australia, Wilkinson (1959-E387) chemically analyzes rocks and minerals separated from rocks in the Black Jack teschenite sill, New South Wales. After some 22 pages of results and comparison of the compositional data, the author concludes that "fractional crystallization was the differentiation mechanism" that caused the observed variations in the rock and mineral series.

In contrast to their mechanistic counterparts, almost all the mathematical explanations are from physics and astrophysics. Of all the scientific disciplines in our sample, these appear most concerned with establishing lawlike relationships for the physical universe, expressed in the language of mathematics.

The first such article in our sample is a collaboration between the German physicist A. Sommerfeld and the American H. Frank (1931-E077).[8] The article runs 42 pages and has 22 references, two line graphs, and four tables of data, but a whopping 294 equations representing the electric and magnetic behavior of metals down to very low temperatures. Despite the impressive mathematical complexities of this article, the authors make their case largely by a set of comparisons among the new theory, the existing classical theory, and experiment:

8. The word "collaboration" is not quite accurate. In an unusual move, Sommerfeld announces, in the first footnote in the text, "the parts of this report as far as they carry further than the results of my paper, Zeits. f. Physik **47,** 1, 1928, are due mainly to Dr. Frank, on whom the credit and responsibility thereof fall."

> We see that for these normal metals the agreement [between theoretical calculations and measurement] is satisfactory as far as the order of magnitude is concerned. There are several reasons why a better agreement cannot be expected. (p. 20)
>
> Summarizing the results, we can say that the new theory affords a somewhat better explanation of the galvanomagnetic effects than the classical theory gave. (p. 27)
>
> [A]nd here we see that the new theory is in better agreement with experiment than the classical theory. (p. 29)
>
> The agreement [between theoretical calculations and measurement] is certainly all that can be expected. (p. 32)

Sometimes such comparisons are highly speculative, a degree of imaginative construction that is not always welcome. In a long astrophysical article similarly packed with equations, Herbert Dingle compares different mathematical models of the physical universe with the available evidence (1934-E375). According to Dingle, cosmological theorists of his time created numerous assumptions "in order to make discussion possible in the almost complete absence of observational knowledge." Dingle is suspicious of this practice and tries to put these theorists in their place by a mathematical argument more tightly constrained by the empirical evidence (Kragh 1996, pp. 69–71). From the vantage of the late 20th century, however, we now know that cosmological theorists have had some major successes by yoking mathematics with what would appear to be far-fetched assumptions.

Reviewing Arguments

The scientific review journal arose in the 19th century, responding to the flood of published literature (Kronick 1985, pp. 46–48). The nine reviews in our 20th-century sample cover such broad topics as the effects of radiation (1928-E059), the mechanism of plant nutrition (1957-E458, 1966-E457), techniques for measuring cosmic rays (1964-E448), and the passage of insulin into bodily fluids other than blood (1974-E063). Their arguments have two basic components: an introduction designed to secure the attention of some research front, and an evaluation of the recent texts within that front. This second component informs readers of the state of current research on a specialized topic and heightens the importance of some knowledge claims over others. It forms a second-order stratum of judgment, supplementing that of peer review.

What distinguishes the review article from other types is that it is written solely on the basis of other texts. The first review article in our sample is 91 pages long, with 10 pages listing more than 475 references about equally divided among French, English, and German publications. The author, Henry Laurens, systematically reviews the published literature on the physiological effects of radiation on skin, wounds, eyes, blood circulation, and metabolism (1928-E059). Laurens does not offer any new facts or explanations, but sifts through and weighs those of others.

Articles like Laurens's do not offer new science. This does not mean, however, that they do not shed new light on problems at a research front. In the introduction for a review of the state-of-the-art receivers for cosmic radio waves, Robinson informs his readers that "[t]he major part of the review is devoted to a discussion of the basic types of radio astronomy receivers. Argument has continued for a decade about the relative sensitivity of various receiving techniques. An attempt will be made here to present a unified approach to the question" (1964-E448). As a consequence of analyzing and synthesizing the various arguments in the literature, Robinson is able to conclude with practical advice, such as "[f]or most of the receiving techniques discussed, some favourable characteristics are lost if the output is not strictly proportional to the increment of input power." Argumentatively, this review article differs little from other scientific articles except that its "materials" are other texts rather than test tubes, spectrometers, fossils, and the like.

In the most argumentatively explicit of all the articles in our 20th-century sample, the Russians Dolgov and Zeldovich (1981-E033) review the contributions of astronomy to particle physics, including such matters as equations for particle densities in the universe, the lifetime and mass of the neutral lepton, and "how our beautiful and stable (with respect to annihilation) world was created from an explosive initial state." Throughout, the authors remind their readers that arguments are being constructed, their own and those of others: "Various arguments forbid" (p. 7), "Arguments are presented in favor" (p. 7), "The arguments are the following" (p. 9), "It is noteworthy that with the same arguments" (p. 11), "Cosmological arguments lead to" (p. 13), "Clearly the arguments presented above" (p. 18), "They argued that" (p. 20). In this particular case, the authors mine the arguments of others to create arguments of their own.

Visual Argument

It is impossible to conceive of the argumentative practices in 20th-century science without their visual representations (tables and figures). The underlying argument might be characterized as, "If you don't believe what I've written, see for yourself" (Latour 1990, p. 36). Visuals highlight theoretically vital features, arrange streams of data so that they can be categorized and taken in at a glance, help communicate how an experimental apparatus works, and illustrate complex relationships not easily communicable in regular prose (Cleveland 1994, Tufte 1983). These attractive characteristics have meant that, as the scientific article evolved, not only has the number of visuals increased, but also with that increase, assertions tied to visual evidence have become a routine part of scientific argument.

Our analysis of 20th-century articles reveals that figures and tables occupy a sizable proportion of the article's surface area, an average of 26% (18% figures, 8% tables). More dramatic, only 12% of the articles in the sample were without figures or tables, as compared with 52% in the 19th century, and the percentage of articles with numbered visuals integrated into the main text has steadily increased over the past century (see table 8.6). This has conferred upon 20th-century visuals an imposing presence largely absent in articles from earlier centuries.

To illustrate the close interconnectedness of the visual and verbal in modern scientific prose, we chose one of our botanical articles, on the evolution of the oak family (Fagaceae). This article combines evolutionary theory, taxonomic description, and analysis of fossil samples with the aid of an electron microscope. Visually, it contains one taxonomic tree and 31 electron-micrographic photographs of a plant fossil discovered in Tennessee. Note in the following paragraph how each verbal assertion is linked to its visual evidence:

> Fruits were typically dispersed without cupules (fig. 18–22). They are rounded-triangular in lateral aspect and triangular in cross section (fig. 18–21). At the angles, fruits have prominent wings up to 3 mm in width (fig. 18). Dispersed fruits are frequently preserved as though the suture at the angle had opened (fig. 16, 17, 20, 21). This phenomenon can also be observed in dried fruits of modern trigonobalanoids (fig. 25). The ovary is inferior with a perigon terminating the apex (fig. 16–22) and styles are occasionally preserved. There are three styles per ovary that expand into terminal, capitate, presumably stigmatic areas (fig. 21, 22). A final notable feature of fruits dispersed without their cupules is the pronounced triangular attachment scar (fig. 19, 20), also seen in modern trigonobalanoids and *Fagus.* (1989-E422)

The placement of the figure references in parentheses does not signify subordination; rather, the figure references are portals to an alternative universe, one populated by visual images. With its parenthetical reference to figures embedded within each sentence, this illustrative passage is obviously an extreme case. Yet the exception tests the rule: in our 20th-century sample of complete articles, very few statements regarding new facts or explanations are made in the absence of visual evidence. Passages like the above simply do not appear in our samples from earlier centuries.

The visuals in our 20th-century sample fall into four broad categories: graphs for representing data trends in two- or three-dimensional grids, tables for displaying and comparing data sets by means of rows and columns, schematic diagrams for presenting simplified versions of nature and experimental arrangements, and photographs and realistic drawings for picturing nature and the instruments of the laboratory. We will now discuss each type separately.

Graphs

The reigning monarch of 20th-century visuals is the Cartesian graph: 57% of articles in our total sample have at least one such graph, 72% after 1950. Hankins (1999) has documented the extraordinary flowering of graphical techniques that occurred during the late 18th and 19th centuries. These were codified and championed by, among others, William Playfair in England, James Joseph Sylvester and J. Willard Gibbs in America, Johann Heinrich Lambert in Germany, and Étienne-Jules Marey in France. Graphs found applications not only in the "pure" sciences, but in medicine, economics, engineering, and mathematics as well. According to our data, however, it was not until the 20th century that graphs became so closely integrated into the scientific article as to become routine.

In this remarkably fecund visual form, the author typically plots some independent variable, such as time, on the abscissa (horizontal axis) and some dependent variable, such as a physical or chemical property, on the ordinate (vertical axis).

This arrangement, as well as its many permutations, is ideally suited for communicating multiple data points at a glance, visually representing change as well as cause and effect, uncovering trends in a large mass of data, and making comparisons among multiple data sets (Cleveland 1994).

A new twist on the Cartesian graph plays a pivotal role in the earliest complete article in our 20th-century sample. In it, Hugh Ramage builds upon Mendeleev's periodic principle for the chemical elements and Ryberg's mathematical law for the hydrogen spectrum; using Cartesian graphs, he plots the spectra he measured for 29 metal elements. In this *Proceedings of the Royal Society of London* article, Ramage's two graphs represent complex trends among 19 elements divided into five groups, a representation quite beyond the powers of ordinary prose. Here is how Ramage describes his graphical method and its heuristic advantages:

> It is apparent, when comparing the [flame] spectra of each group, that the positions of the strongest lines, and of the others in order, change regularly with the increase of atomic mass of the metals. The change in position is apparently so simple that it suggested a graphical method of representing the spectral lines as functions of atomic mass. The lines were plotted as abscissa, and the atomic masses as ordinates. Two diagrams were drawn at first, one from the oscillation frequencies of the lines, and the other from the wave-lengths. Connecting lines were then drawn through the corresponding lines in homologous spectra. . . . [It] was thought that the equations to these curves might be discovered by further study, and also that some relation might possibly be discovered between the equations. (1902-E222)

Indeed, Ramage's interpretation of his graphs leads him to "the following facts," the first already established, the second, new: "1. The metals considered may be classified into groups, according to their spectra. The fact is not new, but the diagrams make its truth most obvious. 2. The connecting lines between the members of the groups are not continuous: there are certain breaks in them." His subsequent discussion seeks to explain the significance of the breaks in the spectral lines, an observation unlikely to have been made, absent the patterns revealed by his visuals. This early-20th-century article illustrates the prime importance of visuals in the process of scientific discovery and argument construction. Variations on Ramage's graph of spectral lines constitute a major visual form in the modern chemical literature.

In many of our 20th-century articles, the proof of a knowledge claim resides firmly within their graphs. The center of attention in a biological article from the 1920s is not the chickens under study, but five graphs plotting the relationship between their brain temperature and circadian rhythm. One of them shows brain temperature as a function of time of day and depth in the brain tissue; the authors' interpretation follows:

> The records in fig. 2 indicate that brain temperature is never stable but is continuously fluctuating with a periodicity which is often close to 15 min (Aschoff, Aschoff & Saint Paul 1973a). In general, the fluctuations occur synchronously at all sites, although occasionally they are out of phase with each other. The extent of these fluctuations is seldom less than 0.2°C and can be as much as 0.6°C, especially in the deeper parts of the brain. (1973-E124)

The authors' concern here is not with "the unanaesthetized adult male chickens" whose lives were sacrificed in the name of scientific progress, but the mechanism of thermoregulation in mammals. And that mechanism is revealed by visualization.

Here is an example of a central and sophisticated use of the line graph from a German article on quantum physics by the Nobel laureate Wilhelm Wien, "Concerning the Illumination of Canal Rays at High Pressures and the Question of the Delay Time" (1925-G552). In this example, Wien is concerned with the "significant question of whether both the decay of the light-process according to the wave theory of light and a statistical delay time of the electron in a quantum trajectory, caused by the emission, must be accepted, or whether only one of these assumptions is to be made." Another investigator has interpreted a series of experiments conducted in a vacuum as indicating support for simultaneity; Wien proposes to conduct another series under high pressure in order to obtain more accurate measurements. He concludes from his observations that "no cause exists for us to make the simultaneous assumption of delay time and decay. Certainly the former is small, smaller than one percent of the latter. Hence decay and delay time behave as if they were only two descriptions of the same process."

A comparison of his observations with theoretical predictions clearly implies this conclusion. To make his case, Wien plots his theoretical calculations of intensity (in lumens) versus pressure (in atmospheres) for eight sets of conditions, involving variations in the free path of the perturbation for the decay under pressure, $\lambda_1°$; the free path-length for the delay time under pressure, $l_1°$; and the free path-length of the delay time, l. (For our purposes, we need not go into the mathematics of how these variables are related.) The result is eight easily compared, theoretically derived curves. As shown figure 9.1 (Wien's fig. 1), only if both decay and delay time are infinite (curve 8) will the intensity rise to a high point and plateau, at least up to two atmospheres. But "if both delay time and decay are finite [curves 1–7], the intensity curve must climb to a maximum and then drop down, while the observations show that up to a relatively high pressure, no drop in intensity occurs." From this finding, Wien concludes that at least one of these two factors must be infinite for observation and theory to be consistent. This conjecture is then substantiated by Wien in another graph (his fig. 5, not reproduced here).[9]

Tables

The number of articles with tables has increased steadily over the last 335 years: over half our 20th-century sample contains at least one table, while less than 10% of our 17th-century sample does. We attribute the robustness of tabular presentation to the fact that tables are an easy nonverbal means by which scientists can present their data "using visual organizational resources to enable meaning relations to be recovered from bare thematic items in the absence of grammatical constructions. There is always, however, an implied grammar, and a recoverable textual sentence or paragraph for every table" (Lemke 1998, pp. 96–101). Like their close relative the graph,

9. In interpreting this passage the first author received some help from Roger Steuewer, who is not responsible for any muddle.

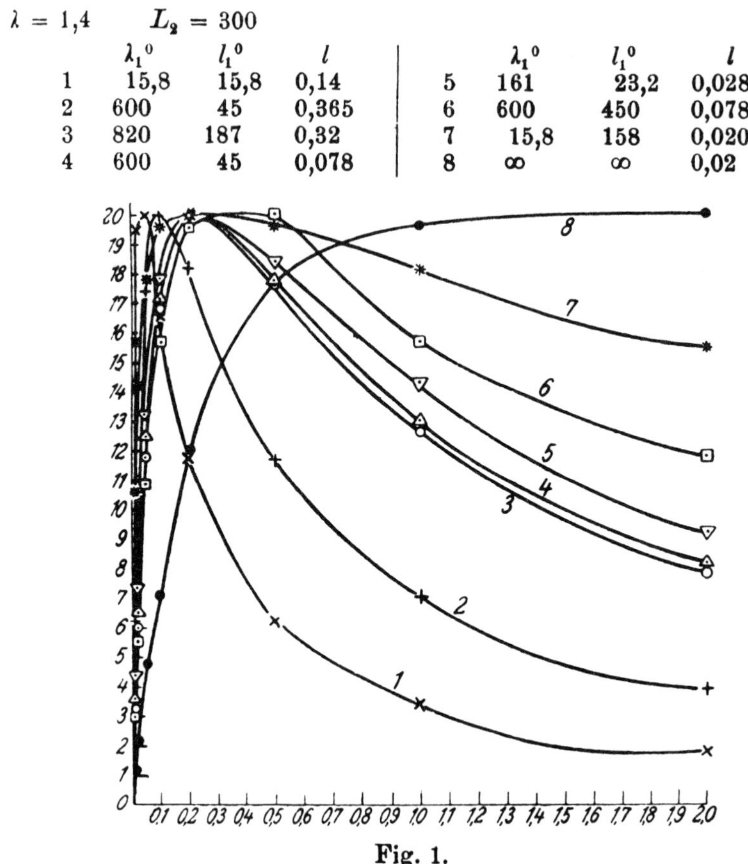

$\lambda = 1{,}4 \qquad L_2 = 300$

	λ_1^0	l_1^0	l		λ_1^0	l_1^0	l
1	15,8	15,8	0,14	5	161	23,2	0,0286
2	600	45	0,365	6	600	450	0,0783
3	820	187	0,32	7	15,8	158	0,0207
4	600	45	0,078	8	∞	∞	0,02

Figure 9.1. Graph (figure 1) from Wilhelm Wien, "Concering the Illumination of Canal Rays at High Pressures and the Question of the Delay Time" (1925)

tables are invaluable as a means of segregating the quantitative into a specially built examination space, one designed to facilitate detecting data trends and comparing data sets.

In an article in the *Annales de Chimie* (1923-F489), Guntz and Benoit frequently resort to tables in order to display their measurements and theoretical calculations concerning the reactions of alkali earths with gases. Typical is their simple table comparing calorimetric measurements with theoretical calculations for the heat of formation involved in the reaction between solid barium and gases with nitrogen and hydrogen:

	Theory			*Measurement*		
Ba %	90.16	89.92	89.94	89.76	89.98	90.70
NH_3/Total Alk	0.333	0.325	0.324	0.334	0.338	0.341

Emboldened by the excellent agreement between theory and measurement, they then undertake a series of calorimetric measurements with different weights of BaNH dissolved in hydrochloric acid, also presented in tabular form. These displayed data then permit the authors to shift their argument from data to chemical equations:

$$\text{Ba solid} + \text{NH}_3 \text{ gas} = \text{BaNH solid} + \text{H}_2 \text{ gas} + 42.16 \text{ cal}$$

$$\text{Ba solid} + \text{N} + 1/2\ \text{H}_2 = \text{BaNH solid} + 54.4 \text{ cal}$$

The data at the end of each reaction are heats of formation, the final product of their argument. The authors repeatedly employ this same argumentative strategy—integrating the visual and the verbal, comparing measured and theoretically calculated results, deriving and displaying reactions—throughout the entire article.

Schematics

About 22% of our sample contains a schematic that illustrates a mechanical explanation, like the schematic in figure 9.2, which illustrates Winckler et al.'s mechanical explanation of why, on 3 September 1960, the sun's cosmic rays arrived on planet

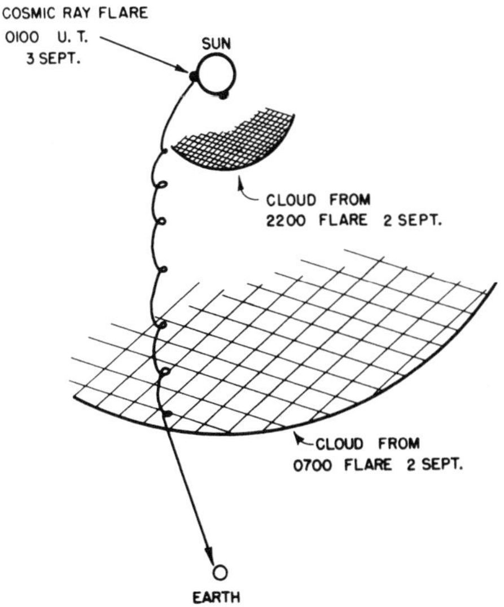

FIG. 1. Disturbances from two flares in the region approximately 30°W of central meridian were in transit at the time of the cosmic-ray flare. Particles from the cosmic-ray flare on the east limb were propagated through or around the magnetic cloud from the 0700 flare.

Figure 9.2. From J. R. Winckler, P. D. Bhavsar, A. J. Masley, and T. C. May, "Delayed Propagation of Solar Cosmic Rays on September 3, 1960," *Physical Review Letters,* vol. 6, p. 489 (1961). Reproduced with permission of authors and American Physical Society.

earth a little later than normal (1961-E122). Their explanation involves two magnetic clouds created by different solar flares (15 hours apart) on 2 September, the preceding day. In the figure, the authors represent the sun and earth as circles of different sizes, the magnetic clouds as cross-hatched slices of circles, and the cosmic ray flare as a solid semicircle on the sun's surface from which emerges an attached squiggly line falling to the earth, its trajectory. This graphic reconstruction of an event in interplanetary space is "realistic" in the same sense that Huygens's drawing of his air pump is (see chapter 3). Both are simplified versions of objects: one to better explain a unique natural phenomenon, the other to better reveal the inner working of the author's experimental apparatus. Unlike Huygens's figure, every item in this modern one is clearly labeled, and its essence is distilled in its figure caption. Similar mechanistic schematics in our 20th-century sample illustrate the decay of a neodymium isotope (1963-E267) and collisions of subatomic particles (1960-E268).

Realistic Renderings

About 30% of our 20th-century articles contain realistic renderings—largely photographs or drawings of the microscopic world in animal and plant biology.[10] One such is a photograph that establishes the fact that dorsal root ganglia from mice embryos, under the cell culture conditions reported in the methods section, will grow large, isolated neurons (figure 9.3, from 1977-E299). On this micrograph the authors have placed arrowheads to direct the reader's attention to the key evidence for their claim; they have also added a short vertical bar to indicate scale (length of bar equivalent to one micrometer; not shown). The figure caption further educates the reader on how to interpret the images in this photograph, as does a short explication in the main text. Cumulatively, the 10 micrographs in this article tell the story behind a new neuronal mechanism.

As pointed out by Myers (1990) and supported by our own observations, visual representations redefine space, "wiping it clean of all irrelevant details and structuring it so that each mark has meaning only in relation to the presentation of the claim" (p. 235). Even photographs, which of necessity contain some details gratuitous to the argument at hand, are nonetheless selected and arranged on the page so that they support the author's claim with the least possible distraction. But visual representation not only reduces extraneous details, it also adds something. In the words of Lynch (1990), it "includes methods for *adding* visual features which clarify, complete, extend, and identify conformations latent in the incomplete state of the original specimen. Instead of reducing what is visibly available in the original, a sequence of reproductions progressively modifies the objects visibly in the direction of pedagogy and abstract theorizing" (p. 181). That is accomplished by identifying the important components in an image, fitting curves and adding error bars to experimental data in two-dimensional Cartesian graphs, extrapolating a curve to higher or lower abscissa values, adding identifying labels and scale bars to photographs, and

10. Photographs have largely replaced the realistic renderings of past centuries. The first photograph in our sample appears in 1923. Five articles have them before 1950, 11 after.

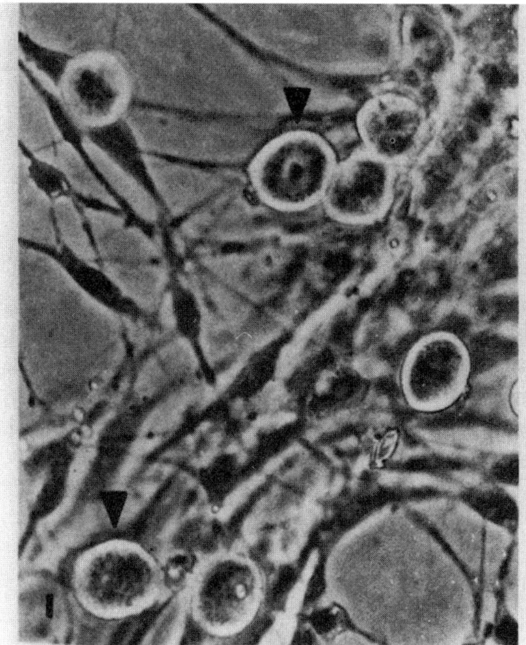

FIGURE 1 15-day-old embryo mouse DRG's, 1 wk after explantation. Neurons appear as isolated spherical cells with birefringent edges growing on top of collagen substrate, fibroblasts, and Schwann cells (arrowheads). × 400.

Figure 9.3. From N. K. Gonatas, S. U. Kim, A. Stieber, and S. Avrameas, "Internalization of Lectins in Neuronal GERL," *Journal of Cell Biology*, vol. 73, p. 3 (1977). Reproduced with permission of authors and Rockefeller University Press.

so on. So the process of preparing visual representations involves both removing extraneous details and inserting amplifying features in order to establish facts and explain them.

The Structure of Scientific Argument

In chapter 8 we discussed the typical arrangement of the 20th-century scientific article. We can now tie this arrangement (excluding the front and back matter) into the features of scientific argument we have just discussed. First in the standard arrangement is an introduction establishing the scientific context in which the authors are working, including a current problem in need of solution. Next comes a methods and materials section detailing the methods, measuring instruments, and other paraphernalia employed for acquiring new facts. After that, a results and discussion section presents new facts acquired by the methods described and explains these facts in the light of past scientific facts and theories. Explanations for the facts usually come in the form of a mechanism or set of mathematical equations, and sometimes both. Particularly when the author anticipates the new knowledge claim will be controversial, explaining the results involves presenting and "impeaching" any plausible weaknesses or gaps in the explanation or any threatening alternative explanations (Suppe 1998). Finally, a conclusion section, paragraph, or sentence reiterates the author's knowledge claim and asserts its importance or relevance to the scientific community. This format is not an argumentative straightjacket, but more of a highly flexible prototype out of which authors fashion numerous variations, depending upon their own preferences as well as those of their specific journal or discourse community.

We will illustrate the flexibility of this argumentative structure by examining two historically significant articles that happened to appear in our random sample, both from the physical sciences. In the first, C. T. R. Wilson (1911-E209) reports experimental results from his newly modified cloud chamber. In the second, Arthur H. Compton (1923-E147) relates his adaptation of the then-new and controversial quantum theory to explain anomalous experimental results on the scattering of X-rays. Both are arguments in which visuals provide key evidence for the claims of new knowledge.

Wilson's New Facts and Method

Wilson's article was first read before the Royal Society of London on May 11, 1911, and then published six months later in its *Proceedings*. The article has three parts: (1) introduction, (2) method, and (3) results and discussion, which is subdivided by type of radiation inhabiting Wilson's cloud chamber (none, α-, β-, γ-, and X-rays). As part of his research, the experimenter had reproduced "natural" clouds in his laboratory apparatus and then observed and recorded their behavior, under different radiation conditions. The drops of water from the clouds made the paths of ionizing particles visible for the first time.

The article's title, "On a Method of Making Visible the Paths of Ionising Particles through a Gas," suggests that the author's argumentative goal might be to establish his method as a legitimate fact-gathering tool for the subatomic world. The first few sentences of the introduction, however, make it clear that the author takes for granted that his cloud chamber, an earlier version having been developed, refined, and tested during the 1890s, provides a "true picture" of the "tracks of individual α- or β-particles, or of ionising rays of any kind." Thus the discussion of methods seems fairly sketchy. Wilson assumes his readers already possess intimate knowledge of his apparatus and its operation. "On a Method . . ." actually pays little attention to Wilson's method—not even bothering with a specific reference to his earlier work other than "the method described in former papers." Wilson does, at least, mention two important innovations to his cloud chamber: the lining of its glass bulb with a gelatine that prevented fogging of the glass and, more important, the addition of a high-speed camera that captured images of the cloud formations frozen in time for later analysis and quantification. Overall, though, he does not provide helpful information to other researchers wishing to repeat or build upon his work.

The third and final part, results and discussion, is largely devoted to establishing facts generated by Wilson's apparatus, for example, that β-rays generated "absolutely straight thread-like lines of clouds," while γ-rays "produced . . . a cloud entirely localized in streaks and patches." The main facts manufactured by means of Wilson's apparatus not only are communicated by his written observations, but also are visually represented by two photographic images. These somewhat murky figures give "but a poor idea of the really beautiful appearance of these clouds," yet they offer strong indirect proof that Wilson's apparatus actually makes the subatomic world visible to the naked eye, as his title proclaims. To the naive viewer, these photographs resemble a black-and-white abstract painting of threadlike lines and curves of no particular significance; to a cloud maestro like Wilson, however, they reveal the wonders of the subatomic world in a way never before possible. Here the visual representations do triple duty: they picture nature, they permit the researcher to investigate the invisible world behind natural appearances, and they support an implicit argument, namely, that Wilson's apparatus has enormous potential in the future manufacture of new knowledge claims.

Wilson does not explain the significance of the facts created by his cloud chamber until the article's end, where, in carefully hedged statements, he suggests possible mechanical explanations for his X-ray results only. A typical such statement, an argument by comparison, is that his results are "in agreement with **Bragg's view** that the whole of the ionisation by X-rays **may be** regarded as being due to β- or cathode rays arising from the X-rays" (boldface added). Because of the minimal explanation of the acquired facts throughout the article, however, the reader at article's end may be left somewhat perplexed about the main claim or argumentative purpose.

Overall, Wilson's article reads like the preliminary communication it is, establishing Wilson's priority for his modified apparatus and its application without revealing the full story. In many respects, this article is more typical of fact-driven articles from earlier centuries. Indeed, an article of Wilson's on the same subject published a year later (1912) is more representative of 20th-century practice. Wilson gave this later article nearly the same title as the first and reproduced almost the same basic arrangement, but he reported far more methodological details, periodically offered mechanical explanations after the critical buildup of gathered facts, and appended a series of breathtaking photographs of the subatomic world clearly made visible. Together, these articles set in motion a new methodology that would grow into a major research front of physics, one based not upon mathematics and high theory, but the creation and analysis of images generated by the experiment itself (Galison 1997, pp. 106–120).

Compton's New Theoretical Explanation

Wilson's 1911 article has no abstract, no problem-setting introduction, no conclusion, and no formal references to work by others. Readers are thus left to tease out the author's argument and possible explanations for the stated facts as best they can. By contrast, Compton's 1923 article in *Physical Review* has all of the above; thus it is more characteristic of the 20th century, particularly its second half. In contrast to Wilson's title, Compton's delivers on its promise: the author will indeed mount an argument for "A Quantum Theory of the Scattering of X-rays by Light Elements." The unusually long abstract (about 550 words) gives us the Cliffs Notes version of that argument: in brief, compared with classical electrodynamic theory, then-new quantum theory yields much superior "*agreement between experiment and theory*" (italics in original) regarding the scattering behavior of X-rays and γ-rays when they collide with electrons. The abstract also summarizes Compton's mechanical and mathematical explanations for this behavior.

The article falls into four main parts: a problem-setting introduction, a theoretical discussion formulating the "quantum hypothesis of scattering" to solve the problem, a test of this hypothesis by comparing theoretical calculations with previously reported experimental results, and a conclusion elevating the status of the main claim from a hypothesis to a theory. In some respects, Compton is simultaneously building upon and arguing against his own past work, as reflected in the references to five of his own earlier articles (cited 10 separate times), published while he still believed in classical electrodynamics as the explanation for the X-ray scattering.

The article's opening sentence gets right to the heart of the matter: "J. J. Thomson's classical theory of the scattering of X-rays, though supported by the early experiments of Barkla and others, has been found incapable of explaining many of the more recent experiments." His research niche created, Compton then goes on to detail the ways in which the classical theory "is difficult to defend" and "improbable," a controversial assertion at the time. Implicit in the discussion is that Compton's solution is about to be revealed; it is indeed the subject of the next section, which uses quantum theory to derive a "hypothesis" (a set of alternative mathematical equations and mechanical explanations) for the scattering effects inadequately explained by the classical theory. The third section, putting Compton's quantum hypothesis to the test, is one long argument by comparison: Compton compares results from classical electrodynamics with experimental results, classical theory with his quantum hypothesis, and his quantum hypothesis with experimental results.

For these comparisons, Compton relies heavily upon visuals (four figures and one table) to make his case as strongly as possible. One of his figures (figure 9.4) is a relatively simple Cartesian graph plotting the effect of a change in wavelength on the absorption of X-rays due to scattering. The crosses are derived from experimental data, the horizontal line from classical electrodynamics, and the solid curve from the quantum hypothesis. Clearly, the experimental data at wavelengths below 0.5 angstroms agree ("perhaps within the experimental error" to use the technical parlance) with the quantum hypothesis, and not nearly so well with classical theory. For wavelengths above 0.5 angstroms, however, neither method appears to do a particularly good job of fitting the data. In the accompanying text, Compton explains that, according to experimental results from three independent research groups, "excess scattering" of the X-rays becomes significant at the higher wavelengths, and this effect accounts for the divergence of the experimental results from the quantum hypothesis.

Here we have a very powerful example of a visual simultaneously providing a mathematical explanation for a previously unexplained phenomenon and establishing a fact by a multilayered comparison. With comparisons of this kind, Compton is in a well-fortified position to open his concluding section with the following statement: "This remarkable agreement between our formulas and the experiments **can**

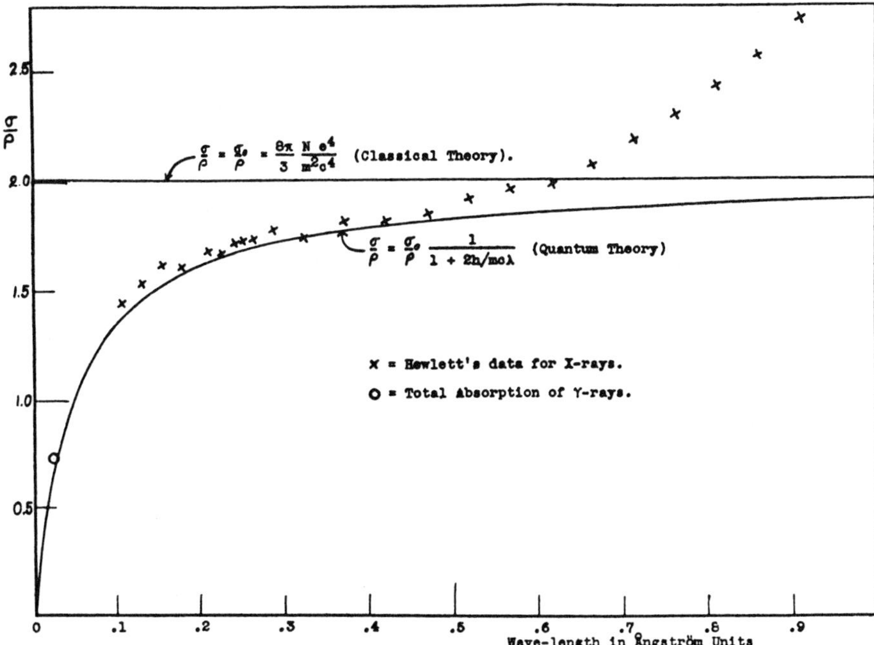

Fig. 6. The absorption in carbon due to scattering, for homogeneous X-rays.

Figure 9.4. Graph (figure 6) from Arthur H. Compton, "A Quantum Theory of the Scattering of X-rays by Light Elements" (1923)

leave little doubt that the scattering of X-rays is a quantum phenomenon." The very slight hedging of the predicate phrase in boldface (as opposed to the more definitive "leaves no doubt") is more a sign of social politeness than any real lack of conviction. In the remaining few paragraphs, Compton feels comfortable in elevating the epistemic status for his quantum hypothesis: "the present **theory** accounts," "the present **theory** depends," "the experimental support of the **theory** indicates very convincingly," "the quantum **theory** of scattering applies."

By reinterpreting recent experimental results from a new theoretical perspective, this article established the first empirical proof for quantum theory—a new theoretical method for exploring nature that future physicists would have to master for their own arguments in this research territory to be taken seriously. We should note that Compton's well-wrought argument did not bring all argument to a close. A few authors openly challenged it, as one might expect for a paradigm-breaking knowledge claim. And others, including Compton, continued to refine it both theoretically and experimentally over the next several years (Bazerman 1988, pp. 191–225). Like most modern scientific articles, Compton's is set *in medias res;* that is, it emerges from the triumphs and failures of past research and looks hopefully to the future for continued refinement and, most important of all, for positive citations indicating community acceptance.

Conclusion

Ever since the first publication of Thomas Kuhn's revised version of *The Structure of Scientific Revolutions* (in 1970), there has been nearly continuous debate concerning what he meant by such key terms as "paradigm," "revolutionary science," and "normal science." In the course of that debate, so-called postmodernists have preferred a radical interpretation, one that calls into question such notions as "progress." Some postmodernists also appear to regard science as but one belief system among others of equal value. At the other end of the spectrum, the so-called realists have insisted to the death that science captures truths about the material universe by means of direct observation, experiment, and reason. It is not our task to enter into this debate. Nevertheless, our discussion of the communicative and argumentative practices of science does bear on one of the terms in the debate over Kuhn's book, "progress."

In our concluding chapter we will offer an evolutionary explanation for the changes of scientific communicative and argumentative practices over time. Evolutionary theories are incompatible with any notion of progress that implies successive betterment, one that says, for example, Neanderthals, good; Cro-Magnons, better; *Homo sapiens*, best. The only notion of "better" that any evolutionary theory can tolerate is that of "better adapted" to prevailing conditions. In our conclusion to this chapter, we anticipate our final evolutionary chapter by asserting that the facts we have amassed concerning communicative and argumentative practices in science support the hypothesis that current practices are a consequence of the selective survival of practices that were, persistently, better adapted to the changing environments of the various scientific disciplines over time.

In all three languages studied, style reacted by adapting the resources of natural languages to the special needs of describing a complex material world: it placed that world more and more in the privileged position of sentences, the subject position; it exploited the structure of the noun phrase as a carrier of more and more cognitive content; and, at the same time, it simplified syntax by reducing the sentence length and corresponding number of clauses per sentence.

Presentation reacted by creating a master finding system and standard arrangement, one that conserved the scientist's reading time. That finding system and standard arrangement acts like a map allowing readers to easily direct their attention to select components within the argument being made.

In contrast to earlier centuries, the modern scientific argument, embedded as a consequence of its citations in the context of some research front, has two well-defined strata: verbal and visual. The verbal stratum typically consists of a problem-setting introduction, detailed information on research equipment and procedures for solving the problem, quantitatively based facts deduced from the applied equipment and procedures, theoretical explanations of the facts, and summaries of the new knowledge claims generated by the procedures. The pattern of citations that, in contrast with earlier centuries, underlies every section of the modern scientific article suggests that argument itself has become as much social as individual. While earlier centuries tilt in this direction, especially after 1700, in the 20th century this considerable tilt becomes a tectonic shift. The number of articles with citations in the

17th and 18th centuries remains under one-half; in the 19th century this rises to about two-thirds; in the 20th century, virtually every article contains citations—many of them. Scientists can no longer create a new argument without placing it overtly in the context of the past arguments of others.

Argument shifts as well to the visual. Along with equations, the visual text establishes facts and explanations by means of data arranged in columns and rows and graphs depicting data trends and mechanisms, as well as schematics and photographs. Indeed, we contend that it is the interaction of visual and verbal texts, an interaction enabled and facilitated by devices of style and presentation, that constitutes the heart of scientific argumentative practices at the end of the 20th century. While the "computer revolution" will undoubtedly continue to facilitate this interaction, we do not think this heart will look, or beat, very differently at the end of the twenty-first century.

CHAPTER 10

Explaining the Development of the Scientific Article

In chapter 1 we compare two scientific articles published three centuries apart as a means of representing, in dramatic form, the scientific article as a developing textual entity, characterized by changes in style, presentation, and argument. Chapters 2–9 describe these changes century by century, drawing upon our analysis of a large and diverse sample covering three languages and many scientific disciplines. We have now reached the point where it is time to attempt to explain what we have described. This is a more perilous venture, and what we will offer is more an explanatory sketch than an explanation per se.

In this chapter, we attempt to answer three related questions. First, how does modern scientific prose leave us with the impression that it is the objective and efficient conveyor of cognitive complexity? To answer that question, we draw upon and synthesize information given in the preceding chapters. Second, how did scientific style, presentation, and argument happen to develop in just the way they did? For this, we need a theory of change. Our choice is an adaptation of the evolutionary theory developed by Stephen Toulmin (1972), David Hull (1988a–c), and others to explain conceptual change in science.

Our explanations provoked a third question, what it would take to make our explanations less speculative than they now have to be. For this purpose, we need a "thick description" in Clifford Geertz's (1973) sense, a reconstruction of the social and political context of particular communicative events in science. In the latter part of this chapter, we offer one such reconstruction, taking as our object of study the communications of the first decade of the Kaiserliche Akademie der Wissenschaften (Imperial Academy of Sciences), launched in Vienna in 1847. We try to explain the rapid conformity of the communications of this late-blooming scientific society to European norms in terms of evolutionary theory.

Accounting for Our Impressions

We believe that, in general, modern scientific communication can be characterized as projecting a particular image: that it is an objective, efficient conveyor of cognitive complexity. The question we initially address is, how does it do so? By what textual means? Under the rubric of objectivity, we place those aspects of style that focus attention away from people and toward things. In this category, for example, we place the use of the suppressed-person passive verb and verbs that relate to the activities of things rather than people. We also place in this category the relative absence of the personal pronouns *I* and *we* and expressions departing from a neutral or plain style.

Hedges are another signal that scientific style is object oriented, indicating as they do an authorial concern for the fit between words and the world. This is an epistemic, as distinct from a social use of this device, which is a matter of impression management. Epistemic hedges show a persistent deference to the material world mediated through scientific instruments, including the oldest of these instruments, the five senses. Although theories may be, as Einstein insisted, the free inventions of the human mind, nonetheless these must be tested at the experimental and observational bar. And, as no theory passes this test with a perfect grade, the degree of its success will always be a central issue.

We also identify another set of stylistic features, those that make syntax more efficient. Increasing cognitive complexity has forced the shift in scientific prose to more complex noun phrases in the subject position; as compensation, there has been a corresponding decrease in the length of sentences and in the number of clauses per sentence. It is this double decrease that constitutes syntactic efficiency in our sense. Here is a sentence not atypical of 20th-century practice: "The kinetics of the addition of bromine to a few allyl compounds (allyl bromide, allyl chloride, methallyl chloride, allyl alcohol and allyl acetate) has been investigated in the temperature range 20° to 50°C, using dry acetic acid as a solvent." The difficulties in reading this sentence reside entirely in its noun phrases; its syntax is as simple as its noun phrases allow.

The presentational features of scientific articles also promote readerly efficiency. Among these are titles, introductions, headings, the numbering of equations and figures, the format and placement of citations, and finally, conclusions. We take it that these organizational features promote efficiency by permitting scientists to discover as quickly as possible whether they need to pay attention to an article and, if so, on just what constituents of the article their attention should dwell: Results? Figures? References cited?

The goal of communicative efficiency is particularly evident when we follow changes in presentational features from the 17th century to the 20th. We believe this "selection pressure" accounts for figures migrating from the end of the article or journal volume, with no descriptive captions, to a central position, accompanied by detailed captions; for equations and data moving from running text to a space set apart for their better display; and for citations shifting from running text to footnotes and then to the ends of articles. For a similar reason, headings, used unsystematically in the 17th century, in the 20th century became a convention. Also in the 20th century, all of these features are incorporated into a master finding system.

The objectivity and efficiency of scientific prose have a single purpose: to lay bare for close scrutiny the arguments that scientists make in establishing new facts and explanations about the material world.

Accounting for Change

To account for changes in style, presentation, and argument over time, we need a theory of change. For that purpose, evolutionary theory is an obvious choice because it deals with a historical process of self-organized change. The fact that we are focusing on social rather than biological change certainly complicates our problem. But there is nothing in principle that should prevent the application of evolutionary theory to a cultural product. For clarity, we will call it by its most general form, "selection theory," as suggested by Campbell (1988). Then, evolutionary theory becomes the name only of its biological kind.

In our work, we are extending to matters of style, presentation, and argument the work of two philosophers who have applied that theory to conceptual change in science: Stephen Toulmin and David Hull. In *Human Understanding* (1972), Stephen Toulmin makes the point that "the essential loci of conceptual change . . . [are] not the opinions of individuals, but the collectively attested repertoires of concepts that form the intellectual transmit of disciplines" (p. 289). These repertoires are his units of selection, the traits on which selection works. He also identifies "the twin activities of speculation and criticism" as "the human embodiments of conceptual variation and selection" (p. 296). These constitute his motor for change. In this first attempt, Toulmin establishes the plausibility of selection theory in the analysis of conceptual change in science; he does not transform his insights into a theory of such change. Moreover, Toulmin's level of analysis is so abstract that testing or extending his insights is difficult or impossible. How are we to capture, for the purpose of analysis, a unit of selection so all-encompassing as a repertoire of concepts, or a motor of change so general as speculation and criticism?

David Hull provides us with a theory we can adapt to changes in style, presentation, and argument. In "A Mechanism and Its Metaphysics" (1988a) and in *Science as a Process* (1988c), Hull paves the way for the application of evolutionary theory to cases of conceptual change, first by categorizing evolutionary theory as one of a class of selection theories and then by redescribing conceptual change in science clearly and rigorously in terms of this general theory. According to Hull, in biological evolution, individuals among species interact with one another and the environment. When they do, in sexual species at least, the genetic endowments of individuals combine to produce a next generation, a new cohort on which natural selection has operated and continues to operate in the direction of more nearly satisfactory adaptation to each other and the environment. Generalized and translated into Hull's terminology, selection theory takes the following form: when interactors interact, replicators create lineages by a process of selection. In Hull's words, "when the interplay between replication and interaction causes lineages to change over time, the end result is evolution through selection" (1988a, p. 136).

From the viewpoint of this general theory, science as a whole is readily redescribed: its interactors are scientists, and its replicators, conceptual systems. Its lineages are two: generational trees consisting of mentors and their students, and conceptual trees consisting of concepts and systems of concepts. The generational trees form the living systems that make science possible. The conceptual trees form science itself: "[T]he chief activity of scientists," Hull asserts, "is the production of conceptual systems" (1988c, p. 508). The culture of science and the conceptual systems it generates are both produced by and subject to intense selection pressures in the highly charged competitive environment that, everyone agrees, constitutes science. In terms of selection theory, science advances, not by launching and nurturing a few candidates for its contributions to fact and theory (*K* selection) but by allowing a candidate swarm to compete in an environment in which only a few claims of fact and theory can survive (*r* selection). Science copes by imitating, not mammals or birds, but the oyster, the salmon, the oak.

In "Picturing Weismannism: A Case Study of Conceptual Evolution," Griesemer and Wimsatt (1989) apply Hull's theory to the facts of change in a particular case, a set of diagrams that present August Friedrich Leopold Weismann's central doctrine of the continuity of the germ line. In Griesemer and Wimsatt's view, scientific "concepts" are not the best unit for tracing conceptual development. Because they are expressed in a natural language, they are hard to pin down; moreover, once pinned down, their meaning is still often subject to extended debate. In addition, because they are expressed in words, concepts present no clear boundary between themselves and the surrounding text. As a result, the analysis of the relationship between them and their "environment" is difficult if not impossible. These defects also make concepts hard to compare in detail or to array in lineages. In their paper, Griesemer and Wimsatt argue that, because diagrams suffer from few of these defects, they are an ideal "organism" with which to demonstrate conceptual evolution (pp. 16–21). Weismann diagrams, they contend, behave in good Weismannian fashion: "[T]heory-phenotypes do not directly make more theory phenotypes in the scientists which they infect. Rather what is passed on is a relatively compact generative structure which, in the right conceptual and social environment, generates the theory-phenotype of the next generation" (p. 14). In other words, descent does not necessarily yield exact copies but rather a variety of offspring with the same generative structure. Tracing the descent of the initiating diagram, Griesemer and Wimsatt demonstrate that the "different lineages of these diagrams show a number of interesting evolutionary patterns, including: descent without modification, descent with modification, differential proliferation, adaptive radiation, extinction, relict survival in a changed and specialized niche, and successive simplification for efficient specialization to a simplified niche" (p. 44). We endorse this passage fully insofar as Griesemer and Wimsatt are referring, not to evolutionary theory per se, but to selection theory generally.

With Griesemer and Wimsatt, we have moved a long way from the evolutionary talk of Toulmin, and a genuine step forward from the philosophically rigorous but not rigorously tested theory of Hull. Every term of theory employed by Griesemer and Wimsatt is correlated with specific characteristics in a specific "organism" in the evolutionary tree that they have created for the set of diagrams that has the initial Weismann diagram as its ancestor. Moreover, this redescription has considerable explanatory power.

Griesemer and Wimsatt chose Wiesmann diagrams because they and their fine structure had a discrete identity. This is most emphatically not the case with stylistic features or with argument. About presentational features, we may be slightly more confident. Still, we cannot omit style, presentation, or argument from our analysis without making our object of study—scientific communication—unrecognizable. Thus, we fall short of the philosophical rigor that Griesemer and Wimsatt achieve.

The groundwork laid, we can now turn our attention to explaining how selection theory might be applied to the scientific article. In evolutionary theory, the organism, the individual living creature, is the traditional locus of change. In Hull's terminology, this is an "interactor—an entity that interacts as a cohesive whole with the environment in such a way that this interaction *causes* replication to be differential" (1988a, p. 134). In the case of the scientific articles, the analogous unit is the individual article.[1]

Each organism is an instance of its overall phenotype, or general bodily design. As part of their bodily design, for example, human beings have two ears, one on each side of the head; so placed, these constitute a character of the human phenotype. Suites of characters of the phenotype are any intuitive grouping of phenotypical features that have collectively evolved. The set of Caucasian facial features, for example, constitutes a character suite of the human phenotype. Analogously, the phenotype of the scientific article consists of those features of style, presentation, and argument we have discussed in the preceding chapters. Each of these is a character, and style, presentation, and argument are the names for suites of characters.

The *genotype* is the set of generative structures by means of which the organism inherits phenotypes and suites of characters. In Hull's terminology, the genotype is a replicator, "an entity that passes on its structure largely intact in successive replications" (1988a, p. 134). In the case of the scientific article, the genotype is a set of predispositions: to create arguments, the vehicles by means of which Hull's "conceptual systems" are built, to transform these arguments into sentences and paragraphs, and finally, to order these sentences and paragraphs according to well-recognized organizational constraints. These predispositions are behavioral tendencies generally shaped by learning;[2] they function just like any skill we have, like violin playing or carpentry. When the situation calls for it, scientists activate these predispositions to create a scientific article.

While evolution works on individual organisms, it is the species as a whole that is affected. The species is a group of organisms that produce progeny relatively uniform in phenotype because they are relatively uniform in genotype. Evolution works

1. It is not, of course, the copies of the article in each issue of the journal that was printed. This a form of reproduction with which we are not concerned.

2. Most matters of style and presentation can be taught; in the 20th century, they also have become the subject matter of style manuals and textbooks. But this is not true of syntactic efficiency. It is hard to imagine writers routinely exercising conscious control of the length and complexity of noun phrases or of sentences to meet present norms.

because, within species, there is variation among organisms in their ability to cope in their niches, the environments within which populations of organisms interact. It is on this variation that selection works. Selection is the differential reproduction of variants as a consequence of environmental pressures within a niche. In Hull's words, this is "a process in which the differential extinction and proliferation of interactors *cause* the differential perpetuation of the replicators that produce them" (1988a, p. 134). It is this process that creates a lineage, a "family tree" of successful variants that selection creates over time: "an entity that persists indefinitely through time either in the same or an altered state as a result of replication" (p. 135).

While selection works on variants among individual scientific articles, it is the species of articles as a whole that is affected. It is this species that changes over time, a differential reproduction that is a consequence of environmental pressures within a niche, constituted in its innermost space by a scientific discipline or subdiscipline and in its outermost by science as a whole. This process creates the lineage of scientific articles, a family tree that exhibits the changes we have chronicled in this book. Such rapid change in so short a period is possible because social control and learning enter into the process, two factors that are not part of biological evolution.

To sum up, the communicative *phenotype* of the article is constituted by three *suites of characters*: style, presentation, and argument. Over time, these characters vary, and through their *genotypes,* these *variants* selectively reproduce as a consequence of the varying needs of the different scientific disciplines, the article's *niche.* It is this process of *selection* that creates the communicative *lineage* whose history our theory is designed to explain.

Unlike biological evolution, the evolution of the scientific article is teleological: the goals are objectivity and efficiency. The shift toward objectivity in scientific style is easily understood: science is primarily about objects, while ordinary prose is, primarily, about people. Efficiency, a goal of both style and presentation, is easily understood by reference to the growth of the scientific periodical. From 1700, when their number was a mere 10, scientific periodicals increased by a factor of 10 every 50 years at least up the mid–20th century (de Solla Price 1961, pp. 92–124). Given a bang so big, it is little wonder that scientific style and presentation opted for efficiency of comprehension. Of course, both objectivity and efficiency themselves evolve over time: they are not the same as they were in the 17th century.

Just as with biological features, the selection of new communicative and argumentative features over time takes on a logical, almost inevitable appearance only in retrospect. The scientific article has evolved, not in the sense of becoming better (or worse), but in the sense of changing to cope with the communicative and argumentative needs of an evolving set of disciplines whose messages have become ever more complex and have, consequently, strained to the utmost the resources inherent in natural languages.

The Vienna Academy of Science

We are now in a position to present a case that will test the explanatory and heuristic potential of our selection theory. To make our case, we gathered and analyzed a random sample drawn from the 10 volumes issued within the first decade of *Sitzungsberichte der Mathematisch-Naturwissenschaften Classe der Kaiserlichen Akademie der Wissenschaften* (Proceedings of Mathematical Natural Sciences from the Imperial Academy of Sciences), founded in Austria in 1847.[3] As a general rule, the data from a sample of articles parallel the data we have for European science at that period. We will not bore the reader with this recital, since what is most interesting about this case is what is unique to it: the very rapid movement in the first decade of the Academy from a prose of informal communication to a prose roughly analogous to the scientific prose of those nations in which science as a profession was more advanced—England, France, and the German states. This change cannot be accounted for on the basis of selection pressures that altered the style, presentation, and argumentation in English, French, and German articles over the preceding centuries. The change is much too rapid. This case highlights instead the importance of a single component of our selection theory, the possibility of learning. We claim that the Austrians learned by imitating German models; German models form the requisite selection pressure.

Background

Some historical background is necessary to understanding our point. Hans Schlitter, the historian of the Vienna Academy, cites with approval an Academy planner who "turned his eyes toward Austria—the Academy must be founded in Vienna, the Imperial City that must form the center of German culture!" (1921, pp. 27–28). But despite this ideal location, and despite an interest that begins as early as Leibniz, the Academy was not incorporated until 30 May 1847 and did not hold its first meeting until 25 November. That this long delay had a baleful effect on the state of Austrian science is clear from two travelers' accounts, one by Charles Sealsfield in 1828 and another by William Wilde in 1843. Sealsfield finds that intellectual labors free of censorship are impossible in Austria and, indeed, are forbidden for professors, who often act as state spies to ferret out student deviation (Taschwer 1997, p. 11). Things had not improved in 1843, as Wilde's observations indicate:

> There are many able professors in [Vienna's] university, besides numerous directors of cabinets and museums, eminent naturalists, celebrated travelers, distinguished physicians, and several private individuals of acknowledged literary and scientific ability—some of whom have long since earned European reputations, but there is no central point of interest, no common rallying place, no general or special scientific society, where such persons may meet for mutual instruction and the general propagation of knowledge—in one word, there is no academy of science in Vienna. It certainly sounds strange, and loudly demands inquiry, why the imperial city should be the only capital in Europe without an academy for the cultivation of science, more especially as such institutions are permitted to exist in other parts of the empire, as at Prague, Pesht [Budapest], Venice, and Milan. Numerous and incontrovertible proofs could be adduced of there being sufficient material for the

3. We followed similar sampling and analysis procedures to those detailed in appendixes A and B. We selected 38 passages and 39 complete articles.

> formation of such an institution in Vienna, although in conversation we have often heard the contrary advanced. . . .
>
> . . . Were such an academy in existence it would generate a spirit and create a desire for scientific knowledge and investigation, as experience amply proves it has been done in other countries; moreover, it would advance and give greater scope to the mind of that class who naturally feel that Austria is not a free country—the thinking and the educated. (Wilde 1843, p. 84)

Wilde goes on to lament the current decline in Austrian astronomy, botany, and mineralogy since the deaths of Littrow, Jacquin, and Mohr. Chemistry and astronomy are dead, as is mineralogy, with the exception of Haidinger. Physiology is but a name, and geology and comparative anatomy are not yet born (Tashwer 1997, p. 12). The message of general stagnation is clear from both of these travelers' accounts.

When we look at the early *Proceedings* of the Academy, those from 1848 and 1849, we may legitimately feel that the views of Sealsfield and Wilde are not without substance. In 1848, we have something that looks like a newsletter, full of announcements and academy business, programmatic and political statements, and recycled science. In the first volume, Schrötter reports on a letter in which Professor Nendtvich relates that Herr Mollnár has established without a doubt the existence of platinum in the sands of Oláhpiáner. He also outlines a plan for expanding the reach of the Academy to include "political studies" and "theoretical medicine." Fenzl petitions the Academy for funds to rescue a naturalist stranded in Mexico. Haidinger reports on research in mineralogy that he has already published elsewhere. But by 1852, only four years later, contributions of this sort have disappeared, to be replaced by original papers and, on occasion, by brief communications from governmental agencies, such as the ministries of agriculture and trade. If professional identity is measured in part by the steady production and publication of original scientific work, the Academy increased markedly in professional identity in its first decade.

Evolutionary Change

We now examine the presentational features of the scientific articles of the early Vienna Academy insofar as they are forerunners of present-day presentation, insofar, in other words, as they form a master finding system. We focus on these features because, in this short period, they are the most significant markers of evolutionary change.

As a general rule, it is a mistake to read history backward in this way, but we see no other explanation for these changing characters than the need to make the comprehension of the content they organize more efficient for scientist-readers. In saying this, we do not mean to imply that this was a conscious aim of the scientists involved; indeed, we believe that unconscious conformity to norms is the more likely explanation.

In our examination, we looked at titles, citations, and introductions. Table 10.1 summarizes some of our results.[4] From these data, we can see at a glance that in the

4. The initial year of the Academy was eliminated because it consisted almost entirely of short notices.

Table 10.1. Titles and Citation Placement in *Proceedings* of the Vienna Academy of Sciences

Time Period	*Vague Titles*	*Detailed Titles*	*Citations at Bottom of Page*	*Citations within the Text*
1848–1852[a]	62%	38%	24%	76%
1853–1856	23	77	50	50

[a]The initial year of the Academy was eliminated because it consisted almost entirely of short notices.

first decade titles became more specific, in-text citation placement diminished, and substantive headings became less frequent while formal ones became more so.

The shift in titles toward specificity may be exemplified by contrasting a title of 1851, Fitzinger's "Concerning the Avar [Asiatic nomad] Skull," with a title of 1855, von Hauer's "Concerning the New Bondings of Chlorcadmium with the Basic Metallic Chloriates." Headings are another important index of rapid evolutionary change. In the manner of a literary essay, Fitzinger's "Concerning the Avar Skull" contains no headings; in the manner of a modern scientific article, von Hauer's "Concerning the New Bondings" contains two levels of heading, general and specific:

Representation of the Salts.
I. Chlorbariumbicadmiate.
II. Chlorstrontiumbicadmiate.
III. Chlorcalciumbicadmiate.
IV. Chlorcalciumhemibicadmiate.
V.Chlormagniumbicadmiate.
VI. Chlormagniumhemibicadmiate.
VII. Chlormanganesebicadmiate.
VIII. Chlorferrobicadmiate.
IX. Chlorcobaltbicadmiate.
X. Chlornickelbicadmiate.
XI. Chlorcupromonocadmiate.

A line following the headings acts as a surrogate heading in that it divides the article proper from its conclusion.

Both articles contain citations. In von Hauer's case, they are at the bottom of the page in the more modern manner, one that permits full citation with a minimum of interruption to the reader. In Fitzinger's case, citations are incorporated into sentences within the text, a clumsy procedure: "In 1843 in Müller's Archiv Rathke published the description and illustration of a specimen of a nearly intact cranium of a skull, which bears a striking resemblance to that of the Graffenegger skull."

Introductions are an additional index of rapid evolutionary change. Table 10.2 indicates a shift away from narrativity and toward full exposition in our sample. In the first five years, narrative and expository introductions are about equally divided. In the next three years, expository introductions as a whole sweep the board, edging out the narrative variety completely. The effect of these quantitative differences can be experienced by comparing the introductions in the above two articles by von Hauer and Fitzinger. In the introduction to his article, Fitzinger writes about the discovery of a skull belonging to an Avar, a member of an Asiatic tribe of nomads. But the introduction tells us nothing about the significance of the skull, nor does it preview the contents of the article:

> In 1820 at Feuersbrunn near Grafenegg encircled by the Manhart mountains in lower Austria, a mile east of Krems, not far from the outlet of the Kamp river into the Donau, farmer laborers, while working the fields, found a skull with an unmistakably human shape at only a slight depth. August, Count of Breuner, heir of Grafenegg, who always has given special attention to the study of nature, added the skull to his collection and made it available to domestic and foreign natural philosophers who asked about it, so that they might become familiar with that rare find.

In this second, contrasting introduction, von Hauer is concerned with newly discovered bondings of chlorcadmium with the metallic chloriates:

> In one of the last proceedings of this highly esteemed society, I published an article concerning a new series of double bondings of chlorcadmium with other metallic chlorides. In this article, only the general properties of these crystallized bondings were indicated, so as to suggest a nomenclature similar to the one Bonsdorff introduced in the case of the double salts of mercury- and gold chlorides, which proved decisively analogous to the chlor-bondings of antimony, zinc, etc. I therefore chose the name chlorcadmiate on the assumption that these were the same double salts in which chlorcadmium takes the place of the electro-negative component.
>
> The naming of the three groups, into which the salts are divided in virtue of their chemical composition, which was proposed in my earlier article, as well as of each of the individual salts themselves, which is adopted in the following discussion, arises as a necessary consequence of the point of view stated above and needs no further justification. The chemical formulas for the individual salts were constructed according to these assumptions.
>
> It follows from what has been said that the constitution of the double bondings of the chlorcadmiums, which are now to be described in detail in the following discussion, were understood in accordance with the theory of salts.

In the first introduction, the structure is clearly narrative. Emphasized are the setting in which the skull was found and the generosity of its noble owner. In the second introduction, the structure is clearly expository. Its only narrative element is in its first sentence, devoted partly to deference to von Hauer's "highly esteemed" colleagues, and mostly to the outline of his research program. Aside from this, the

Table 10.2. Character of Introductions in Academy Articles

	Narrative Introduction	*Full Expository Introduction*	*Minimal Expository Introduction*	*No Introduction*
1848–1852	45%	55%	0%	0%
1853–1856	0	71	18	11

introduction conforms to the structure that Swales (1990) has determined is the norm for 20th-century scientific articles: establish an intellectual territory, define a niche in that territory, and inhabit that niche. The territory in this case is these double-bonded compounds, the niche is von Hauer's possible contribution to this area of inorganic chemistry, a niche he fills by showing that his newly discovered double-bonded compounds fit in nicely with the existing theory of the salts.

It may appear from this analysis that narrative and exposition cannot cohabit the same introduction, that a narrative introduction cannot fulfill Swales's criteria. Such is not the case in principle, nor is it the case in fact. In our Vienna Academy sample is an 1856 article on snails by Frauenfeld. It has a strong narrative structure, telling of a longtime interest in Dalmatian snails, an interest finally satisfied by a journey to the grottos from which the snail specimens originated, a journey that permits Frauenfeld "in the matter of identifying characteristics, which are subject to very great variation in these creatures, a clearer and more certain judgment." The introduction simultaneously fulfills both the narrative conventions and those that Swales enumerates. Thus, the virtual absence of narrative elements in the 20th century cannot be accounted for by their incompatibility with the expository forms that eventually prevailed. Rather, full expository forms conform to a worldview in which the knowledge sought takes place in a world from which time, which is the essence of narrative, is excluded; indeed, this may well be the explanation for the eventual predominance of full expository forms. That they eventually predominate, however, is not in question.

It is true that all events, including all scientific events, occur in chronological order. In a general sense, all modern scientific articles are "stories" of past events. What differentiates these from those we more comfortably refer to as "narrative"? Science relates sequences of events whose essential character is their typicality as means of doing science, as in the case of methods and materials sections, or their exemplification of some lawlike property of nature, as in the case of results sections. This is true even in the so-called historical sciences, such as geology and biology, which traffic in unique events. It is not the uniqueness of these events that is relevant to science, but their lawlike character; only those details that subtend to that character are deemed relevant in the modern scientific article. In contrast, the narrative aspects that we have just highlighted, aspects that diminish in scientific prose over time, are neither typical of the way science is done nor exemplary of its lawlike character. They concern the activities of particular human beings who *happen* to be doing science.

What may we say about general trends in presentation in our selection of Vienna Academy *Proceedings*? There is a definite movement toward composing scientific articles in well-articulated parts in the modern manner, and toward trying, by such devices as titles, headings, citational practices, and introductions, to convey as much information as efficiently as possible. These trends have in common a theory of the way scientists read: to gain the most information in the least possible time.

Accounting for Rapid Change

What is the source of the changes we have just documented? We would like to argue that this source was local, that it resided in the social and political conditions that characterized the Austro-Hungarian Empire in midcentury, the time of the Vormärz, the revolution, and the counterrevolution. This claim may at first glance seem to have about it a paradoxical air, for we want to assert that the local conditions in a time of political and social turmoil enabled the foundation of a science with universal standards of communication.

We do not pretend to account for the rapid growth of Austrian science as a whole. This is an enormous task that must trace the rise from modest beginnings—only three founding members of the Academy are in the *Dictionary of Scientific Biography*—to the elevated heights of Bolzmann and Mach. The links are certainly in place: Bolzmann's teacher was Josef Stepan, elected to full Academy membership in 1865; Andreas von Ettinghausen, another original member, was Mach's teacher. But while lineages can be traced, they tell us nothing about what makes such lineages possible: the laboratories, professorships, journals, textbooks, courses of instruction—in short, the social structures necessary to create a mature science. In this chapter, we attempt to account only for the changes in the means of communication; we attempt to account for one of the conditions necessary for the maturation of any complex intellectual enterprise.

It might seem at first glance that the Vormärz, far from fostering science, actually inhibited it. It is certainly true that the conditions created by the Vormärz delayed the Academy's foundation. It is equally true that censorship was rife during this period. To forestall revolution, Austro-Hungary had become, in effect, a police state (Taylor 1948, p. 55; Taschwer 1997, pp. 12–14). But Prince Metternich's policy toward the Academy actually protected it by narrowing its scope. As he says himself: "While his Majesty the Emperor, once and for all on the basis of good reasons and important political considerations, has strictly limited the scope of the Imperial Academy of Learning in Vienna, this is only to prevent from the start many inconveniences which could not have been easily avoided, given the current mood of agitation, were theological, philosophical, and juridical concerns open to it" (Meister 1947, p. 217; see also p. 63). In fact, under these conditions, the Academy was made free of "generally prescribed censorship" (Meister 1947, p. 63). These circumstances are especially important in view of the virtual eclipse of the University of Vienna between 1848 and 1868 (Schorske 1998, p. 115).

The evidence suggests that the regime was generally supportive of the Academy as long as it remained politically conservative. While the revolutionary period is reflected in its *Proceedings*, revolutionary influence is always marginal to its concerns. A revolutionary Germany criticized the Academy's reactionary reputation (Meister 1947, pp. 71–72); the first volume of the *Proceedings* reports that the Academy debated whether it should send a representative to the Frankfurt "National Assembly" despite the fact that no invitation had been forthcoming. But regime approval never really flags. In this same volume Schrötter talks about adding "political studies" to the studies of the Academy; the Academy suggests "state studies" instead, and official concurrence is eventually received. During the revolutionary occupation of Vienna, Ettinghauser is accused of collaboration with the revolutionary forces, and Schrötter of making guncotton for them. The anonymous accusation against Ettinghauser is never pursued, however, and the case against Schrötter is dropped when he explains that he rendered the guncotton deliberately defective (Meister 1947, pp. 75–76).

But did this supportive behavior have an enduring intellectual provincialism as its price? There is certainly evidence of what seems to be Academic provincialism. In 1849, Boué gives a lecture with the title "For the Advance of Knowledge, What Can and Must Be Most Useful for the I[mperial] Academy of Science? Should It Set Aside Money only for Geological Journeys or for the More General Purposes of Natural History?" In it he says:

> What do botanists and zoologists need most today? The most accurate knowledge of local flora and fauna, together with a detailed understanding of the characteristics of their ranges. What will lead to the greatest advances in the comparative anatomy and physiology of plants and animals? An increase of researches into the details of local and individual variation.
>
> The very same method is supremely capable of deciphering alpine geology, whether the researcher is travelling or virtually glued to the spot. Only in this way can the necessary detailed knowledge be achieved, and important fossils found. On this point, indeed, I may almost go so far as to affirm that perhaps in the case of Austria the detailed study of a single ten-mile cross-section from Eisenerz to the Danube, as in the work of Herr Unger (Neues Jahrbuch für Mineralogie, 1848, table 5), would more likely lead to very certain and important results than a summer's excursion throughout all of the Austrian Alps.

In this same 1849 volume of *Proceedings*, moreover, 17 out of 68 reports, or 25%, are on local topics. Typical titles are "Concerning the New Foraminifera from Tertiary Strata of the Austrian Basin" and "Concerning the Occurrence of an Alkaline Substance in the Smelting Compartment of the Iron Blast Furnace at St. Leonard in Carinthia." In the 1854 *Proceedings*, eight out of 41 reports, or 20%, are on local topics. Typical titles are "Report on the Knowledge of the Family *Capricorniae* in the Austrian Alps" and "Relationships among Vegetation in Austria in 1853." Thus, it may seem that Boué's advice to focus on the local is consistently followed.

If so, however, it is not with a provincial intent; indeed, that is not Boué's intent either. When read carefully, Boué's is a call for the creation of a universal science in Austria, a possibility because Austrian flora, fauna, and geology are varied enough for the purpose. Moreover, the intent seems generally realized; for example, von Hauer's article on Alpine fossils, "Report on the Knowledge of the Family *Capricorniae* in the Austrian Alps," is local only in the sense that the fossils must be somewhere. Otherwise, this is simply an article on fossil taxonomy, no more, no less: "In a manner similar to that in an earlier publication on heterophylls, I have tried in the following pages to describe the ammonites from the family *capricorniae,* that have been discovered up to now in our Alps." The local is merely a means to the universal.

Local sites could be exploited in the interests of universal standards because a model of such standards was readily available in German science, a science all the more available because of the predominance of German influence in Austro-Hungary. In the Academy, lip service is paid to the multiethnicity of the Austro-Hungarian empire; for example, the rules of the society stipulate that papers submitted may be in any language of the Empire, in addition, of course, to Latin (Meister 1947, p. 225). In fact, in our sample with one exception, a paper in Italian, all papers are in German, a clear indication of German hegemony. As Robert Kann

Table 10.3. Selected Stylistic Features of Academy and German Scientific Articles

	Academy 1848–1856	*Germany 1801–1900*
Evaluative expressions	0.6	0.6
Hedges	1.1	1.1
Sentence length	42.0	45.0/38.5[a]

[a]This represents the following periods: 1826–50/1851–75.

(1950) points out, "[T]he Germans played a hand, and had interests at stake, not only on the high level of central administration of the empire but also in the regional units of the crown lands and the historico-political entities" (p. 56). Under these circumstances, it is not unreasonable to infer that the Academy existed within "the concept of the Austrian state and the Austrian idea of embracing many nationalities, bound together by a German-directed cultural and administrative superstructure under the supreme union of the crown" (Kann 1973, p. 290).

We hypothesize that German hegemony is the cause of change in the specific instance with which we are here concerned, the communicative practices of the early Vienna Academy. Our evidence for German hegemony derives primarily from citational patterns.[5] From 1853 to 1856, citations in German increase from a trickle of 2.5 per article to a steady stream of 9.8. While bibliographic information makes it impossible to differentiate adequately between those sources in German and those from Germany, a careful study of the citations in a full session of the 1854 *Proceedings* indicates that Swiss and Austro-Hungarian sources account for only 28% of citations.[6] A full 47% of citations are in German and from Germany.[7]

Further evidence for this hegemony comes from the conformity of Academy scientific articles with selected stylistic and presentational features of German scientific articles of the period, as tables 10.3 and 10.4 illustrate. In table 10.3, evaluative expressions and hedges are given per 100 words, and sentences by average length in a 10-line sample. Table 10.4 compares German and Academy practices in terms of percentage of articles containing selected organizational features: headings, specific titles, complete introductions and conclusions, citations, and visuals. While parallel tables could be presented that would show an almost identical conformity with English and French scientific prose, the relative paucity of citations from English and

5. Our hypothesis would fail if the authors we are dealing with were predominately German themselves, despite the predominance of Austro-Hungarian citizens in the Academy rolls. But authors were predominately Austro-Hungarian. There are 35 authors in the sample, 25 of whom are definitely from Austro-Hungary, four of whom are probably so, based on their topic or on dialectical differences in their prose. Only one is definitely German.

6. A volume reprints the content of the meetings of the Academy during the past year—that is, its sessions.

7. It needs also to be said that bibliographic assignment was in many cases far less than optimal: sometimes by location of journal, sometimes by object of study (e.g., a mountain range in Germany), and sometimes by the place of publication of works of the author other than those cited.

Table 10.4. Percentage Occurrence of Selected Presentational Features in Academy and German Scientific Articles

	Academy 1848–1856	*Germany 1801–1900*
Headings	34%	40%
Specific titles	66	81
Complete introductions	93	98
Complete conclusions	31	33
Citations	68	69
Visuals	52	52

French sources—for example, French and English together account for only 20% of citations in 1854—argues for a paucity of influence as well.

This evidence for German hegemony seems conclusive. The evidence for a causal relationship, however, is only suggestive. The evidence suggests that, especially for those features of style and presentation that can be placed under personal or social control, such as those mentioned in tables 10.1 and 10.2, rapid assimilation of a model is possible when that model is readily available and subject to considerable deference. Although no explicit instruction takes place, under the influence of a powerful model, behavioral dispositions alter in subtle though definite ways.

Conclusion

In this chapter, we have suggested a version of selection theory as an explanation for the changes in style, presentation, and argument in scientific communication from the 17th to the 20th century. At this point support for our theory must be regarded as suggestive only—there is some fit between our theory and the evidence. Regardless of the ultimate truth of our formulations, our theory has heuristic potential: in our case study of Viemese science, it located a selection pressure—the hegemony of German science—for which we were able to find enough historical evidence to tell a plausible causal story linking social pressure to communicative change. This modest success suggests a general procedure for linking communicative and argumentative change to the social, political, and economic niches in which, and in interaction with which, the change takes place.

Epilogue: Past, Present, Future

> Now, in the [late] 20th century, we look forward to applying electronic technology to scientific communication. Certainly the editors and scientists who started this whole process more than 300 years ago would be astounded at the scope of the worldwide scientific endeavor. But I doubt that they would have any difficulty recognizing the basically similar characteristics of the system they started.
>
> Eugene Garfield
> *Current Contents* (25 February 1980)

In this book we have traced the development of the scientific article's progress: its style, its presentation of text and graphics, and its way of arguing from the late 17th century to the end of the 20th century in English, French, and German, the three major languages of science.

We have found that the very first scientific articles are typically brief reports describing an individual's encounter with nature through observation and, much less often, experiment. In late-17th-century England, such articles tend to be a run of Baconian "facts," loosely connected with theory, if at all. In general, they seek to establish the authors' credibility more by means of reliable testimony than by descriptive adequacy, more by qualitative experience than by quantitative experiment and theory. In contrast, the early professionalization of French science through the Académie Royale des Sciences led early on to a heightened emphasis on several features familiar in late-20th-century practice: quantification, mathematical and mechanical explanations for acquired facts, and use of observations and experimental results as stepping stones to theory. Also consistent with the early professionalization, the 18th-century French sample scored lower on our measures of personal expression and higher when the components of a master finding and organizing system were at issue.

Looking at our combined data from the 17th through the 19th century, we spotted several trends common to the samples for all three languages. First, scientific style moves from the occasionally and overtly social and personal to the mostly impersonal. Second, scientific style becomes more nominal than verbal. In this style, the complex noun phrase pushes out the simple one in the subject position. Third, sentence syntax becomes simpler, at least as measured by sentence length and clausal density. Finally, presentational features move away from the bare minimum one would expect in a letter or news item; evident in this transformation are a variety of formal elements for better displaying complex information (headings, figure captions, a numbering system for citations and visuals, etc.) and of substantive elements that assist in reader comprehension (e.g., introductions that contextualize a research problem or niche). Despite the existence of central tendencies, we also found much variety, as one would expect from a prose aimed at a diverse audience—a loosely knit community of amateurs and some professionals united by an interest in learning more about the natural world and how it works.

In the 20th century, we find the scientific article growing considerably more uniform across national boundaries and scientific disciplines. Most striking of all, "scientific English" has become the international discourse of science, which involves not only a specific language but also a suite of stylistic features: relatively short, syntactically simple sentences containing complex noun phrases with multiple modification, verbs in the passive voice, noun strings, technical abbreviations, quantitative expressions and equations, and citational traces. French and German scientific articles also conform to this basic style, with some variations. For example, French and German scientific prose has resisted the noun string; each of these languages employs several grammatical structures that avoid the passive voice yet maintain an objective tone. Whatever the language or discipline, the style is streamlined to focus the reader's attention on the things of the laboratory and the natural world beyond the printed page, rather than to draw attention to the text itself or its author. And in contrast to earlier centuries, the intended audience, as indicated by the specialized style and implied scientific knowledge, is almost exclusively other professionals engaged in similar research.

This uniformity involves presentational features as well as stylistic ones, particularly in the latter half of the 20th century, when the proliferation of scientific style manuals encouraged the rapid development of a large suite of presentational features. From the title at the beginning to the references at the end, the modern scientific article is designed to convey its claim efficiently to its targeted audience.

The content of specific arguments, which is the subject matter of science, is not our concern. Rather, we have focused on the general form arguments take—the kinds of claims authors make, and the kinds of evidence they adduce in support of these claims. In the 17th century, claims are mostly claims of fact. Their basis is naked-eye observations of natural objects or experimental results; sometimes observations are enhanced by microscope or telescope. The nature of these claims means that hedging is infrequent. When they exist, explanatory claims tend to be immediate and mechanical, though there are some speculative explanations at the micro-level. Such explanations are general, not discipline-specific. What counts as evidence is still an open question, and a forensic model involving witnesses and testimony is still an option. During the late 18th century and throughout the 19th century—in conjunction with the establishment of special-interest journals and societies and the growth of career opportunities within universities and newly created research institutes—each scientific discipline starts developing explanatory structures appropriate to its enterprise. There are chemical explanations, geological explanations, physical explanations, biological explanations. By the 20th century, only a few sciences, such as plant and animal taxonomy, heavily rely upon naked-eye observations; explanatory claims range widely and tend to be specific to specific sciences; and epistemic hedging has become a flexible resource to fine-tune claims to evidence. Finally, in 20th-century scientific argument, there is a preference for comparison of large data sets; in addition, mathematics is applied, seemingly whenever possible.

An often-overlooked complement to the verbal text are its accompanying visuals: the evidence they contain and the explanations they suggest. As a result of this increased visual component, the modern scientific article has now become almost as much about interpreting information in figures and tables as about reading straight text.

Overall, then, our results support the hypothesis that the scientific article has evolved in the following directions:

- the representation of science as an objective enterprise through a style increasingly designed to focus the reader's mind on the things of the laboratory and the natural world,
- the development of stylistic and presentational devices for the more efficient communication of science in partial compensation for its growing complexity,
- increasing concern with mounting an argument that not only establishes new facts but also offers theory-based mechanical or mathematical explanations for them, and
- the increasing prominence of visual representations, and their integration into argument.

Translated into evolutionary language, selection pressures favor a style that represents science as an objective enterprise, foster more efficient communication, and produce stronger, more flexible argumentative strategies. These result in either a gradual and continuous change in some feature over time—as in the general decline of personal pronouns and corresponding rise of passive voice—or a relatively abrupt change—as in the emergence of a heading abstract or the fused noun string.

We now turn our attention away from the past. While we own no crystal ball, we can hazard some views on what the future holds for the scientific article based on our sense of its development. Despite many proclamations about the demise of print culture, while more than half the journals in our 20th-century sample now publish Web-based articles, none does so to the exclusion of print. The significant journals of science still remain firmly entrenched in the traditional way of publishing. And the scientific community and publishers still apparently view "e-journals" such as *Psycoloquy* and the *Online Journal of Current Clinical Trials* as interesting novelties. Yet, clearly, the scientific article is entering an era in which it will be increasingly dominated by the opportunities and problems created by the personal computer and its global network consisting of e-mail and the World Wide Web.[1]

1. Much has been written on the subject. See, for example, Lederberg (1996), Boyce and Dalterio (1996), Brody (1996), and Harnad (1990, 1991, 1992, 1999).

This technology is rapidly changing the way in which the scientific manuscript is prepared by authors, put through peer review, produced in final form, distributed to interested readers, and perused by those readers. Indeed, the 21st century, what Harnad (1991) calls the "post-Gutenberg era," may very well witness the extinction of the scientific journal distributed by publishers on actual paper.[2] For example, one can easily foresee the day when customized e-journals will regularly turn up in scientists' e-mail box. These journals may house links to articles selected by a computerized search known as "collaborative filtering," which takes into account the recipient's past preferences and those of others with similar interests.

During the past decade, many have proclaimed that this new technology will "revolutionize" scholarly publishing. Typical is this statement by Schaffner (1994): "It is clear to all involved—from the most astute students of electronic publishing to the most casual observer—that we are approaching a time when new information technologies will cause profound and elemental changes in scholarly communication. While these changes will eventually affect communication in all areas of scholarship, the sciences seem likely to be affected first" (p. 239).

These revolutionary claims mainly have to do with the dissemination of articles and the economics of publishing. The question of special interest to our endeavor is whether electronic publishing holds the analogous promise of revolutionizing communicative and argumentative practices per se. Our guess is, in some ways, without a doubt, and in others, probably not much.

Web publication will unlikely have much direct effect on style. Whatever the language, we believe the trend toward shorter sentences with fewer clauses will continue, as will the continual pressure on the natural languages to adapt to the demands of the growing complexity in science. Presentation is another matter. The future scientific article will look noticeably different from the current printed version. Web publication will accelerate modularization. Links will allow readers easier access to the material they are most interested in, whether it be an abstract, a figure or table, bibliographic information, or biographies of and other publications by the same authors.[3] The basic units of the modular arrangement will become even more self-contained than they are now, as scientists come to recognize they are writing what is, in essence, a hypertext document that will seldom be read front to back. The Web will also alter the "intertextual" status of texts: readers will be able to move backward from an article to the articles it cites and forward to the articles that cite it (Caplan and Arms 1999). Links may send readers to additional data gathered by the authors in the course of their research project and to more detailed methodological descriptions. Visual images will undergo a similar transformation: there will

2. It seems highly probable, however, that many readers will print out articles of special interest for detailed scrutiny. The scientific "paper" will still have the advantage of easy portability.

3. At the present time, the *Astrophysical Journal* offers one of the more advanced electronic finding systems. Its articles possess tables of contents linked to appropriate text, references cited in text linked to the references in the list at the end, references at the end linked to cited articles, and mention of tables and figures in text linked to actual table and figures. As one might expect given their present-day prominence and worldwide circulation, *Science* and *Nature* also offer similarly evolved electronic articles. Unfortunately, and this is one of the real limitations with the present economic arrangement, all three journals are accessible to subscribers only.

be links to the data and methods used to generate figures; there will be visual images that move and make sounds; and there will be three-dimensional images that the scientist-reader can manipulate to view from different perspectives. Color photography will likely flourish, especially in specialties such as astronomy and molecular biology. Editors and graphic designers will adapt the layout of the scientific journal and its articles to their new primary medium: the computer screen.

The pace of argument may also change. Since it will be easy to append reader criticisms and queries along with the author responses, agonistic forums may become commonplace. It is not clear, however, that this will constitute an improvement. We already know that electronic communication, at least in one notorious episode, has had the interesting consequence of increasing the pace of informal scientific communication (e-mail, fax, and bulletin boards) to the point of *destabilizing* knowledge. According to Bruce Lewenstein's (1995a, 1995b) study of electronic communication and the cold fusion controversy of 1989, "the barrage of conflicting material about cold fusion led to what the media called 'fusion confusion.' . . . Communication times were shorter, but the communication itself was more complex, chaotic and intense" (1995a, pp. 417, 429). No one knew whose information to trust. The knowledge claims about cold fusion eventually stabilized once the faster, informal channels were surpassed by traditional published papers in journals and conference proceedings. These old but reliable communicative means reduced, though did not eliminate, "the chance of receiving conflicting or competing information" (1995a, p. 429). They also permitted speculation to coalesce into stable knowledge claims supported by a consensus of the relevant scientific community.

The 21st-century electronic world will also have social consequences pertinent to the scientific article. Thanks to e-mail and other forms of electronic communication, scientists can much more easily collaborate with colleagues around the world without having to leave their home institutions. With the formation of these "collaboratories," it is not unreasonable to predict that bylines will take on an increasingly international flavor. Furthermore, once the constraints imposed by the competition for available space in print journals are lifted, in certain specialties at least, amateur scientists in much greater numbers may contribute observationally based facts to the scientific literature—sightings of astronomical bodies, new species of flora and fauna, new geological specimens, and so on.

Despite the utopian picture painted by Harnad and others about the post-Gutenberg era and the brave new World Wide Web, there are still considerable economic, technical, and institutional hurdles that must be overcome before electronic publication can reach its full potential. One can easily assemble a grab bag of nagging questions. Will the Web evolve into something other than "an overstuffed, underorganized attic full of pictures and documents that vary wildly in value" [not a bad description of the early days of the printed scientific article] (Brody 1996)? Who will foot the bill for the production and long-term maintenance of Web articles? Will commercial publishers allow all Web users fast and affordable access to the articles? Hundreds of years from now will scholars and scientists be able to access articles prepared with obsolete electronic technology? Will the powerful search engines and a never-ending stream of information tempt scientists to narrow rather than broaden the scope of their reading, leading to a "balkanization of the global village" (Van Alstyne and Brynjolfsson 1996)? In those disciplines where speed of publication is a genuine concern, what will be the role of peer and editorial review? If anyone can post an article on the Web, how will readers know whether the information in a particular article is trustworthy?

These problems and others await the electronic article on the Web. Whatever its future, we can rest assured that the scientific article will continue to change in response to the demands of individual disciplines and scientific communities, as well as in response to new communicative technologies. And whether in the form of ink on paper or pixels on a computer screen, the scientific article will remain the medium of choice for establishing new knowledge claims generated by and for—to quote the title page for the first *Philosophical Transactions*—"the ingenious in many considerable parts of the world."

APPENDIX A

Method for Sampling Scientific Texts

As mentioned in the Introduction, our sample consists of 10-line passages and whole articles drawn from the significant journals of science identified by Gascoigne (1985) for the period 1665–1905 and Garfield (1976) for the period 1901–1995. We allocated the short passages and whole articles as described in table A.1 and labeled them as described in chapter 2, note 6. The number of passages per journal was loosely based on weightings given in Gascoigne (1985) and Garfield (1976). The passages for analysis were chosen by random number generation for year of publication, page number, and first line on the page. (For this purpose, we designed a Microsoft Excel spreadsheet with columns of random numbers within selected ranges. For example, to obtain year of publication for articles in 18th-century journals founded before or in 1801, we generated a column of random numbers between 01 and 100, which signified the last two digits in the year. If the journal was founded after 1801, we used as the minimum year the last two digits of the founding year in calculating the random numbers. We followed a similar procedure for the other centuries.) If the page selected was in not a scientific article but an obituary or some other type of document, we skipped to another random number. Also, we started our line count at the beginning of a sentence and stopped at the end of a sentence. If the randomly selected first line did not begin a sentence, we advanced to the closest line that did, counted 10 lines down, then stopped at the next period ending a sentence. So, strictly speaking, our passages seldom covered exactly 10 lines.

The whole articles were a random subset of the articles from which we randomly selected passages. In deciding upon the number of passages and whole articles per century, we rejected the approach of distributing them in some proportion to the number of total articles published as a function of time. Given the exponential increase in the number of journals since 1665 (de Solla Price 1986, p. 8), that would almost certainly have meant that nearly all our

Table A.1. Sample Composition

Years Covered	*English Passages*	*French Passages*	*German Passages*	*Total Passages*	*Number of Whole Articles*
1665–1700	100	98	0[a]	198	100
1701–1800	122	217	143	482	126
1801–1900	188	122	214	524	104
1901–1995[b]	486	52	62	600	100
Total	896	489	419	1,804	430

[a]No German-language journals appear in Gascoigne's (1985) list for the 17th century.
[b]The final year is not 2000 because our 20th-century sample was gathered in 1994–95.

sample would have been from the 20th century. And we wanted to make certain we had a fair representation of the 18th and 19th centuries since past studies in the communicative and argumentative practices of science have largely ignored these centuries. We arrived at the numbers in table A.1 for both articles and passages because they gave us a reasonable distribution of text samples across each century and represent significantly more than earlier studies have attempted. Furthermore, we projected that, with the present numbers, we could finish our textual analyses over a two-year period—an important practical consideration.

The remainder of appendix A gives our method for choosing journals in each century and the number of 10-line passages for each journal. Appendix B discusses our method for analyzing the selected texts.

17th-Century Sample

For the period 1665–1700, we sampled 100 passages from the *Philosophical Transactions*, 71 from the *Mémoires de l'Académie Royale des Sciences*, and 27 from the *Journal des Sçavans*. While this does not quite match Gascoigne's (1985) weightings of 2.47, 2.02, and 0.30, respectively (pp. 91–96), we felt it was the best way of achieving a balance among the sources of 17th-century periodical science; this slight deviation in favor of equal balance seemed justified because Gascoigne's weightings include most of the 18th century. Concerning the French sample from the *Mémoires*, of course, "periodical science" is, strictly speaking, a misnomer. Few of the articles in our sample were actually published before the 18th century, and those few generally appeared in the *Journal des Sçavans*. Moreover, until 1699, the Académie rules frowned on author identification. Nonetheless, despite their 18th-century publication date, the articles chosen from the *Mémoires* were in the vast majority of cases identified by date and author as products of the 17th-century Académie. For ease of comparison, the 100 complete articles selected for analysis were divided equally between the French and English passages.

18th-Century Sample

The sample for the period 1701–1799 is smaller than 500 because of difficulties in obtaining some periodicals in the French and German samples.

English	**Passages**	**Whole articles**
Philosophical Transactions	110	41
Transactions of the Royal Society of Edinburgh	6	1

English (*continued*)	Passages	Whole articles
Memoirs of the Manchester Literary & Philosophical Society	3	1
Transactions of the Royal Irish Academy	3	1
Total	122	44

French	Passages	Whole articles
Mémoires de l'Académie des Sciences	168	41
Observations et Mémoires sur la Physique (Rozier's Journal)	27	8
Mémoires des Savans Étrangers	15	3
Annales de Chimie	7	2
Total	217	54

German	Passages	Whole articles
Chemische Annalen	77	15
Astronomisches Jahrbuch	43	8
Bergmanisches Journal	23	5
Total	143	28

19th-Century Sample

English

Because of skewing, we had to oversample the early part of the 19th century. We also had to substitute for periodicals not available to us.

	Passages	Whole articles
Philosophical Magazine	28	6
American Journal of Science	23	4
Philosophical Transactions	17	3
BAAS Reports	15	3
Royal Society, Proceedings	12	2
Monthly Notices of the Royal Astronomical Society	11	2
Journal of Botany	9	1
Transactions of the Royal Society of Edinburgh	8	2
Science	6	1
Zoologist	6	1
Nature	5	1
Quarterly Journal of the Geological Society of London	5	1
Zoological Society of London, Proceedings	4	1
The Gardener's Chronicle	3	1
Rhodora	3	1
Science Gossip	3	1

(*continued*)	Passages	Whole articles
The Annals and Magazine of Natural History	2	—
The Auk	2	1
Bulletin of the Torrey Botanical Club	2	—
Chemical News	2	1
Proceedings of the Academy of Natural Sciences	2	1
The Geological Magazine	2	—
American Journal of Physiology	1	—
The Astrophysical Journal	1	—
Bulletin of the British Ornithologists Club	1	—
Bulletin of the Geological Society of America	1	—
Entomological News	1	—
The Entomologists Monthly Magazine	1	—
The Ibis	1	—
Journal for the Society of Chemical Industry	1	—
Journal of the American Chemical Society	1	—
Journal of the British Astronomical Association	1	—
The Journal of Physiology	1	—
The Nautilus	1	—
The Observatory	1	—
Pharmaceutical Journal and Transactions	1	—
Popular Astronomy	1	—
Proceedings of the Biological Society	1	1
Proceedings of the Chemical Society	1	1
Transactions of the Entomological Society of London	1	1
Total	188	37

French	**Passages**	**Whole articles**
Comptes Rendus Hebdominaires	27	5
Annales de Chimie	12	2
Journal de Physique (Rozier's)	11	2
Comptes Rendus, Société de Biologie	9	1
Annales de la Société Entomologique de France	8	2
Bulletin, Académie Royale des Science, Brussels	8	2
Mémoires, Société d'Arcueil	6	1
Archives des Sciences Physiques	5	1
Bulletin, Société Botanique de France	5	1
Bulletin, Société Géologique de France	4	1
Mémoires de l'Académie Royale de l'Institute	4	1
Mémoires du Muséum d'Histoire Naturelle	3	1
Révue Generale des Sciences	3	1

Journal de Pharmacie et des Sciences Accessoires	3	1
Mémoires de la Société d'Histoire Naturelle	3	—
Journal de Physiologie Experimentale	3	—
Bulletin, Muséum d'Histoire Naturelle	2	1
Bulletin, Société Chimique de Paris	2	—
Bulletins, Société Anatomique de Paris	1	1
Annales de Chimie Analytique	1	—
Annales de la Société Linnéene de Lyons	1	—
Journal de Pharmacie et de Chimie	1	1
Total	122	25

German	**Passages**	**Whole articles**
Annalen der Physik	33	9
Sitzungsberichte der Kaiserlichen Akademie der Wissenschaften	20	3
Astronomische Nachrichten	17	3
Journal für die Chemie, Physik und Mineralogie	11	3
Archiv für Anatomie, Physiologie und Wissenschaftliche Medicin	11	2
Monatsberichte der Königlichen Preussichen Akademie der Wissenschaften	8	1
Verhandlungen der Gesellschaft Deutscher Naturforscher und Ärzte	8	1
Zeitschrift für die Gesammten Naturwissenschaften	7	1
Jahresbericht des Physikalischen Vereins	6	1
Verhandlungen der Physicalisch-Medicinischen Gesellschaft	6	—
Berliner Entomologische Zeitschrift	5	1
Botanische Zeitung	5	—
Chemische Annalen	4	—
Neues Jahrbuch für Mineralogie, Geognosie Geologie und Petrefaktenkunde	4	1
Zeitschrift der Deutschen Geologischen Gesellschaft	4	1
Archiv für die Gesammte Physiologie	3	1
Berichte der Deutschen Botanischen Gesellschaft	3	—
Berichte der Deutschen Chemischen Gesellschaft	3	—
Neues Journal der Pharmacie für Aerzte, Apotheker und Chemiker	3	—
Journal für Praktische Chemie	3	2
Archiv der Pharmacie	2	1
Archiv für Mikroskopische Anatomie	2	—
Archiv für Pathologische Anatomie und Physiologie	2	—

German (*continued*)	Passages	Whole articles
Jahrbuch der Chemie und Physik	2	1
Journal für Technische und Ökonomische Chemie	2	—
Gartenflora	2	1
Naturwissenschaftliche Rundschau	2	—
Neues Jahrbuch der Chemie und Physik	2	1
Ornithologische Monatsschrift	2	1
Physikalische Zeitschrift	2	—
Verhandlungen des Zoologisch-Botanischen Vereins	2	2
Zeitschrift für Analytische Chemie	2	1
Zeitschrift für Physiologische Chemie	2	—
Anatomische Hefte	1	1
Anatomischer Anzeiger Centralblatt	1	—
Archiv für Entwickelungsmechanik der Organismen	1	—
Archiv für Experimentelle Pathologie und Pharmakologie	1	—
Bericht über die Versammlung Deutscher Naturforscher und Ärzte	1	1
Berlinisches Jahrbuch für die Pharmacie und für die damit Verbundenen Wissenschaften	1	1
Biologisches Centralblatt	1	—
Botanische Jahrbücher für Systematik, Pflanzengeschichte	1	—
Botanisches Centralblatt	1	—
Centralblat für Allgemeine Pathologie und Pathologische Anatomie	1	—
Deutsches Jahrbuch für die Pharmacie	1	1
Elektrotechnische Zeitschrift	1	—
Entomologische Zeitschrift	1	—
Meteorologische Zeitschrift	1	—
Monatshefte für Chemie	1	—
Tageblatt der Gesellschaft Deutscher Naturforscher und Aerzte	1	—
Verhandlungen der Physikalischen Gesellschaft zu Berlin	1	—
Zeitschrift für Angewandte Chemie	1	—
Zeitschrift für Chemie und Pharmacie	1	—
Zeitschrift für Krystallographie und Mineralogie	1	—
Zeitschrift für Physikalische Chemie	1	—
Zeitschrift für Untersuchung der Nahrungs- und Genussmittel	1	—
Zeitschrift für Wissenschaftliche Zoologie	1	—
Zoologische Jahrbücher	1	—
Total	214	42

20th-Century Sample

We gathered the 20th-century sample of 10-line passages from Garfield's (1976) list of most-cited journals for 1974 (pp. 610–613). First, the five most-cited journals were chosen in seven categories: (1) general sciences, (2) chemistry/biochemistry, (3) physics, (4) biology, (5) botany, (6) astronomy/earth sciences, and (7) review. (For the review category, we picked the most-cited review journal in categories 2 through 6.) Next, 10-line passages from 72 articles were collected from these five journals in each of the seven categories; both the article itself and the passage within the article were randomly chosen by the method described at the beginning of appendix A. We proportionally distributed the 72 passages in a given category according to a "journal impact factor" reported by Garfield. As in the 19th century, we had to oversample the early 20th century to avoid skewing, since many of the journals in our sample did not exist at the beginning of the century. Finally, for each of the journals in our seven categories, we randomly selected two whole articles from among the articles with randomly selected short passages. In total, our initial sample included 35 journals (5 general, 25 specialized, and 5 review), short passages from 504 articles, and 70 whole articles.

General Sciences	**Passages**	**Whole articles**
Proceedings of the National Academy of Science of the U.S.A.	30	2
Science	18	2
Nature	14	2
Proceedings of the Royal Society of London	8	2
Comptes Rendus	2	2
Chemistry/Biochemistry		
Journal of Biological Chemistry	24	2
Journal of the American Chemical Society	18	2
Biochimica et Biophysica Acta	12	2
Journal of Chemical Physics	12	2
Journal of the Chemical Society	6	2
Physics		
Physical Review Letters	26	2
Physical Review	14	2
Nuclear Physics	13	2
Physics Letters	11	2
Journal of Applied Physics	8	2
Biology		
Journal of Molecular Biology	22	2
Journal of Cell Biology	20	2
Journal of Physiology	14	2
Journal of Bacteriology	8	2
American Journal of Physiology	8	2

Botany		
Planta	21	2
Plant Physiology	21	2
American Journal of Botany	11	2
Phytopathology	10	2
Phytochemistry	9	2

Astronomy/Earth Science		
Astrophysical Journal	19	2
Geochimica et Cosmochimica Acta	19	2
Journal of Geophysical Research	12	2
Monthly Notices of the Royal Astronomical Society	12	2
Astronomy and Astrophysics	10	2

Review		
Reviews of Modern Physics	25	2
Physiological Reviews	16	2
Chemical Reviews	13	2
Annual Review of Astronomy and Astrophysics	10	2
Annual Review of Plant Physiology	8	2

An unanticipated problem with our initial 20th-century sample was the almost complete absence of passages in French or German. Few foreign-language journals appear on Garfield's list, and most of the ones that do changed to English in the latter part of the century. So we consulted Gascoigne's (1985, pp. 109–114) list of ranked journals for the period 1901–1905 and selected three highly ranked French journals and three German ones (total of 96 foreign passages and 30 whole articles, evenly distributed among the six journals). These additions raised our sample size to 600 short passages and 100 whole articles.

French- and German-Language Journals	**Passages**	**Whole articles**
Comptes Rendus	16	5
Annales de Chimie	16	5
Journal de Physique	16	5
Zeitschrift für Physiologische Chemie	16	5
Annalen der Physik	16	5
Annalen der Chemie	16	5

APPENDIX B

Method for Analyzing Scientific Texts

For each of the four centuries covered by our survey, we analyzed the stylistic features in 10-line passages randomly chosen by the sampling methods outlined in appendix A. We also analyzed the presentation and argument in whole articles chosen as a random subset of the articles from which we selected the passages. In total, we examined short passages in 1,804 articles for style alone and 430 whole articles for presentation and argument. Listed below are the textual features we sought to quantify, organized under our hypothesized trends. At the start of our project (circa 1994), we formulated a tentative set of trends, along with the accompanying textual features we employed to track change over time. We established these trends on the basis of the published literature informed by our own intuitions. Key source materials included Allen et al. (1994), Bazerman (1988), Berkenkotter and Huckin (1995), Bostian and Hollander (1990), Charney (1993), Day (1988), Dear (1985), Dillon (1991), Fahnestock (1986), Gross (1990), Halliday (1993a–c), Harmon (1992b, 1994), Holmes (1989a), Lakoff and Johnson (1980), Lakoff and Turner (1989), Myers (1989), Quirk and Greenbaum (1972), Rodman (1991, 1994), Rudwick (1976), Shapin (1984), Swales (1990), and Wilkinson (1991). The data we subsequently acquired allowed us to modify, expand upon, and better understand these trends.

As the alert reader will immediately recognize, evaluating some of the textual features given below depends on the judgment of the analyzer and the historical context (e.g., does "electron orbit" count as poetic metaphor or ordinary language?). And we have found that even such seemingly simple tasks as counting illustrations in an article or total words in a selected passage prove more complicated than they first appear (e.g., should four figures arranged into a single figure with four parts count as one or four figures? Should contractions—say, the French *c'est*—be counted as one word or two?). However, unlike most scientific experiments, we were not interested in the here unobtainable goal of exact measurements, only in a reasonably reliable and consistent means of establishing change in a large collection of scientific texts over time. In the parlance of science, we sought not so much quantitative results as "trends."

To facilitate data management and analyses, we developed a Microsoft Excel (version 5.0) spreadsheet program consisting of linked worksheets (with considerable help from Suzanne Gross and Audrey Styer). We used this program in calculating ratios, sums, ranges, averages, and standard deviations, and in sorting and plotting the data to determine communicative and argumentative trends over time. Further details on this computer program will be provided by the authors upon request.

Style

Trend: *In conformity with a philosophy that embraces experiment and theory as the best means for acquiring new knowledge and that disdains emotional or overtly literary expression, the style of the scientific article has evolved toward the impression of "objectivity."*

We used 10-line passages to analyze style.

We counted the number of personal pronouns (*I, we, je, nous,* etc.) and proper names (*Newton, Lister, Lavoisier, Monod,* etc.) divided by the total number of words in the 10-line segment. We did not include names appearing as part of an author-date referencing style.

We counted the number of evaluative expressions, divided by the number of words in the 10-line segment. For example, two instances occur in the following: "I placed my Prisme . . . that it might be thereby refracted to the opposite wall. It was at first *a very pleasing divertisement,* to view the *vivid and intense colors* produced thereby" (Newton 1672, p. 3076).

We counted the number of poetic metaphors or similes (e.g., "a creature shaped like a shoe") divided by the number of words in the 10-line segment.

We counted the number of other expressions departing from normal scientific discourse divided by number of words in the 10-line segment. We included this feature to cover any register shifts not covered by the first three features above.

We counted the number of instances of the passive voice divided by the number of words in the 10-line segment, for example, "ten animals *were injected* with the AIDS virus" and "the mixture *was decanted.*" We differentiated between the "suppressed-person passive" (person as implied agent of action) and "objective passive" (thing or concept as implied agent).

We counted the number of dummy subjects (*it* or *there*) divided by the number of words in the 10-line segment.

We counted the number of hedging expressions divided by the number of words in the 10-line segment, for example, "this *seems to be* DNA," "this *is probably* DNA."

We did a census of finite verbs in the 10-line segment. We divided them into verbs indicating things people do and things matter or mathematics does. In counting verbs, we ignored helping verbs (e.g., "have been developing" = develop) and all nonfinite verbal structures—infinitives, participles, and gerunds.

Trend: *As a by-product of the growth of cognitive complexity in science itself, various aspects of the style in scientific articles have become more complex.*

We counted the number and type of noun phrases (NPs) in the 10-line segment. We determined the following ratios for the subject and complement positions: simple/total NPs, pronouns and proper names/total NPs, complex/total NPs, and multiple modifications/total NPs, as defined by Quirk and Greenbaum (1972). As an example of our method for counting NPs, take the sentences: "*The clouds* [simple NP] are viewed *through the roof of the cloud-chamber, which is of glass, coated below with a uniform layer of gelatine* [multiple modification NP]. *The floor* [simple NP] is also covered *by a layer of gelatine, in this case blackened by the addition of a little Indian ink* [multiple modification NP]" (1911-E209). This passage contains four NPs: two simple and two multiple modifications. The NP ratio would thus be 50% simple (in the subject position) and 50% multiple modification (in the complement position). For additional details, see Appendix C.

We counted the number of noun strings with words not separated by function words (e.g., "catalyzed high temperature partial oxidation reformer") divided by the number of words in 10-line segment.

We counted the number of quantifying expressions (e.g., "about the four-hundredth part of the weight of water") and equations (e.g., "$x > y$") divided by the number of words in the 10-line segment. We did not count, as quantifying expressions, either reference numbers or the word "equation," "table," or "figure" followed by a number.

We counted the number of abbreviations (e.g., "ICP-MS analysis," "ft"), acronyms (e.g., "CERN"), and eponyms (e.g., "Joule's law") divided by the number of words in the 10-line segment. We did not count any abbreviations already counted as a quantifying expression, such as "50 gal/min," or common expressions like "M." for "monsieur" or "&" for "and."

We counted the number of citations divided by the number of words in the 10-line segment. We defined a citation as any reference to a specific work whether in the text, in footnotes, or in a list of references, whether or not there is complete bibliographic information.

Trend: *Within the boundaries imposed by the increasing complexity of science, style has evolved toward more efficient communication.*

We calculated the average sentence length in 10-line segments.

We calculated the clausal density as assessed by the number of finite clauses divided by the number of sentences per 10-line segment and per 100 words. For example, six clauses appear in the following quotation from Martin Lister (1697): "It [the milk of *Lactuca syl. costa spinosa*] springs out [1] of the Wound as thick as Cream and Ropes, and is [2] White, and yet the Milk which came out [3] of the Wounds, made [4] towards the top of the Plant, was plainly streaked or mixt [5] with purple Juice, as though one had dashed or sprinkled [6] Cream with a few drops of Claret." This clausal density is 11 per 100 words.

Presentation

Trend: *Presentation has gained in communicative efficiency by evolving a master system for finding and organizing information.*

Presentation for 20th-Century Articles

If this article is experimental, methodological, or observational, does it exhibit the arrangement of Abstract, Introduction, Materials and Methods, Results, Discussion, Conclusion (or Summary), Acknowledgments, References?

If this article is theoretical, does it exhibit the arrangement of Abstract, Introduction, Theorem, Proof of Theorem, Conclusion (or Summary), Acknowledgments, References?

If this article possesses one of these arrangements or some obvious variation, what is the relative weight of the sections, as measured by their length in pages and fractions of a page over total pages?

If neither arrangement is present, what is the organizing principle? How are the sections distributed as measured by their length in pages and fractions of pages over total pages?

Does this article employ consecutively numbered graphics (*any* kind of drawn object) or tables? If so, we separately determined the number of tables, plots of numerical data, illustrations of scientific equipment, and any other kind of illustration, as well as the percentage of the article occupied by these items.

Does this article employ equations? If so, how are they displayed?

Is the organizing principle of the article's arrangement revealed by the use of headings? Are the headings general ("Introduction," "Methods," "Experimental") or specific ("Effects of Temperature on Thermal Conductivity")?

Does the article have consecutively numbered tables or graphs?

How are the citations presented? Does this article employ uniformly formatted citations referred to in the text and presented with bibliographic information at the page bottom or gathered at the article end? How many citations appear in the first third of the article? second third? final third? (not including any reference list)?

Does the article's title bear a close resemblance to its major claim? That is, can the title be recast into the article's major claim with only minor wording changes (e.g., "Inverse Relation between Pressure and Volume in Gases")? If not, is the title a general or specific description of the subject matter (e.g., "On Gases" vs. "The Behavior of Ideal Gases")?

If there is an abstract, is it informative or indicative (as defined in Wilkinson 1991, pp. 348–349)? If none, is there a separate summary at the end of the article?

If there is introductory material, to what extent does it contain the elements identified by Swales (1990, pp, 137–166): (1) establishing an intellectual territory, (2) establishing a niche in that territory, and (3) occupying that niche, and in what order?

If there is a conclusion, does it contain any of the following: (1) original claims from having occupied the niche, (2) wider significance to intellectual territory, and (3) recommendations on future work to validate the claim or expand the niche? If so, which ones and in what order?

Presentation for Pre-20th-Century Articles

In centuries other than the 20th, there is no neat division of sections, and printing practices generally precluded the integration of text and visuals and rendered the allocation of space to visuals devoid of significance. Another, analogous set of questions seemed advisable:

Does the title refer to the article's theme, or specify the article's theme or claim?

If there is an introduction, does it establish an intellectual territory or a niche in that territory? Does it occupy that niche?

If there is a conclusion, does it contain niche-occupying insights, reflect on their wider significance, or make recommendations for the future of research?

If there are citations, are they in the margins, at the bottom of the page, or incorporated in the text?

If there are book citations, do they contain author name, date of publication, page numbers, and/or any other information? For article citations, do they contain author name, title, journal name, volume number, date of publication, page number, and/or any other information?

If there are headings, are they general or substantive? Are they in the text, in the margin, or, oddly, at the *bottom* of the page?

Are the graphics numbered in Arabic or in Roman? Are they accompanied by legends?

Are there footnotes, and if so, are they numbered?

Are there equations, and if so, are they numbered?

Argument

Trend: *Scientific arguments will become increasingly complex in the following ways.*

Arguments will shift from expression through narrative and description to expression through exposition and explanation.

Arguments will shift from individual to social, as indicated by changes in citation patterns.

Arguments will show an increased concern for accuracy and precision, as manifested in their hedges.

Explanations will shift from those that are qualitative and generally mechanical to those that are quantitative, mathematical, and generally specific to disciplines, for example, biological explanations or chemical explanations.

Arguments will shift from those centered on words to those centered equally on words and on tables and visuals.

Argument-Related Questions

Our argument chapters focus on examining the above shifts in the randomly selected whole articles for each century. To that end, we rely upon a traditional close reading and interpretation of the texts. As a quantitative aid to these interpretations, we gathered supplementary data by asking the following questions of each text:

> Is the article's content mainly a) experimental? b) theoretical? c) methodological? d) observational? e) observational/theoretical? f) experimental/theoretical? g) experimental/methodological? h) medical/surgical? i) mathematical?
>
> Is the article's main claim a) observation? b) experimental results? c) mechanical explanation? d) mathematical rule? e) mathematical explanation? f) making or improving equipment?
>
> Is there any mention of witnesses to an observation or experiment?
>
> If there is a graphic, is it of a) equipment? b) experimental arrangements? c) a natural object? d) is it a list? d) a table? e) a mathematical relation?
>
> If there is a graphic, does it support a) an observation? b) an experimental result? c) a mechanical explanation? d) a mathematical relation? e) a mathematical explanation? f) improving equipment?

APPENDIX C

Noun-Phrase Analysis

The most troublesome of the textual features we analyzed is the noun phrase. Our analysis method here is derived from the work of Quirk and Greenbaum (1972), who performed a quantitative analysis of 17,000 contemporary noun phrases taken from informal speech, fiction, serious talk and writing, and scientific writing.

Quirk and Greenbaum defined two types of noun phrase (NP), "simple" and "complex." The simple type encompasses pronouns (e.g., *I, we*), proper names (e.g., *Newton, Darwin, Einstein*), and nouns with no substantive modifiers (e.g., *tentacles, the tentacles*). Within this category, Quirk and Greenbaum also separately tracked the subset of pronouns and proper names. The complex NP includes nouns with one or more modifiers, which could be as little as a noun followed by a prepositional phrase (e.g., *a series of tentacles*) or preceded by an adjective (e.g., *velar tentacles*). Within this category, Quirk and Greenbaum also separately counted the subset of nouns with "multiple modification" (e.g., *the main facts which a theory of superconductivity must explain*). Finally, they also kept track of whether or not the NP served as a grammatical subject in a sentence.

To give a better sense of how this analysis works, we detail below the NP distribution in sample passages drawn from the 17th and 20th centuries. In both passages, simple NPs are underlined, complex ones in boldface. The first passage comes from Martin Lister (1697):

> It [the milk of *Lactuca syl. costa spinosa*] springs out of **the Wound as thick as Cream and Ropes**, and is White, and yet **the Milk which came out of the Wounds, made towards the top of the Plant**, was plainly streaked or mixt with **purple Juice**, as though one had dashed or sprinkled **Cream with a few drops of Claret**. And indeed, **the Skin of the Plant** thereabouts was purplish also, perhaps with Veins. Again,

in the Shell I drew it, it turned still yellower and thicker, and by and by curdled, that is, **the white and thick caseous part** did separate from a **thin purple Whey**. So **the Blood also of Animals, whilst warm** remains liquid and alike, but so soon as cold, it cakes and has **a *Serum* or Whey separated from it.**

This passage has 8 simple NPs and 9 complex; of these, 6 (35%) are pronouns and proper names, while 7 (41%) have multiple modifiers. The subject position has 5 (29%) simple NPs and 4 (24%) complex; the nonsubject position has 3 (18%) simple NPs and 5 (29%) complex, as follows:

Subject Position

Simple, Pronouns/Names: it, one, I, it, it (5)

Complex, without Multiple Modifications: the Skin of the Plant (1)

Complex, with Multiple Modifications: yet the Milk which came out of the Wounds, made towards the top of the Plant; the white and thick caseous part; the Blood also of Animals, whilst warm (3)

Nonsubject Position

Simple: Veins, the Shell (2)

Simple, Pronouns/Names: it (1)

Complex, without Multiple Modifications: purple Juice (1)

Complex, with Multiple Modifications: the Wound as thick as Cream and Ropes; Cream with a few drops of Claret; thin purple Whey; a *Serum* or Whey separated from it (4)

The second passage comes from Howard M. Goodman and Alexander Rich (1962), "Formation of a DNA-Soluble RNA Hybrid and Its Relation to the Origin, Evolution, and Degeneracy of Soluble RNA":

It has been known for **a long time** that **transfer or soluble RNA (sRNA*) molecules** play **a central role in the organization of amino acids into polypeptide chains during protein synthesis. Individual sRNA molecules** combine with **a particular amino acid** to produce **a complex which is active on the ribosomal particle. Recent experiments** make it likely that **a sequence of nucleotides in sRNA** carry **the specificity for determining the position of the amino acid in the polypeptide chain.** However, as yet little is known regarding **the origin of sRNA. These molecules** could arise from **DNA** in **a manner similar to the production of messenger RNA.** On the other hand, it has been demonstrated that **the sRNA molecule** is largely folded back upon itself with a **regular system of hydrogen bonding**, and this has given rise to **the suggestion that RNA may act as a template for manufacturing itself.**

This passage has 18 complex NPs, as compared with only 6 simple ones. Of these, 15 (63%) have multiple modifiers (34%) and 5 (21%) are pronouns/proper names. The distribution in the subject position is 4 (17%) simple and 8 complex (34%); for the nonsubject position, 2 (8%) simple and 10 (42%) complex, as follows:

Subject Position

Simple: little (1)

Simple, Pronouns/Names: it, it, this (3)

Complex, without Multiple Modifications: Recent experiments; These molecules (2)

Complex, with Multiple Modifications: individual sRNA molecules; transfer or soluble RNA molecules; (sRNA*); a sequence of nucleotides in sRNA; the sRNA molecule; RNA (6)

Nonsubject Position

Simple: none

Simple, Pronouns/Names: it, itself (2)

Complex, without Multiple Modifications: a long time (1)

Complex, with Multiple Modifications: a central role in the organization of amino acids into polypeptide chains during protein synthesis; a particular amino acid; a complex which is active on the ribosomal particle; the specificity for determining the position of the amino acid in the polypeptide chain; the origin of sRNA; DNA; a manner similar to the production of messenger RNA; a regular system of hydrogen bonding; the suggestion that RNA may act as a template for manufacturing itself (9)

REFERENCES

Allen, Bryce, Jian Qin, and F. W. Lancaster. 1994. "Persuasive Communities: A Longitudinal Analysis of References in the *Philosophical Transactions* of the Royal Society, 1665–1990." *Social Studies of Science* 24: 279–310.

Allen, D. E. 1993. "Natural History in Britain in the Eighteenth Century." *Archives of Natural History* 20: 333–347.

American Chemical Society. 1959. "Notice to Authors of Papers." *Journal of the American Chemical Society,* vol. 81.

Appel, Toby A. 1987. *The Cuvier-Geoffroy Debate: French Biology in the Decades before Darwin.* New York: Oxford University Press.

Atkinson, Dwight. 1999. *Scientific Discourse in Sociohistorical Context: The Philosophical Transactions of the Royal Society of London, 1675–1975.* Mahwah, N.J.: Erlbaum.

Austin, John L. 1966. "Three Ways of Spilling Ink." *Philosophical Review* 75(4): 427–440.

Barnes, Sherman B. 1934. "The Scientific Journal, 1665–1730." *The Scientific Monthly* 38: 257–260.

Bazerman, Charles. 1988. *Shaping Written Knowledge: The Genre and Activity of the Experimental Article in Science.* Madison: University of Wisconsin Press.

———. 1998. "Emerging Perspectives on the Many Dimensions of Scientific Discourse." In Martin and Veel, pp. 15–28.

Beer, John J. 1958. "Coal Tar Dye Manufacture and the Origins of the Modern Industrial Research Laboratory." *Isis* 49: 123–131.

Ben-David, Joseph. 1971. *The Scientist's Role in Society: A Comparative Study.* Englewood Cliffs, N.J.: Prentice Hall.

Berkenkotter, Carol, and Thomas N. Huckin. 1995. *Genre Knowledge in Disciplinary Communication: Cognition/Culture/Power.* Hillsdale, N.J.: Erlbaum.

Birn, Raymond. 1965. "Le Journal des Savants sous l'Ancien Regime." *Journal des Savants*. Janvier–Mars 1965: 15–35.

Blum, Ann Shelby. 1993. *Picturing Nature: American Nineteenth-Century Zoological Illustrations.* Princeton, N.J.: Princeton University Press.

Boig, Fletcher S., and Paul W. E. Howerton. 1952a. "History and Development of Chemical Periodicals in the Field of Organic Chemistry: 1877–1949." *Science* 115 (11 January): 25–31.

———. 1952b. "History and Development of Chemical Periodicals in the Field of Analytical Chemistry: 1877–1949." *Science* 115 (23 May): 555–560.

Bostian, Lloyd, and Barbara Hollander. 1990. "Technical Journal Editors and Writing Style." *Journal of Technical Writing and Communication* 20: 153–163.

Boyce, Peter B., and Heather Dalterio. 1996. "Electronic Publishing of Scientific Journals." *Physics Today* 49: 42–47. Available at: http://www.aas.org/~pboyce/epubs/pt-art.htm.

Brody, Herb. 1996. "Wired Science." *Technology Review,* 99(7): 42–45. Available at: http://209.58.177.220/articles/oct96/toc.html.

Broman, Thomas. 1995. "Rethinking Professionalization: Theory, Practice, and Professional Ideology in Eighteenth-Century German Medicine." *Journal of Modern History* 67: 835–872.

Brose, Eric Dorn. 1997. *German History 1789–1871: From the Holy Roman Empire to the Bismarkian Reich.* Providence, R.I.: Berghahn Books.

Burnham, John. 1990. "The Evolution of Editorial Peer Review." *Journal of the American Medical Association* 263: 1323–1329.

Campbell, Donald T. 1988. "A General 'Selection Theory,' as Implemented in Biological Evolution and in Social Belief-Transmission-with-Modification in Science [Response to Hull]." *Biology and Philosophy* 3: 171–177.

Cannon, Susan Faye. 1978. *Science in Culture: The Early Victorian Period.* New York: Dawson and Science History Publications.

Caplan, Priscilla, and William Y. Arms. 1999. "Reference Linking for Journal Articles." *D-Lib Magazine,* Vol. 5, Nos. 7/8. Available at: http://www.dlib.org/dlib/july99/07caplan.html.

Cardwell, D. S. L. 1972. *Turning Points in Western Technology.* New York: Science History Publications.

———. 1980. "Science, Technology, and Industry." In *The Ferment of Knowledge: Studies in the Historiography of Eighteenth-Century Science.* G. S. Rousseau and Roy Porter, eds. Cambridge: Cambridge University Press, pp. 449–483.

Carr, Jeffrey. 1973. "Martin Lister." In *Dictionary of Scientific Biography.* New York: Scribner's, pp. 415–417.

Charney, Davida. 1993. "A Study in Rhetorical Reading: How Evolutionists Read 'The Spandrels of San Marco.'" In Selzer, pp. 203–231.

Christie, John R. R. 1974. "The Origins and Development of the Scottish Scientific Community." *History of Science* 12: 122–141.

Cicero. 1942. *De Oratore.* E. W. Sutton and H. Rackham, trans. Vol. 2. Cambridge, Mass.: Harvard University Press.

Cleveland, William S. 1994. *The Elements of Graphing Data.* Summit, N.J.: Hobart Press.

Cohen, H. Floris. 1994. *The Scientific Revolution: A Historiographical Inquiry.* Chicago: University of Chicago Press.

Collins, Randall. 1998. *The Sociology of Philosophies: A Global Theory of Intellectual Change.* Cambridge, Mass.: Harvard University Press.

Crosland, Maurice. 1978. *Historical Studies in the Language of Chemistry.* New York: Dover.

———. 1992. *Science under Control: The French Academy of Sciences 1795–1914.* Cambridge: Cambridge University Press.

———. 1995. "Explicit Qualifications as a Criterion for Membership in the Royal Society." In *Studies in the Culture of Science in France and Britain since the Enlightenment.* Aldershot, U.K.: Variorum, pp. 167–187.

Daston, Lorraine, and Katharine Park. 1998. *Wonders and the Order of Nature: 1150–1750.* New York: Zone Books.

Day, Robert A. 1988. *How to Write and Publish a Scientific Paper.* 3rd ed. Phoenix, Ariz.: Onyx Press.

Dear, Peter. 1985. "*Totius in Verba:* Rhetoric and Authority in the Early Royal Society." *Isis* 76: 145–161.

———. 1995. *Discipline and Experience: The Mathematical Way in the Scientific Revolution.* Chicago: University of Chicago Press.

de Solla Price, Derek J. 1961. *Science since Babylon.* New Haven, Conn.: Yale University Press.

———. 1986. *Little Science, Big Science . . . and Beyond.* New York: Columbia University Press.

Dillon, Andrew. 1991. "Readers' Models of Text Structures: The Case of Academic Articles." *International Journal of Man-Machine Studies* 35: 913–925.

Dodart, Denis. 1731. "Mémoire pour Servir à l'Histoire des Plantes." In *Mémoires de l'Académie Royale des Sciences depuis 1666 jusqu'à 1699*, tome IV, pp. 121–333.

Eklund, Jon. 1975. *The Incompleat Chymist, Being an Essay on the Eighteenth-Century Chemist in His Laboratory, with a Dictionary of Obsolete Chemical Terms of the Period.* Washington, D.C.: Smithsonian Institution Press.

Ereshefsky, Marc. 1997. "The Evolution of the Linnaean Hierarchy." *Biology and Philosophy* 12: 493–519.

———. 1999. "Species and the Linnean Hierarchy." In *Species: New Interdisciplinary Essays.* R. Wilson, ed. Cambridge, Mass.: MIT Press, pp. 285–305.

Fahnestock, Jeanne. 1986. "Accommodating Science: The Rhetorical Life of Scientific Facts." *Written Communication* 3: 275–296.

———. 1998. *Rhetorical Figures in Science.* New York: Oxford University Press.

Finney, David John. 1960. *An Introduction to the Theory of Experimental Design.* Chicago: University of Chicago Press.

Fisher, Ronald A. 1971. *The Design of Experiments.* 9th ed. New York: Hafner Press.

Fleck, Ludwik. 1979. *Genesis and Development of a Scientific Fact.* Fred Bradley and Thaddeus J. Trenn, trans. Chicago: University of Chicago Press.

Flesch, Rudolf. 1962. "Our Shrinking Sentences." In *The Art of Readable Writing.* New York: Collier Books, pp. 119–130.

Fox, Robert. 1992. *The Culture of Science in France, 1700–1900.* Aldershot, U.K.: Variorum.

Fox, Robert, and George Weisz, eds. 1988. *The Organization of Science and Technology in France, 1808–1914.* Cambridge: Cambridge University Press.

Franck, Georg. 1998. *Ökonomie der Aufmerksamkeit, ein Entwurf.* München: Carl Hanser Verlag.

———. 1999. "Scientific Communication—A Vanity Affair?" *Science* 286: 53–55.

Fulcher, Gordon S. 1920. "Preparation of Abstracts." *Astrophysical Journal* 51: 255–256.

———. 1921. "Scientific Abstracting." *Science* 54: 291–295.

Galison, Peter. 1987. *How Experiments End.* Chicago: University of Chicago Press.

———. 1997. *Image and Logic: A Material Culture of Microphysics.* Chicago: University of Chicago Press.

———. 1998. "Judgment against Objectivity." In *Picturing Science, Producing Art.* New York: Routledge, pp. 327–359.

Gaonkar, Dilip Parameshwar. 1993. "The Idea of Rhetoric in the Rhetoric of Science." *The Southern Communication Journal* 58: 258–295.

Garber, Elizabeth. 1999. *The Language of Physics: The Calculus and the Development of Theoretical Physics in Europe, 1750–1914.* Boston: Birkhäuser.

Garfield, Eugene. 1976. "Significant Journals of Science." *Nature* 264: 609–615.

———. 1996. "When to Cite." *The Library Quarterly* 66: 449–458.

———. 1998. "Mapping the World of Science." Paper presented at the 150th anniversary meeting of the American Association for the Advancement of Science, Philadelphia. Available at: http://www.the-scientist.library.upenn.edu/eugene_garfield/papers/mapsciworld.html.

Gascoigne, John. 1995. "The Eighteenth-Century Scientific Community: A Prosopographical Study." *Social Studies of Science* 25: 575–581.

Gascoigne, Robert Mortimer. 1985. *A Historical Catalogue of Scientific Periodicals, 1665–1900, with a Survey of Their Development.* New York: Garland.

Geertz, Clifford. 1973. *The Interpretation of Cultures.* New York: Basic Books, pp. 3–30.

George, A. L., and T. J. McKeown. 1985. "Case Studies and Theories of Organizational Decision Making." In *Advances in Information Processing in Organizations: A Research Annual.* R. F. Coulam and R. A. Smith, eds. Greenwich, Conn.: JAI Press, pp. 21–58.

Gilbert, G. Nigel, and Michael Mulkay. 1984. *Opening Pandora's Box: A Sociological Analysis of Scientists' Discourse.* Cambridge: Cambridge University Press.

Goodman, Howard M., and Alexander Rich. 1962. "Formation of a DNA-Soluble RNA Hybrid and Its Relation to the Origin, Evolution, and Degeneracy of Soluble RNA." *Proceedings of the National Academy of Sciences of the U.S.A.* 48: 2101–2109.

Gopen, George D., and Judith A. Swan. 1990. "The Science of Scientific Writing." *American Scientist* 78: 550–558.

Gopnik, Myrna. 1972. *Linguistic Structures in Scientific Texts.* The Hague: Mouton.

Gould, Steven Jay, and Richard C. Lewontin. 1979. "The Spandrels of San Marco and the Panglossian Paradigm: A Critique of the Adaptationist Programme." *Proceedings of the Royal Society of London, B: Biological Sciences* 205: 581–598.

Griesemer, James R., and William C. Wimsatt. 1989. "Picturing Weismannism: A Case Study of Conceptual Evolution." In *What the Philosophy of Biology Is: Essays Dedicated to David Hull.* Michael Ruse, ed. Boston: Kluwer Academic, pp. 1–60.

Gross, Alan G. 1990. *The Rhetoric of Science.* Cambridge, Mass.: Harvard University Press.

———. 1996. "Preface: The Rhetoric of Science 1996." In *The Rhetoric of Science,* 2nd ed. Cambridge, Mass.: Harvard University Press.

Gross, Alan G., and William M. Keith, eds. 1997. *Rhetorical Hermeneutics: Invention and Interpretation in the Age of Science.* Albany, N.Y.: SUNY Press.

Gunnarsson, Britt-Louise. 1997. "On the Sociohistorical Construction of Scientific Discourse." In *The Construction of Professional Discourse,* Britt-Louise Gunnarsson, Per Linell, and Bengt Norberg, eds. London: Longman, pp. 99–126.

Hagge, John. 1997. "Disciplinary Style Manuals as Reliable Guides to Scientific Discourse as Norms." *Technical Communication* 44: 129–141.

Hahn, Roger. 1971. *The Anatomy of a Scientific Institution: The Paris Academy of Sciences, 1666–1803.* Berkeley: University of California Press.

Halliday, M. A. K. 1993a. "On the Language of Physical Science." In Halliday and Martin, pp. 54–68.

———. 1993b. "Some Grammatical Problems in Scientific English." In Halliday and Martin, pp. 69–85.

———. 1993c. "The Analysis of Scientific Texts in English and Chinese." In Halliday and Martin, pp. 124–132.

———. 1998. "Things and Relations: Regrammaticising Experience as Technical Knowledge." In Martin and Veel, pp. 185–235.

Halliday, M. A. K., and J. R. Martin, eds. 1993. *Writing Science: Literacy and Discursive Power.* Pittsburgh: University of Pittsburgh Press.

Hankins, Thomas L. 1999. "Blood, Dirt, and Nomograms: A Particular History of Graphs," *Isis* 90: 50–80.

Harmon, Joseph E. 1992a. "An Analysis of Fifty Citation Superstars from the Scientific Literature." *Journal of Technical Writing and Communication* 22: 17–37.

———. 1992b. "Current Contents of Theoretical Scientific Papers." *Journal of Technical Writing and Communication* 22: 357–375.

———. 1994. "The Uses of Metaphor in Citation Classics from the Scientific Literature." *Technical Communication Quarterly* 3: 179–194.

Harmon, Joseph E., and Alan G. Gross. 1996. "The Scientific Style Manual: A Reliable Guide to Practice?" *Technical Communication* 43: 61–72.

Harnad, Stevan. 1990. "Scholarly Skywriting and the Prepublication Continuum of Scientific Inquiry." *Psychological Science* 1: 342–343.

———. 1991. "Post-Gutenberg Galaxy: The Fourth Revolution in the Means of Production of Knowledge." *Public-Access Computer Systems Review* 2: 39–53.

———. 1992. "Interactive Publication: Extending the American Physical Society's Discipline-Specific Model for Electronic Publishing." *Serials Review, Special Issue on Economics Models for Electronic Publishing,* pp. 58–61. Available at: http://cogsci.soton.ac.uk/harnad/Papers/Harnad/harnd92.interactivpub.html.

———. 1999. "Free at Last: The Future of Peer-Reviewed Journals." *D-Lib Magazine,* Vol. 5, No. 12. Available at: http://www.dlib.org/december99/12harnad.html.

Harris, Randy Allen. 1997. "Rhetoric of Science." Unpublished paper. Available at: http://www.ece.uwaterloo.ca/~jgwilkin/if/winter97/mar25/article.html.

Hayes, Donald P. 1992. "The Growing Inaccessibility of Science." *Nature* 356: 739–740.

Heilbron, J. L. 1983. *Physics at the Royal Society during Newton's Presidency.* Los Angeles: William Andrews Clark Memorial Library, University of California.

Higham, Nicholas J., ed. 1993. *Handbook of Writing for the Mathematical Sciences.* Philadelphia: Society for Industrial and Applied Mathematics.

Hill, John. 1751. *A Review of the Works of the Royal Society of London, Containing Animadversions on such Papers as Deserve Particular Observation.* London: Griffiths.

Hoffmann, Roald. 1988. "Under the Surface of the Chemical Article." *Angewandte Chemie* 27: 1593–1602.

Holmes, Frederic Lawrence. 1989a. "Argument and Narrative in Scientific Writing." In *The Literary Structure of Scientific Argument.* Peter Dear, ed. Philadelphia: University of Pennsylvania Press, pp. 164–181.

———. 1989b. *Eighteenth-Century Chemistry as an Investigative Enterprise.* Berkeley: Office for History of Science and Technology, University of California.

———. 1991. *Hans Krebs: The Formation of a Scientific Life, 1900–1933.* Vol. 1. Oxford: Oxford University Press.

Homberg, Ernst. 1998. "Two Factions, One Profession: The Chemical Profession in German Society, 1780–1870." In Knight and Kragh, pp. 39–76.

Hooke, Robert. 1665. *Micrographia: or, Some Physiological Descriptions of Minute Bodies Made by Magnifying Glasses.* London: Martyn and Allestry.

Hufbauer, Karl. 1982. *The Formation of the German Chemical Community (1720–1795).* Berkeley: University of California Press.

Hull, David L. 1988a. "A Mechanism and Its Metaphysics: An Evolutionary Account of the Social and Conceptual Development of Science." *Biology and Philosophy* 3: 123–155.

———. 1988b. "A Period of Development: A Response." *Biology and Philosophy* 3: 241–263.

———. 1988c. *Science as a Process: An Evolutionary Account of the Social and Conceptual Development of Science.* Chicago: University of Chicago Press.

Hyland, Ken. 1998. *Hedging in Scientific Research Articles.* Amsterdam: Benjamins.

Jacob, Margaret C. 1997. *Scientific Culture and the Making of the Industrial West.* New York: Oxford University Press.

Jevons, W. Stanley. 1874. *The Principles of Science: A Treatise on Logic and Scientific Method.* London: Macmillan.

Johns, Adrian. 1998. *The Nature of the Book: Print and Knowledge in the Making.* Chicago: University of Chicago Press.

Johnson, Kurt, and Steve Coates. 1999. *Nabokov's Blues: The Scientific Odyssey of a Literary Genius.* Cambridge, Mass.: Zone Books.

Jones, Richard Foster. 1982. *Ancients and Moderns: A Study of the Rise of the Scientific Movement in Seventeenth-Century England.* New York: Dover.

Kann, Robert. 1950. *The Multinational Empire: Nationalism and National Reform in the Habsburg Monarchy: 1848–1918.* New York: Columbia University Press.

———. 1973. *A Study in Austrian Intellectual History from Late Baroque to Romanticism.* New York: Octagon.

Kargon, Robert H. 1977. *Science in Victorian Manchester: Enterprise and Expertise.* Baltimore: Johns Hopkins University Press.

Katz, Michael J. 1985. *Elements of the Scientific Paper.* New Haven, Conn.: Yale University Press.

Kelves, Daniel J. 1978. *The Physicists: The History of a Scientific Community in Modern America.* New York: Knopf.

Kennedy, George A. 1991. *Aristotle* On Rhetoric: *A Theory of Civic Discourse.* New York: Oxford University Press.

Killingsworth, M. Jimmie, and Michael K. Gilbertson. 1992. *Signs, Genres, and Communities in Technical Communication.* Amityville, N.Y.: Baywood.

Kitcher, Philip. 1991. "Persuasion." In *Persuading Science: The Art of Scientific Rhetoric.* Marcello Pera and William R. Shea, eds. Canton, Mass.: Watson, pp. 3–27.

Knight, David, and Helge Kragh, eds. 1998. *The Making of the Chemist: The Social History of Chemistry in Europe: 1789–1914.* Cambridge: Cambridge University Press.

Knorr-Cetina, Karin D. 1981. *The Manufacture of Knowledge: An Essay on the Constructivist and Contextual Nature of Science.* Oxford: Oxford University Press.

Kragh, Helge. 1996. *Cosmology and Controversy: The Historical Development of Two Theories of the Universe.* Princeton, N.J.: Princeton University Press.

———. 1998. "Afterword: The European Commonwealth of Chemistry." In Knight and Kragh, pp. 329–341.

Kronick, David A. 1976. *A History of Scientific and Technical Periodicals: The Origins and Development of the Scientific and Technical Press, 1665–1790.* Metuchen, N.J.: Scarecrow Press.

———. 1985. *The Literature of the Life Sciences.* Philadelphia: ISI Press.

———. 1991. *Scientific and Technical Periodicals of the 17th and 18th Centuries: A Guide.* Metuchen, N.J.: Scarecrow Press.

Kuhn, Thomas A. 1970. *The Structure of Scientific Revolutions.* 2nd ed. Chicago: University of Chicago Press.

Laeven, Hub. 1990. *The* "Acta Eruditorum" *under the Editorship of Otto Mencke (1644–1707): The History of an International Learned Journal between 1662–1707.* Amsterdam: Holland University Press.

Lakoff, George, and Mark Johnson. 1980. *Metaphors We Live By.* Chicago: University of Chicago Press.

Lakoff, George, and Mark Turner. 1989. *More Than Cool Reason: A Field Guide to Poetic Metaphor.* Chicago: University of Chicago Press.

Latour, Bruno. 1987. *Science in Action.* Cambridge, Mass.: Harvard University Press.

———. 1990. "Drawing Things Together." In *Representation in Scientific Practice.* Michael Lynch and Steve Woolgar, eds. Cambridge, Mass.: MIT Press, pp. 19–68.

———. 1992. "Pasteur on Lactic Acid Yeast: A Partial Semiotic Analysis." *Configurations* 1: 129–145.

Latour, Bruno, and Steve Woolgar. 1986. *Laboratory Life: The Construction of Scientific Facts.* Princeton, N.J.: Princeton University Press.

Leatherdale, W. H. 1974. *The Role of Analogy, Model and Metaphor in Science.* Amsterdam: North-Holland.

Lederberg, Joshua. 1996. "Options for the Future." *D-Lib Magazine,* vol. *2,* no. *5.* Available at: http://www.dlib.org/dlib/may96/05lederberg.html.

Lemke, Jay. 1998. "Mutiplying Meaning: Visual and Verbal Semiotics in Scientific Text." In Martin and Veel, pp. 87–113.

Lesch, John E. 1984. *Science and Medicine in France: The Emergence of Experimental Physiology, 1790–1855.* Cambridge, Mass.: Harvard University Press.

Lewenstein, Bruce V. 1995a. "From Fax to Facts: Communication in the Cold Fusion Sage." *Social Studies of Science* 25: 403–436.

———. 1995b. "Do Public Electronic Bulletin Boards Help Create Scientific Knowledge? The Cold Fusion Case." *Science, Technology, and Human Values* 20: 123–149.

Licoppe, Christian. 1997. "Théâtres de la Preuve Expérimentale en France aux XVIIIe Siècle: De la Pertinence d'un Lien entre Sciences et Sociabilités." *Bulletin de la Société d'Histoire Moderne et Contemporaine* 3–4: 29–35.

Lister, Martin. 1697. "An Account of the Nature of the Juices, more particularly, of our English Vegetables." *Philosophical Transactions* 19: 365–383.

———. 1967. *A Journey to Paris in the Year 1698.* Raymond Phineas Stearns, ed. Urbana: University of Illinois Press. (Original work published 1699)

Locke, David. 1992. *Science as Writing.* New Haven, Conn.: Yale University Press.

Lundgreen, Peter. 1988. "The Organization of Science and Technology in France: A German Perspective." In Fox and Weisz, pp. 311–332.

Lynch, Michael. 1990. "The Externalized Retina: Selection and Mathematization in the Visual Documentation of Objects in the Life Sciences." In *Representation in Scientific Practice.* Michael Lynch and Steve Woolgar, eds. Cambridge, Mass.: MIT Press, pp. 231–265.

MacLeod, Roy. 1996. *Public Science and Public Policy in Victorian England.* Aldershot, U.K.: Variorum.

Martin, J. R. 1998. "Discourses of Science: Recontexualisation, Genesis, Intertextuality and Hegemony." In Martin and Veel, pp. 3–14.

Martin, J. R., and Robert Veel, eds. 1998. *Reading Science: Critical and Functional Perspectives on Discourses of Science.* New York: Routledge.

McClellan, James E. 1979. "The Scientific Press in Transition: Rozier's Journal and the Scientific Societies in the 1770s." *Annals of Science* 36: 425–449.

———. 1985. *Science Reorganized: Scientific Societies in the Eighteenth Century.* New York: Columbia University Press.

McCutcheon, Roger Philip. 1924. "The *Journal des Sçavans* and the *Philosophical Transaction* of the Royal Society." *Studies in Philology* 21: 626–628.

McKie, Douglas. 1948. "The Scientific Periodical from 1665 to 1798." *Philosophical Magazine,* Commemorative Issue, pp. 122–132.

Meister, Richard. 1947. *Geschichte der Akademie der Wissenschaft in Wien: 1847–1947.* Wien: Adolf Holzhausens.

Menard, Henry W. 1971. *Science: Growth and Change.* Cambridge, Mass.: Harvard University Press.

Montgomery, Scott L. 1996. *The Scientific Voice.* New York: Guilford Press.

Moss, Jean Dietz. 1993. *Novelties in the Heavens: Rhetoric and Science in the Copernican Controversy.* Chicago: University of Chicago Press.

Myers, Greg. 1989. "The Pragmatics of Politeness in Scientific Articles." *Applied Linguistics* 10: 1–35.

———. 1990. "Every Picture Tells a Story: Illustrations in E. O. Wilson's *Sociobiology*." In *Representation in Scientific Practice.* Michael Lynch and Steve Woolgar, eds. Cambridge, Mass.: MIT Press, pp. 231–265.

Neufeld, Arthur. 1986. "Reproducing Results." *Science* 234: 11.

Newton, Isaac. 1672. "New Theory about Light and Colors." *Philosophical Transactions* no. 80: 3075–3087.

Nye, Mary Jo. 1996. *Before Big Science: The Pursuit of Modern Chemistry and Physics 1800–1940.* New York: Twayne.

Nyhart, Lynn K. 1995. *Biology Takes Form: Animal Morphology and the German Universities, 1800–1900.* Chicago: University of Chicago Press.

Oldenburg, Henry. 1970. *The Correspondence, 1670–1671.* A. Rupert Hall and Maria Boas Hall, eds. and trans. Vol. 7. Madison: University of Wisconsin Press.

Oldroyd, David R. 1990. *The Highlands Controversy: Constructing Geological Knowledge through Fieldwork in Nineteenth-Century Britain.* Chicago: University of Chicago Press.

Ornstein, Martha. 1928. *The Role of Scientific Societies in the Seventeenth Century.* Chicago: University of Chicago Press.

Peebles, P. J. E., and Joseph Silk. 1990. "A Cosmic Book of Phenomena." *Nature* 346: 233–239.

Pera, Marcello. 1994. *The Discourses of Science.* Clarissa Botsford, trans. Chicago: University of Chicago Press. Revision of *Scienza e Retoica,* published in 1991.

Perelman, C., and L. Olbrechts-Tyteca. 1969. *The New Rhetoric: A Treatise on Argumentation.* John Wilkinson and Purcell Weaver, trans. Notre Dame: University of Notre Dame Press.

Perrault, Claude. 1671. *Mémoires pour Servir à l'Histoire Naturelle des Animaux.* Paris: Académie Royale des Sciences.

Poovey, Mary. 1998. *A History of the Modern Fact: Problems of Knowledge in the Sciences of Wealth and Society.* Chicago: University of Chicago Press.

Porter, Roy. 1978. "Gentlemen and Geology: The Emergence of a Scientific Career, 1660–1920." *The Historical Journal* 21: 809–836.

Portugal, Franklin H., and Jack S. Cohen. 1978. *A Century of DNA: A History of the Discovery of the Structure and Function of the Genetic Substance.* Cambridge, Mass.: MIT Press.

Prelli, Lawrence J. 1989. *A Rhetoric of Science: Inventing Scientific Discourse.* Columbia: University of South Carolina Press.

Quirk, Randolph, and Sidney Greenbaum. 1972. *A Grammar of Contemporary English.* New York: Seminal Press.

Rappaport, Rhoda. 1969."Government Patronage of Science in Eighteenth-Century France." *History of Science* 8: 119–134.

Riley, Kathryn. 1991. "Passive Voice and Rhetorical Role in Scientific Writing." *Journal of Technical Writing and Communication* 21: 239–257.

Roberts, Lissa. 1989. "Setting the Table: The Disciplinary Development of Eighteenth-Century Chemistry as Read through the Changing Structure of Its Tables." In *The Literary Structure of Scientific Argument.* Peter Dear, ed. Philadelphia: University of Pennsylvania Press, pp. 99–132.

Rodman, Lilita. 1991. "Anticipatory *It* in Scientific Discourse." *Journal of Technical Writing and Communication* 21: 17–27.

———. 1994. "The Active Voice in Scientific Articles: Frequency and Discourse Functions." *Journal of Technical Writing and Communication* 24: 309–331.

Roger, Jacques. 1997. *Buffon: A Life in Natural History.* Sarah Lucille Bonnefoi, trans. Ithaca, N.Y.: Cornell University Press.

Rothschuh, Karl E. 1973. *History of Physiology.* Guenter B. Risse, trans. Huntington, N.Y.: Robert E. Kreiger.

Rudwick, Martin J. S. 1976. "The Emergence of a Visual Language for Geological Science, 1760–1840." *History of Science* 14: 149–195.

———. 1985. *The Great Devonian Controversy: The Shaping of Scientific Knowledge among Gentlemanly Specialists.* Chicago: University of Chicago Press.

Schaffner, Ann C. 1994. "The Future of Scientific Journals: Lessons from the Past." *Information Technology and Libraries* 13: 239–247.

Schlitter, Hanns. 1921. *Gründung der Kaiserlichen Akademie der Wissenschaften (Ein Beitrag zur Geschichte des Vormärzlichen Österreichs).* Wien: Universitäts-Buchhändler.

Schorske, Carl E. 1998. *Thinking with History: Explorations in the Passage to Modernism.* Princeton, N.J.: Princeton University Press.

Secord, James A. 1986. *Controversy in Victorian Geology: The Cambrian-Silurian Dispute.* Princeton, N.J.: Princeton University Press.

Selzer, Jack, ed. 1993. *Understanding Scientific Prose.* Madison: University of Wisconsin Press.

Shapin, Steven. 1974. "The Audience for Science in Eighteenth Century Edinburgh." *History of Science* 12: 95–121.

———. 1984. "Pump and Circumstance: Robert Boyle's Literary Technology." *Social Studies of Science* 14: 481–520.

———. 1994. *A Social History of Truth: Civility and Science in Seventeenth-Century England.* Chicago: University of Chicago Press.

Shapin, Steven, and Simon Schaffer. 1985. *Leviathan and the Air-Pump: Hobbes, Boyle, and the Experimental Life.* Princeton, N.J.: Princeton University Press.

Shapiro, Alan. 1996. "The Gradual Acceptance of Newton's Theory of Light and Color, 1672–1727." *Perspectives on Science* 4: 59–140.

Silliman, Robert H. 1974. "Fresnel and the Emergence of Physics as a Discipline." *Historical Studies in the Physical Sciences* 4: 137–162.

Simons, Herbert W., ed. 1990. *The Rhetorical Turn: Invention and Persuasion in the Conduct of Inquiry.* Chicago: University of Chicago Press.

Sprat, Thomas. 1667. *History of the Royal Society of London.* London: J. Martyn and J. Allestry.

Stewart, Larry. 1986. "The Selling of Newton: Science and Technology in Early Eighteenth-Century England." *Journal of British Studies* 25: 178–192.

Stimson, Dorothy. 1968. *Scientists and Amateurs: A History of the Royal Society.* New York: Greenwood Press.

Stratton, Charles R. 1984. *Technical Writing: Process and Product.* New York: Holt, Rinehart, and Winston.

Stroup, Alice. 1990. *A Company of Scientists: Botany, Patronage, and Community at the Seventeenth-Century Parisian Royal Academy of Sciences.* Berkeley: University of California Press.

Suppe, Frederick. 1998. "The Structure of the Scientific Paper." *Philosophy of Science* 65: 381–405.

Swales, John. 1990. *Genre Analysis: English in Academic and Research Settings.* Cambridge: Cambridge University Press.

Taschwer, Klaus. 1997. "Wie Die Naturwissenschaften Popülar Wurden: Zur Geschichte der Verbreitung Naturwissenschafticher Kenntisse in Österreich zwischen 1800 und 1870." *Spurensuche* 1–2: 4–31.

Taylor, A. P. J. 1948. *The Habsburg Monarchy, 1809–1918: A History of the Austrian Empire and Austria-Hungary.* London: Hamish Hamilton.

Taylor, J. Herbert, ed. 1965. *Selected Papers on Molecular Genetics.* New York: Academic Press.

Tebeaux, Elizabeth. 1997. *The Emergence of a Tradition: Technical Writing in the English Renaissance, 1475–1640.* Amityville, N.Y.: Baywood.

———. 1999. "Technical Writing in Seventeenth-Century England: The Flowering of a Tradition." *Journal of Technical Writing and Communication* 29: 209–253.

Thomas, Francis-Nöel, and Mark Turner. 1994. *Clear and Simple as the Truth: Writing Classical Prose.* Princeton, N.J.: Princeton University Press.

Tilling, Laura. 1975. "Early Experimental Graphs." *British Journal for the History of Science* 8: 193–213.

Toulmin, Stephen. 1972. *Human Understanding: The Collective Use and Evolution of Concepts.* Princeton, N.J.: Princeton University Press.

Trelease, Sam F., and Emma Sarepta Yule. 1927. *Preparation of Scientific and Technical Papers.* Baltimore: Williams and Wilkens.

Tufte, Edward R. 1983. *The Visual Display of Quantitative Information.* Cheshire, Conn.: Graphics Press.

U.S. Geological Survey. 1916. *Suggestions to Authors of Papers Submitted for Publication by the United States Geological Survey with Directions to Typewriter Operators.* 3rd ed. George McLane Wood, ed. Washington, D.C.: U.S. Government Printing Office.

Valle, Ellen, 1997. "A Scientific Community and Its Texts: A Historical Discourse Study." In *The Construction of Professional Discourse.* Britt-Louise Gunnarsson, Per Linell, and Bengt Norberg, eds. Longman: London, pp. 76–97.

Van Alstyne, Marshall, and Erik Brynjolfsson. 1996. "Could the Internet Balkanize Science?" *Science* 274: 1479–1480.

Van Maanen, John. 1988. *Tales of the Field: On Writing Ethnography.* Chicago: University of Chicago Press.

Vinay, Jean-Paul. 1995. *Comparative Stylistics of French and English: A Methodology for Translation.* Jean Darbelnet, trans. Amsterdam: J. Benjamins Translation Library.

Watson, James D. 1966. *The Double Helix: A Personal Account of the Discovery of the Structure of DNA.* New York: Atheneum.

Watson, Jeffrey. 1985. "English, the International Language of Science." *CBE Views* 8(2): 15–24.

Weinberg, Alvin. 1967. *Reflections on Big Science.* Cambridge, Mass.: MIT Press.

Westfall, Richard S. 1993. *The Life of Newton.* Cambridge: Cambridge University Press.

Wetzel, Walter. 1998. "Origins of and Education and Career Opportunities for the Profession of 'Chemist' in the Second Half of the Nineteenth Century in Germany." In Knight and Kragh, pp. 77–94.

Wiener, Philip P. 1951. *Leibniz Selections.* New York: Scribner's.

Wilde, William. 1843. *Austria: Its Literary, Scientific, and Medical Institutions: With Notes upon the Present State of Science, and a Guide to the Hospitals and Sanitary Establishments of Vienna.* Dublin: William Curry.

Wilkinson, Antoinette M. 1991. *The Scientist's Handbook for Writing Papers and Dissertations.* Englewood Cliffs, N.J.: Prentice Hall.

Wilson, C. T. R. 1912. "On an Expansion Apparatus for Making Visible the Paths of Ionising Particles through a Gas." *Proceedings of the Royal Society of London A* 87: 277–290.

Wolf, A. 1939. *A History of Science, Technology, and Philosophy in the Eighteenth Century.* New York: Macmillan.

INDEX